What's Fair?

What's Fair?

American Beliefs about Distributive Justice

JENNIFER L. HOCHSCHILD

Harvard University Press
Cambridge, Massachusetts, and London, England

10   9   8   7   6   5   4   3   2

Library of Congress Cataloging in Publication Data

Hochschild, Jennifer L., 1950-
    What's fair?

    Includes bibliographical references and index.
    1. Income distribution — United States.   2. Distri-
butive justice.   I. Title.
HC110.I5H62   339.2'0973   81-6272
ISBN 0-674-95086-0 (cloth)   AACR2
ISBN 0-674-95087-9 (paper)

To Tony

Acknowledgments

With a book this long in the doing, the list of people and institutions that have contributed to it is also very long. But those who stand out deserve special mention.

First, my thanks to colleagues and students in the Political Science Department of Yale University and the Institute of Policy Sciences and Public Affairs of Duke University. They have been unfailingly empathetic and encouraging, and sometimes usefully impatient. Second, my thanks to various sources for funding the research, analysis, and clerical work: the Public Health Service of the National Institutes of Mental Health (Fellowship Number 1 F31 MH 05634-01), the Aeolian Fellowship of Oberlin College, the Psychology and Politics Program of Yale University, the Political Science Department of Columbia University, and the Hochschild Family Foundation.

Certain people have been especially helpful at various stages of this work. They will surely recognize their influence and the improvements they induced. I am very grateful for their intellectual contributions and even more gratified by their friendship. They are: Deborah Baumgold, Lance Bennett, Thomas Biersteker, Elizabeth Bussiere, David Cameron, Robert Dahl, Edwin Dorn, Lloyd Etheredge, James Fishkin, Judith Gruber, Roderick Kieweit, Lucy Knight, Charles E. Lindblom, Craig MacLean, John McConahay, David Mayhew, Michael Murray, David

Price, James Scott, Charles Whitmore, John Witte, and Mary Witte. Marilyn Hogge, Sandra Strauss, Kathleen Capehart, and Arianne Bahnson were invaluable in helping me translate scribbles on paper into neat and accurate prose and citations.

This book would not have been possible without a few people whom I would like particularly to thank. They are: my parents, Barbara and George Hochschild, for urging me to finish for years, but accepting it when I did not; Robert Lane, for giving me the inspiration and later the guidance to conduct such a study; twenty-eight respondents, without whom this book could not have been written; Douglas Rae, without whom the book probably would not have been written; and Tony Broh, for everything.

J.L.H.

Contents

Tables

Figures

What's Fair?

1 Why There Is No Socialism in the United States

"Is there any point to which you would wish to draw my attention?"
"To the curious incident of the dog in the night-time."
"The dog did nothing in the night-time."
"That was the curious incident," remarked Sherlock Holmes.[1]

Holmes solved his case when he realized that Colonel Ross's watchdog had not barked when the evidence suggested that it should have. Watson's awe at Holmes's reasoning suggests that we are not in the habit of examining closely things that do not occur. There are obvious reasons for this. But, as Holmes points out, when evidence leads us to expect something that then does not happen, an investigation may be warranted.

Such an important nonevent in the history of the United States is the absence of a widespread socialist movement among poor Americans. Werner Sombart asked, "Why is there no socialism in the United States?"[2] I will examine a part of the answer — the fact that the American poor apparently do not support the downward redistribution of wealth. The United States does not now have, and seldom ever has had, a political movement among the poor seeking greater economic equality. The fact that such a political movement could succeed constitutionally makes its absence even more startling. Since most of the population have less than an average amount of wealth — the median level of holdings is below the mean[3] — more people would benefit than would lose from downward redistribution. And yet never has the poorer majority of the population, not to speak of the poorest minority, voted itself out of its economic disadvantage.

Economic Inequality in the United States

Holmes would recommend that we begin our investigation by examining the known facts. After all, if existing inequalities are small and lessening, or if even the poor feel that they are "pretty well off," then the silence of the nonwealthy majority is hardly surprising. The dog doesn't bark because it has no reason to be disturbed. Some analysts make that claim. Thirty years ago, Joseph Spengler concluded that "available statistical data indicate that over-all income inequality in the United States has been diminishing since the late 1920's."[4] More recently, Robert Lampman argues that by adding nonmonetary transfer payments to income data, "one can conclude that the goal of eliminating income poverty as stated by President Johnson in 1964 had been virtually achieved before the onset of the 1974–75 recession."[5] Best known, of course, is Alexis de Tocqueville's thesis, stated in the unequivocal first sentence of *Democracy in America*: "No novelty in the United States struck me more vividly during my stay there than the equality of condition."[6] One hundred years later, Louis Hartz adopted Tocqueville's viewpoint to argue that "the historic ethos of American life [is] its bourgeois hungers, its classlessness, the spirit of equality that pervade[s] it."[7]

But the empirical support for these claims is at best ambiguous, and much evidence suggests that they are simply false. In order to evaluate whether the poor "should" demand downward redistribution — that is, whether economic inequality is actually great and persistent — we must look briefly at data on income and wealth distributions. We are looking for evidence on several points: (1) Has economic inequality in the United States increased or decreased during the twentieth century? (2) How great are the absolute differences between the wealthiest and poorest Americans? (3) How accurately does monetary income measure true disposable income and real wealth? Knowing at least generally how material well-being is distributed in the United States will permit us to evaluate whether it would be reasonable to expect the poor to demand redistribution.

First, consider the absolute differences in income among Americans and how those differences have changed over the last five decades. Table 1 shows the percent share of aggregate income (before taxes but after transfer payments) received by quintiles of the United States population

Table 1 Percent share of aggregate pretax income received by each quintile of Americans, 1929-1977.

Year	Lowest fifth	Second fifth	Third fifth	Fourth fifth	Highest fifth[a]
1929[b]	12.5		13.8	19.3	54.4
1935-36[b]	4.1	9.2	14.1	20.9	51.7
1947[c]	3.4	10.5	16.8	23.8	45.5
1957[c]	3.0	10.3	18.1	25.2	43.4
1967[c]	3.7	10.5	17.2	24.7	43.9
1977[d]	4.3	10.3	16.9	24.7	43.8

a. "The mean income of households with greater than $100,000 [income] was assumed to be $100,000 exactly." This assumption has the effect of making the share of the wealthiest 20 percent smaller in the table than it actually is, since it measures the income of someone who actually makes $500,000 as $100,000. U.S. Bureau of the Census, "Household Money Income in 1975 and Selected Social and Economic Characteristics of Households," *Current Population Reports (CPR)*, P-60, no. 104 (Washington, D.C.: U.S. Government Printing Office, 1977), p. 76.

b. U.S. Bureau of the Census, *Income Distribution in the United States*, by Herman P. Miller (Washington, D.C.: U.S. Government Printing Office, 1966), p. 21. Data are aggregated by families and unrelated individuals.

c. Edward C. Budd, "Postwar Changes in the Size Distribution of Income in the U.S.," *American Economic Review, Papers and Proceedings* 60 (May 1970): 253. Data are aggregated by families and unrelated individuals.

d. U.S. Bureau of the Census, "Money Income in 1977 of Households in the United States," *CPR*, P-60, no. 117, p.19. Data are aggregated by household; this change in unit of analysis has the effect of slightly decreasing the measured amount of inequality.

for the past fifty years. The shares received by the two poorest quintiles have changed little; the poorest 20 percent and second-poorest 20 percent continue to receive about 4 percent and 10 percent respectively of the total income. The largest change has been a transfer of money from the richest quintile to the third and fourth quintiles. The middle and upper-middle classes are gaining at the expense of the rich, but the downward redistribution is not trickling down to the poor and near-poor.

David Cameron has analyzed these and other Census Bureau data and concludes that "we see some diminution [of inequality, as measured by the difference between the incomes of the top 20 percent and bottom 40 percent] from the late 1940's to the mid-1950's, then an increase in inequality during the early 1960's, followed by another decrease during 1966–68. But since that period the gap between the top and bottom income recipients has increased."[8] He notes that such persistent inequality is particularly striking in light of six changes that have occurred in the United States since the 1940s, all of which should have had an equalizing effect. These changes are: an increase in the rate of participation in the labor force, an increase in the educational attainment of the population, a reduction in the differential between white and nonwhite family incomes, an increase in governmental transfer payments, an increase in the share of national income received by labor through wages and all other compensation, and a decline in the share of national income received by capital in the form of corporate profits and interest. These changes should, when combined, considerably reduce income inequality. But they have not done so.

Next, consider whether these data on income distributions accurately describe people's disposable incomes. To make this picture more accurate, we must consider two factors that change incomes — nonmonetary transfers that add to disposable income and taxes that subtract from it. Let us look first at the effect of nonmonetary transfers on the total distribution of income. The Census data cited above include money transfers; thus Aid to Families with Dependent Children (AFDC), Supplemental Security Income (SSI), Social Security, unemployment compensation, and pensions have already been considered. But in-kind services and subsidies, which are not included in the Census data, could substantially reduce inequality. They do in the short run, but not in the long run. The best study on this subject compared the distribution of income in 1950, 1961, and 1970 after allocating the burdens of tax payments and the benefits of government expenditures by income class. It shows that "inclusion of all government spending and taxation in household incomes significantly reduces effective income differences among income classes in each year but that dispersion in these post-fisc income distributions has not changed significantly between 1950 and 1970."[9] In other words, government actions have an equalizing effect on incomes in any given year, but this effect does not produce real change in income inequality over time. Explanations for this "interesting puzzle" include the fact that total taxes are becoming less progressive and may now be regressive, and the fact that "most government benefits are distributed independent of income and depend upon characteristics like being a farmer or aged or a veteran, or driving an automobile, or going to a public college."[10] Another study agrees that "redistribution through in-kind transfers consists of shuffling a great mass of money and resources about, mainly in the dense middle of the distribution. The poor gain some in the process, but not enough to have any substantial impact on overall measures of income inequality."[11] In fact, it finds a strong positive relationship between income and in-kind benefits. A gain of 1 percent in income produces, on an average, a gain of 0.22 percent in transfers.[12]

Other analyses also suggest that transfer payments primarily re-distribute upward or within one class; for example, Social Security transfers money from young to old middle-class citizens. Low college tu-ition transfers money from old to young middle-class citizens. Agricul-tural price supports and western water projects transfer wealth from con-sumers to agribusiness.[13]

The picture looks somewhat different when we consider the impact of nonmonetary transfers only on poverty. Timothy Smeeding finds that "when adjustments for federal taxes paid, income underreporting, and in-trahousehold income-sharing are combined with in-kind transfers eval-uated at their cash equivalent, the official Census poverty gap of $12.0 billion [in 1972] is reduced to $5.4 billion."[14] In terms of total numbers of people below the poverty line, he finds that in-kind transfers reduce the number of poor from 18,805,000 to 12,854,000.[15] Smeeding also finds, however, that in-kind transfers are inefficient devices for reducing pov-erty, in the sense that they deliver only thirty-one cents of antipoverty effect per dollar of program cost; that is, over two-thirds of the money spent to reduce poverty in fact is transferred to the nonpoor.[16] Finally, Smeeding also estimates that the target efficiency of in-kind transfers to aid the poor has decreased since 1972, so that as antipoverty programs expand, the proportion of money they allocate to the nonpoor also ex-pands.[17]

Nonmonetary transfers are not the only factors that affect the accu-racy of the data on income distributions presented in table 1. Taxes also affect disposable income, so we must briefly consider the distributive effects of taxes. The aggregate incidence of taxation is regressive for the very poor, proportional for most citizens, and progressive only for the very rich. Individual income taxes are progressive and their proportion of total taxation has greatly increased over the past fifty years. They are, however, nowhere nearly as progressive as the tax rates suggest, and their progressivity is declining. Corporate income taxes are probably regressive in the lower half of the income distribution and progressive in the upper half. Sales and property taxes are regressive, but their inci-dence is declining; payroll taxes are regressive and their incidence is in-creasing.[18] The very poor, whether welfare recipients or not, pay a much higher rate of taxes as their income increases to $10,000 than the rest of the population.[19] Overall, even making the most progressive assump-tions possible about the incidence of taxation, Joseph Pechman and Ben-jamin Okner estimate that in 1966 the poorest fifth of the population paid about 19 percent of their income in taxes, the middle 70 percent paid 21 to 24 percent, and the richest tenth paid about 30 percent.[20] Roger Herriot and Herman Miller concluded that the tax rate in 1968 varied from 50 percent for those with incomes below $2,000, to 29–34 percent for those with incomes between $2,000 and $50,000, and back to 45 percent for those with more than $50,000. Their figures differ from Pechman and Okner's because of different methods of measurement, but one conclusion seems clear: taxation appears to follow Director's law by redistributing from the very rich and the very poor to the middle income classes.[21]

Finally, consider whether the data on income distribution, even when corrected for nonmonetary transfers and taxes, accurately represent the distribution of wealth. Briefly, they do not. Data on wealth — that is, all property, possessions, and income — are inferential and incomplete, and therefore much less reliable than data on income. But they consistently suggest much greater differences between the richest and poorest than income data indicate. Table 2 shows the most recent estimates for the distribution of wealth among income tax payers.

There are several things to notice about these data. First, those in the lowest income categories hold an even smaller share of wealth than of income. The poorest 24 percent of taxpayers own less than 8 percent of the

Table 2 Distribution of wealth among American taxpayers, 1970.

Adjusted gross income (AGI)	Percent of people filing income tax returns	Percent of all wealth	Wealth per dollar of income
$ 0– 2,999	24.31	7.63	$26.39
3,000– 5,999	20.17	11.49	5.49
6,000– 8,999	18.00	11.85	3.74
9,000– 11,999	14.97	12.30	3.35
12,000– 14,999	9.65	9.97	3.27
15,000– 19,999	7.46	11.24	3.74
20,000– 24,999	2.57	6.78	5.06
25,000– 29,999	1.03	4.23	6.39
30,000– 49,999	1.24	9.29	8.56
50,000– 99,999	0.47	8.02	10.92
100,000–199,999	0.084	3.63	14.00
200,000–499,999	0.017	2.02	17.57
500,000–999,999	0.0024	0.70	18.67
1 million +	0.0009	0.85	18.75
Total	99.9743[a]	100.00	

Source: Adapted from Stanley Lebergott, *The American Economy* (Princeton: Princeton University Press, 1976), pp. 242, 245.

a. Figures do not add up to 100 percent because of rounding.

nation's total wealth, whereas the wealthiest 5 percent hold over 35 percent of the nation's wealth. Next, note that the ratio of wealth per dollar of income increases as income increases; that is, for incomes between $12,000 and $15,000, each dollar of income yields $3.27 of wealth; for incomes between $30,000 and $49,000, each dollar of income yields $8.6 of wealth; and for incomes over $1,000,000, each dollar of income adds $18.75 of wealth. Finally, the very poorest in income, those with less than $1000 (not shown in the table), have the greatest wealth per dollar of income — $62.37. They tend to be "entrepreneurs . . . and older persons . . . who retain wealth 'appropriate to' higher permanent levels of income."[22] Both this oddity at the bottom of the income scale and the much greater inequalities of wealth than of income should caution us that income measures do not adequately reflect material well-being.

We know little about changes in the distribution of wealth for the whole population during the twentieth century, but scholars have carefully studied the top wealth-holders. Wealth inequality reached its peak in America before World War I, until "wealth concentration had become as great in the United States as in France or Prussia, though still less pronounced than in the United Kingdom."[23] Wealth became less concentrated during World War I, more during the 1920s, less in the 1930s and 1940s, and "has remained essentially unchanged since 1945."[24] Since scholars and policymakers usually focus only on changes around the poverty level, whereas this book compares a sample of near-poor with a sample of near-rich, a closer look at the very wealthy seems appropriate. Estimates of holdings among the wealthiest Americans are shown in table 3. Although the shares of the wealthiest have declined, the rich still possess a disproportionate share of the nation's holdings, at least from the egalitarian perspective we initially imputed to Holmes's dog.

In a final point about the current distribution of income and wealth, it is significant that some evidence suggests that "cost-of-living movements have moved in a fashion which serves to reinforce the nominal distribution trends,"[25] that is, as the cost of living rises, the rich get richer and the poor get poorer.

These data demonstrate, I believe, that the dog's silence is not that of an egalitarian contented with the American economic scene. Even after monetary transfer payments, income is distributed unequally, and the poor and near-poor are not gaining on the rich and near-rich. Nonmonetary transfers improve the standard of living of the poor, but they help the middle classes and rich just as much. The time series data of table 1 show that, at least so far, welfare has not given the poor enough of a boost to improve their relative position. Taxes are at best a stand-

Table 3 Share of personal wealth held by the wealthiest one-half percent of Americans, 1922-1972.

Year	Percent
1922	29.8
1933	25.2
1945	20.9
1953	22.7
1962	21.6
1972	20.9

Source: Adapted from Jeffrey Williamson and Peter Lindert, *American Inequality: A Macroeconomic History* (New York: Academic Press, 1980), p. 54. Because they are computed differently, the figures from 1962 and 1972 are not strictly comparable to the figures from 1922 to 1953.

off: the very rich and very poor help the rest of the population to maintain their position. Data on private wealth holdings are, perhaps not coincidentally, extremely sketchy, but they show much more inequality than income figures do. Economic inequality in America may not be excessive—to make that judgment one must use further evaluative criteria—but surely we can conclude that the United States falls far short of Tocqueville's vaunted equality of condition.

Should We Expect Redistributive Demands?

Even if we agree that the dog's silence is not that of a contented egalitarian, we have not yet justified our surprise at its silence. After all, people may be ascetic, or self-effacing, or masochistic, so that they are happy to be worse off than others. In that case, their silence in the face of inequality would need no explanation. But surely most people are not predominantly masochistic or ascetic. Furthermore, we have specific reasons for expecting them to protest persistent hardship.

I can suggest seven bases for expecting redistributive demands. They range from classical political theory to recent Gallup polls and have been espoused by radicals and reactionaries alike. First, political thinkers since Aristotle have worried that the many poor would revolt against the few rich in a democracy. "Sometimes [the masses] attack the rich individually, [and] sometimes they attack them as a class," but in either case extreme differences in wealth make democracies unstable.[26] Hundreds of years later, John Adams concurred:

Suppose a nation, rich and poor . . . all assembled together . . . If all were to be decided by a vote of the majority, [would not] the eight or nine millions who have no property . . . think of usurping over the rights of the one or two million who have? . . . Perhaps, at first, prejudice, habit, shame or fear, principle or religion, would restrain the poor . . . and the idle . . . but the time would not be long before . . . pretexts [would] be invented by degrees, to countenance the majority in dividing all the property among them . . . At last a downright equal division of everything would be demanded, and voted.[27]

A century after the United States was founded, during an era of dramatically rising inequality, Lord Macaulay warned Americans that "your government will never be able to restrain a distressed and discontented majority. For with you, the majority is the government, and has the rich, who are always a minority, absolutely at its mercy."[28]

Some political thinkers, in fact, praise democracy precisely because they hope that it will lead to the changes that Aristotle and Adams so feared. In 1831 Stephen Simpson urged: "Let the producers of labor but once fully comprehend their injuries and fully appreciate their strength at the polls, and the present oppressive system will vanish like the mists of the morning before the rising sun. The power to remedy the evil is unquestionable; it resides in the *producers* of wealth, who constitute so overwhelming a majority of the people, when not carried away by the infatuation of faction."[29] One hundred years later, Senator Huey Long hoped to be elected president on the strength of his program to "share the wealth." It would have set a minimum and maximum family estate and yearly income, and would have financed extensive social welfare programs by stiff taxes on the rich. He claimed that biblical law, American history, and the support of millions of voters were behind his plea on the Senate floor: "But, oh, Mr. President, if we could simply let the people enjoy the wealth and the accumulations and the contrivances that we have . . . If we could distribute this surplus wealth, . . . what a different world this would be."[30]

It is not surprising that such diverse political thinkers have argued, despite continual disconfirmation, that a democracy would redistribute wealth.[31] Most of them adopt certain empirical assumptions which, if true, would cause the poor to demand redistribution. These empirical claims constitute the second reason for expecting such demands. Liberal democratic theorists see people as motivated by the pursuit of private, self-interested goals.[32] People are assumed to be rational and self-conscious in that they always prefer more, rather than the same or fewer, material goods, *ceteris paribus.* Thus everyone should favor redistribution from others to themselves, and a properly functioning democracy should translate these desires into political demands. The poor particularly might favor redistribution both because their absolute need is greater and because the rich have more effective ways to get richer.

Furthermore, even when liberal theory focuses on the need for stability and reasonableness as foundations for freedom and the pursuit of happiness, it can lend itself to arguments for redistribution. A nation with a large, poor, alienated, unemployed, distinct ethnic underclass is hardly a stable nation. Bismarck and Disraeli understood this principle a century ago; more recently, liberals like Gunnar Myrdal, Martin Luther King, and members of the Kerner Commission have agreed.[33] Stability may require judicious redistribution. In addition, social science research[34] and the testimony of the poor[35] lead reasonable people to conclude that poverty and wealth depend less on personal skill and motivation than on structural biases or random events. In that case, we should not blame or praise others for their economic circumstances, and we should mitigate the ills produced by blind luck and severe biases, if only to maintain a stable democratic society. Thus empirical assumptions within liberal theory about individual motivation and social structure could easily lead one to expect demands for redistribution and policies to meet those demands.

A third reason for expecting demands for redistribution stems from normative, not empirical, aspects of liberal theory. Democrats, especially Americans, have always valued the ideal of equality, and its range, domain, and definition seem to be expanding over time. The range of people who warrant equal treatment has grown over three centuries from propertied white males to the entire adult population; the domain of goods to be distributed equally has grown from narrowly circumscribed political rights to a wide range of civil and social rights. We now hear powerful arguments for even further expansion to include equal psychological and environmental well-being. Most important, equality is increasingly defined as equal substantive outcomes, whether as ends in themselves or as prerequisites of true liberty and equality of opportunity. A strong argument for redistribution, then, is perfectly consistent with the traditional American insistence on freedom, individualism, and opportunity for advancement.[36]

Fourth, much psychological theory also predicts that the poor would demand redistribution of wealth. Social psychology stresses our profound and continual need for comparison with others and our past,[37] our propensity to feel relatively deprived and envious,[38] our focus on achieved over ascribed characteristics,[39] our need to be validated by participating in socially rewarding — and rewarded — activities,[40] our need for social and economic security,[41] our altruism toward sufferers similar to ourselves,[42] our propensity to attribute worldly success to personal traits and behaviors,[43] our need to perceive the world as just,[44] and our need to believe that we have received a fair return for our efforts and achievements.[45] All of this suggests that demands for redistribution might come as the political acting out of psychological impulses.

Fifth, since World War II other highly industrialized nations have used progressive taxation and social welfare policies to redistribute downward. In 1966, for example, nine European nations spent between 16 percent and 21 percent of their gross national product (GNP) on social welfare policies; eight more Western nations spent over 10 percent, and of 22 industrial nations, only Japan spent less than the United States' 7.9 percent.[46] Similarly, income is less equally distributed in the United States than in most other highly industrialized nations. Table 4 presents data on the distribution of pretax income by quintiles for ten nations belonging to the Organization for Economic Cooperation and Development (OECD).

The poorest 40 percent of the United States citizens have less than the poorest two-fifths of all other nations. Although in absolute terms these differences in shares for the poorest quintiles "may be thought small, in relative terms the bottom decile in Japan receives twice as much of total income as does the bottom decile in Canada, the United States, and France."[47] Furthermore, the Gini coefficient is higher for the United States

Table 4 Percent of aggregate pretax income received by each fifth of the population in ten industrial nations, and Gini coefficient of inequality, 1966-1973.

Country	Year	Lowest fifth	Second fifth	Third fifth	Fourth fifth	Highest fifth	Gini coefficient
France	1970	4.3	9.9	15.8	23.0	47.0	0.416
United States	1972	3.8	10.0	16.8	24.5	44.8	0.404
Germany	1973	5.9	10.1	15.1	22.1	46.8	0.396
Netherlands	1967	5.9	10.9	15.8	21.6	45.8	0.385
Canada	1969	4.3	10.9	17.3	24.2	43.3	0.382
Norway	1970	4.9	11.6	18.0	24.6	40.9	0.354
Sweden	1972	6.0	11.4	17.4	24.3	40.5	0.346
United Kingdom	1973	5.4	12.0	18.1	24.2	40.3	0.344
Japan	1969	7.6	12.6	16.3	21.0	42.5	0.335
Australia	1966-67	6.6	13.5	17.8	23.4	38.9	0.313

Source: Adapted from Malcolm Sawyer, "Income Distribution in OECD Countries," *OECD Economic Outlook: Occasional Studies* (Paris: Organization for Economic Cooperation and Development, 1976), pp. 14, 16. Data using pretax income are presented here for ease of comparison with table 1; posttax distributions are "broadly similar." See ibid., p. 14, for distribution of posttax income.

than for any other nation except France. This indicates greater inequality across *all* levels of income in the United States than in most comparable nations. Non-Western, nonliberal nations such as the People's Republic of China, Yugoslavia, and Tanzania have moved even further than OECD nations to flatten wage structures. That Americans are not clamoring to follow the lead of Tanzania is understandable, but we do have close historical, cultural, and political ties with Europe. And yet on this issue, both masses and elites in the United States differ sharply from their European counterparts.

The sixth reason for anticipating demands for redistribution from the American poor is the fact that we are now receding from an era of rising expectations. The 1960s brought economic expansion, government activism, and personal and political optimism to most of the country. In 1964, for example, respondents to a Gallup Poll evaluated their personal lives at 6.0 for the past, 6.9 for the present, and 7.9 for the future on a self-anchoring scale from 1 to 10. They were similarly optimistic about the "situation for our country"; they rated it at 6.1 for the past, 6.5 for the present, and 7.7 for the future. Blacks, workers, city dwellers, the poorly-educated, and the near-poor (those with incomes from $3,000 to $5,000) were the most optimistic.[48] By the mid-1970s, however, things had changed. In January 1975, over half of those with annual family incomes below $10,000 saw their financial position as only "fair" or "poor"; more than half of the population expected their family's financial situation to worsen or to stay the same.[49] In 1978, the average figure given by respondents with incomes below $5,000 for the "smallest amount of money a family of four needs to get along" was $10,348. Fifty-four percent of that 1978 sample, including over 60 percent of those with incomes below $7,000, expected prices to rise more than their incomes during the succeeding twelve months.[50] From 1974 onward, at least half of the population consistently cited financial problems as their greatest worry. Paralleling this decline in optimism have been marked declines in the nation's economic growth rate and productivity, and rises in both unemployment and inflation. In the 1980s, the economic problems of the poor and middle classes are likely to worsen. Finally, during the past two decades of rising, then falling, optimism and prosperity, government at all levels became steadily more involved in social welfare issues. In 1954, domestic expenditures at all levels of government accounted for 13.6 percent of the nation's GNP; in 1964, they accounted for 17.7 percent; and by 1974, they had risen to 25.0 percent.[51] Thus we see a pattern of rising expectations, followed by a failure to realize them, accompanied by a steadily more visible governmental presence in economic affairs. Relative deprivation theory suggests that the poor might respond to this pattern with discontent and demands for redress.[52]

People often point to equality of opportunity as the great safety valve of American politics; they argue that Americans do not seek equality because they hope to become unequal. This claim leads to the seventh and final reason why we might expect the poor to make demands for redistribution—the hollowness of the equal opportunity claim and the severe consequences of its limitations. I have already cited evidence showing that upward mobility does not depend solely, or even largely, on individual merit. But even if it did, as Stanley Lebergott points out, "The probability that anyone will rise from the lower 99 percent to the top 1 percent of the wealth distribution is less than 0.0002."[53] Intergenerational mobility across all socioeconomic levels is consistently upward, but also consistently modest. David Featherman and Robert Hauser show that in 1962 nonblack adult men held occupations that averaged about 11 points higher in status than their fathers' occupations did, on a 100-point scale devised by Otis Dudley Duncan. In 1972, the rate of upward intergenerational mobility had risen only one point, despite all the social and economic changes of the previous decade.[54]

Shifting from consideration of the chances for mobility of unspecified individuals to the actual achievements of particular groups, we find that groups traditionally discriminated against have made little headway compared with more privileged groups in the past three decades. Specifically, women have lost ground in comparison with men, and blacks have gained only a little ground from the 1950s to the 1970s. Consider tables 5 and 6. Furthermore, not only did youth unemployment rise from 9 percent in 1968 to 13 percent in 1978, but unemployment among minority youth rose even more—from 19 percent in 1968 to 35 percent in 1978.[55] Given the widespread and urgent endorsement of better life chances for blacks and women in the past two decades, we should not be surprised if they were now to protest our nation's failure to translate the rhetoric of equal opportunity into reality.[56]

Albert Hirschman describes how the safety valve of a belief in equal opportunity might give way, letting loose a full head of steam in opposition to it. An expanding economy, as ours generally was from World War II to the early 1970s, improves the position of many people without an equal and opposite downward effect on others. Those left behind— women, blacks, Hispanics, many of the poor and working class—expect, in the absence of other information, their own position similarly to improve in the near future. Hirschman calls this optimism a "tunnel effect," as when drivers of cars in a traffic jam in a tunnel are initially pleased

Table 5   Median income of women as a percent of median income of men, for full-time, year-round adult workers, 1955–1978.

Year	Percent
1955	64
1960	61
1965	60
1970	59
1974	57
1978	59

Sources: 1955-74: Department of Labor, Women's Bureau, *The Earnings Gap between Women and Men* (Washington, D.C.: U.S. Government Printing Office, 1979), p. 6. 1978: David E. Rosenbaum, "Working Women Still Seek Man-Sized Wages," *New York Times*, July 27, 1980, sec. 4, p. E3.

Table 6   Median income of black families as a percent of median income of white families, 1952-1977.

Year	Percent
1952	57
1957	54
1962	53
1967	59
1972	59
1977	57

Source: Edwin Dorn, *Rules and Racial Equality* (New Haven: Yale University Press, 1979), pp. 34-35. The absolute difference between black and white incomes is also rising, even when measured in constant dollars. The constant dollar difference (in 1967 dollars) in 1952 was $2234; in 1977, it was $3976. The current dollar difference in 1952 was $1776; in 1977, it was $7177. "Black" income from 1952 to 1962 is actually "Negro and Other Races" in these census data.

that cars in the adjacent lane are beginning to move. The tunnel effect "operates because advances of others supply information about a more benign external environment; receipt of this information produces gratification; and this gratification overcomes, or at least suspends, *envy* . . . As long as the tunnel effect lasts, everybody feels better off, both those who have become richer and those who have not."[57] At some point, however, those left behind come to believe that their heightened expectations will not be met; not only are their hopes now dashed, but they are also left in a relatively worse position than when the upward mobility began. "Nonrealization of the expectation ['that my turn to move will soon come'] will at some point result in my 'becoming furious,' that is, in my turning into an enemy of the established order."[58] This reversal of sentiment does not require any particular event to set it off, so that the tunnel effect is "treacherous" to elites, since they may receive no "advance notice about its decay and exhaustion . . . On the contrary, they are lulled into complacency by the easy early stage when everybody seems to be enjoying the very process that will later be vehemently denounced and damned as one consisting essentially in 'the rich becoming richer.' "[59] It does not seem farfetched to see the 1940s, 1950s, and 1960s as an era of expansion and optimism, and to see the 1970s as an era of slowing down and of increasing pessimism. That leaves the 1980s poised for an explosion of anger and demands for change among those left behind earlier.

Attitudes toward Redistribution

We now have seven reasons, ranging from the authority of great thinkers, to plausible extrapolations from liberal theory, to comparisons with similar nations and our own recent past, to expect the poor to demand redistribution to mitigate their persistent and substantial inequality. And yet the dog doesn't bark — or does it? Before we proceed on the assumption that this piece of conventional wisdom is true, we must examine it more closely. It is time to step back from speculation and theory, and follow our mentor Holmes in closely considering the known facts about support for redistribution.

Redistribution of holdings has seldom been a major political issue in the United States. Trade unions have sought better wages, working conditions, and benefits — but seldom reductions in wage differentials or ties between corporate profits and wages.[60] Socialists have demanded public ownership of industries, the creation of opportunities for oppressed groups, and changes in American foreign policy — but seldom a fundamental reordering of status and wage relations.[61] Henry George, Eugene Debs, and Huey Long did have large national followings, but in retrospect, at least, it is clear that they never seriously threatened the American political order. George's Single-Tax Clubs did not daunt the robber barons or Horatio Alger; Debs's Socialist Party received, at its height, 6 percent of the national vote; Huey Long was elected to the Senate but found little sympathy there; Norman Thomas's Socialist Party won only 2 percent of the national vote in 1932 — in the depths of the Depression.[62] The United States has no viable socialist party at present; at most, one wing of the Democratic Party is mildly social democratic.[63] Anarchists, not egalitarians, have dominated American radicalism;

American radicals are more likely to oppose government infringement on individual autonomy than to seek government aid in the creation of substantive equality.[64] Even egalitarian communal movements have insisted on voluntary membership and freedom from outside intervention.[65]

Redistribution has been so far from the national consciousness that even voracious pollsters and doctoral students have, for the most part, ignored it. As a result, we know little about how most citizens actually feel about distributive changes. In the past forty years, only eight questions on national surveys have investigated some aspect of redistribution of income. Only three of the eight mention wealth. The findings from these questions are contained in table 7.

These results show several things. First, support for redistribution is strongest among the poor, unemployed, and blue-collar workers—a fact that is hardly surprising. At most, however, only 55 percent of the poor strongly support a program for their benefit. Other survey data confirm this finding: more poor than rich support progressive taxation and anti-poverty measures, but seldom do a majority of the poor do so.[66] Second, the more radical ideas of equalization (question E), limits on incomes (questions D and H), or confiscating wealth (question C) produce dramatically decreased support at all income levels. Third, when Schlozman and Verba compare answers to questions B and G, they find "greater average agreement in 1976 than in 1939, agreement that varies little across social groups . . . It is as if the entire nation has adopted the more liberal position held in the 1930's by the more disadvantaged groups in American society." That finding is not at all borne out by questions E or F, however. Furthermore, in comparing questions D and H, Schlozman and Verba find "the pattern . . . quite different. There was . . . more receptivity to this radical change in 1939 than today."[67]

These data give us no clear general picture of support for redistribution—never mind consistent and intelligible details. Are variations in support a result of the way questions were worded or of substantive differences in ideology or circumstance? Has there been any real change in the past forty years? Why do those who would benefit from redistribution, but not from welfare, support the latter more than the former? How do supporters and opponents within one class differ? What specific policies do supporters and opponents of redistribution prefer? Why do some of the wealthy support downward redistibution? Most important, why do so many people with incomes below the mean oppose policies that would benefit them substantially?

These poll data, scanty as they are, serve as the appropriate point from which to start considering support for redistribution. Analyzing question F, Hansen demonstrates that income, occupation, education, subjective status, degree of optimism, attitudes toward the beneficiaries of redistribution, and most attitudes toward government all have at most a "surprisingly weak" relationship to attitudes toward redistribution. She does find age to have an effect.[68] Analyzing question E, Feagan finds that an increase in education leads to a decline in support for redistribution, but that age, region, and religion have little effect.[69] Analyzing questions G and H, Schlozman and Verba find that occupational level significantly affects support for redistribution and for limits on incomes, but that employment status does not. They find a relationship between education and economic conservatism among older respondents, but not among younger ones.[70] All three sets of scholars find that blacks support redistribution more than whites do.

We can conclude at this point that race, income, and occupation certainly affect attitudes toward redistribution, but that the effects are weaker than the theoretical discussion above would lead us to expect. That result leaves us just about where we started—why do the poor not support redistribution more strongly? The surveys confirm our political and historical knowledge that most people with incomes below the mean do not believe in policies that appear, at first blush, to be in their self-interest. The survey analyses also give some evidence on variables that do not work very well to explain this nonbelief. But that is not very satisfying, and the polls do not even begin to answer our other questions. Opinion polls tantalize, but do not satisfy, our detective instincts.

My Research

If poll data do not even concur on how often the dog barks, never mind on when and why, perhaps we should turn for answers to other explanations and data. Scholars have explained the absence of a movement for redistribution, or more generally of an American socialist movement, in various ways. Some explanations are historical. America lacked a feudal aristocracy against which to react; virtually all Americans came from, or quickly became members of, the property-holding middle class; our two-party political system solidified before a working-class party could develop; the frontier served as an outlet for the discontented and landless; the Socialist Party and leftist radicals were unable to work together in their historic moment of opportunity in the late nineteenth century; and slavery caused an irreconcilable split within the proletariat.[71]

Table 7 Percent of the United States population supporting redistribution of income and wealth, and their income and occupation levels, 1937-1976.

Response to poll question	Income level[a]				Occupational level[b]				
	Lowest	Second	Third	Highest	Unem- ployed	Blue- collar	Lower white- collar	Upper white- collar	Total

A. 1937. Do you think that the federal government should follow a policy of taking money from those who have much and giving money to those who have little? (N not reported)

Yes	43[c]	—	—	18	44[d]	—	—	22[d]	30

B. March 1939. Do you think that our government should or should not redistribute wealth by heavy taxes on the rich? (N = 2102)

Should	46	34	28	17	54	44	32	24	35

C. March 1939. Do you think that our government should or should not confiscate all wealth over and above what people actually need to live on decently, and use it for the public good? (N = 2102)

Should	24	14	7	5	28	24	12	6	15

D. Dec. 1939. Do you think there should be a law limiting the amount of money any individual is allowed to earn in a year? (N = 2048)

Yes	32	24	18	10	42	32	22	13	24

E. 1969. Every family in this country should receive the same income, about $10,000 a year or so. (N = 1002)

Agree	14	17	16	7	—	—	—	—	13

F. 1974. Some people think the government in Washington ought to reduce the income differences between the rich and the poor, perhaps by raising the taxes of wealthy families or by giving income assistance to the poor. Others think that the government should not concern itself with reducing this income difference between the rich and the poor. Where would you place yourself on this scale? (N = 1428)

Government should do something (scale position of 1 on 7 point scale)	55	44	45	27	—	47	31	29	37

G. 1976. The government should tax the rich heavily in order to redistribute wealth. (N = 1370)

Agree	—	—	—	—	47	51	42	39	47

Table 7, continued

Response to poll question	Income level[a]				Occupational level[b]				Total
	Lowest	Second	Third	Highest	Unemployed	Blue-collar	Lower white-collar	Upper white-collar	

H. 1976. The government should limit the amount of money any individual is allowed to earn in a year. (N = 1370)

Agree	—	—	—	—	9	6	7	7	9

Sources: A: "The Fortune Quarterly Survey: X," *Fortune Magazine*, October 1937, pp. 154, 159; B and C: "The Fortune Survey: XXII," *Fortune Magazine*, June 1939, p. 68, and Sidney Verba and Kay Lehman Schlozman, "Unemployment, Class Consciousness, and Radical Politics," *Journal of Politics* 39 (May 1977): 302; D: "The Fortune Survey: XXVIII," *Fortune Magazine*, March 1940, p. 98, and Verba and Schlozman, "Unemployment," p. 302. For a detailed analysis of the methodology and substance of the 1939 *Fortune* surveys, see Verba and Schlozman, "Unemployment"; E: Joseph Feagin, "Poverty: We Still Believe That God Helps Those Who Help Themselves," *Psychology Today*, November 1972, p. 108; F: Susan Hansen, "Public Opinion and the Politics of Redistribution," unpublished paper, Urbana, University of Illinois, 1977, table 2; G and H: Kay Lehman Schlozman and Sidney Verba, *Injury to Insult* (Cambridge, Mass: Harvard University Press, 1979), pp. 202, 220, 221.

a. For questions A, B, C, and D, *Fortune Magazine* divided its sample into categories of Poor, Lower Middle-Class, Upper Middle-Class, and Prosperous, "as determined by a classification of homes by value or rental" (*Fortune*, July 1935, p. 65). It also had an economic category entitled "Negro," which has been eliminated from this analysis. Thus the percentages and totals reported here are only for white respondents.

For question E, the income categories in the original report of the data were: under $4000; $4000 to $5999; $6000 to $9999; and over $10,000. Those categories are reported here under the columns of Lowest, Second, Third, and Highest, respectively.

For question F, the income categories in the original report of the data were: under $4000; $4000 to $7000; $7000 to $10,000; $10,000 to $15,000; and over $15,000. The first three categories are reported here under the columns of Lowest, Second, and Third, respectively. The final two categories were combined in a weighted average under the column of Highest.

b. For questions A, B, C, and D, *Fortune Magazine* divided its sample into categories of Unemployed, Wage Worker, Lower White-Collar, and Upper White-Collar. See Verba and Schlozman, "Unemployment," 1977, for a discussion of these divisions. These categories are reported here under the columns of Unemployed, Blue-collar, Lower white-collar, and Upper white-collar, respectively.

For question F, the reported occupational categories are Unskilled, Semiskilled and Skilled, White-collar, Managerial, and Professional. The first two categories were combined in a weighted average in the column Blue-collar. The category of White-collar is reported here as Lower white-collar, and the categories Managerial and Professional were combined in a weighted average under the column of Upper white-collar.

For questions G and H, the reported categories were Unemployed, Blue-collar, Lower white-collar, and Upper white-collar. They are reported verbatim.

c. All cell entries are the percent agreeing with the question from that category.

d. These figures are interpreted from a verbal description of the data in the original report.

Other explanations are economic. If capitalist systems have "historically always been characterized by great inequalities in the distribution of income and wealth,"[72] then, in choosing capitalism, Americans may in some sense have deliberately chosen aggregate gain over distributive or collective goals. Furthermore, the coincidence of the nation's founding, the industrial revolution, and sudden access to vast natural resources has permitted great economic expansion and widespread individual gain since the nation's founding. Most people could become better-off than their parents were; a few could become much better-off.[73] Finally, the polity's dependence upon capitalism gives the market a remarkably free rein to "mold volitions."[74]

Still other explanations are political. The founding fathers, after all, deliberately designed a constitutional structure that would foster factionalism based on region of the country, occupation, and opinion — anything to avoid the dreaded mischief of broad class conflict.[75] More pointedly, some argue that political and legal equality through representative democracy is "the principal ideological lynchpin of Western capitalism" because its "very existence deprives the working class of the idea of socialism as *a different type of state.*" Because "the bourgeois state 'represents' the totality of the population, *abstracted* from its distribution into social classes, as individual and equal citizens, . . . the economic divisions within the 'citizenry' are masked by" their apparent political equality. The distinction between economic hierarchy and political equality "is then constantly presented . . . to the masses as the ultimate incarnation of liberty." There is, finally, classic pluralism; American politics substitutes group antagonisms and payoffs for class-based ones.[76]

Some explanations are structural. Ira Katznelson describes the dominant feature of American society as the unchallenged serial nature of class relations. We see the community, workplace, and state as separate arenas; each uses a different vocabulary, has different institutional expressions, and legitimates different patterns of demand and reward. In other Western nations, socialist parties have developed a world view that overcomes this separation; but Americans see class relations, if at all, as only one among many components of public life. Even if they do not like their class position, they can escape it when they leave the narrow arena of the workplace.[77] In addition, in bureaucratic and industrial settings, where most people spend most of their time, authority is faceless, organization is hierarchic, and minute divisions foster conflict among peers — all of which mitigate against working-class unity. Collective action costs individuals more than they gain from it, and the structural means to overcome that barrier seldom exist.[78] The educational system tracks students, elevating the intelligent and capable leaders out of the working class into the bourgeoisie.[79]

Finally, some explanations are ideological and psychological. Workers generally accept, even if they have some doubts about, the American ethos of rugged individualism and the American dream of upward mobility. They fear equality; they have little or no class consciousness; they believe the world is just and people get what they deserve; the poor limit their aspirations and dreams to reduce dissonance between desires and possibilities.[80]

Surely we have an embarrassment of riches here.[81] Why embark on yet another study of the same subject? I have two replies. First, as noted above, very few of these works address the specific question of redistribution of income and wealth; socialism is usually defined in terms of nationalization of industries, workers' control, or class conflict. Even among socialists (who perhaps take their cue from Karl Marx himself), questions of distribution are at best subsidiary and at worst ignored. Second, these studies do not tell us enough about individual beliefs. As we saw in table 7, surveys that compare rich with poor barely begin to answer our questions about beliefs concerning distribution. Qualitative studies that could have answered these questions do not compare rich and poor; therefore they cannot draw conclusions about the relations between economic status and beliefs concerning distribution.

I propose to fill these two gaps in our knowledge of American political values by focusing on issues of redistribution and by comparing rich and poor respondents in a way that can fully explore their beliefs about distribution — through intensive, qualitative interviews with a small set of people.

The methodological value of comparing rich to poor in explaining why the poor do not protest their lot is clear.[82] The value of a small sample of unstructured, intensive interviews is perhaps less so and therefore requires some discussion. Topics as complex and slippery as beliefs about income, property, justice, equality, and the role of the government in the economy and vice versa require a research method that permits textured, idiosyncratic responses. The researcher must permit — even induce — people to speak for themselves and must be wary of channeling their thoughts through his or her own preconceptions about what questions to ask, how answers should be shaped, and what coding categories best subdivide the responses. The channeling comes later. As Robert Redfield points out, the student of an unfamiliar culture must take two positions, in the proper sequence, in order to generate and then communicate his or her findings. First, "the investigator has to see the meaning, understand the valuation, and feel the feeling connected with object or act in the mind of the native." Only after understanding the respondent's point of view may the investigator "change his viewpoint and look at that object or act — together with the meaning and value it has for the native — as an object of scientific interest now to be described from the outside and related . . . to other things according to the demands of a more detached and abstract understanding."[83] The interviews need to be open enough to allow for unanticipated value judgments and unorthodox world views, but structured enough to permit comparisons among respondents and obedience to the discipline of a "more detached and abstract understanding."

To achieve this balance between openness and discipline, I have conducted intensive open-ended interviews with twenty-eight working adults chosen at random in New Haven, Connecticut. To choose the subjects, I used block census data to identify the lowest-income and highest-income among predominantly white neighborhoods in the Standard Metropolitan Statistical Area (SMSA) of New Haven.[84] I then used a street directory and voting lists to identify the adult residents of the two neighborhoods. Subjects were selected from that list by assigning each a number and then randomly selecting numbers. I sent each potential subject a letter explaining my purpose and followed this up with telephone calls and visits to their homes. I offered the poor respondents thirty dollars for participating. Out of thirty-six wealthy subjects contacted, twelve participated, for a response rate of 33 percent. Out of forty-three poor respondents contacted, sixteen participated, for a response rate of 37 percent.

Thus I spoke with eight men and eight women with incomes ranging from $2,000 to $12,000 and with six men and six women with incomes above $35,000.[85] Most of the poor did not own their own home, had less than a high school education, and worked as unskilled or skilled laborers. They all lived in a city neighborhood that is in transition from middle-class ownership to rental by ethnic white families, the elderly, and increasingly, blacks and Puerto Ricans. It is a run-down neighborhood, rapidly losing young adults and hope. All of the wealthy owned their own home and two to twenty acres of land, had at least a high school education (and in some cases postgraduate degrees), and worked as executives or professionals. A few women in this group were not employed outside the home. They lived in an exclusive, virtually all-white suburb, which has grown over several decades from a rural village to the most desirable bedroom community for New Haven. It is zoned to permit only single-family dwellings on at least two acres of land. Many of the wealthy also owned their own businesses and employed up to thirty people.

Each interview consisted of three sessions of about two hours each; all were taped and transcribed verbatim. The topics of conversation ranged from the distribution of money and authority within the family, school, and workplace; to views on fair incomes, the class structure, the electoral system, and government policies; to the meaning of justice, equality, and democracy. The idea of equalizing incomes and holdings was extensively discussed several times. My questions sought perceptions, explanations, and evaluations of existing conditions, as well as changes the respondent would make if he or she were "assistant God," as one woman put it. There were detailed probes, forced choice questions, and opportunity for rambling anecdotes.[86]

This research method permitted respondents to reveal their convictions and uncertainties, their reasoning processes and emotional reactions, their foci for passion and indifference, their expertise and ignorance. From the interviews, I was able to evaluate the content, complexity, and strength of individual beliefs about justice, as well as the circumstances in which they occurred and their effects on respondents' political and economic views. The thread uniting all of these facets was an attempt to understand how people feel about being poorer than over half or wealthier than nine-tenths of the nation's population.

But knowing how twenty-eight people feel is not of great value to most readers. I must therefore clarify what *is* of value to them in this book — what they can and cannot expect to learn from intensive interviewing of a few people. Obviously, one cannot safely generalize from a sample of this kind to a national population; it would be worthless, for example, for me to point out what percentage of my sample sought more or fewer government services for the poor. Since I make no attempt to establish proportions of people who support a particular policy or hold a particular belief, it matters little whether this group is a representative sample of all United States citizens. Thus a concern that a disproportionate number of the wealthy (or poor) respondents are Jewish, or Italian, or over fifty years old, or whatever, would be misplaced. These demographic considerations become important only when one seeks to infer from a sample, as survey researchers can do, how many and what kinds of respondents seek more or less downward redistribution.

Since I cannot generalize from this sample to a population, what *can* I claim from intensive interviewing? One can make four claims, ranging from cautious to bold. The first and most cautious is Karl Lamb's, that "the reader [should] . . . accept the material [acquired through intensive interviews] for its intrinsic interest and make judgments about its wider applicability on the basis of its resonance with his own experience." Intensive interviewing thus "suggests" or "implies" truths about American politics, but it never "proves" them.[87]

This claim is so cautious as to be indisputable, but it is hardly a convincing reason to devote hours to the pages ahead. A slightly more powerful claim, as described by Harry Eckstein, "holds that case studies may be conducted precisely for the purpose of discovering questions and puzzles for theory, and discovering candidate-rules that might solve theoretical puzzles."[88] Intensive interviews are a device for generating insights, anomalies, and paradoxes, which later may be formalized into hypotheses to be tested by quantitative social science methods.

This claim, as Eckstein says, "identif[ies] perfectly legitimate uses of case study and methods of carrying them out. [It is] . . . implicit in a host of meritorious political studies . . . [and] is the standard defense of case study by theory-oriented social scientists."[89] But it both exaggerates and underestimates the merits of small samples and intensive probes. It exaggerates because case studies are simply one limited tool for generating theory; the best theorists might be just as successful — or more so — with a different tool, and the poor theorists are not helped much by it. Thus this claim permits us only to say that "there is no special reason for either making or not making such studies."[90]

But this argument also underestimates the value of intensive interviews, which leads to the third claim. They can fill in gaps left by opinion research through providing data that surveys are unable to produce. In opinion polling, the *researcher infers* the links between variables; in intensive interviewing, the researcher induces the *respondent* to *create* the links between variables as he or she sees them. For example, polls show that most of the population usually does not support programs leading to the downward redistribution of wealth. Surveyors explain this finding through the correlation between wealth and support; the researcher interprets the relationship and infers that the rich do not support certain programs because these programs would hurt their economic position. Intensive interviewers explain this finding by discussing with respondents what they expect and how they would feel about the effect of redistributive programs on their lives. The researcher interprets respondents' statements to draw conclusions about what redistribution means to people in various economic positions. The conclusions from both types of research may be equally valid, even identical, but they emerge from different types of data, which are collected in different ways to yield different types of explanations for the same phenomenon.[91]

The fourth and boldest claim for intensive interviewing modifies the conclusion just reached by arguing that intensive interviews can generate findings that survey research does not. This sentence implies two differences between the third and fourth claims. The former holds that the same conclusion may be reached by different paths; the latter holds that different conclusions may be reached by different paths and that the conclusions of intensive interviewing may more accurately capture reality. The third claim also argues that the methods of the two types of research necessarily determine the kinds of explanation they generate — differences between explanations do not stem from poor polling or interview techniques, but from the nature of the two enterprises. The fourth claim, in contrast, argues that polls could perhaps generate the results that interviews provide, but that pollsters may too often be limited by either a failure of imagination or the exigencies of statistical techniques.

An example will illuminate this claim. Imagine two independent dimensions: support for equality in the home and support for equality in the workplace. Both dimensions vary along a scale ranging from low to high support for equality. Survey research would correlate values along both scales; the relationship would be a high positive correlation if most people fell along the diagonal in the boxes marked X in figure 1 (that is, if most people felt the same about equality in the home and in the workplace).[92] Those people who do not appear on the diagonal (that is, those in the boxes marked 0) would reduce the correlation; they would be defined as part of the unexplained variance. But intensive interviews might discover that many respondents support equality at home and oppose it in the workplace, or even that some support equality at home *because* they oppose it at work. They view the relationship between home and work differently from those along the diagonal, and differently from the surveyor. Thus what is error for the survey researcher becomes a finding for the intensive interviewer. Intensive interviews may find results where surveys find only noise.

One can, I believe, subscribe to all four claims for intensive interviews without contradiction; that at least is my position. Responses from these twenty-eight people may resonate with events or feelings in the lives of the readers; particular responses or sets of responses may engender hypotheses in the minds of social scientists; responses may flesh out the skeletal findings of the pollster; responses may even justify rejection of some interpretations of survey results. It is not necessary to decide a priori which of these or other claims for small samples is the most defensible.[93] The proof is in the reading.

Support for equality in the home

		Low	Moderate	High
	Low	X	O	O
Support for equality in the workplace Moderate		O	X	O
	High	O	O	X

Figure 1   Hypothetical findings about attitudes toward equality in the home and in the workplace.

But drawing conclusions from the interviews, responding to "the demands of a more detached and abstract understanding," is the second step according to Redfield. Let us begin with his first step — taking the "inside view of things." Chapter two reveals some of the blooming, buzzing confusion of the conversations, which I shall briefly examine before seeking to make social science sense of them. Of this our mentor Holmes might approve, since he always preferred to view the scene of the crime before retiring to his study with pipe, files, violin, and Dr. Watson.

2 Support for and Opposition to More Equality

In this chapter I introduce eight respondents approximately as they presented themselves during the interviews. My purpose here is not to analyze their views, but to convey the flavor of our conversations, with their intense and quiet moments, predictable and anomalous opinions, revealing and obscuring comments. I hope thereby to draw the reader into the context from which the later social science analyses emerge.

Opponents of Redistribution

Consider Maria Pulaski, who cleans other people's homes. (First and last names that begin with the letters A through L are used for the wealthy; letters M through Z are used for the poor.)[1] Her husband, a skilled laborer, was demoted during the 1974 recession. She feels lucky that he was not laid off, but she badly misses his former salary. After taxes and an unknown amount that her husband allots to himself, Maria has about $7,000 a year (in 1976 dollars) from both incomes to fully support herself and her husband, and to partially support one son, his wife, and his six children. She is acutely conscious of her poverty. She can think of nothing "that made me real happy. I'd be happy if I can just get along, pay my bills, and live normally, without have to worrying [sic] about everything, about all my bills and utilities. It's very difficult." She also cannot even imagine a future "worse than what I'm in now. The way things are now, this *is* the worst for me."

Maria feels that wealthy employers underpay and occasionally cheat her, and "that bothers me a lot. They're making their money, and then when you ask them for a raise, they almost die — 'The cost of living!' Well, the cost of living for me too! It doesn't seem fair." She is also angry about taxes. The government, she says, should not "take so much taxes out. Take it from the other people that have it, the richer people. They get away without paying the taxes. And *we* have to pay the taxes." Not only are tax rates too high and biased toward the rich, she feels, but also the wealthy are better at manipulating tax laws: "My husband's afraid to deduct things. [He says] 'No, I'm not getting in trouble.' And yet these wealthy people, they take out everything. They give to charity, but then they'll say, 'Well, we'll deduct it from my taxes.' They exaggerate, too."

Yet Maria is not calling for a program to dispossess the rich. Her employers earn $60,000 a year, but "they worked for it, why not? You work for it, it's fair. If I got a good education and I'm doing a different job [than you] and a harder job, I deserve more. But if you deserve it, you deserve it. I don't believe in this equal, all equal." Even those who did not work for it, who "got it through their parents," deserve to keep their wealth. "Sure. If I had money, and I gave it to my children, that's good. Good luck to 'em."

For the first eight hours of interviews, Maria also showed no sign of wanting major changes in the government. After the tape recorder was turned off, however, she suddenly volunteered an observation about the need for such a change: "I only hope things get better, instead of what they are now. Change the government — no, I shouldn't say that, huh?" Changing the government "just might" improve matters, "because the way things are now, I don't know, they're fluky." She had no specific recommendations: "I don't even know what you'd have to do to change it. Get all these men out that (pause) then put the new ones in? I wonder if it would make a difference. Maybe it wouldn't." But the potential for political activism seems to be there:

MP: Can't be just one person doing it [changing the government] or two persons. You all gotta get together and go around, talking with the people, and try to let them understand things.
JH: Would you get involved in something like that?
MP: Sure I would. If I thought it was going to help. Why not?

Although she does not expect the rich to go along with these changes, she thinks that if "the middle-class people get together and discuss the things what have to be discussed, maybe *they'll* all go for it." Still she is pessimistic: "But what can you do? Actually, you don't see anything like that happening though. Nope."

Does Maria seek major political and economic change? Apparently not. But does she enthusiastically endorse present distributions of wealth and authority? Hardly. There are discrepancies between what she acquiesces in and what she dimly envisions. Because she can neither fully endorse the status quo as she sees it nor fully imagine a desirable alternative, Maria is ambivalent and often retreats into confusion, bitterness, and pessimism.

Maria's pessimism is only one form of nonsupport for major political or economic change. Some of the poor vehemently oppose it. At age twenty-seven, Sally White is unemployed after holding six clerical jobs in nine years, mainly in small companies that have failed. Despite this dismal record and her average annual income of about $6,000, Sally believes wholeheartedly in free enterprise. Her many jobs have given her "good experience," she loves "wheeling and dealing," and she has no doubts about her own ability to succeed: "People *can* make money if they put their minds to it and get off their little rear ends. People get lazy, but I have no doubt that I will make out well. Because I'm very ambitious, so if there's something I want, I'll do it." She and her friends are "always onto the newest idea — 'Let's see how to make money here!' "

Like Maria, Sally rejects the idea of equalizing incomes across occupations. She also rejects the concept of equal pay within occupations: "Not all secretaries are the same. This person may work at a better speed and be more profitable for you, so he *should* get paid more. When I was in control, it was always the person that could do the best for *me* that would get the raise." But Sally exempts some people from this canon of pay for productivity. Some company presidents "just step in, Daddy owns the business, and here comes Junior and [he] gets a $50,000 a year job and he does nothing." But even though Junior has a boondoggle, "Somebody worked to get there in his family, and if they want to give it to him, really, it's their business." Other company presidents who have "worked [their] way up" may eventually take it easy, but they still deserve high salaries. "I know if I got my business going and I decided to be lazy and have someone else [run it], I would still expect my full share of the profits. *I'm* the one that got the whole thing going." Thus while Sally believes that workers' pay should depend upon fine gradations of productivity, she believes that pay for company presidents requires only family connections or previous effort. Why does someone who will probably remain a worker, and who almost certainly will not become a company president, hold this view?

Sally gives two reasons for "hating" the idea of flattening pay scales. First, "It would take all of the fun out of life. There would be no point in pushing yourself to achieve if you can't get any gain from it." Second, she believes that self-interest ultimately benefits everyone: "By pushing *yourself* up, you're also bringing people with you. Say you own a business, and you're making it more prosperous. Well, then, the people working for you, you're also making [them] more prosperous. But you have to do it for *you* first. And if everybody's doing everything at once, it pulls together, it raises everything. But everybody is out there doing it for themselves."

Unlike many free enterprise enthusiasts, Sally does not want the government to withdraw from the economic realm. In fact, quite the reverse. The American economy is healthy, and all Americans have a chance to advance precisely because of government aid: "You have your SBA [Small Business Administration] to help people out. There's all kinds of help — education programs, and training and job programs and — there's everything! There's *no* reason why people can't get out and work nowadays." All she wants now is enough restraint on government action to ensure that there will always be wealthy citizens. As she puts it, "What would be the sense of pushing if I couldn't get rich by doing it?"

Sally White is not ambivalent about present distributions or pessimistic about the future, as Maria Pulaski is. In fact, whereas Maria impels us to think about acquiescence and suppressed opposition, Sally leads us to consider a very different research question: How can some of the poor be optimistic and entrepreneurial in light of their personal economic failure?

But we are not yet ready to draw lessons from Maria or Sally. To place their views in perspective and to see the relationship between economic position and political opinions, we need to compare them to a group of rich respondents. Only with such a comparison can we discuss the relationship between poverty and attitudes toward redistribution. Furthermore, the wealthy are also an important research subject in their own right, since they exercise a disproportionate share of social, economic, and political power, and since they are so seldom studied.

Common sense, historical evidence, liberal theory, and survey data all lead us to expect the rich to oppose the downward redistribution of wealth; generally my interview data concur. But as Redfield counsels, we need to see the wealthy through their own eyes before we analyze them through the lens of social science.

Consider Isaac Cohen, age forty-eight. Through "hard work and luck," he has risen from a childhood of poverty and anti-Semitism to ownership of a business that supports his gracious suburban life and the postgraduate education of two children. (He would not reveal his income; I estimate it to have been at least $70,000 annually, in 1976 dollars.) He is a "workaholic," driven by a need for security and enough money never again to have material worries for himself and his dependents. His immediate family "is the beginning and end of my obligation," but he takes that obligation very seriously: "I wouldn't hurt anyone deliberately, but you fight like hell to defend, and you use *anything* at your means to defend yourself. *Anything.*"

Isaac wants society to care for "our sick, our infirm, our less fortunate, those who can't take care of themselves." But "if you're healthy there's no reason why you can't work and earn." He has no sympathy for the "drones" inevitable in any society: "I'm willing to accept this, but I refuse to pay them a living wage. You have to suffer. You have to have an *incentive* to get out of the dirt." To the "shiftless and lazy," he says only "Well goddammit, 'Suffer! I don't want to pay you to continue living this way.' " Isaac sees welfare as ultimately harmful to the poor because it teaches them to accept a dole rather than to develop a work ethic. Society thereby loses potential talent, money is wasted, and the poor are infantilized.

Indeed, Isaac argues, not only should we leave the shiftless and lazy to shift for themselves, but also we should not overpay manual workers: "Some of us simply aren't fortunate enough to have the capacity to reason and understand and plan. They shouldn't be paid what I am paid. I would resent it. Frankly, their income should be commensurate — a living wage, nothing more than that. Why *should* they have the opportunity to buy a new car or live in a house with more rooms than are absolutely necessary?" Finally, Isaac flatly rejects the idea of equal incomes: "There has to be a difference. I have to have something that you *do not* have. The sameness can kill me."

So far, this viewpoint seems straightforward enough. Nothing here would be hidden from a good survey. But Isaac suddenly announces, "Frankly, I can't justify my own income. On the grand scheme of things, judging what I need to live comfortably on, I earn entirely too much money." In fact, he continues, "I don't believe anyone should have anything in excess. It's wasteful." He accepts the policy implications of this view by endorsing confiscatory inheritance taxes and stricter personal and corporate tax laws. "Family fortunes should not be perpetuated in any form. Society gave me what I had, and my incentive built up the security and good life that I have. That good life does not belong to my children by right. I owe society something. I have to give it back. This is contradictory, I know, but I mean it." Isaac is not about to relinquish his holdings unilaterally: "My business doesn't have to be as profitable as it is, okay, but that's society. We measure success with dollars. The name of the game is dollars." But his belief is as sincere as it is surprising, and part of my analytic task is to understand the distributive implications of such an apparent anomaly.

Finally, Isaac's judgments sharply distinguish between family members and everyone else. He believes that all people, especially blacks and the poor, are greedy and unscrupulous, but he is very proud of his family's "honor box." Instead of giving his children an allowance, he supplies a box with up to twenty dollars in change. He keeps the box filled, but does not monitor it. "And my kids have always been encouraged to use it when they need it for something. Not to abuse it, but it is there, and I will never question the level of that box. And it has never been abused." Again, a sharp and nonobvious distinction, which raises the question of "double standards" in beliefs about distribution.

Isaac leads us to ask about some kinds of discrepancies within a belief system; another rich respondent suggests others. Barbara Azlinsky, age fifty, is a legal paraprofessional married to Ian, a career civil servant; they have an elegant suburban home, three cars, three children in college, and a joint annual income of about $37,000. Barbara shares Isaac's work ethic, condemnation of the lazy poor, vague hostility toward the undeserving rich, and flat opposition to equalizing incomes. She gives two reasons for her opposition. First, material equality would "homogenize the country," which would lead to "no personality, no character. You're limiting them [people] right away. How can they do what they want?" Her second reason is revealed in this exchange:

BA: It would be nice to have everyone equal, but let's face it, you give someone $10 and you give another one $10,000, each one will do what they want with it. So I don't think there's any equality. I don't think you can attain it. That [trying to equalize incomes] is impractical, I think, knowing human nature.

JH: What if you give everybody $10,000? Some will . . .

BA: Drink it.

JH: And some will . . . ?

BA: Save it. Okay, so where are you? You're right back to where you started.

This seems clear enough — until she adds: "Except they have the freedom and happiness to do what they wanted to do. That's what I was thinking when you said about, ah, utopia." Midsentence, her opposition to equality turns into a wistful perception of it as ideal, but impossible to achieve. Which is her "true" view? The question is unanswerable as posed: the important point is ambivalence.

A similar shift in Barbara's views occurs when we discuss the poor. She opposes a minimum wage because for "everyone who can think, self-preservation would be there [as a motivation], and you would do something to work, to get money. If it's given to them [the poor], I don't think they value it as much as if they worked for it. When I think about *our* income, and how *we* skimped and saved and did without, I would like to see some other people do it." She is particularly incensed at welfare exploiters, such as a woman "who was having children because the state was supporting her on welfare," and "tremendous[ly]" fat women who buy "tremendous baskets full of food with food stamps." Welfare recipients who shop for groceries "with *taxis* waiting for them — that irritates me. When I didn't have a car [and had three children less than four years old], I wouldn't dream of getting a cab to help me with shopping." Again, this view seems clear — until she suddenly adds, "Looking on and watching this, it's nice [to criticize], but being in *their* place, I imagine this is a necessity, the food shopping and the taxi, because they *don't* have a car."

Barbara has the same mixed feelings about the rich. Generally, "if you work for it, you deserve it. Someone that's developed land or *done* things is entitled to profit. That's private enterprise." But she also feels that many of the wealthy — her neighbors, most doctors, Muhammed Ali — do not deserve their holdings. Her comments about lawyers' salaries best capture her ambivalence; her confused language reflects the contradictions in her thoughts:

BA: They deserve their money, but sometimes they take advantage of you.

JH: What makes them deserve the high salary?

BA: Well, they have their education. Some of them don't deserve the money that they have, but they're entitled to it, because they have studied. They have worked hard for it. There are *some* lawyers, they think they're next to God, but they're *not.* I mean, I dislike someone that (pause). You can have a fine attorney who is very good, a good prosecutor deserves what he's getting. But if he thinks he's the best — and he probably isn't — he doesn't deserve so (trails off).

The ambivalence within each of Barbara's attitudes may reflect the changes her beliefs have undergone in the past thirty years. She feels "more materialistic now in my old age" and less of a "humanitarian" than she was in her youth. She is angry that coworkers have been promoted over her, that her husband was recently demoted, and that her children need financial help she cannot give. Furthermore, she always believed that "by the time I reached this age and stage in life, I would have some security, and I don't. We don't have anything really." She is "upset" by the discovery that her childhood rule — "You work hard, you get your reward" — simply "is not so." She concludes, "I've gotten bitter, because I was brought up 'Do good, do good,' all that. But I don't think that should be the rule, one's way of living. Can't be sweet all the time." Thus in bare outline Barbara agrees with Isaac's rejection of economic equalization, but the nuances of her values and her feelings about them differ greatly from his.

Some Developing Themes

In one sense, all four of these vignettes merely illustrate the fact with which I began: neither rich nor poor seek redistribution of wealth. To stop there is to miss the point, however. Values relating to distribution are much more complicated than the simple statement "People do not support income equalization" suggests. The reasoning, judgments, and emotions behind this statement are complex, confusing to both speaker and hearer, and at least as important for the social scientist as the bald opinion. These vignettes suggest at least four themes for further investigation.

First, some repondents are ambivalent; they simultaneously hold contradictory opinions about one subject. Maria Pulaski resents her wealthy employers, but respects their right to be wealthy. Barbara Azlinsky feels contemptuous toward and angry about welfare cheats, but she also sympathizes with their plight. These ambivalent beliefs often are associated with confused or unhappy emotions. Maria is bitter, hesitant, and pessimistic; Barbara is bitter, angry, and often incoherent. What kinds of ambivalence recur among respondents, and what political effects does ambivalence have?

Second, some respondents hold not contradictory opinions about one subject, but startlingly different opinions about different subjects. I characterize these views as disjunctions, rather than as ambivalence. Different domains of life are especially likely to call forth different views. Isaac Cohen is permissive about money at home, rigid about it at work and in society in general. Sally White supports with equal enthusiasm rugged economic individualism, social hedonism, and a political welfare state. These disjunctions are less likely to be associated with confused or unhappy emotions. Isaac and Sally are both cheerful, optimistic, and unconcerned about their apparent inconsistencies. What kinds of disjunctions recur among respondents, and what political effects do disjunctions have?

Third, the quality of nonsupport for equalizing incomes varies among respondents. Isaac Cohen and Sally White both vehemently "hate" the idea. Barbara Azlinsky rejects it, but makes wistful comments about how nice it might be. Maria Pulaski rejects it, but makes defiant comments about the need for egalitarian tax reforms and political change. The strength of opposition does not depend on economic position. The two strongest opponents are a wealthy industrialist and an unemployed secretary; the two weakest opponents are a wealthy professional and a struggling cleaning woman. What kinds of opposition to redistribution of wealth recur among respondents, and what political effects do these variations have?

Fourth, respondents vary in their interpretations of their environment and of its effects upon their beliefs. In the face of a long series of failures, both her employers' and her own, Sally White insists that free enterprise works and that any day now she will attain success. In the face of a lifetime of upward mobility and current success, Barbara Azlinsky claims that the free enterprise system does not work as it should and that economically she is a failure. What is the relationship between external circumstances and beliefs about distribution, and what political effects does this relationship have?

Before I turn to these themes and questions, however, and respond to "the demands of a more detached and abstract understanding," I must finish obeying Redfield's injunction to "see the meaning . . . and feel the feeling . . . in the mind of the native."[2]

Supporters of Redistribution and Abstainers from Opinion

Opposition, whether vehement or muted, is not the only possible or actual response to the idea of redistributing wealth. Some poor and some rich *do* support equalizing holdings; others in both groups refuse even to consider the question of fairness in the distribution of holdings.

Consider Rod Thompson, who is nineteen years old, works in his father's small grocery store, has one year of college education and no future plans. His parents give him room, board, and spending money; he would like to earn "$20–30,000 someday," but is content right now.

Rod draws on his experience at the YMCA to evaluate the worth of various professions. "FBI agents, and lawyers, and doctors and things like that" who "probably make $100,000 a year" have "some amazing long lunch breaks at the YMCA." Asked if they nevertheless deserve their pay, he concludes, "No. Well, if the opportunity arises that they need 'em, they *are* qualified. But I guess they don't need them very often, if they are playing basketball every afternoon at least for five hours." Similarly, "Athletes are way overpaid. $325,000 a year, what are you going to do with that? I suppose you'd go nuts for awhile, but there's not enough time to spend that kind of money. So why should they get it?" There "definitely" should be a limit on incomes. "There's no reason why people can't live comfortably on, Jeez, $40,000." He later raised his preferred maximum to $100,000, then lowered it: "You don't have your yacht for everyday, forty Mercedes. But you could live with your three meals a day and do whatever you want on $20,000. I like that." His figures are hazy, but his conviction is strong and consistent. Asked about a minimum income, he comes to the same conclusion from the other direction: "Between $10,000 and 20,000, I'd say. Better yet, you could have everybody make the same thing."

What reasoning underlies Rod's unconventional values? At times, he seeks the greatest good for the greatest number and assumes the diminishing marginal utility of wealth. He corrects me when I ask why people "deserve" equal incomes, saying "Some of them don't *deserve* it, but . . ." He accepts a revision asking why people "ought" to have equal incomes and answers: "There's so many people that need it that don't have it. There's so many people that have it that don't need it. So you might as well bring it in towards the middle, so that you could set a standard. So that you can make people relatively happy." At other times, he focuses on the consequences of equality for community sentiment. With similar incomes, "People would be more together, helping each other out," and they would develop interests "that you don't have to make money out of. You just do them for the enjoyment of them."

Rod foresees problems in implementing redistribution. First, it will never happen because "there's too much power. The people that would [make it] possible to make that law are the people with the high salaries. They would never do that. (pause) You could get up a petition. (pause) Those things never work." Second, he feels that those with important, difficult, or productive jobs may really deserve more than the lazy or unskilled. But his greatest concern is with incentives. People, including himself, whose earnings were limited might not work hard because "everybody's incentive now is their economic stature." Even the best possible society would have people "that don't want to do nothin' or aren't happy in what they're doing." He struggles for a solution to this problem: "I used to think about how Adolf Hitler — morbid, I know, but — burned Jews and turned them into soap. You can't do that, but he sorta had the right idea. But he just got a little outa hand. Maybe you put all the renegades in their own little world and let them try to function." Rod here is, in effect, proposing concentration camps for those who will not work for the social good. Soon he retreats, embarrassed, from this position and asks me to ignore it. Upon reflection, in fact, he decides that people *would* develop nonmonetary work incentives in an egalitarian society. After all, when he had a part-time job with no work:

RT: I thought it'd be great, sitting around for six, seven, eight hours. But after awhile it was horrible. Mostly slept. I was embarrassed to take their money, as a matter of fact. I would have given anything to have some work.

JH: Do you think other people would end up like that?

RT: Yeah, I guess they'd really miss working.

Rod Thompson strongly, if confusedly, seeks equality. He gets diverted by alternatives and objections, but he always comes back to his basic conviction that people should not have more or less money than they need to live comfortably.

In contrast to Rod, Phillip Santaguida refuses even to consider alternatives to the way things are. In 1976, he was sixty-eight and a door-to-door salesman. His wife Marion works part-time, and together they earn $11,000 annually. They have few immediate financial worries, but they have high fixed costs, and their only plans for retirement are to keep working as long as possible.

Phillip neither favors nor opposes economic inequality. Its existence is not, in his eyes, subject to reform or moral evaluation. For example, unskilled laborers are underpaid because they "can replace them so easily. 'Cause there's more unskilled workers than there are skilled workers, and that's what makes it so cheap, the price." His explanation of wealth has similar Marxist overtones: "An honest man never makes it, have to be a thief. That's how you get the big money, by manipulating, gypping somebody. Above the law or within the law. The small businessman has maybe three [employees]. And if you can manipulate three people, get a good pay out of three people — what if you can manipulate *fifty* people, get *fifty* pay slips to work with. The rich can manipulate more. Money is power."

And yet he does not believe that society should confiscate these ill-gotten holdings. After all, "It's their money to do as they please. If a guy got rich [by having] people working for him just robbing banks of all that money — that's *his*. *He* took all these chances. Nobody gets to tell him what to do with it." Besides, the poor are no more virtuous, only less successful: "The fella working in the shop, he's trying to gyp his boss out of a day's work, and *he's* dishonest." In fact, unrelenting competition is ubiquitous: "There's always going to be conflict, jealousy. Every country wants more from a smaller country. The smaller country wants more from the *tiny* country. Everybody's out to beat everybody, and it's just human nature to try to get away with everything you can." No more than wealthy thieves should nations be condemned: "Countries are doing it — it's a good thing. People are fighting each other — it's a good thing. The more he fights, the more rewards he gets."

Phillip explains that his refusal to make judgments is deliberate psychological self-protection. Manipulation "doesn't make me mad. After you get to think about it, you say, 'Well, *I* could be up there too. It's all open for me too, if I was able to *get* there.' Then I back up. Then I run off, I don't get mad." He knows that, in fact, he never had much chance to "get there." He compares his own deeply poor, immigrant background to the opportunities he would have had as a member of "the Woolworth family." A Woolworth child "would see how this worked at home. We'd have our little talks and find out [how] to manipulate this money, make three out of nothing." Nevertheless, "I don't let things like that bother me. Otherwise I would be in the nuthouse."

Phillip adds further that equality would be impossible to achieve and undesirable anyway. If incomes were equalized, we would "turn out to be a bunch of cannibals. We'd be stealing from each other, killing each other, trying to take away from the ones that *are* satisfied. It can't be." Even though it "doesn't sound right," he concludes: "That's the way it's gotta be. Because it'd be a hell of a world to live in if we didn't have some rich and some poor. You gotta have all classes. Who'd do your housework then? Who'd go picking up the garbage? You gotta have people with money that you have to look up to and do work for. Most of the people don't like rich people, [but] that's what's gotta be."

Despite this grim outlook, Phillip is contented and gentle. He loves, respects, and shares everything with his wife; he spoils his grandchildren shamelessly. Moreover, he is deeply distressed about poverty. "Nobody deserves to be poor": they are poor only because "they're not in a position to take [advantage of] the breaks in life. Sometimes [it's] circumstances, and sometimes people don't even know they're poor. They think that's their *life*. But today, in America, there shouldn't be *any* poor people. Nobody."

How does Phillip live with both his "cannibalistic" view of human nature and his personal compassion? What are the implications of his insistence that what is, must be? The answers to these questions are crucial for our understanding of Americans' beliefs about distributive justice.

Finally, in this series of appetizers, consider the wealthy who support greater economic equality, thereby opposing their own apparent self-interest.

Craig Cabot, age thirty-seven, is the patrician of the group. He descends from a long line of wealthy professionals, attended elite schools from first grade through law school, married a woman with equal status and even greater wealth, and recently moved to New England to become a judge. He is also the philosopher of the group. He discourses on natural versus manmade law, the social contract, legal justice versus economic policy, and individual rights versus the public good. He hesitates only when pinned down on specific circumstances or practical details.

For Craig, the worst possible society is one that would "prevent an individual from freedom of choice and opportunity." Conversely, the good society is one that would "give an individual a chance to make it, whatever that 'it' is for him. Whatever turns him on, that's the whole basis for human happiness. I'm no psychiatrist, I don't know the first thing about it. But to the extent that that's frustrated or inhibited, the person is going to be unhappy."

These two measures of good and bad inform the rest of Craig's discussion of desirable distributions. On the one hand, the government should not "hand everybody everything and say 'Hey, here's your cupcake—be happy! What else do you want? I've just given you a cupcake.' Good Lord!" On the other hand, it should provide "a level beneath which people should not be allowed to drop." Setting that level at "mere survival" is insufficient: "Decency, humanity would say that you have to do more than that. 'Minimal' to me would be enough support so that people could live with reasonable dignity. Dignity—really that says it. People are entitled to live with self-respect and the respect of other people. They're entitled to be free from the anxiety of a pauper state, a dependent state."

Craig does not fear that such a guaranteed income without mandatory work requirements would destroy work incentives. After all, most people would "rather work than be paid off. Their sense of dignity—if it is allowed to be healthy and mature, if society doesn't crush that urge—it'll be enough for people to want to work." Certainly "a percentage" will "cheat the system," just as "a percentage goes to crime." But, he points out, just as we hire police to control bank robbers, rather than closing down banks, we could hire police to control malingerers, rather than rejecting an otherwise desirable system. In a perfect society, no welfare cheats—or bank robbers—would exist, and we could eliminate police and courts. But the perfect society will never arrive, and meanwhile we should beware of a double standard that insists that a welfare system, but not a banking system, must be invulnerable to attack before it is allowed to operate.

Craig does, however, endorse a guaranteed jobs program in order to bolster the morale of the unemployed. "A person who had been working has a natural urge to have something to do, to have self-respect and respect from others. Losing a job has got to be crushing to that kind of an individual." But work should not be required. Welfare mothers, for example, should be encouraged to stay home and care for their children. After all, society will not "benefit from the reduction in the pittance we're talking about [that is, a guaranteed income] to make her work and sacrifice the emotional stability of her children and of the family unit."

Craig rejects the imposition of a ceiling on incomes as strongly as he supports an income floor. He gives three reasons. First, "Why should the government inhibit an individual from going as far as his energy will take him? If he is working within the system, and he happens to be very lucky, energetic, or both, good luck to him." Second, although great inequality of incomes is "evil," the alternative is "more evil." Eliminating great inequality would create a "horrible bureaucratic structure, the inherent evil of a managed population, a constituency which is governed by a mechanical formula." Finally, upon reflection, he concludes that unequal incomes are not so awful after all:

cc: My gut reaction is that it would not be good for government to go to the extent of bulldozing, filling in the holes and levelling off the mounds, and giving us total uniformity. I don't think there's anything inherently positive about total uniformity. In the arts, in politics, in anything else, total uniformity seems not to be a virtue.

jh: If we had more uniformity of incomes, would we end up with more uniformity . . .

cc: Of everything? I think so, not uniformly but to a substantial extent. Particularly if that were protracted over generations.

Thus Craig Cabot does not seek as much equality as Rod Thompson does, but he does seek substantial improvement in the position of the poor. He knows that such improvement can come only from higher taxes on the rich, including himself. Why does Craig support a program that could only cause absolute as well as relative damage to his economic position? Where do his views come from? What sustains them? Would he act on them if he could? How does he reconcile them with his present life? What do they imply for political change?

To complicate the picture a bit more before answering these questions, let us consider Bruce Abbott, who seeks the reverse of Craig's good society — a low income ceiling and no income floor. Aged forty-six in 1976, he first worked as a psychologist in several small colleges, but decided in 1964 that "I wanted to get involved in the movement toward black equality." He took a 25 percent reduction in pay, when he had four young children, to become a guidance counselor at a black inner-city school.

Bruce believes simply that "nobody's worth more than $50,000." That amount is "more than enough for anybody to live decently, morally." Under that ceiling, the pay structure in the ideal society would "be very concerned about skill, contribution, risk, and effort." Nurses should earn more than performers. Boring jobs should have high pay and short hours; perhaps "the more interesting, exciting the job is, the less you ought to be paid." Even though executives have "important" skills — "I don't want to jump on their chests and all" — still "I just don't think they're worth a hell of a lot more than I am."

Bruce believes, however, that some people "deserve to be poor." They are those who "chose to be poor, in the sense that they don't value working, [those] for whom it [poverty] is not a badge of failure or a bad way to live. Ivy League professors' sons and daughters who already got it made and say 'The hell with it. I'm not going to work, I'm going to go and enjoy life in the sunny beautiful day.' If the kid wants to do that, fine, but you do not have the freedom to go off and live by yourself *and* be supported by society." Even ghetto children, whose destructive socialization he fully understands, fall ultimately under the same rule. Bruce would "walk more than one or two miles or three miles with that person who's not going to contribute," but finally, someone who does nothing of value merits nothing from society. He rejects Craig's argument that simple human existence warrants at least minimal support. After all, "People exploit one another." At some point, "You can't be a goddamn fool, just say 'Yeah, I'll hand out everything to you.' There's a certain 'taking advantage of the white liberal do-gooder' attitude and you [don't] do them any good" by playing into it. In the final analysis, one must "draw the line between compassion and what is beyond compassion."

Bruce's concern about exploitation stems from his conviction that the good of all must finally outweigh the good of the individual. Even though "individual fulfillment is vitally important," we must not forget that "there's also a social dimension in one's existence. Therefore, as a member of society, you are expected to contribute in a social way, do something of value to other people in order to benefit from the labor of others." Social contribution can be broadly defined: "Talking to people is of value if it's a supportive, loving, sharing kind of thing." But what one contributes to society must equal what one draws from it, and one person's welfare must be balanced against that of others: "We've got more and more to realize that what we expend to keep elderly people and sociopaths alive is so much out of proportion with what other people have that there's no sense of justice that I can find there at all. Therefore we ought to make decisions on very tough issues."

Bruce knows that he is walking a tightrope. On the one hand, personal benefits must not outweigh the social, and even the natural, good: "I don't value human life ultimately anymore as I did when I was younger. Because to put ultimate value on human life means that we're not going to have any more whales or fish, pollution's going to be so bad. I don't think that man has the right to rape the universe for his own sake." On the other hand, individual fulfillment is a basic value: "The most important thing is the right not to be poor and the right to develop oneself, pursue happiness as Jefferson meant, to make something out of one's mind. There's no greater slavery than to be deeply deprived in terms of health, food, and all that kind of thing." Bruce recognizes, even demands, that we must confront these contradictions. He has no answers beyond a hope that conflicting values can be balanced. Although "we've got to swing back in the direction" of doing "the public thing" rather than "doing your own thing," he insists that "we can do that and *still* let me keep my dignity and identity as a thinking person." At a minimum, that balance requires more economic equality, since extremes of poverty and wealth are inimical to both the social and the individual good. But a guaranteed income would help only a few individuals, hurt more, and damage the social fabric. So the ideal income range is something like $0 to $50,000.

More Developing Themes

The second set of vignettes confirms the need to expand beyond a narrow question of support for redistribution to consider other distributive issues, several income classes, and various theories of distributive justice. Three of these respondents support redistribution, and yet the differences among them are almost as great as the differences between supporters and the four opponents described earlier. The fourth, who claims to have no opinion, differs from both groups. Specifically, these descriptions point to four more themes for investigation.

First, some respondents do seek greater economic and political equality. Rod Thompson, Craig Cabot, and Bruce Abbott all consistently and strongly seek more equality, and all know that their views are approaching the boundaries of American mainstream thinking. Their support for more equality raises a host of questions. Why do some of the rich support a program that would absolutely and relatively harm their position? How do respondents feel about marching to a different drummer? What do they do about it? What would it take to get them involved in political action? In short, why do some respondents support greater equality, and what political effects does egalitarianism have?

Second, the nature of support for equalizing incomes varies among respondents as much as opposition varies. Rod Thompson wants incomes to range from $10,000 to $50,000; Craig Cabot wants a range of about $10,000 to infinity; Bruce Abbott wants a $0 to $50,000 range. Craig seeks a policy of guaranteed incomes supplemented by guaranteed jobs in order to help the unhappily unemployed. Bruce says that guaranteed incomes would simply legitimate exploitation; a jobs program will both benefit its recipients and, more importantly, benefit society. Rod has no idea of what policies should be used to equalize holdings. What kinds of support for redistribution recur among respondents, and what political effects do these variations in policy preferences have?

Third, some respondents are indifferent to the whole question of distributive justice. Phillip Santaguida demonstrates one form of indifference: a deliberate refusal to become involved in questions of right and wrong concerning matters which he sees as inevitable. A few other respondents are indifferent because they simply do not care, or because their value system does not accord distributive justice a very important place. What forms of withdrawal from distributive issues recur among respondents, and what political effects does indifference have?

Fourth and finally, people differ from others and even within themselves in their emotional responses to their own beliefs about distribution. Questions of justice for Rod Thompson are a source of wry, flippant humor; justice for Craig Cabot and Bruce Abbott is a source of moral questioning and personal guilt. As we saw earlier, Sally White is cheerfully and confidently opposed to equality; Barbara Azlinsky is defensively and ambivalently opposed to equality. Respondents vary internally as well: Phillip Santaguida is indifferent to excessive wealth but dismayed by poverty; the loving, humanistic, gentle Bruce Abbott would steel himself to unplug kidney dialysis machines; the casual, mocking Rod Thompson toys with the idea of putting bad people into concentration camps. What emotional patterns recur among respondents, and what political effects do feelings about distributive values have?

Plan of Action

I am, finally, ready to begin to answer these questions. Up to this point, I have obeyed Redfield's first injunction — to get inside the respondents, understand their view of the world, and convey it to the reader. So we have Maria's bitter resignation, Phillip's amused cynicism, Barbara's frustrated confusion, Bruce's totalitarian humanism. Each person opposes, ignores, or supports the redistribution of wealth for different reasons and in combination with different emotions, perceptions, and evaluations. These perspectives, captured in 200 pages of transcript and eight hours of conversation apiece, are what the raw interview data provide.

But this is only the beginning. The point of this book is not to examine a series of individual psyches. I am not, finally, studying Rod's aimlessness, or Isaac's intransigence, or Sally's optimism. The point is to use these individual portraits to generate arguments that apply to other people and settings. I must move to Redfield's second injunction and respond to "the demands of a more detached and abstract understanding." Individuals are subordinated to typologies, idiosyncrasy to pattern, in order to see how people think and feel about distributive justice.

My basic premise is that attitudes about the redistribution of wealth derive from an individual's general norms of distributive justice used in specific circumstances. People's views vary in their clarity, sophistication, robustness, and complexity. Respondents apply different norms to different circumstances, hold underlying principles of equality or acceptance of differences, and sometimes reject normative analysis completely. But each person seeks what is "fair." More formally, everyone makes sense of his or her environment partly by applying beliefs about distributive justice to specific circumstances. Thus attitudes toward redistribution are best understood in a broader context of norms of distributive justice.

The rest of the book explores this general proposition and the themes that follow from it. Chapter three sets up the framework for analyzing the data. It describes the underlying principles of equality and differentiation, the norms of distributive justice that derive from them, and the domains of life to which they apply. Chapter four shows that people generally use a principle of equality, and thus egalitarian norms, in the socializing domain — the arena of home, family, school, and neighborhood. Chapter five shows that people generally use a principle of differentiation, and thus differentiating norms, in the economic domain — the arena of the workplace, marketplace, and social structure.

Chapter six shows that people generally return to a principle of equality, and thus to egalitarian norms, in the political domain—the arena of tax and social policies, political rights and authority, and visions of utopia. Chapter seven shows that some people do not follow the dominant three-part pattern of beliefs. They follow alternative patterns, consistently using either a principle of equality or a principle of differentiation. Throughout chapters four through seven, I show that people's emotional responses to their own beliefs vary and that they are often ambivalent about their beliefs. Chapter eight examines recurring types of ambivalence and discusses how they affect the dominant pattern of distributive beliefs. Chapter nine concludes with a discussion of the political orientations that result from combining distributive beliefs, emotions, and ambivalence. It shows how the question of redistribution of wealth involves intense conflict for most respondents and speculates about the implications for political action and policy change of the entire set of findings.

3 Norms of Distributive Justice and Three Domains of Life

The Analytic Framework

Chapter two makes clear that we cannot classify individuals as either supporters or opponents of the redistribution of wealth, since people have apparently contradictory views about equality. Similarly, we cannot group economic classes according to support of or opposition to redistribution. Some poor and some rich generally oppose more equality; some poor and some rich generally favor it.

If neither individual ideology nor class position is a good criterion for assigning egalitarian or differentiating views, we need a more subtle classification. But first, we must clarify the relationship among equality, differentiation, and justice. Ordinary language in liberal societies often equates justice and equality — justice means ensuring equal opportunity, giving equal pay for equal work, guaranteeing equal protection under the law, or avoiding favoritism and scapegoating among one's children or students. But this usage blurs concepts that should be kept separate. Hence I reserve the term *equality* for a particular principle of distributive justice — that which starts from a prima facie assumption that all people may legitimately make the same claims on social resources. Thus equality is a subset of, not a synonym for, justice.

Differentiation is also a subset of justice and has the same logical status as equality in my analytic framework. Briefly, justice as differentiation starts from a prima facie assumption that people may legitimately make varying claims on social resources. Differentiation, like equality, is a basic principle—a value judgment that its holder may not be aware of and that is not susceptible to rational explanation or contradiction.

The analytic framework has a further subdivision. Within each principle, of equality or differentiation, are particular *norms of distributive justice*. These are more precise than first principles and are "prescriptions regarding . . . and prohibitions against certain patterns of behavior and belief . . . when such statements are generally accepted in a society and when each individual has the sense that they are generally accepted by others."[1] Norms have both a social and an individual component: the norm itself is a widely held social value, but the use of a particular norm in a specific allocative decision is an individual choice. The relationships among these concepts are displayed in figure 2.

Finally, we recall from chapter two the concept of domains of life—the categories of activity and thought that make up a person's daily existence. The three relevant here are the socializing, economic, and

Figure 2   Distributive justice, distributive principles, norms of distributive justice, and specific allocative decisions.

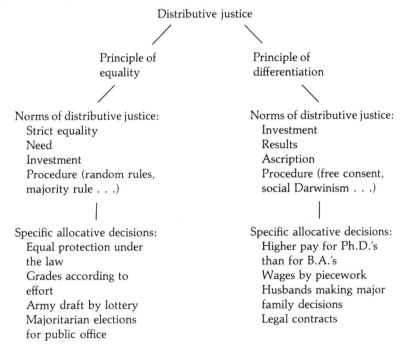

Distributive justice

Principle of
equality

Principle of
differentiation

Norms of distributive justice:
  Strict equality
  Need
  Investment
  Procedure (random rules,
  majority rule . . .)

Norms of distributive justice:
  Investment
  Results
  Ascription
  Procedure (free consent,
  social Darwinism . . .)

Specific allocative decisions:
  Equal protection under
  the law
  Grades according to
  effort
  Army draft by lottery
  Majoritarian elections
  for public office

Specific allocative decisions:
  Higher pay for Ph.D.'s
  than for B.A.'s
  Wages by piecework
  Husbands making major
  family decisions
  Legal contracts

political domains. This last set of terms brings me to my explanation of support for equality and differentiation. People use different norms in different domains, so that the explanatory variable of support for or opposition to equality is neither individual ideology nor class position, but rather the specific decision in question. More particularly, people generally use norms that derive from a principle of equality in the socializing and political domains, and generally use norms that derive from a principle of differentiation in the economic domain. This hypothesis is pictured in figure 3.

Thus individuals begin from an assumption that they are equal to all others in their home life, school, community, political rights, and policy interests; however, they begin from an assumption that they are either better or worse than — at any rate, not necessarily equal to — all others in their economic and social worth. Justice, then, requires differentiation in economic matters but equality in personal and political matters; justice is not a matter of finding the right rule for all occasions.

This three-part pattern is blurred in two ways. First, a few people do not follow it: they are consistently differentiating or egalitarian. Second, even those who do follow it feel ambivalent about some or many aspects of their normative judgments. This ambivalence is systematic, explainable, and just as important a finding as the dominant pattern itself.

· Using an egalitarian norm does *not* automatically imply that one seeks to redistribute downward, and, correspondingly, using a differentiating norm does *not* automatically imply that one seeks to redistribute upward. The distributive consequences of using a particular norm vary with the circumstances of its use.

Finally, this analytic framework shows why respondents are so often uncomfortable in discussing the downward redistribution of wealth. When they view redistribution as an economic question, they argue from a principle of differentiation and oppose it. When they view it as a political question, they argue from a principle of equality and sometimes favor it. The *political* redistribution of *economic* goods, by definition, straddles two domains and forces people to confront the disjunctions in their beliefs about distributive justice. Most often, particularly in a polity that has never seriously considered downward redistribution, the best way to deal with this ideological disturbance is to repress it or to deny its existence. Thus most people refuse to consider the possibility of, or "oppose," redistribution even though it would materially benefit them.

This chapter explores these concepts, focusing on the norms of justice for two reasons. First, when respondents say, for example, that they give the same allowance to all their children, or that an allowance depends on

Figure 3   The dominant three-part pattern of beliefs about distributive justice.

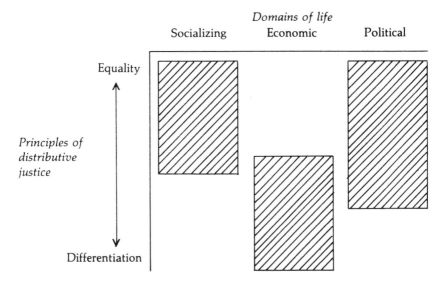

the child's needs that week, or that they give the older ones more than the younger ones, we will be able to recall the philosophical and political implications of such apparently mundane comments. Knowing the underlying premises and likely pitfalls of a casually used norm enriches our understanding of the respondent's arguments about fairness.

Second, people's beliefs reflect the distinct world view or "social construction of reality" of their society. Each society has its own perspective, which structures the world for its members so that they do not continually have to question or create a basic understanding of their environment: "I apprehend the reality of everyday life as an ordered reality. Its phenomena are prearranged in patterns that seem to be independent of my apprehension of them and that impose themselves upon the latter. The reality of everyday life appears already objectified, that is, constituted by an order of objects that have been designated objects before my appearance on the scene."[2] Marxists add that a dominant class — be it priesthood, bourgeoisie or proletariat — controls the political, economic, and ideological institutions of a society. This class "uses its privileged access . . . to propagate values which reinforce its structural position . . . [by] defin[ing] the parameters of legitimate discussion and debate over alternative beliefs, values, and world views . . . [Its] parameters . . . define what is legitimate, reasonable, sane, practical, good, true, and beautiful."[3]

The norms described here are the parameters of legitimate discussion of distributive justice in American society. They have in common assumptions about individualism, the nature of causation, the approximate amount and kind of goods available for distribution, and the relationship of citizens to each other and to government. Within this common framework, however, they differ in significant ways. Thus these norms give both the range and the limits of possibilities for distributive justice as seen by virtually all Americans — certainly by my philosophically untrained sample.[4]

In short, these norms are the intellectual tools with which contemporary Americans make distributive judgments. Obviously, laborers and business executives do not read Plato or John Rawls; nor did Rawls consult with laborers and executives in formulating his maximin principle. Nevertheless, the philosophers discussed here articulate the moral and political choices available to my respondents.

Principles of Equality and Differentiation

Sometimes people's distributive judgments derive from a *principle of equality* among persons, that is, they assume that every person may legitimately make equal claims on social resources, despite differences in race, sex, ancestry, prior holdings, talents, achievements, conduct, rules of the game, or luck.[5] The purest form of this principle is the norm of giving equal social resources to all. A more complex form argues that movements away from strict equality of outcomes must be justified in a way that reinforces the fundamental equality of persons. All claims may not be equally met, and all persons may not end up with equal shares of social resources, but each person has a prima facie right to make equal claims. Three conditions determine how the principle of equality is applied: the boundaries of the community of equals, the type of resources to be distributed, and the translation of the general principle into particular claims that may call for distributions that diverge from strict equality.

At other times, people begin with a *principle of differentiation* among persons, that is, they assume that differences in race, sex, ancestry, and so on create legitimately different claims on social resources. The purest form of this principle is the norm that ascriptive traits determine a person's worth and that the distribution of social resources should vary accordingly. A more complex form argues that "justice is an equality of proportion between persons and 'things' assigned to them . . . [Justice is] an adjustment in which differences of persons (in whatever respect) is made a basis of corresponding differences of treatment."[6] The principle of differentiation permits equal allocations to persons with the same claim, but it assumes that persons are inevitably different in ways that usually call for unequal allocations. The same three conditions of boundaries, goods, and particular claims determine how the principle of differentiation is applied.

The crux of the difference between the two principles is that the principle of equality assumes that people begin with equal value and can make equal claims on society. Differences in treatment must be justified. The principle of differentiation assumes that people begin with different value and therefore can make different claims. Identical treatment must be justified.

Aristotle's dictum "Treat equals equally" is useless until we specify *who* is equal to whom, *what* goods are subject to the dictum, and what equal treatment means in a particular case. These three forms of specificity are the three conditions for applying the general principles.[7] The first defines who is to be equal to whom, the boundaries of the relevant community. The community may be as small as the children of a family or as large as the human race. But once it is defined, the principle is restricted to its members. Thus South Africa can claim to follow the principle of strict equality—blacks are treated equally among themselves, and whites are treated equally among themselves. As the example suggests, this condition may permit the principle of equality to yield dramatically unequal results, but this paradox is a problem of boundaries, not of definition.

The second condition concerns what goods are subject to allocative choice. Social resources must be substantial, comparable, and divisible to be within the purview of distributive justice. Thus romantic love, whose objects are not comparable (or chosen justly), and national defense, which is not divisible, are not considered in this analysis.

The third condition specifies what equal treatment means or identifies the particular claim to be used in a particular distributive process. One might begin, for example, from an assumption of prima facie equality of all students, but decide that equality does not in this case require that everyone use the same textbook. The general principles of equality and differentiation need to be translated into a specific rule for the division of resources.

The translation of general principles into particular allocations takes place through norms of distributive justice. Six distinct and conflicting claims will be considered here. In figure 4, they are arrayed along a continuum from equality to differentiation.[8]

Briefly, the norms of distributive justice are:

(1) *Strict Equality:* All community members deserve equal amounts of the good being divided. Alternatively, members should sacrifice equally when necessary.

(2) *Need:* All needs of community members deserve equal satisfaction. Alternatively, members should sacrifice equal amounts of satisfaction when necessary.

(3) *Investments:* Community members deserve rewards in proportion to what they put into the community. This norm forms the midpoint of the continuum. It is egalitarian if the investment is equally available to all and always renewable (for example, effort, virtue). It is differentiating if the investment is not equally available to all and need not be renewed once obtained (for example, education, training).

(4) *Results:* Community members deserve rewards in proportion to their productivity or social contribution, usually, but not necessarily, measured by market value. This is the first clearly differentiating norm.

(5) *Ascription:* Community members deserve rewards according to relevant ascriptive traits, such as age, sex, race, class, or religion.

(6) *Procedures:* Community members deserve rewards according to the results of specified processes, such as free consent, random rules, the market, or social Darwinism. This norm does not seek patterned results; therefore, without further information, it cannot be placed on the continuum. The choice of a procedure, however, often depends on the basic principle being followed. Majority rule and random rules assume initial equality of persons; social Darwinism and a free market assume differences.

Figure 4   Norms of distributive justice.

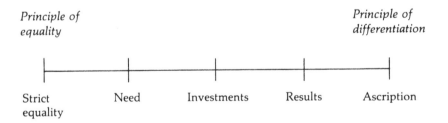

The location of the Procedures norm along the continuum depends on the procedure used.

Norms of Distributive Justice

Norms are prescriptions or prohibitions that a society uses to create fair relations among its members. Each norm could, in theory, be embraced to the exclusion of all others; each prescribes different actions and would lead to different outcomes from the others. Norms are also prescriptions or prohibitions that individuals can use to promote or measure justice within their society. Individuals, like societies, can embrace one norm to the exclusion of all others or can try to juggle conflicting prescriptions and their equally conflicting outcomes. Individuals may pursue norms that differ from or even conflict with their society's norms.

Each norm has four elements. First is a philosophy, the kind of distribution it prescribes, and the reasons for this prescription. It deals in values, ethics, and moral judgments. Second is a psychology, the kind of society the norm endorses, and the elements of human nature that it seeks to foster. This facet deals in emotions, motivations, and personal interactions.[9] Third are characteristic problems — perversions or distortions to which the norm is especially susceptible, silly consequences that it cannot easily avoid, facts that it ignores or values that it violates. Fourth, even as it raises new problems, each norm resolves some of the problems raised by other norms. Let us consider now the six norms, from egalitarian to differentiating.

Strict Equality of Outcomes: Objective Equality   The norm of strict equality assumes that "the human worth of all persons is equal, however unequal may be their merit" or any other trait.[10] Some take it on faith that "all men are equal — now and forever, in intrinsic value, inherent worth, essential nature."[11] Others justify this assumption by specifying the equally worthy human attributes: "Each man is to himself equal to the great world of his own experience. In what matters most to men this world has the same import to all; it teaches each the lesson of his own infinite worth. And so men, who are equal to the same thing, are equal to each other. One being of infinite worth cannot be greater or less than another of infinite worth."[12] Others more soberly cite natural rights, descent from God, or rational wills as evidence of our equal worth.

Each justification of strict equality implies different community boundaries and different social resources to be distributed. If inalienable rights prove our equal worth, the community is usually bounded by the state. Relevant resources are those things necessary to ensure these rights, whether they be life, liberty, and property (Locke), life, liberty, and the pursuit of happiness (Thomas Jefferson), or equality, liberty, security, and property (Declaration of the Rights of Man). For one writer, at least, this assertion is all that is necessary: "In the United States . . . *all men are equal in their rights, . . . it is impossible to make them otherwise . . .* This point once settled, every thing is settled."[13] Of course, specifying the social resources necessary for equal rights is often politically controversial. For example, which is needed to pursue happiness — an equal right to property or a right to equal property?[14] Is downward redistribution of income and wealth necessary for liberty or anathema to it?[15]

If our status as children of God proves our equal worth, the community boundaries expand to include all Christians or even all potential Christians: "There is no such thing as Jew and Greek, slave and freeman, male and female; for you are all one person in Christ Jesus."[16] Early Christians believed that all material goods should be distributed equally. As the Church became an institution, the scope of relevant resources narrowed; with the Reformation, it again broadened, but only to encompass intangible goods. Reformers sought the right to read scripture, communicate directly with God, and seek their own salvation. Secularized, these resources became education, participation in government, and personal autonomy. Thus whereas proponents of equal rights seek political and legal goals, proponents of religious equality seek broader social and psychological goals.

Those who claim that our equal worth lies in our equal ability to reason, choose, and act morally pursue still broader community boundaries and the division of still more resources. For Kantians, the community of equals includes all people and all resources crucial to self-development; everyone must be treated as an end, never as a means. Thus "a society practicing equal respect [for 'basic human needs and capacities'] would be one in which there were no barriers to . . . autonomous persons . . . who are equally free from political control, social pressure, and economic deprivation and insecurity . . . [The community] focuses on equalizing the rewards and privileges attached to different positions, not on widening the competition for them."[17]

Even Kantians, however, do not insist that "all social inequalities are unnecessary and unjustifiable and ought to be eliminated."[18] Babeuf does: "Let there be no other difference between people than that of age or sex. Since all have the same needs and the same faculties, let them henceforth have the same education and the same diet. They are content with the same sun and the same air for all; why should not the same portion and the same quality of nourishment suffice for each of them?"[19] Once relevant social resources are expanded so that everything except age or sex is to be distributed equally, however, community boundaries must shrink drastically. Egalitarian utopians envision small communities set off from the world; egalitarian societies have been small, self-contained, isolated, voluntary, and usually short-lived. At Brook Farm, for example, "The community members all stand in social equality," and all work was paid the same in order "to give outward expression to the great truth, that all labor is sacred, when done for a common interest."[20] Its members realized that Brook Farm would remain very small, however, since "minds incapable of refinement will not be attracted into this association. It is an Ideal Community, and only to the ideally inclined will it be attractive . . ."[21] Thus utopian communities often expect an inverse relationship between the extent of strict equality and the size and stability of membership — and history usually confirms their expectations.

Psychologically, a norm of strict equality seeks to enhance "cooperative relations in which the fostering or maintenance of enjoyable social relations is a primary emphasis."[22] Strict egalitarians argue that purely expressive social relations require mutual respect, which in turn requires equal status and holdings. They reason that "when the parties involved in any transaction are unequal in status, the relationship is likely to be one-sided, and the interests of one party to suffer."[23] In fact, both parties may suffer if unequal status leads to self-devaluation, self-aggrandizement, or conflict over the distribution of status and holdings. Thus winners as well as losers are hurt by material inequality. Richard Tawney says it best: "Practical equality is necessary . . . because a community requires unity as well as diversity, and because, important as it is to discriminate between different powers, it is even more important to provide for common needs . . . Social well-being . . . depends upon cohesion and solidarity. It implies the existence, not merely of opportunities to ascend, but of a high level of general culture, and a strong sense of common interests, and the diffusion throughout society of a conviction that civilization is not the business of an elite alone, but a common enterprise which is the concern of all."[24]

Strictly equal distributions may also serve as a strategy for decreasing envy and defusing rivalry. If all community members have enough standing so that they should not or cannot be squelched, if they all intransigently demand fair treatment, and if the desired resources are fixed and divisible, then a strictly equal division is the best way to satisfy everyone. In fact, in such a situation they are not likely to feel satisfied, but strict equality at least ensures that none will have cause to be more dissatisfied than another.

If strict equality prevents some disasters, it invites others. The first problem is that, as the progression from equal political rights to equal material resources to identity in all things but age and sex suggests, the norm of equality is vulnerable to an extreme and ridiculous interpretation. If Rudolf Serkin receives a piano, must Bjorn Borg also? If equality is not identity, how are we to compare social resources to ensure equal values? Market worth, elite decisions, or an arbitrary standard are obviously unsatisfactory measures. Relying on their own judgment encourages recipients to devalue goods dishonestly in an attempt to receive more of them.

Comparing social resources is one problem; dividing them is another. Even if people recognize that some desirable goods cannot be divided, "There is a risk that, in the pursuit of equality, good things which there is difficulty in distributing evenly may not be admitted to be good."[25]

A more profound danger is that the norm of equality may violate its own intention of treating individuals as inherently valuable. Equality does not reward — and may not even recognize — individual excellence or idiosyncrasy. But scarce abilities or unconventional traits make people unique and of value to the community. As Bertrand Russell put it: "It has always been difficult for communities to recognize what is necessary for individuals who are going to make the kind of exceptional contribution that I have in mind, namely, elements of wildness, of separateness from the herd, of domination by rare impulses . . . Unjust societies of the past gave to a minority opportunities which, if we are not careful, the new society that we seek to build may give to no one . . . If there had not been economic injustice in Egypt and Babylon, the art of writing would never have been invented."[26] Can we endorse, then, a norm that authorizes society to ignore all individual characteristics in the name of respecting the individual?

Some people fear that equality may not only ignore excellence, but also that it may dampen or even penalize it. The norm hardly requires this outcome, but a society that seeks solidarity and fears envy could foster conformity and mediocrity. Who can forget Tocqueville's nightmarish vision of the consequences of democratic equality:

> I see an innumerable multitude of men, alike and equal, constantly circling around in pursuit of the petty and banal pleasures with which they glut their souls . . . Over this kind of men stands an immense, protective power which is alone responsible for securing their enjoyment and watching over their fate . . . It does not break men's will, but softens, bends, and guides it; it seldom enjoins, but often inhibits, action; it does not destroy anything, but prevents much from being born; it is not at all tyrannical, but it hinders, restrains, enervates, stifles, and stultifies so much that in the end

each nation is no more than a flock of timid and hardworking animals with the government as its shepherd . . . Equality has prepared men for all this, predisposing them to endure it and often even regard it as beneficial.[27]

In short, "Equality, by itself, is not enough to make a good society."[28]

Responding to Need: Subjective Equality   The problems raised by a norm of strict equality are partly answered by a norm of need, which would allocate resources so as to satisfy equally all needs. Because people do not have exactly the same number or kind of needs, the equal satisfaction of needs will lead to unequal distributions of goods among persons. The degree of final inequality and the direction of redistribution from the status quo depend on the community boundaries, the type of needs that call for response, the priorities among needs, and the social resources used to respond to them. Thus a norm of need begins from a principle of equality, but does not necessarily lead to downward redistribution.

The norms of need and equality have the same philosophical premise, namely, that "the human worth of all persons is equal, however unequal may be their merit."[29] Thus one person's well-being has the same value as everyone else's. But it is well-being, not resources, that are to be equal, and some people need more resources than others to be equally satisfied. Thus "the equal concern for the good lives of its members . . . requires society to treat them differently."[30] According to this reasoning, different distributions according to need lead to "the most perfect form of equal distribution."[31]

To illustrate this apparent paradox, Gregory Vlastos argues that justice requires New Yorker X, who is seriously threatened by Murder Inc., to be guarded so well that his chances for survival are the same as those of all other New Yorkers. The community undertakes this extra expense "precisely *because* X's security rights are equal to those of other people in New York . . . Hence in these special circumstances, where his security level would drop to zero without extra support, he should be given this to bring his security level nearer the normal."[32] In one passage, Tawney agrees: "Equality of provision is not identity of provision. It is to be achieved, not by treating different needs in the same way, but by devoting equal care to ensuring that they are met in the different ways most appropriate to them . . . The more anxiously, indeed, a society endeavors to secure equality of consideration for all its members, the greater will be the differentiation of treatment which, when once their common human needs have been met, it accords to the special needs of different groups and individuals among them."[33]This seems clear, until one focuses on the "special needs." If strict equality founders when one must decide what will be distributed equally, then equality of needs stumbles when one must decide which needs will be satisfied first. Even in conditions of scarcity, "As long as it is a question not of actual starvation but of insufficiency, the rule has everywhere been that all should go short alike."[34] When starvation set in, "the effort was made to preserve the children, and after them the aged and infirm."[35] The most basic needs are to be met first for everyone, and the needs of the neediest take precedence even then. One can dispute Hobhouse's apparently empirical claim, but the prescription itself is clear.[36]

At this level of need, the community is usually very broadly defined: people seldom ignore urgent feelings of hunger or cold even of complete strangers. Yet scarcity may have the opposite effect: a community may decide that charity begins at home and draw its boundaries closer.

It is after urgent needs are met that the allocation of further resources raises difficulties. We can agree that, abstractly, everyone needs "the conditions of full physical, mental, and spiritual development,"[37] but specifying those conditions raises questions of different desires, abilities, and requirements. What if some people need more food than others to be satisfied; or more problematically, what if some need more elaborate food to feel equally gratified? Proponents of a need norm recognize, even insist, that equal well-being requires unequal shares, but they seldom face its highly inegalitarian, even elitist, implications.

A second problem of the norm of needs is the fact that equalizing well-being requires interpersonal comparisons of utility — a notorious can of worms. Even if people are honest about the intensity of their needs, even if all needs beyond physical urgency are equally deserving, and even if false consciousness does not exist, how can preferences and satisfactions that are felt internally be compared externally? And of course, these assumptions are heroic.[38] Intersubjective measures of need are controversial, vague, and idiosyncratic. Very small communities may have enough resources and self-restraint to avoid this problem, but larger groups probably do not. Who chooses deserving needs, and how? The possibilities for highly elitist control and dramatic redistribution upward are obvious.[39]

A third problem is the danger of interpreting the need norm so as also to subvert the norm's underlying principle of equality. Expanding the total supply of social resources is presumably in everyone's interest. Growth-oriented societies will probably develop job specializations and the corresponding belief that "every one of whom a given function is required may claim . . . the conditions necessary to its performance . . .

Thus different functions imply different special needs."[40] We cannot, however, objectively measure how difficult or important any job is and how many resources it requires. In these circumstances, those in control may define their own jobs as particularly needy and crucial and thereby justify a stratified society with highly unequal rewards.[41]

Psychologically, proponents of a need norm seek "cooperative relations in which the fostering of personal development and personal welfare is the primary goal."[42] Up to a point of excessive personal risk, community members are obliged to help others with exceptional needs or strong desires. The norm assumes neither equal needs and strengths among community members nor proportionality between a person's needs and his or her value to the community. It also does not assume that aid will be reciprocated. It *does* assume that if people need certain resources fully to develop their potential, they should receive them regardless of their merit or the size of others' allocations.[43] "A baby in the family is equal with others, not because of some antecedent and structural quality which is the same as that of others, but in so far as his needs for care and development are attended to . . . [Response to need] is equitable because it is measured only by need and capacity to utilize, not by extraneous factors which deprive one in order that another may take and have."[44] If babies and other community members do not receive the resources they need, they will become worse-off, and they will contribute less to the community in the future. Thus a community that cares about each person's well-being would be doubly hurt by ignoring needs. According to this reasoning, some people may, for the most part, give, and others receive, but the welfare of all is promoted equally.[45]

The norm of needs, unlike the norm of strict equality, bases mutual esteem not on equal status, but on ties of reciprocal nurturance and growth. The goals are not solidarity and respect, but responsibility, gratitude, and intimacy. Total dependence may be forbidden; Louis Blanc, Karl Marx, and Edward Bellamy all insist that everyone contribute according to ability in order to receive according to need. But worth is not determined by ability or dependent upon equal status; all community members are, by definition, equally worthy of giving and receiving aid.

If the norm of need is divorced from the assumption of equal human worth or of contribution according to ability, it suffers from a psychological perversion. Morton Deutsch's "direct and explicit responsibility for . . . the welfare of others in the group"[46] can turn into self-righteous charity, which "prescribe[s] that one person forego resources previously enjoyed, for little or no return, in order that another may benefit."[47] Introducing the element of unrequited giving shifts the tone from justice between interdependent intimates to benevolence and obligation between patron and client. This form of social responsibility may be virtuous, mature, altruistic, and system-stabilizing — but it is not particularly just.[48] Thus the mutual benefits between mentor and protégé(e) become one-sided paternalism from patron to client if the basic premise of equal worth and the corresponding right to equal well-being are forgotten.

Investments: Proportional Justice No. 1   The problems of excessive demand and paternalism raised by a norm of need are resolved by a norm of investments, which allocates resources in proportion to members' investments in the community. Once relevant investments are defined — whether as time, effort, virtue, education, training, or money — those who invest equal shares deserve equal rewards, regardless of the results of their actions, their needs, or any other traits.[49] Like the norm of needs, the norm of investments may not generate an equal division of resources. Whether its use leads to upward or downward redistribution will depend on the definition of relevant investments.

The norm of investments lies at the midpoint on the continuum between the principles of pure equality and pure differentiation. Those who start with an assumption of prima facie equality define relevant investments as those traits that everyone possesses. Wealth, talent, and family connections are not such traits. But reason and automony are; all people (except philosophers' bugaboos, infants and idiots) can be held responsible for their volitions and actions. According to this view, the community should not penalize members for needing extra time or failing to accomplish a goal, since achievement depends on uncontrollable variations in skill or holdings. But all people can equally control their *effort* to accomplish something; therefore judging members' efforts does not violate their fundamental equality.

Those who start from an assumption of prima facie differences among people define relevant investments as things that people possess unequally, which are acquired through prior actions or holdings, and which, once acquired, retain their value forever. Education and vocational training have these characteristics. They are not inherent attributes that everyone can always call upon; their acquisition depends on skill, intelligence, connections, geography, and ancestry. Furthermore, the value of a diploma or license lasts a lifetime. Thus all people cannot equally make certain investments in the community; rewarding those investments implies acceptance of the principle of differentiation.

The resources to be distributed and the community's boundaries affect what investments are valued and thus whether the norm will tilt toward equality or toward differentiation. In his letter to the Galatians, Paul defines the community as the children of God, that is, all those who accept God's guidance as best they can. To be rewarded with salvation one need not successfully obey a rigid set of laws. Rather, one must have faith and strive to understand and obey God's will: "If we do not slacken our efforts, we shall in due time reap our harvest. Therefore, as opportunity offers, let us work for the good of all, especially members of the household of the faith."[50] In the succeeding 1500 years, the Catholic Church increasingly rewarded material contributions and tangible, non-renewable achievements until Martin Luther reintroduced the distinction between faith and good works. He claimed that all people, however poor and lowly, were equally able to achieve salvation by using faith to combat sin and carnal desires, not by producing good works or demonstrating virtue.[51] Thus the history of the Christian use of the investment norm demonstrates its location as a midpoint. It is highly egalitarian in the hands of Paul and Martin Luther, but highly differentiating in the hands of the pre-Reformation bishopric.

Edward Bellamy is the strongest American proponent of the egalitarian version of this norm. In his utopia, everyone has an equal income because the society requires "precisely the same measure of service from all, . . . that each shall make the same effort; that is, we demand of him the best service it is in his power to give."[52] Questioned about the role of varying talents, resources, and achievements, Bellamy's protagonist answers: "The amount of the resulting product has nothing whatever to do with the question, which is one of desert. Desert is a moral question, and the amount of the product a material quantity. It would be an extraordinary sort of logic which should try to determine a moral question by a material standard . . . A man's endowments, however godlike, merely fix the measure of his duty . . . A man who can produce twice as much as another with the same effort, instead of being rewarded for doing so, ought to be punished if he does not do so."[53] Bellamy would, however, distribute only material goods according to an investment norm; his utopia has an elaborate system of differentiated praise, honor, status, and power in order to induce everyone to work equally hard. He does not deny that incentives to work are essential; he does deny that they should be monetary.

Egalitarian investments may include, besides faith and effort, other forms of work, virtue, or training equally accessible to all. John Locke, for example, follows an investment norm when he argues that in a well-ordered society, differences in wealth result mainly from differences in virtue and enterprise. A honest merchant both should and would have more customers than a shyster, a diligent worker more land than a laggard.[54]

Investments valued from a differentiating perspective include educational credentials, training, and possibly money. Economists, for example, calculate how much each year of college education is worth in future income; those who use these analyses to prescribe more education use a differentiating investments norm. Similarly, those who argue against taxing interest on savings accounts or stocks, because such taxes penalize sober investors more than frivolous consumers, use a differentiating investment norm. Finally, those who argue that only students who complete law school, pass a bar exam, and become duly licensed lawyers may legitimately file divorce papers for others use a differentiating investment norm.

Money and its equivalents lie right on the boundary between the norms of investment and results. On the one hand, one invests money in order to obtain rewards in exactly the same way as one invests effort, virtue, or time in the classroom. On the other hand, one cannot be held responsible for, and therefore be praised for, deciding to invest money, as one can be praised for deciding to invest effort or time. This ability to straddle a boundary may suggest why money holds such a powerful place in our values. Rewarding its use satisfies the moral demands of two norms as almost nothing else in society does.

Psychologically, the norm of investments seeks to foster individual autonomy, maturity, and responsibility. People unite with others for the sake of neither fellowship nor nurturance, but to help themselves. Giving and receiving help may be sincere and enthusiastic, but it is also instrumental. In a society governed by a norm of investments, all people would be able to earn respect and rewards, but they must *earn* them, not be given them. People control, and are therefore responsible for, their own actions, and society's main responsibility is to give them the opportunity and motivation to act.

The psychology of a norm of investments also has a less stern side, because it insists only that people must pursue a goal, not that they must reach it. According to this norm, "Success is to be measured not so much by the position that one has reached in life as by the obstacles which he has overcome while trying to succeed."[55] Thus one competes against oneself or against external barriers, not against others or a predetermined standard; achievement is relative, not absolute. After quoting the passage above, President Emil Danenberg of Oberlin College told the

1980 graduates, "Having worked to teach you that neither wealth nor social background nor sex nor racial origins determine a person's worth, now we add to the list: grade point average. Society honors its great achievers, even as we do today, but Oberlin's greatest concern is not in how great you become, but in how narrow you can make the gap between the person you are and the person you can be."[56] By this criterion, the student at the bottom of the class or the worker at the bottom of the corporate ladder may be the most successful and the most worthy of social reward if he or she has traveled further than all other students or workers.

The dual psychology of a norm of investments — one is responsible for one's actions, but one is not responsible for their results — reflects the position of this norm at the midpoint of the equality-differentiation continuum. It can be forgiving or harsh, evidence of a soft heart or a stiff backbone, depending on the definition of relevant investments. But no matter what its tone, a society using a norm of investments depends less on a conscious sense of community than societies using the first two norms do. Equality without community becomes mindless uniformity; response to need without community becomes paternalism and dependency. Rewarding investments without community perhaps loses some appeal, but it does not eliminate its essential quality of justice. This norm assumes that individuals can — must — stand alone, and that the community's job is only to provide paths for these separate individuals to travel along. Of course, providing equal opportunity can be an enormous task if, for example, one argues that only equal holdings ensure an equal chance to obtain education and training or to express virtue and faith. But even in this case, the community's role is adventitious, not essential.

Like the others, the norm of investments is subject to perversions. First, one may perceive this norm to be not prescription but accomplished fact, so that people's holdings are seen as accurate measures of virtue. In 1901 the greatest spokesman for this "gospel of wealth," Bishop William Lawrence, proclaimed that "to seek for and earn wealth is a sign of a natural, vigorous, and strong character . . . Only by working along the lines of right thinking and right living can the secrets and wealth of Nature be revealed . . . Godliness is in league with riches."[57] The psychological counterpart to the gospel of wealth is the "just world syndrome," the belief that people always get what they deserve. In this view, victims of bad luck or structural biases must somehow have been evil or stupid, just as the wealthy must somehow be moral or smart. Believers in a just world even blame themselves for their own adversity, apparently finding impotence in the face of aimless chance more distressing than guilt or shame in the face of intelligible causation. Such a belief turns a personalistic, volitional norm into an elitist or fatalistic one.[58]

Hobhouse points out a second problem with an investment norm: we sympathize with unproductive hard workers more than with skilled lazy workers, but what about skilled *and* hardworking laborers — do they not deserve extra reward? Do we really want to reward stupidity as much as intelligence, failure as much as success? Should the buyer of a product have to pay for the greater labor time of an inefficient worker?[59]

Finally, the norm poses a more profound, if less teasing, problem. It assumes that effort and virtue are volitional, that "desert pertains to the moral will alone."[60] But are people responsible for their moral will any more than for their intelligence or talents? People can control and develop their moral will — but perhaps the same is true for intelligence and skill. Perhaps one is born with a given aptitude for effort or virtue, just as one is born with talents or wealth. In that case, a norm of investments merges with a norm of results.

Results: Proportional Justice No. 2   The norm of results answers the problems of a norm of investments by mandating distribution in proportion to achievements, defined as productivity or social contribution. This is the first clearly differentiating norm, since it assumes that people have different capabilities and worth and that their social rewards should differ accordingly.

Liberal philosophy often confounds investment and results norms by assuming that intentions correspond to achievements. "If at first you don't succeed, try, try again"; effort and success are links in one chain, with one distributive consequence. The linkage is not automatic, however, and the elements need to be kept separate. The investment norm cares only about intentions; in the norm of results, the "value of any action always lies in its consequences."[61] Thus the norm of results endorses "the type of differentiation that comes from unequal intellectual and moral strengths, unequal applications of resolve and aspiration, and unequal benefactions of luck."[62] In short, the investment norm rewards effort, whereas the norm of results commends effort, but rewards only success.[63]

Liberals justify the norm of results by claiming that the supreme political value of individual freedom "needs to have roots in social differentiation," which follows directly from individual accomplishments and their rewards.[64] Just as we may not deserve two good eyes but are entitled to use them,[65] so we may not strictly deserve our talents and resources but must be free to reap the benefits of their use: "The purpose of societal arrangements is to allow the individual the freedom to fulfill his own purposes — by his labor to gain property, by exchange to satisfy his wants, by upward mobility to achieve a place commensurate with his talents . . . Individuals will differ — in their natural endowments, in their energy, drive, and motivation, in their conception of what is desirable — and society should establish procedures . . . to fulfill these diverse desires and competences."[66]

Some proponents urge freedom so that we may benefit from individual traits: "Differences in the readiness to take advantage of economic opportunities are of great significance in explaining economic differences in open societies . . . It is obviously just to penalize those who have contributed less."[67] Others urge freedom so that we may benefit from unequal inheritances and even luck: the ability "to initiate, to create and to do" depends on characteristics "we are . . . born with . . . Plainly chance, contingency, luck play a great role in liberty understood in this sense. Equality is nonexistent here."[68]

Whether they emphasize merit or chance, those who claim that a norm of results best fosters freedom insist on the sanctity of private property. The community may even be defined as that area within which property rights are protected. Property is both a reward for and a means to further productivity. It has the same conceptual status as ability, ambition, and luck — none is worth anything if not put to use, and all are tools, the free use of which defines political freedom. Equality, or even a principle of prima facie equality, threatens property rights that are essential to liberty; therefore it must be kept within strict conceptual and political limits.[69]

A second justification for a norm of results is more instrumental: a community that relies upon it increases the total supply of social resources, thereby benefiting all. The "Captain of Industry" was a "man of workmanlike force and creative insight into the community's needs, who stood out on a footing of self-help, took large chances for large ideals, and came in for his gains as a due reward for work well done in the service of the common good, in designing and working out a more effective organization of industrial forces and in creating and testing out new and better processes of production."[70] To achieve this common good, exceptionally productive people need exceptional resources with which to produce and exceptional rewards to remain motivated. If the state always acted to foster the "best human purposes," such individual exceptions would be superfluous. But states are "rather stupid and commonplace"; therefore "it is positively a good thing for the community that a considerable fraction [of wealth] should remain at the disposal of the most capable men, among whom . . . a proportion . . . will find good social use for it . . . Thus it is in the larger interest of the common good itself that private interests should maintain themselves."[71] Private vices become public virtues, and the highly individualistic, self-interested norm of results can be pressed into the service of the public interest and the community good.[72]

Despite his rejection of desert as grounds for a claim of justice, John Rawls's theory of justice seems at least a close cousin to this line of argument.[73] His "maximin" principle permits social and material inequalities that provide the greatest benefit to the least advantaged members of society, as long as these inequalities are "attached to positions and offices open to all," and as long as the community provides each member with "the most extensive total basic liberty compatible with a similar liberty for others."[74] The latter two conditions obviously fit into a liberal norm of results, but it is the maximin principle that is both most distinctive and most interesting here.

Rawls explains that "all social values — liberty and opportunity, income and wealth, and the bases of self-respect — are to be distributed equally unless an unequal distribution of any, or all, of these values is to everyone's advantage."[75] The underlying principle here may be egalitarian, even socialist,[76] but its effects are likely to be differentiating. "Differences in wealth and power *are* justified in two ways (a) as incentives to attract candidates into certain jobs and then to encourage them to do well and (b) as facilities for providing required services to the rest of the society."[77]

Furthermore, the subsidiary concept of chain connection also justifies differences according to a norm of results. "At least in the longer run," enhancing the position of the best-off, and presumably most productive, will expand the total amount of goods, some of which will trickle down to the poor.[78] "The poor can only be made richer if the rich are also made richer, and the rich can only be made poorer by impoverishing the poor further as well."[79] The maximin principle does not require that a chain connection hold, but Rawls assumes that it generally does. Even without assuming a chain connection, the maximin principle clearly endorses differentiation according to certain results of one's actions — which is at least a modified version of a norm of results.

A third justification of a norm of results relies on a simple claim of payment: a person should get back "that proportion of the national wealth that he has himself created."[80] In its most rigorous form, this is "a principle of commutative justice requiring repayment of debts, return of borrowed items, or compensation for wrongly inflicted damages . . . So the return of contribution is not merely a matter of merit deserving reward. It is a matter of a maker demanding that which he has created and is thus properly his."[81]

These three justifications of a norm of results all assume that a free, competitive market best measures the value of goods and therefore of their owners. To some, the market process is itself just: "It is the basic premise of a liberal-capitalist society that a fair distribution of income is determined by the productive input — productive as determined by the market — of individuals into the economy."[82] To others, laws of supply and demand are only "operative facts," not "ethical principles."[83] Still others argue that the market distorts the worth of results by using a price mechanism rather than measuring social contribution. Garbage collectors and police, for example, are invaluable to cities and may deserve more reward than athletes or lawyers. Or workers who build automobiles may contribute more than their foremen or designers of cosmetic alterations. By changing the measure of value, a norm of results may be made downwardly redistributive.

Psychologically, the norm of results is best suited to "cooperative relations in which economic productivity is a primary goal."[84] Proponents of this norm assume that people are independent, self-interested, and motivated mainly by rewards. Community members compare themselves to others to determine if their shares are equitable, that is, if they have the same ratio of rewards to contributions as do other community members. To each according to his or her productivity.[85] Thus in contrast to a norm of investments, people measure their worth through comparisons with others or possibly with an external standard of accomplishment. Success is measured absolutely or in relation to others, not to oneself.

The norm of results relies less on a conscious sense of community than does the norm of investments and indeed less than all of the other norms except the procedural one. In fact, its users often extol the value of the individual freethinker, standing apart from or even against his or her community. Its users also tend to be insistent methodological individualists, although there is no necessary link between a norm of results and an epistemology of methodological individualism.[86]

Strictly speaking, economic rationality requires only that people receive as many resources as they can use for the benefit of all; however people learn quickly to apply economic values to the rest of a culture, so that they come to believe that efficient producers deserve rewards, not only resources. Furthermore, efficient producers may use their status to obtain control of their community and to appropriate even greater rewards to themselves. Self-interest overwhelms altruism and fraternity,[87] and efficiency becomes synonymous with justice, in the eyes of both winners and losers.[88]

At this point, other market-oriented values come to dominate many features of individual psychology. People grow accustomed to impersonal dealings with interchangeable others, and they value others for their usefulness and exchange value.[89] Mutual self-interest, not fellowship or nurturance, induces interdependence: "Egoism can motivate one party to satisfy the expectations of the other, since by doing so he induces the latter to reciprocate and to satisfy his own [expectations] . . . We owe others certain things because of what they have previously done for us."[90] Division of labor and interchangeability among workers permit people to be economically interdependent while remaining emotionally independent.

At an extreme, defining justice as equity, demanding that everyone give and get in the same proportion as everyone else, becomes pathological. Unchecked, economic values lead to an unmitigated meritocracy in which the rich are seen as successes and good, and the poor as failures and bad. The devastating effects for both rich and poor are obvious. People refrain from activities with no market value; they blame themselves excessively for poverty and praise themselves excessively for wealth; they become one-dimensional and estranged: "A person becomes alienated from his possessions and creations when he learns to regard them as utilities which have value because other people desire them; he becomes alienated from other people when they are perceived as competing with him for scarce goods; and he becomes alienated from himself when he sees his own value as a utility based on the desires of others."[91]

One problem is having too much opportunity to rise or fall; another is having too little. Whether deliberately or not, the rich and powerful may bias the allocation system to continue to reward themselves even after they are no longer productive. More subtly, the need (described earlier) to believe in a just world creates an assumption that the rich have done valuable things and the poor have done worthless things. People with this view assume erroneously that luck is distributed equally, that opportunity is broad and equal, that wealth and poverty have no cumulative effects, and that activities have objective worth. At a further stage of reification, the distinctions among effort, achievement, and reward are lost. People combine norms of investment and results and assume not only that achievements are always rewarded, but also that efforts always lead to achievement. There is no psychological room here for honoring a virtuous debtor or condemning an unscrupulous millionaire. Goodness, productivity, and holdings correlate exactly. This pathology culminates finally in a belief that, by definition, whatever the rich do is moral and valuable and whatever the poor do is immoral and valueless. Otherwise, their positions would be reversed. In my terms, a norm of ascription masquerades as a norm of results: "To begin with, a criterion such as sex or age [or class] may serve as one of several indicators of a person's fitness. Gradually more and more stress is placed on this indicator and finally it becomes the only criterion and is considered decisive even when considerations of fitness pull in the opposite direction . . . [A] further development may take place so that references to fitness become superfluous and are replaced by the belief that it is in itself right to attach importance to status."[92] The flexible libertarian norm that gives everyone a chance to better himself or herself becomes rigid and elitist through distortion of its own best principles.

A final distortion leaves the norm itself intact, but applies it to the wrong elements in the community. The United States changed during the nineteenth century from an agrarian, small-scale, and relatively egalitarian society to a nation of corporate capitalism, huge institutions, and vast differences in wealth. During this period,

> through a highly successful case of ideological transfer, the Lockean defense of private property, which in the agrarian order made good sense morally and politically, was shifted over intact to corporate enterprise . . . The corporation took on the legitimacy of the farmer's home, tools, and land, and what he produced out of his land, labor, ingenuity, anguish, planning, forbearance, sacrifice, risk, and hope. The upshot was that the quite exceptional degree of autonomy the farmer members of the demos had enjoyed under the old order, an autonomy vis-à-vis both government and one another, was now granted to the corporation.[93]

This "extraordinary ideological sleight-of-hand" had two deleterious consequences. "First, the new order generated much greater differences than the old in political resources, skills, and incentives within the demos itself." Second, "the internal government of the corporation was . . . hierarchical and often despotic . . . An increasing proportion of the demos would live out . . . their daily existence, not within a democratic system but instead within a hierarchical structure of subordination."[94] Thus the extension to inappropriate bodies of the liberal tenets of private property, a mandate for profit-making, and opportunity to advance has stifled individuals' chances to use the same tenets justly to acquire their share of goods.

Ascription One solution to the problems of conflating and reifying effort, achievement, and reward in a norm of results is simply to eliminate any reliance on volition or accomplishment; that is, just distributions may depend solely on ascriptive traits, which are fixed at birth, permanent, socially important, easily ascertained, and ranked in value. Examples of these attributes are race, sex, class, and age.[95]

The fullest version of this norm is the medieval metaphor of a great chain of being, in which all living things have an appointed place in a hierarchy of value. Just as animals are a higher form of life than plants, the heavens rise over the earth, and the soul surpasses the body, so is the pope superior to the emperor, clergy to laity, and nobility to peasantry. Reason, divine law, and natural analogies reveal the proper social order. A correct hierarchy, in which each class receives benefits and obligations from the class above and gives them to the class below, yields a just and harmonious society.[96]

Secularized, the great chain of being becomes Edmund Burke's "Old Whig" world, in which each segment of the community has clearly defined authority, privileges, and duties.[97] Leaders of the community have a particularly difficult and crucial task, for which only a few qualify and for which the resources and rewards must be especially great. A society can be governed well only if it is "in that state of habitual social discipline in which the wiser, the more expert, and the more opulent conduct, and by conducting enlighten and protect, the weaker, the less knowing, and the less provided with the goods of fortune."[98] Leaders can acquire this wisdom, expertise, and opulence only under special circumstances:

> To be bred in a place of estimation; to see nothing low and sordid from one's infancy, . . . to stand upon such elevated ground as to be enabled to take a large view of the wide-spread and infinitely diversified combinations of men and affairs in a large society, . . . to be led to a guarded and regulated conduct, from a sense that you are considered as an instructor of your fellow-citizens in their highest concerns . . .; to be employed as an administrator of law and justice, and to be thereby amongst the first benefactors to mankind . . .: these are the circumstances of men that form . . . a *natural* aristocracy, without which there is no nation.[99]

The natural aristocracy need not be a hereditary aristocracy, but "the circumstances that form a natural aristocracy" occur only when property and rank are secure and devoid of vulgarity — that is, inherited. Furthermore, a law of primogeniture is essential because the "defensive power" of property "is weakened as it is diffused," that is, redistributed downward.[100] Thus with a few exceptions, the "natural aristocracy" is hereditary.

If aristocrats need to learn to use their wealth wisely, common people must be "taught to seek and to recognize the happiness that is to be found by virtue in all conditions." In the happiness of a "protected, satisfied, laborious and obedient people" lies "the true moral equality of mankind, and not in that monstrous fiction [of material equality] which, by inspiring false ideas and vain expectations into men destined to travel in the obscure walk of laborious life, serves only to aggravate and embitter that real inequality which it can never remove."[101] If each class "perform[s] its allotted function," it will be "secured such a livelihood, and no more than such a livelihood, as was proportioned to its status."[102] But a lower-class attack on "rank, and office and title and all the solemn plausibilities of the world"[103] would "confound . . . the best men with the worst; and weaken . . . and dissolve . . ., instead of strengthening and compacting, the . . . visible and regular authority of the state."[104]

An ascriptive norm persists, at least in diluted form. Contemporary advocates argue that some must command and others obey; no social order can long function without authoritative and stable leadership, which probably arises from a hereditary elite. In a few exceptional cases, people may climb to the top or fall from the heights, but usually people become what they are born to be. Constant striving by common people toward unattainable goals simply frustrates them needlessly; but freed from the anxieties of both useless ambition and possible destitution, they could pursue their given vocations to the best of their abilities. The just society is achieved when obligations balance rewards, when people are gratified by their appointed role, and when they exercise the freedom that comes from stability, security, and discipline.[105]

Even in supposedly classless America, "The tendency toward hereditary stratification is so deeply rooted . . . that if one could miraculously eliminate every trace of it today it would begin to creep back tomorrow." Both of the "newer principles," equality and meritocracy, are hard to live with regularly. At times, everyone "is delighted to accept some good thing . . . simply because he stood in a family relationship to the donor, or occupied a certain position in the community, or was a member of the same club as the donor."[106] Local elites, political and corporate nepotism, and particularly "aristocracies of professions" testify to the persistence of hierarchy. By even the second generation of an academic, military, or banking family, a private world of presuppositions, exclusiveness, endogamy, and superiority flourishes.[107]

Moving away from class categories, we find recurring arguments that inherent differences between the sexes call for differences in treatment. In voicing his fears of a nuclear holocaust, Erik Erikson offered the hope that "if women would only gain the determination to represent as . . .

lawyers what they have always stood for privately . . . they might well . . . add an ethically restraining . . . power to politics."[108] The details of his psychoanalytic argument that "girls emphasize . . . inner and . . . boys outer space"[109] are less important here than his assumption that sex should and does crucially influence a person's value structure, obligations, and privileges. Robert Jay Lifton argues that woman's triple role as nurturer, temptress, and knower is partly created by male fantasy and cultural institutions, but basically "emanates" from the "focus . . . [of] woman's psychological life, . . . close identification with organic life and its perpetuation."[110] Others argue that women's special traits make them best suited for nurturing and preserving the family, while men are best suited to jobs outside the home which require aggression, physical strength, or analytic thought.[111]

The idea of community plays two roles in an ascriptive norm. Sometimes ascriptive traits define the community to which some other norm is applied. In South Africa, the black and white communities have internal political equality, but vast differences in political rights and power separate the two. Similarly, parents may treat all children equally, but reserve for themselves, the adults, the right to decide on that treatment. At other times, other criteria, such as the course of a river or the outcome of a battle, determine community boundaries, and the norm of ascription then applies to its members. Burke, after all, made ascriptive claims only for Britain and Britons. The resources to be distributed do not affect the nature of the norm, but dramatically affect its importance to a society. A caste system in India and Jim Crow laws in the United States are philosophically similar, but empirically very different.

The norm of ascription has two complementary psychological components — noblesse oblige and deference. Those who top the social hierarchy "regard themselves as so much set apart as to belong to a totally different class of human beings — a class naturally designed to impose its will on all inferior classes."[112] But at least before democratic revolutions, they "derived, from the very extent of the respect they inspired, a motive for not abusing their power. The nobles, placed so high above the people, could take the calm and benevolent interest in their welfare which a shepherd takes in his flock. Without regarding the poor as equals, they took thought for their fate as a trust confided to them by Providence."[113] The elite is not simply a power elite; it must accept the responsibility for seeing past personal or sectional interests to rule for the good of all.

In medieval times, claims Tocqueville, those who ranked lower in the social hierarchy "accepted benefits from their [leaders] . . . and did not question their rights. They loved them when they were just and merciful

and felt neither repugnance nor degradation in submitting to their sever-
ities, which seemed inevitable ills sent by God."[114] In the modern era, ascriptive claims are more tied to merit. The "better sort" of the lower
classes defer to men of "rank and wealth" in the belief "that those who
were superior to them in these indisputable respects were superior also in
the more intangible qualities of sense and knowledge."[115] This claim
demonstrates the transformation of a norm of results into an ascriptive
norm; the social hierarchy is the outcome of a slow, inexorable sorting
process, at the end of which merit and rank co-vary. What is a problem
for a norm of results becomes a virtue for a norm of ascription.

Deferential workers need not be self-abnegating, since they see themselves as part of "an organic entity in which each individual has a proper
part to play, however humble. Inequality is seen as inevitable as well as
just, some men being inherently fitted for positions of power and privilege. To acknowledge the superiority of such people is not to demean or
belittle oneself, since all must benefit from their stewardship of
society."[116] If "all who properly fulfill their stations in life contribute
worthily to the common good," then deferential workers are "the moral,
if not the social, equals of the elite."[117]

Collectivities play two important roles in the psychology of ascriptive
social relations. First, classes are active social units. Laborers are linked
to other laborers by more than employment: they share a culture, norms,
and behaviors. Classes are stable, partly isolated, semiautonomous.
Friendships and marriage occur within one or between closely related
groups.[118] A society without the peculiarities and distinctions of classes
"would be as useless as a rankless army and as dull as a wine list that gave
neither the name of the vineyards nor the date of the vintages."[119]

Second, class conflict — as distinguished from class differences — is
unnecessary and pernicious. It is the job of the elite to rule in everyone's
interests; class conflict indicates its failure. If conflict continues, the
masses may legitimately abandon the old elite and give their allegiance to
a new, more effective one.[120]

Like the other norms, the ascriptive norm can succumb to perversions
and exaggerations. A caste system is an obvious distortion; closer to
home, so is a view that blacks deserve freedom, but not equality with
whites. Abraham Lincoln held such a view:

> I have no purpose to introduce political and social equality between
> the black and white races . . . Physical difference between the two
> . . . will probably forever forbid their living together upon the
> footing of perfect equality, and inasmuch as it becomes a necessity
> that there must be a difference, I . . . am in favor of the race to

which I belong, having the superior position . . . He [the Negro] is not my equal in many respects — certainly not in color, perhaps not in moral or intellectual endowment. But in the right to eat the bread, without leave of anybody else, which his own hand earns, *he is my equal and the equal of . . . every living man.*[121]

The claim that women differ significantly from men in ways that should affect each sex's vocation, privileges, and responsibilities is not a distortion of an ascriptive norm. It *is* an ascriptive norm. But the argument that women deserve less pay for the same jobs or less important and lucrative jobs does pervert the norm.[122] The perversion lies in the fact that this claim gives most of the privileges to one sex and most of the burdens to the other. An assertion that one ascriptive group is categorically superior to another destroys the distinctive quality of ascriptive justice — that rewards and obligations must be balanced. When sexual differences become sexual inequalities, ascription loses its moral force and becomes merely dominance and exploitation.

To the charges of racism and sexism implicit in the paragraphs above, some answer that affirmative action policies are themselves a misplaced use of ascriptive criteria. These policies are designed to end and partially compensate for past discrimination by setting targets for employing minorities and women in proportion to their representation in the relevant population subgroup. Opponents call this a retreat from achievement to ascriptive criteria: "The principle of professional qualification or individual achievement is subordinated to the new ascriptive principle of corporate identity. . . *The liberal and radical attack on discrimination was based on its denial of a justly earned place to a person on the basis of an unjust group attribute . . .* But now it is being demanded that one must have a place primarily because one possesses a particular group attribute."[123] Proponents of affirmative action see this view as naive or hypocritical; successful white men do not realize that affirmative action policies merely expose and correct for an underlying preference for white males that has always bolstered a supposed norm of achievement.[124]

The most serious danger inherent in an ascriptive norm is that a rigid hierarchical society may persist long after the elite has abandoned its responsibilities and the common people their pride in place. At that point, differences in rank persist only because the elite can retain power and wealth and, more subtly, define the legitimating values to benefit itself.[125] Thus professions require licensing of members in order to restrict access; promotions depend partly on intangible "character traits," appearance, or family connections; job categories flooded by women are downgraded. A ruling class with privileges but no merit or duties, and a subordinate class with duties and talents but no privileges, is a frightening but plausible inversion of the norm's intent.

Procedures   One possible solution to the rigidities of a hierarchical ascriptive norm is to maintain the use of ascription (thereby avoiding the problems of norms of need, investments, and results), but to abandon the hierarchical distinctions. All people, by virtue of their birth, deserve the same share of social goods as all other people — a norm of strict equality. Thus the circle is complete. Yet one might choose instead to abandon all norms that prescribe distributive outcomes. In that case, one might seek only to guarantee that the distributive *process* is fair, letting the distributive *outcomes* fall where they may. The use of procedures is thus a sixth possible norm. The first five norms start from a desired result and devise processes to approach it; the sixth norm starts with a valued process and sees the final result merely as derivative.

A procedural norm is qualitatively different from the others and does not fit along the continuum illustrated in figure 4. But since one's choice of a procedure may depend on one's choice of a principle of equality or differentiation, particular variants of the norm can themselves be located on the continuum.

The first procedure to be considered uses a principle of equality to produce differentiated results. Users of this procedure argue that although people have fundamentally equal worth, in some circumstances it is impossible to treat them equally. Rather than try to do so and inevitably fail, we can respond to their basic equality more fairly by subjecting them all to a procedure that randomly chooses winners and losers.

For example, proponents of selection by lottery argue that cumulative inequalities always pervert meritocratic intentions, so that the apparently open norms of investments and results merely delude and damage both winners and losers. With a lottery, social resources are still distributed unequally, but all community members have the same probability of receiving them, and no one is able wrongly to attribute success or failure to his or her own character. Everyone has an equal chance fairly to achieve unequal results.[126] Alternatively, some see a lottery as a substitute for an impossible egalitarian norm, not for a flawed meritocratic one. When a valued social resource is indivisible, an equal distribution, though desirable, may be unattainable. A lottery gives everyone an equal chance to receive the reward and thus justifies the unequal distribution it ultimately produces.

Other procedural rules, although not strictly random, are also intended to yield fair outcomes by ignoring individual characteristics and rejecting all final patterns. Examples are chronological waiting lists, queues, and unassigned places at the dinner table or in the classroom.[127]

A second procedure mixes principles of equality and differentiation and generally yields differentiated outcomes. This is the procedure of free consent, for which Robert Nozick is the strongest contemporary advocate.[128] In his formulation, justice follows from adhering to the twin principles of private property and entitlement. As long as holdings are legitimately acquired initially, legitimately used, and legitimately transferred, any configuration that results from that history is just. People are entitled to keep what they can fairly get — no matter how much or how little that is.[129]

Nozick gives two reasons for making free consent necessary and sufficient to legitimate property acquisition and transfer.[130] First, free consent is the essential foundation of liberty and rights, which in turn are the essential foundations for a system of social justice. Second, exchanges that are not fraudulent or coerced benefit everyone involved; otherwise they would not enter into them. Thus interfering with a freely chosen exchange on behalf of some patterned result or group both intolerably violates human rights and inhibits the achievement of the greatest possible happiness for all.

Others agree that justice is synonomous with free consent, although they may reject Nozick's Lockean premises or libertarian conclusions. For Thomas Hobbes, "When a covenant is made, then to break it is *unjust*: and the definition of *Injustice* is no other than *the not performance of covenant*. And whatsoever is not unjust is *just*."[131] For Jeremy Bentham, "When the question of slavery is not considered, there is little to say respecting the conditions of *master* and its correlative conditions, constituted by the different kinds of servants. All these conditions are the effects of contracts; these contracts the parties interested may arrange to suit themselves."[132] For some modern philosophers too, "Free consent can render any situation just . . . Where inequalities of reward . . . are undeserved, only actual consent to their existence . . . render[s] those inequalities, and the society in which they exist, completely just."[133] Thus differences in reward between master and servant, owner and worker, the deserving and the undeserving are all just as long as each party agrees that they are just.

A community relying on freely contracted exchanges includes all those people with enough ability and resources to bargain, even if their only resource is their labor power. As Bentham suggests, slaves are simply defined out of the community, since they cannot freely consent to anything; for analogous reasons, imbeciles and children are also not full members.

Besides slavery and imbecility, however, there may be more subtle impediments to free consent, such as brainwashing, ignorance, stupidity, threat, economic duress, and certain moods.[134] And the norm has other dangers. What about the ill or handicapped, who do not have even labor power to exchange? And can an exchange between an impoverished worker and a millionaire employer be truly fair? May one sell oneself into slavery? What if one does not know, or does not agree to, the consequences of one's agreements? What of the unintended effects of an agreement on fellow citizens or on unborn generations? Finally, there is the "Rawlsian fallacy: . . . that if something is an individual good it is *ipso facto* a collective good."[135] After all, "Exchanges between freely consenting individuals can result in an economic structure that for various reasons members of the society acting as a collectivity might wish to alter."[136]

The procedure of free consent is egalitarian in its assumption that all people are equally able to make choices and equally responsible for living by the choices they make. But it is differentiating in its assumption that those who are better negotiators, or who happen to have more goods to exchange, deserve to reap the full benefits of their favored position. Its effects will almost certainly be differentiating, since its use is likely to magnify existing differences in holdings, abilities, and luck.

A third set of procedures relies solely on a principle of differentiation. It draws an analogy between human society and Darwin's law of natural selection, which is "hourly scrutinizing, throughout the world, the slightest variations; rejecting those that are bad, preserving and adding up all that are good; silently and insensibly working, *whenever and wherever opportunity offers*, at the improvement of each organic being."[137] This law is inevitable, just, and ultimately benevolent: "From the war of nature, from famine and death, the most exalted object which we are capable of conceiving, namely, the production of the higher animals, directly follows. There is grandeur in this view of life, . . . that, . . . from so simple a beginning endless forms most beautiful and most wonderful have been, and are being evolved."[138]

Herbert Spencer most eloquently transforms Darwinian evolution into human social justice. Society is an organism with life and purpose; perfection of the species dominates any personal claim. Conflict between individuals and within societies will force them to adapt until people become perfectly attuned to one another and strife disappears. Only then can moral law be an absolute claim; until then, moral law changes as conditions for survival change. Our only right at present is to use our capacities, pursue happiness, and overcome others.[139]

Unrestrained conflict not only will lead to perfection, but also defines justice at the present time. Spencer assumes that some people are simply smarter, stronger, more energetic than others. An ideal world would reward merit, but ours is not yet an ideal world. Therefore it is just for people to retain whatever they can get, by whatever means they choose. Any other distributive rule merely enables the weak to drag down the strong and slows the evolutionary process: "Is it not cruel to increase the sufferings of the better that the sufferings of the worse may be decreased?"[140]

William Graham Sumner softens Spencer's harshness by combining the law of nature with a norm of results. The two norms differ, since the latter creates a process in order to reward skills and ambitions, whereas the former justifies a process that rewards victory; that is, rewarding productivity is the intent of one norm and a possible but unintended consequence of the other. But grafting them together yields a hybrid that equates victory with productivity, dominance with social contribution, strength with virtue:

> Competition . . . is a law of nature. Nature is entirely neutral; she submits to him who most energetically and resolutely assails her. She grants her rewards to the fittest, therefore, without regard to other considerations of any kind. If, then, there be liberty, men get from her just in proportion to their works . . . Such is the system of nature . . . If we try to amend it, there is only one way in which we can do it . . . We can take the rewards from those who have done better and give them to those who have done worse . . . We cannot go outside of this alternative: liberty, inequality, survival of the fittest; not-liberty, equality, survival of the unfittest. The former carries society forward and favors all its best members; the latter carries society downwards and favors all its worst members.[141]

Communities further soften the harsh law of nature by regulating market competition, so that the best and strongest win the most, but the worst and weakest are not destroyed. As long as everyone follows certain rules and abstains from certain behaviors, results of the market process may be unfortunate, but not unjust or immoral. One can be called hardhearted, but not unfair, in driving a hard bargain with a failing competitor or in raising prices in a ghetto store. Similarly, producing an expensive commodity that loses popularity may be cause for pity or lamentation, but not for cries of foul play.

Unlike the first two processes, the law of nature does not exclude from the community those who cannot or choose not to participate. Handicapped or reluctant members are part of the process and are simply eliminated early—either physically, according to Spencer, or economically, in the market.

The dangers of the law of nature, even modified into a market, are obvious. Inequalities cumulate. Rampant self-interest reigns. There is no room for dignity in weakness, humility in strength, or collective action for the common good. At most, this process is murderous anarchy; it is at least coldhearted and ruthless. The strong get stronger, and the weak or self-abnegating simply lose.

Underlying the psychology of a procedural norm is an assumption that community members are competitive and interdependent; they "share a bond but one which is antagonistic or has a clear conflict of interest."[142] Interdependence combined with conflict over goals or social resources that everyone values creates a "comparative or contesting set [that] implies winning-losing, better-worse outcomes, inferior-superior status."[143] The degree of competition and the importance of victory vary, however, thereby determining which distributive process is used.

The simplest resolution of competitive interdependence is Pareto's principle, which mandates all changes that help at least one person and hurt none, disregarding the legitimacy of envy and assuming that the starting point is fair. Thus Nozick endorses exchanges that free individuals agree will benefit them both, and others are puzzled by "resistance to the idea that 'profit' is available to both seller and buyer in the same transaction."[144]

Yet there are problems even with the Pareto principle. First, assuming that all starting points are fair begs a crucial issue of distributive justice. Why should we assume that any particular distribution is not the result of prior unfair actions and thus in itself unfair? Second, does an exchange that benefits only the advantaged trader have exactly the same moral status as an exchange that benefits only the disadvantaged trader? Third, dismissing envy simply evades the problem of interpersonal comparisons of utility and ignores most of what we know about psychology. Finally, Pareto's principle is usually irrelevant: in most exchanges involving scarce resources, some gain and others lose.

Before considering direct competition, however, we should consider indirect competition, or relative deprivation. It occurs "when people striving for the same goal, and achieving it *independently*, nevertheless rank and measure their standing relative to each other by using the goal as a common standard."[145] Thus one person's success does not preclude another's; runners race against time, not each other, and they cannot shorten their own time by lengthening that of others. People are, however, apt to measure success relatively, not absolutely: runners *feel* that they are competing with each other, not the clock. Similarly, participants in random procedures such as a lottery, waiting list, or coin toss do not "beat" or "lose to" each other, although they perceive that they do. As the goods being distributed broaden from material goods to "goals, values, ways of thinking, being,"[146] the feeling of relative deprivation runs an increasing risk of becoming personally and socially destructive.

Moving up the scale of degrees of competition, we come to direct competition, in which perceptions coincide with facts. A loss is absolute as well as relative, since one succeeds by taking from others as well as by advancing oneself. Here competitors have no independent measure of success, no chance for joint or partial success. The extent of one person's victory is the measure of the other's defeat.[147] Increasing one's market share in an expanding market is indirect competition; in a stable market, expansion is direct competition. Similarly, theories of class conflict assume direct competition; trickle-down theories or theories of consensual, permeable social strata assume indirect competition. In direct, as in indirect, competition, personal conflict and community instability rise as the value of the goods or goals at stake increases.

Even direct competition has limits, however. Rules of the game assure everyone some share of the total, a voice in later contentions, and a chance to change any outcome. In a majoritarian democracy, for example, the minority accepts the decisions of the majority because it sees the process as just, it never loses an intolerable amount, and it has another chance to compete. If these conditions break down, so does majoritarian democracy.

Removing these limits leads to total conflict, in which victory is complete and final. The loser receives neither a share of goods nor a chance to compete again. "Although one's prior efforts, investment, and costs may elicit some form of condolence or compassion they are not allowed to alter the decision as to who deserves what."[148] Spencer's law of nature rules.

Total conflict occurs when the good at stake is coveted, finite, and indivisible — "the promotion, the fair maiden, the prize."[149] If conflict is extensive enough to reject all rules of social order, it is obviously very destructive to a community. At an extreme, only annihilating the opposition permits stability; life for the losers becomes "solitary, poor, nasty, brutish and short."[150]

Domains of Life

The six norms just described are, of course, much tidier on the page than they are in any human mind. Very few people, whether philosophers or assembly line workers, use only one or make clear choices among several. Instead, people try to combine norms that conflict analytically; they shift ground as they sense difficulties ahead; they resolve dilemmas by fiat; and they jump from one norm to another without knowing that they are doing so. Nevertheless, from this blurring one can sort out distinct patterns of normative use that determine respondents' distributive choices. Understanding these patterns, however, requires a fuller description of the domains of life than I have provided so far.

Three domains are important in this book. The *socializing domain* addresses "everyday life," such as family, school, and friends. It is distinguished by four characteristics. First, the resources to be distributed may be material goods, services, emotions, or authority, but seldom money. Second, community boundaries are clearly defined, and community members are easily identified. Third, people expect to have significant control over actions within this domain. That control may be direct, as in a family, or it may be diffuse and only potential, as in a school or neighborhood association, but the issues here appear intelligible and manageable, even to ordinary people like themselves. Fourth, private, self-interested concerns are legitimate — in fact, for many people they are the *only* legitimate concerns in this domain. Few parents, for example, will support busing of their children for the sake of the national goal of desegregation if they think their children will thereby be harmed; in fact, they would view such support as evidence of being a bad parent.

The *economic domain* addresses issues of earning a living and of finding and knowing one's place in the larger society. Thus it deals with income and authority within one's own and others' workplaces, the social structure and where one fits into it, and the processes by which occupational and class positions are determined. It too has four characteristics. First, the goods to be distributed are pecuniary or obvious money substitutes. Second, community boundaries are broad and vague: communities are interdependent and even indistinguishable. There is no easy way to determine who is or is not a member of the community. Third, most aspects of the economy and society appear to be uncontrollable by anyone. People see them either as parts of the natural world, not subject to human direction, or as Leviathans that should, but cannot, be harnessed. Fourth, private, self-interested concerns are legitimate and may even be the only claims with automatic legitimacy.

The *political domain* addresses issues of citizenship, of the effects of the federal government on one's own life, and of hopes and fears for the future of the United States. It too has four characteristics. First, the goods to be distributed are both pecuniary and nonpecuniary, since they include rights, influence, legal decisions, and authority over values. Second, the community boundaries are broad and vague — communities are interdependent and members often indistinguishable. Third, citizens or their leaders are able to control the outcome of most political questions, although a small, but important, aspect of the political domain is uncontrollable. This aspect is the realm of the future, the ideal society, which exists only in the imagination. Fourth, concerns must be public and not apparently self-interested in order to be legitimate.

These domains and their identifying characteristics are not categories with precise and measurable parameters. Rather, they are heuristic devices, general frameworks within which issues with common traits cluster. A particular issue may not have all four characteristics typical of its domain, but most do, and no single characteristic has more exceptions than any other. In short, these domains are organizing devices for groups of issues, not conceptually distinct units of analysis.

Conclusion

This book contends that we can best understand people's distributive judgments by looking not at their general ideologies or class position, but at the distributive norms they apply to particular domains of life. Respondents usually start from a principle of equality, and use mainly egalitarian norms, when they address the socializing and political domains; they usually start from a principle of differentiation, and use mainly differentiating norms, when they address the economic domain.

The modifiers in the previous sentence, "usually" and "mainly," identify caveats in the basic contention. First, a few respondents do not follow this dominant three-part pattern of beliefs. Second, most respondents feel ambivalent about some or all of it. Finally, except for the endpoints of strict equality and ascription, each norm can be used to redistribute upward *or* downward. A response to need, for example, begins from an assumption of equality, but if we use it to expend all of our resources on kidney dialysis or education for gifted children, then cancer victims or the retarded will be double losers. Similarly, a norm of results is basically differentiating, but if we decide that nurses produce more of value than baseball players, we could use it to redistribute downward.

Setting aside these caveats, however, the dominant three-part pattern goes a long way toward answering Sombart's question of "Why no socialism in the United States?" Americans see socialism, or, more precisely, redistribution of wealth, as an economic matter and thus subject to differentiating norms, or as a mixed economic and political matter, and thus as a muddle between conflicting norms. If there is no political payoff for resolving this muddle, and if its resolution would require a great deal of time, energy, or mental strain, the most rational thing to do is to ignore it — and thus to "oppose" socialism by not supporting it.[151] Finally, this three-part pattern may help to explain why Americans so often seem to hold inconsistent or "unconstrained" political beliefs, since the pattern I propose does not fit along a single political dimension of liberalism-conservatism. The rest of the book examines this contention.

4 The Socializing Domain and the Principle of Equality

It is time finally to obey Redfield's second injunction, to submit the interview data to the "demands of a more detached and abstract understanding." In this chapter, I begin that process by examining respondents' views about justice in the socializing domain. My goal is to show their shared egalitarianism without submerging their individual idiosyncrasies or class differences and without imposing clarity where they feel ambivalence. I will also try to capture the emotional nuances of their feelings about their beliefs and the substantive nuances of their interpretations of a principle of equality.

Equality, Frustration, and the Poor

Poor respondents may find no joy in their support for a principle of equality, for several reasons. Sometimes they support equality because they cannot afford to do anything else; rewarding a job well done is not possible if one has no goods to give as rewards. Sometimes they seek more equality because they hope it will lead them out of poverty; if the mayor gives summer jobs to a lot of teenagers, at least a few may grasp this chance to "make it." Sometimes they are egalitarian because they live on the edge of physical or financial disaster; if one does not respond to an urgent need, the needy person may never recover from the illness or escape the debt collector.[1] Finally, sometimes they are egalitarian simply because they believe in a principle of equality; in that case, they are frustrated because the resources they have to distribute equally are so limited.

Two respondents' views especially illustrate how the fact of poverty and the principle of equality combine to cause bitterness and unhappiness. I have already introduced Maria Pulaski.[2] Her childhood "was rough, very rough. Many times we needed clothes or shoes, we'd have to wait for it until the money came in." Still, "If we needed anything, we [eventually] got it." The fact of need and the obligations entailed by a norm of need dominate her adulthood as they did her childhood. She provides for an extended family on $140 a week and can imagine no worse future than "the way things are now." When her children were young, "anything" they wanted "they got. Even if I didn't have it, I would do housework and I'd get it for them." Although they are now grown, they still "all come to me if they have any problems. If something happens, one of them gets sick, I run. It's always running. And maybe this is why I find it so difficult. I don't know." She works hard to help them rather than easing up in her increasingly onerous housecleaning jobs, "so they can have something which I didn't have. I'd rather see them have it. They're young. I'm getting older."

Although she responds to needs, Maria reserves her enthusiasm for a norm of investments, especially where education is concerned. She and her husband "would have done anything" to educate their children. Their continued support of two grandchildren in parochial high school "is rough because he [her husband] got the cut in pay. But as long as she [a granddaughter] can get a better education and better herself, why not?" Asked why education is so important, she answers acerbically, "Well, what kind of a job could you get now, really, without an education? It's nice to have a nice education, become something — a lawyer, or whatever, doctor. At least get a nice clean job. I can't see them working in a factory when you can better yourself if you're smart enough to do it."

Maria wants to believe that the more readily available, and therefore more egalitarian, investment of hard work is just as rewarding: "If you don't have the education, you can still work and try to make the money. If you want to do it, you'll try hard." But this dictum fails her, since her family's situation is worsening despite her best efforts. So she clings to her old beliefs in hard work and drives herself to satisfy the needs of her family in the desperate hope that the next generation will be able to escape her forced reliance on equality.

Maria wants school teachers also to help the neediest to become less needy. School teachers "*should* help the ones that can't do it, the less smart ones. They need it. I believe in that." Asked why, she reaffirms her guarded optimism about effort, explaining, "So they can, they get something. [Maybe] they can't get ahead. Some of them can, some can't. But I would really try." As at home, compassion is also important: "The teachers shouldn't compare, not in front of the kids. It's embarrassing to the child [who does badly]. It makes the kid feel bad."

But Maria is not all compassion; sometimes she demands results. She is incensed that her granddaughter is allowed to go out without first doing chores at home, and that schools "just push them [failing students] ahead. I can't see them promote someone, can't read, can't write too good." Poor students deserve help, but only successful students deserve A's and promotion.

Politicians who fall down on the job also deserve no compassion. Maria is angry about local politicians' lack of response to their constituents' needs. She asked her alderman, the mayor, and the parish priest for help in admitting her granddaughter to trade school. No help was forthcoming, and Maria became disgusted:

MP: If you need, if you want to talk to someone, you should be able to go and talk, even to the mayor. Or write him a letter.

JH: Do you think he really tried to help or not?

MP: No, I don't think he did. But when they want the votes, they're *all* around you. "He's a good man, he's this, he's that, if you need anything, or you want to talk to him, you can." And then when the time comes for a little favor, you can't get it. So sometimes I get so mad, I don't even want to vote.

Not only do the needy not get extra help, but they also do not even get as much help as the rich and well-connected. Maria is "not prejudiced with the black, but it seems like they're gettin' all the good jobs now." Even worse, it is useless for the poor, black or white, to apply for scholarships from the city because "you wouldn't get it anyway. A doctor's son or a businessman that's *got* the money, their kids get the scholarships. You wouldn't hear anyone that needs, really needed it, got it." She concludes bitterly, "You have to have money, otherwise you don't get it. It's not fair."

Maria's belief that the neediest deserve the most help is a constant burden; she avoids feeling like a martyr to her family only because of her bitter realism, flashes of humorous rebellion, and occasional insistence that others earn their rewards. But she has sacrificed her happiness for the slim hope that her children will benefit from her efforts, and she is incensed when teachers and local leaders do not also accept their obligation to respond to needs. Thus Maria expresses a principle of equality, uses egalitarian norms, and seeks downward redistribution in the socializing domain.

Maria may feel frustrated and bitter, but at least she is coping with her poverty. Vincent Sartori is just as egalitarian in the socializing domain, but he is much more desperate because he cannot manage his poverty at all. He is thirty-five, has two young children and no work: "Some jobs I got laid off, some I got fired, some I just couldn't take no more." He runs an unlicensed snack shop for teenagers, even though he will lose his unemployment compensation if caught. He hopes to make money, but he also hopes that "if the kids are in there, they're not hanging around over near the factory. God, the broken glass—that area is a mess." He permits marijuana, but bans glue sniffing as too dangerous; he sells liquor illicitly only to the oldest teens; he organizes ball games and sends the youngest home by 9:00 P.M.—"all 'cause I got a heart for kids."

Vincent is a gentle man who loves children. But he is also a loser. He cannot keep a job; he is jeopardizing his unemployment compensation; he "blows" his money on liquor or bail; he has a long record of arrests; his family lives on "macaronies"; he cannot afford an essential operation for his son; his wife is unhappy and estranged. He tells the interviewer, a stranger from Yale University with a running tape recorder, that he is considering a bank robbery. Winter is approaching, but his apartment's only source of heat, a gas stove, has been turned off because he owes $350. Vincent's snack shop partner is "simple in the mind" and is "always" trying "to write them [people he feels sorry for] out a check." Nevertheless, Vincent chose him for a partner because "he would give anything in the world just to be as normal as you or me. He's trying to make a dollar. So, hey, what's fair is fair."

Vincent's helpless anger in the face of all this rarely appears in his discussion of family, school, or community. Like Maria, he struggles to respond to his family's needs, but he is too poor. His daughter's bicycle is "just shot," but when she asked for a new one, "I says, 'Yeah, pretty soon we're going to get you a nice one.' Then we try to change her mind off to it. 'Cause, well, we can't do it right now, 'cause we got this bill and we got that bill. It's a pain." He and his wife "didn't even go out to eat in about a couple of years now. A couple of times, I had the landlord's car, we went to McDonalds, took one of those Sunday drives. That was once in a great moon."

Thus Vincent would like to act on a norm of need, but he cannot afford to. All he can do is try desperately to prevent his children from "going through what I'm going through, so they can say, 'Hey, we got something!" He insists, in the face of all his experience, that "dreams, sometimes they come true. Sometimes they don't. But if you *really* put your mind to something you *want* to get, you keep it in your mind, it can be done. And that's why *my* object is to make money. I got almost $100 saved so far."

Like Maria, Vincent occasionally uses a norm of results in his family. Unlike her, he does not use it to hold people up to standards; instead, he uses it to justify rewards. Because his wife earns the family's only steady income, he permits her to make budgetary decisions. "I mean, it's *her* money, *she's* working for it. So I can't tell her what to do with the money."

Vincent has little to say on the subject of justice in education. He regrets having left school early, because "if you want to read a book, there's words in there. I'm not much of a reader, unless it has pictures in the book. As far as sitting down, reading a whole book with just words in it, forget it—I couldn't do it." Nevertheless, he argues forcefully that teachers should "put more attention" to slow students. He uses an athletic analogy to explain why:

> I got feelings for other people. Especially kids that can't do what the other kids are doing. They say, "He's no good, he don't know how to play right." So I talk to the kid: "Don't worry, because everyone has their days. They might say that you stink now. Then when you practice and you start playing with them, then they're going to be saying, 'Well, we should have had him a long time ago!' "

Furthermore, the athletic analogy does not suggest to Vincent that students should be taught to compete. On the contrary, "If the kid really wants to learn, if he puts his mind to it, he can learn. He doesn't have to try and be better than the next one. Just learn what you can learn, so you know what's what." Vincent's norm of responding to needs has limits here: in the final analysis, the child is responsible for his or her own success or failure, and rewards should be commensurate with degrees of success. Thus he tempers a need norm with a mixture of investment and results norms. But even if people are not equally skilled, they are still equally worthy of respect and help.

Vincent's egalitarianism in the neighborhood takes the form of nostalgia for community: "In the fifties, everybody got along better. Like, neighborhoods were neighborhoods." But "ever since [John] Kennedy was assassinated, this whole country just went crazy. The crimes, the economy, neighborhoods are altogether different. Before, you used to turn around and say, 'Sally, how you doing? Come in for coffee.' Now you look at your neighbor, and she snubs you. People are sick today, I'm telling you." His nostalgia, of course, may be empirically unfounded, but normatively it is a clear expression of Tawney's ideal of fellowship.

Again like Maria, Vincent is incensed about illegitimate political differentiation. He castigates the mayor for saying, " 'Well, I'm gonna do more for the black man than I would for the Italians.' What's he got? He's prejudiced? You're running for an office like that, you should just say, 'I'll make everything equal for everybody.' " He tells a long story showing how wealthy and powerful residents of New Haven receive special privileges and legal exemptions, and concludes, "The law today is—it stinks. If you got the money then, hey, you got your freedom."

Vincent knows that many of his problems occur because he gets "suckered in a lot. I just don't have the heart to turn somebody down, if I got it [money] on me." He is now being dunned for the cost of an errant neighbor's furniture for which he cosigned. He is disgusted, "but yet, if he turns around again someday in the future and needs to borrow ten dollars, twenty dollars, like a jerk I'll give it to him. Maybe that's why my brothers are where *they* are and I'm where *I* am. 'Cause they're tight." In the final analysis, however, he does not really envy his "tight" and well-off brothers, "because (pause) I'm different than my brothers actually."

Vincent cannot articulate how he is different, but perhaps we can. He endorses strict equality and response to need even to the point of hurting himself. Egalitarianism for him is not, as it is for Maria, a necessary response to poverty, but rather a belief whose implementation is curtailed by poverty. The most "macho" of my interview subjects, Vincent is the most gentle and idealistic in the socializing domain. He is too poor and disorganized to achieve his ideals, so he becomes bitter, frustrated, and sometimes violent. But he maintains dreams of friendship, security, and happiness—if not for himself, then for his children.

Equality, Contentment, and the Poor

Not all of the poor respondents feel frustrated in their egalitarian beliefs. Some are happy with their lot; they pursue equality because they believe in it. Their poverty prohibits them from redistributing downward as many things as they would like to, but they do not feel that it completely constrains their ability to choose. In part, this difference in emotional reactions is a consequence of degrees of poverty. Most of the contented poor are better-off than most of the frustrated poor. But differences in outlook depend on more than differences in poverty. Without psychiatric evidence, I cannot explain why people react differently to the same stimuli, but I can use two respondents to illustrate how some people are, despite their poverty, content in their use of a principle of equality.

Pamela McLean is thirty-eight years old, a part-time secretary, and a devout Catholic. She has four school-age children and a high school education. Her husband, Pete, is a welder. When he works full-time, they earn about $11,000 (in 1976 dollars), but he has been laid off fifteen of the previous twenty-four months. Thus "last year was just terrible for us. I thought the roof was coming in. We just were really tight on money."

Although Pamela grew up "poor, I never felt that there was anything in the whole world, if I needed it or wanted it badly enough, I wasn't going to get it. Somebody, somehow, someway would get it for me. I was probably spoiled." She views her current situation with similar optimism: "I don't think of myself as poor, even with this financial disaster we've just been through. I think we're fairly upper middle-class. Again, I can never think of anything that I want and I can't figure out a way for us to get it. Except that now it takes a little more time to get it." This confidence that she can provide for her own and her family's needs most distinguishes Pamela from Maria and Vincent. She has more money, but more important is her belief that responding to needs is not an impossible task or almost unbearable struggle. Somehow she will get what she wants; Maria and Vincent can never say that convincingly.

Perhaps because of her confidence, Pamela focuses less on the need norm than on other variants of a principle of equality. She uses the norm of strict equality in two ways. Each child receives certain identical goods, such as a small bicycle at age seven and a large one at age eleven. They get these without question—but no more: "My son has abused his final, big-size bike, and it is in great need of repair. And he just *expected* that somebody was going to get him another bike. And I said, 'Too bad, kid, that's it. You've had two.'" More often, however, equality means sharing all the available goods: "There's very few things that the one particular child owns. We have a large toy room, and it's just stacked full of four kids' worth of collections. Sam's guitar—no one else is allowed to touch that. But for the majority of things, it's community property. We don't have 'mine'; it's mostly 'ours.'" The only exception is special toys such as the guitar, bought with allowances that are carefully calibrated to chores.

Pamela and Pete balance norms of ascription and equality to accommodate differences between them. Pete used to be "*death* on my going to work. Just *never* wanted me to. I think it offended his male pride, to have people think that he couldn't support us." Pamela resisted this sexism — "At one point, it seemed very important to me to go to work only because he was telling me that I couldn't" — but she elaborately arranges her schedule to avoid being "one of these mothers that are never home for their kids." She dominates in decision making, however: "I'm the more persuasive of the two, and don't give in the easiest, and probably talk it to death until he gives in to my way." Pamela and Pete maintain elements of a sexually ascriptive relationship, but both know that they are basically equal.

When the children are involved in decisions, Pamela invokes an egalitarian procedural norm. In disputes over weekend trips, "You say, 'Well, all right, we'll go to your place this time, and it'll be your turn next time, and then *you* can choose after that' — this type thing." Occasionally the children even override their parents, as on a vacation trip to Canada: "It was the kids' decision to go. I didn't want to go in the worst way. I hate the *drive* all the way, and to spend it with all those relatives was just more than I wanted to do! And I was right — it was the worst two weeks we ever had! But the kids kept at us: 'We want to go, we want to go!' So it was more their decision that time than ours. We just kind of fell in."

Pamela is much less egalitarian when she thinks about schools. She expects teachers and parents to give children all the help they need, but most often she uses a norm of results to prescribe stricter academic and social standards in schools. She praises a new school in which "they will teach discipline. They *will* teach reading, writing, and arithmetic. It *will* be taught sitting down at a desk. For God's sake, this [is] what's important." Yet Pamela "really hates" competition among children because it "hurts the ones who aren't able to compete as they'd like to, through no fault of their own." Instead, schools and parents should "just praise the effort that's made," since effort, being voluntary, can be equal: "Carol is so uncoordinated. I'm worried about this baseball thing. She wants so badly to do it, and I don't think she's going to make this team. She's very big for her age, and she's awkward. And although she has the desire and would be a very reliable player, she's just not going to be good. And I *ache* for her. So kids suffer, and that's why I'm happy that they do the best job they can do, and if it's not a winner, fine." She knows that her principles are not completely disinterested: "If I had real athletic-type kids that excelled, or extremely popular children that were natural leaders, I might feel differently." But she concludes that, nevertheless,

"It doesn't matter if you're the best, trying your hardest gets more merit." Thus she balances an insistence that children be made to perform as well as they can with an equally strong insistence that they not be penalized for failures not of their own volition.

Pamela prescribes equality within the community in two ways. First, she is distressed about her own racial prejudice, which she became aware of when she immediately assumed that a group of black teenagers outside her home were troublemakers. Second, she announces proudly that: "I'm a real weirdie when it comes to what people make or how much someone weighs. I never see these things. And it amazes me when someone relates something about age, like 'Oh, I'm so much older than you are.' And it never really dawned on me that there was any difference. So I always think everybody makes the same amount of money, until somebody says, 'Oh, I can't afford to go.'" She sees this lack of awareness of differences as evidence that she is unprejudiced, at least among whites, and egalitarian, and she is proud of those traits.

Thus Pamela's use of a principle of equality is mainly a source of pride and fulfillment to her. She enjoys trying to satisfy her family's needs, sometimes by earning money outside the home, and sometimes by being a good mother inside it. She dominates her husband and children, but she cheerfully lets them override her sometimes. Like Maria and Vincent, she insists on good performance in school, but rejects needless competition. Only when she considers humiliation and prejudice—whether inflicted by someone else or herself—do egalitarian distributive norms cause her distress. Thus Pamela is just as egalitarian in her basic beliefs as Maria and Vincent, but she has slightly different normative emphases and very different emotional responses to her beliefs and the world around her.

Phillip Santaguida was introduced in chapter two as the softhearted cynic. Despite his belief that neither rich nor poor deserve their lot, he shares Pamela's contentment rather than Maria's and Vincent's despair in the socializing domain. And despite his perception of the economy as a Darwinian struggle, he is egalitarian and empathic in this domain. Phillip and his wife Marion's working-class income is a dramatic improvement over that of his childhood: "Always had enough to eat. Never had enough clothes." As a consequence, he is both gratified by his current status and fiercely determined that his children never know deprivation.

Phillip was amused by my questions on childrearing, but his offhand answers reveal a now-familiar pattern of strict equality, need, and results as guiding norms. His two children "fought, they didn't want to share. 'Cause if they wanted to share as they were children, they wouldn't be human. But they were taught to share." Their allowance depended on "how much money I was making at the time, and if they were fresh and they didn't pay attention when I gave out orders," and if they did their chores. But even when resources were scarce, "Kids always came first here."

The casualness of this mix of norms of equality, results, and need contrasts sharply with two arenas of deeply felt egalitarianism. The first is an investment norm: Phillip's only ambition for his children was for them "to get an education," so they would not have to work as hard as he and Marion did: "I worked two jobs to send my kid to college. I bought him everything, so he could look decent and go to school. I says, 'You're not going to be ignorant like *I* was. See that boat — that guy went to school, he got an education. See that guy that's digging that ditch — he didn't go to school. You got the opportunity.' I didn't have the opportunity." Like Maria, Phillip sees education and hard work as alternative ways to "make it," and like her, he finds the former preferable and more reliable; however, Phillip differs from Maria in that his belief is solid and secure, not a desperate clutching at the last possible hope. Their belief in the value of investments is the same; their faith in the rewards of investments is very different.

Second, Phillip values money within a family only because it can gratify needs and wants. If he were richer, he "would help my family more. They don't have as much as us — share it with them." He rejects a norm of results in a rhetorical challenge to Marion. She argues that rather than saving money for their own future, they should give it to the grandchildren who need it now. After all, "If we get sick, we have the house for collateral." Phillip responds:

PS: But Marion, a lot of people say, "I worked hard, let them learn the hard way." Look, if you're gonna be good, you're gonna be good. If you're gonna be ambitious, you're gonna be ambitious. Is Keith gonna be any more lazier or be any more ambitious if I didn't give him the money? Is he gonna be any dumber or anything?

MS: No.

In short, Phillip faces fewer demands and has more resources than Maria and Vincent, so responding to family needs is a pleasure, not a burden, for him: "I got my happiness by giving it to him [his grandson]. After all, you can't take it with you, eh?"

Like Pamela and Pete, Phillip and Marion maintain an image of male dominance in family decision-making despite the basic equality of their relationship. Phillip first claims that "I am the man of the house and I

make a little more decisions," but this quick answer is belied by his behavior. Phillip and Marion listen to each other; they mutually confirm
perceptions of reality and history; they respect and help each other:

PS: We cook together, clean the dishes together, wash the floors, do the
windows together. It's a natural thing. We didn't say, "This is your
job and that's my job." It had to be done—just both done it. Right,
Marion?

MS: Even our money situation. We don't say, "This is yours, this is
mine." It's just ours. Our work is ours and our money is ours.

When they disagree, they "fight it out" until they know "the ultimate of
what the argument was all about, that both of us are gonna be satisfied
with it."

A facile answer is also contradicted by a more thoughtful discussion
when Phillip considers schools. Teachers should encourage competition
because it "is good in *everything*. That gives you the get-up-and-go. If
everything came easy, there would be no incentative [*sic*] to work, to get
better grades. You need competition." When a teacher divides attention,
however, "The one that needs help, that seems to be crippled, that's the
one you give more help to. That's the way *I* did it with *my* kids." Similarly, "The one that's a little bit backward and trying harder needs the
better mark." The smart, successful student "doesn't have to try that
hard—I don't have to give him that much credit. He knows he just gets
that naturally." A clearer choice for rewarding need and effort over accomplishment would be hard to find—although Phillip's praise of competition hints at his dramatically different judgments in the economic domain.

At one point, Phillip struggles to define happiness, the main human
goal for him, and thereby to explicate his social philosophy. He concludes a long conversation with two dicta. First, happiness is unrelated to
wealth. Suppose "you're rich, you got three Cadillacs, a maid, a
chauffeur—if you're down in the dumps, well, that isn't gonna make you
happy. Happiness comes within." Second, people must define their own
happiness—even political science professors can't teach it. "You're dealing with all kinds of people. I can't tell *you* to live like *I* live, see. What
makes you happy makes somebody else sad. You gotta find your own
happiness."

This is hardly an elaborate philosophy, but it does imply a belief in
"the equal . . . human worth of all persons."[3] Everyone deserves happiness; all people deserve equal respect for their idiosyncrasies; wealth is
neither necessary to nor sufficient for happiness. Phillip finds the prin-

ciple of equality to be a source of great satisfaction here; his dog-eat-dog economic views seem very far away.

What do these four cases teach us? First, these people, who were chosen to explicate the views of the poor because they were both representative and articulate, are basically egalitarian in the socializing domain. Within a general principle of equality, they use a variety of specific norms, including strict equality, need, investments, and egalitarian procedures. They are especially egalitarian in the home and community; they support some differentiation in school. There are exceptions to both of these generalizations, since most require chores at home, and all want teachers to give the most help to the neediest students. But the emphasis on equality, with greater or fewer caveats, holds across all aspects of the socializing domain.

Differences among the poor stem from their affective responses to the principle of equality. Sometimes equality seems an inescapable obligation, which they cannot, and those with resources will not, carry out. At other times, it is an impossible ideal, since they have so few resources to allocate, equally or not. For some, however, equality is a gratifying guide by which to care for their family and act morally in the world.

The poor respondents who are better-off are just as egalitarian and much more gratified by equality than those who are worse-off. This suggests that the rich should both support a principle of equality and be very happy. Such a hypothesis would lack support if the rich either are not egalitarian or are egalitarian but unhappy. Let us examine our wealthy respondents to see whether wealth yields egalitarianism, satisfaction, both, or neither in the socializing domain.

Equality, Frustration, and the Rich

Despite commonsense expectations to the contrary, my interviews show that the rich support a principle of equality in the socializing domain just as strongly as the poor do. The interviews show also that gratification from support for equality does not necessarily increase with income, since the rich are not uniformly happy in the exercise of their normative judgments. Instead, like the poor, some are frustrated by their egalitarianism, and others are pleased by it. Up to this point, then, the rich and poor are alike: both classes consistently believe in a principle of equality, and both vary in the emotions accompanying this belief. It is only when one examines the quality of their emotions, or the substance of the issues that frustrate or gratify them, that one can sharply distinguish rich from poor in the socializing domain.

Let us consider two representative wealthy respondents who are egalitarian but frustrated. Barbara Azlinsky, described in chapter two, is one of the most incoherent and unhappy of all my interview subjects. Her first comment, in response to my admiration of her large, elegant home, was, "Ian [her husband] designed it, but it had to be feasible, workable to get a mortgage. And there was a *lot* of compromising, and this is it." This remark illustrates one of the two ways in which she makes normative judgments: she either condemns an unfair situation or praises an unattainable, fair situation. Justice either is not met or cannot be met. Except for flashes of pleasure, Barbara is an angry, unhappy woman.

For example, Barbara expresses her support for strict equality between the sexes by attacking ascriptive judgments. Her mother, who "preferred boys," always favored her brothers and still treats her unfairly: "It's interesting: my brothers work full time, and I do. And yet she'll ask *me* to empty her garbage for her. She won't ask the boys. The kitchen is the female aspect. Isn't that something?" Her own children are now adults, but Barbara is still angry that, despite her job, she had full responsibility for her children when they were young. "So that's where the old school of the wife doing all the cooking and cleaning in the kitchen is still there. It's inbredded [*sic*]. I would never recommend this for a young family."

Sometimes Barbara does directly invoke an equality norm: "Like with Christmas, it got so that I would get one large toy, and they'd take turns. And they were sharing it. You can't get ten different toys for three children, you know." Did this system work well? "Well, it had to." But like Maria, she more often feels compelled against her own will to accept the responsibilities of a need norm. She takes care of her invalid mother, since "she says she gave her life to her children, [so] she demands attention now." But Barbara resents it: "I'm sorry for her, and I *do* stop by as often [as I can]. Her occupational therapy is cooking. So I give her orders, and I buy the food and ask her to cook something, and then I get indigestion for weeks eating it! But it's going to help her, and it helps me because then I don't feel obligated to go there when she's happy."

Sometimes, then, Barbara is angry because strict equality does not exist when it should; at other times she is angry because a norm of need imposes obligations. But she becomes most angry when she contemplates how few people use a norm of investments. She wants people to be rewarded for hard work, decency, and frugality, but rewards seldom match efforts. In her bitterness, she tries to deny an investment norm by asserting that we really do live in a dog-eat-dog world.

Let us see how Barbara expresses this mix of views. She is very proud that her father "was a good humanitarian, [who] didn't care for money, gave different things to all the neighbors," and she "engrained" her children with the same philosophy. But she feels that both she and Ian have been "cheated" out of deserved rewards by unscrupulous coworkers, and that despite their years of "saving and doing without," she can no longer believe "the theory that if I work hard, I will have the money [for retirement]. I see, after all these years, that I don't have it." When she could not afford an expensive antique for a friend's birthday, "It got me very depressed. That's when I realized I couldn't get things I really wanted." As disillusionment grew, so did her materialism, until "now, at my age, I feel I deserve much more." As a result, she now rejects much of her father's generosity and friendliness. Her daughter recently told her: " 'I don't know why we were taught to be punctual and think of other people's feelings, when *nobody* gives a *damn* about being on time with me, or thinking of how to be nice to me.' And I said, 'Well, Helen, it's dog-eat-dog. However it doesn't hurt to be nice.' That was the philosophy *I* was brought up with. But now I realize my father was never a businessman, and I'm telling *my* children, 'Forget about it. It's nice to do this, but if you can't have it in your heart, forget it.' " In short, Barbara believes that the world does not operate according to a norm of investments, because if it did she would be much better off than she is. Therefore she does her best to teach herself and her children that living by such an ideal is as foolish as it is attractive.

Barbara is similarly ambivalent about competition among school children. On the one hand, "Competition [for grades] isn't really good, and it's frightening when you can only give one award. We didn't have competition with the childen knowingly." On the other hand, competitive children did better in school than her own children, who have been "handicapped" ever since. Again, she is disillusioned and angry because her preferred norm is constantly violated, apparently to the advantage of the violators.

Barbara is certain, however, about one relationship among norms: an egalitarian investment norm is an important counterweight to even more egalitarian norms. Specifically, teachers should not have to devote their greatest energies to their neediest students if the students will not try as hard as they can to succeed. As a teacher, you "have to divide your time equally, but you can *enjoy* teaching the more responsive ones. That's what happens with my clients. Those that are complaining, look stern, do not say hello—I'm going to work for them, but I'm going to have a better response with someone that is alert and that will listen to me and respond. Just like an animal. I mean, I walk in the house, the dog greets me—fine, I greet him. The cat ignores me—I don't pet him. I think that's only natural, really. Didn't psychologists say that?" Need in itself is not enough; students, legal clients, and pets should all be aided and rewarded according to their efforts to succeed.

Thus Barbara's egalitarianism generally takes the form of a frustrated belief in a norm of investments. Ascription is bad because it denies some people an equal right to pursue their goals. Needy family members are an obligation, but hardly a source of joy. A properly run society rewards hard work, humanitarian generosity, concern for others, and frugality. But Barbara is so disappointed by the results of trying to live by an investment norm that she verges on abandoning it entirely in favor of a bitter, cynical acceptance of unbridled social Darwinism.

Ernest Berkowitz, like Barbara Azlinsky, is wealthy, egalitarian, and unhappy; however, he reacts to dashed hopes by making an effort to be resigned and philosophical, not bitter and angry.

Ernest has no complaints about his income. He owns two lucrative shoe stores and a large, lavishly furnished house. He would not reveal his income, but I estimate it to be at least $60,000 a year (in 1976 dollars). He is painfully torn, however, between a norm of strict equality and a differentiating norm of ascription. As a result, he is distressed when equality is not achieved, but sometimes even more distressed when it is.

Ernest's parents were wealthier than their neighbors when he was young, but it was ethnicity, not money, that set him apart from his Catholic peers. If a classmate "who might not have had any thought about it before with regard to me as a Jew, looking at me as a person — he said, 'I'm going over to Ernest's house,' the mother said, 'He's a Jew, and you know that the Jews killed Christ.' Now that divorced him from me as an individual." Ernest claims that he learned "how to roll with it, divert them from that standpoint, because otherwise you could be miserable," and he tries hard not to reciprocate religious prejudice. For example, he uses extreme tact when criticizing an aspect of the Catholic Church, and he carefully explains that "I'm not trying to point up the church against the synagogue."

Lack of prejudice is one thing, however; abandoning ascriptive differences is quite another. It was extremely important to him that his children were "brought up religiously, going to Hebrew school, and being Bar Mitzvahed." He describes a lecture on intermarriage in which the rabbi suggested that "you have to tell him [your son] he can only take out Jewish girls. That won't guarantee the fact of getting the marriage to a Jewish person, but you'll be way ahead of the game." Thus for Ernest, all religions may be equally valid, but ascriptive religious and ethnic differences are to be prized and fostered.

A second effort to balance ascription and equality appears when Ernest discusses the proper role of children in family decisions. When they were young, his children had no role: "When we decided we were going to go on vacation and take them to Niagara Falls, we *told* them." But times have changed. "Today, kids who are being told what to do — forget it! They don't want to be told." One cannot now tell a teenager, " 'You're going to Niagara Falls with us tomorrow.' You'd have to ask him, and if he threw a tantrum in the first two minutes, you'd forget Niagara Falls. That's that generation thing that happened. The difference [is] between saying, 'This is what you're going to do' and not getting any flak, and today's asking in the hope that they'll go along with it." Ernest is not sure whether or not he regrets the passing of parental authority. On the one hand, he "accepted very easily" his parents' insistence that he become a shoe salesman instead of a free-lance photographer — "Who the hell was going to be a photographer in those days?" — and he does not regret his submission. On the other hand, he was very sympathetic to a hitchhiker he picked up who had finished college, but was postponing a career. Even though his father "has sweated and worked all his life in a factory to send this kid to college," the son does not owe it to his father to succeed. "After sixteen years of school, which is not easy, they would like a little respite. That's why this whole revolution came around with kids. And that to me makes a lot of sense."

All of Ernest's conflicting views about religious and familial ascription and equality collide when he thinks about his son's recent marriage to a Gentile. He resists talking about it — he is more willing, for example, to discuss his daughter's premarital pregnancy. But he suddenly interrupts the discussion of intermarriage quoted above to say, "We feel strongly about the fact that my son married a girl who wasn't Jewish. But it's not going to tear us apart, whereas older types of Jewish people, different types, it might. But we won't go into detail there." He does, nevertheless, return to the subject again and again. He opposes religious prejudice; he endorses his son's independence; but the results of all this equality dismay him.

Ernest tries to resolve this dilemma by simultaneously denying that an awful thing has happened and that he is responsible for such an awful thing having happened. Thus he claims first that "we're not unhappy with it. What the kids have today, which is great, they look at each other as people today, not from a religious standpoint." Later, he claims that this undesirable marriage simply illustrates the generational changes discussed earlier and thus does not indicate his failure as a parent: "They don't know what they want, but they want something different from our generation or *our* way of life. And it's this *generation.* So it's not my kid by himself. Two out of three [of my friends] have kids with intermarriage—now are you going to blame us? There's no blame, it being so prevalent." If Ernest were less committed to equality as a new and better way to organize a family, or if he were less imbued with the old ways of parental and religious authority, he would be better able to resolve his internal conflict. But he holds conflicting beliefs and will not give up either; therefore he remains hurt and confused.

Ernest is also ambivalent in his distributive prescriptions for schools, but the conflict is much less painful. He tries to use a differentiating norm of procedure to equalize rewards among students by holding the untenable position that everyone can win in a competition:

EB: If you get an A [on a test], and a person who is supposed to have gotten an A got a B, that gives you a lot of self-satisfaction.

JH: Do you think it harms the person who didn't get the A?

EB: No, because that person is going to get the A eventually. If a person has self-confidence, they can accept several defeats, because they'll attribute it to something that just didn't go right, but they'll come back.

But regardless of the virtues of competition in a classroom, cooperation is even more "healthy. Oh yeah, no question, 100 percent. What can be better than getting people to work together? To know people, to know what *their* feelings are about things. Isolation is the worst thing there is, in my opinion." Some children might "slack off, but that's not as much a determinant [that is, as important] as the fact that you are getting kids to talk to each other, help each other possibly."

Ernest concludes with a lecture on the importance of fostering communication and discouraging selfishness and jealousy. As in his discussion of competition, he refuses to face the fact that not everyone can win, that people may continue to disagree even after they communicate. He also has no suggestion for achieving these goals, "because the human mind is too complicated, this is too much a psychological thing. I don't think the human person can be changed." But the elements of an egalitarian social philosophy are there; Tawney would surely agree that increasing understanding and decreasing selfishness and jealousy are basic purposes of an egalitarian community. Thus Ernest's principle of equality is deeply and sincerely held; he becomes angry when religions, or parents, or schools violate it. But his ascriptive norm is just as deeply held, and he is grieved and shaken when his values collide.

Equality, Contentment, and the Rich

Just as the poor sometimes derive gratification from using a principle of equality in the socializing domain, so do the rich. For some wealthy respondents, equality is neither frustrating because it is not carried out, nor disappointing because it is carried too far. Instead, it is a guidepost for making allocative decisions that rewards, as well as directs, its users.

Anne Kaufman is one contented wealth-holder. She and her husband earn over $50,000 a year in their liquor distributorship and package store. Like Ernest, she is adjusting to her son's recent marriage to a Gentile; like Barbara, she worries that hard work and initiative no longer get the rewards they deserve. But her son's marriage did not traumatize her faith or parental role, and diminished rewards have not embittered her. Her subtle and complex normative judgments are not at war with one another or with the world outside, as are Ernest's and Barbara's.

Anne is "very family-oriented," and she evaluates the rest of the world by generalizing from family events. Her parents were "kind disciplinarians, good hardworking people, particularly devoted to their family." She has "really tried to teach [her own children] the same things." This mix of deep love and firm discipline characterizes Anne's norms throughout the socializing domain. She tried to teach her children "discipline: 'When you go out in the world, everybody doesn't give you your own way.' Can't just do anything you want, you have to be considerate of the other people if you're a family unit." In the late 1960s, her college-age son rejected this discipline, along with most other aspects of his upbringing, but Anne struggled to understand rather than condemn him: "I guess Tim represented some of that dissatisfaction, perhaps, of the issue of 'Who am I? Where am I going?' — all of which I think we tried to understand. Children had to oppose their parents, whether it was important or not, for self-expression. But he wasn't a bad kid." Although she patronizes Tim, she does not belittle or resent him as Barbara might or feel betrayed by him as Ernest might. In fact, Tim's rebellion has changed some of her views, as we will see later.

Perhaps this tension between indulgent warmth and high expectations — being a "kind disciplinarian" — does not tear Anne apart because her norms are all variants of a principle of equality. Ernest is torn between equality and ascription, Barbara between investments and zero-sum competition, but Anne moves between need and investments, which are much closer and more easily reconciled than the other two pairs of beliefs.

A balance between compassion and responsibility is not limited to Anne's family. During the Depression, she went from house to house collecting payments for her parents' fuel company, "and I remember times I came to a home where the family was so poor that I didn't ask for any money, I'd call the office and ask my mother to send out more oil to these people. And not that we were charitable to them, because we didn't talk about it." People should respond to others' needs, without forcing them to be grateful. But this very obligation implies a counterobligation: her parents had to be even more diligent in collecting "from the people who *had* steady jobs," in order to meet their own payroll and "help finance it for the others." After all, if they were too generous, they would be able neither to pay employees nor help customers. Need and effort, extending help and demanding payment, concern for others and financial responsibility — these are merely two sides of the same coin for Anne.

Anne's love of knowledge and regret about her own lack of schooling are assuaged by the success of her daughter Sally, who "expended a great deal of effort and always had high marks." In fact, Sally "applied herself *too* much. She would sacrifice a social thing for the sake of school, but there is a happy medium. I told her she was wrong." In contrast, Tim "had all the ability, but he didn't apply himself as hard as he might have." Although she "would be the first to criticize him if he didn't measure up," she blames his teachers for "discouraging him" by rewarding only achievements, not attempts: "He might have done better if they'd appreciated some of the effort that he expended instead of pointing up the times he slipped up." This discussion again shows a mixture of norms that reinforce and modulate each other, rather than canceling each other out as in Ernest's case. Results are the proper standard for reward in school, but they can be overridden by effort or need. Achievement is important, but not at the expense of everything else. A differentiating norm is modified by a series of egalitarian caveats.

Only once does Anne's balancing act fail her and leave her groping for an answer and her usual peace of mind. The question concerned the proper allocation of scarce educational resources. At first, she tried to deny scarcity: "That's sort of straddling the fence, but I think each [group] needs their own. I wouldn't want to say *more*, I'd say *proper* funding." But eventually she tries to balance special needs and high standards — and does not succeed: "It wouldn't be fair to isolate people because they're handicapped. But really, can they keep the pace? And there's also a problem if you have people who are not as capable of learning as faster-learning people. There's frustration on both sides. The top of the class can resent it because they have to slow up for lower ones." She concludes lamely, "I don't know enough about how to separate their abilities. Give them [all] an opportunity." In this case, her norms cannot be reconciled, and she is simply stymied—and, for once, silenced.

Finally, Anne's complex, but integrated, beliefs about her identity as a Jew contrast with Ernest's more ambivalent swings between equality and ascription. Her childhood community was just as anti-Semitic: "No matter what would happen, if you lost in a game or if you did something, someone would say 'Dirty Jew!' " At a movie once, her candy bar wrapper rustled, "and this woman turns around and says, 'Cut out the noise, dirty Jew!' " She was "shocked" and bewildered by such inappropriate ascriptive claims: "I never knew what that had to *do* with it. It was just, we were *people*. If the paper made noise, [just] say 'Be quiet!' " She still struggles to understand religious intolerance—"People put a minority in a demeaning position [to] help their self-esteem. They feel better by putting themselves on an upper echelon"—and proudly cites her Polish Catholic friends and employees as evidence that she is not prejudiced. But recent incidents of anti-Semitism have convinced her "that it is always there," and she shows her own ascriptive values in her dislike of her son's interfaith marriage. "I live with it, tolerate it. But I was disappointed. I *was*, I would be lying to say otherwise." Nevertheless, she is able to say, "I happen to like my daughter-in-law. I never did anything but welcome her into our household. And I *wouldn't* do anything different than that." Although unhappy about and worried by the marriage, she does not feel betrayed and bereft as does Ernest; she concludes, "There's an argument for everything—for and against."

Since Anne is so adept at seeing several sides to any issue, she tones down her occasional differentiating norm of results or ascription with a variety of egalitarian shadings. More often, her search for "a happy medium" leads her to seek a balance between warm indulgence and disciplined responsibility. Since these norms of need and investments are both variants of an underlying principle of equality, she is usually able to be a "kind disciplinarian" and avoid Barbara's and Ernest's unhappy ambivalence. Only when she cannot reconcile her norms (as in the case of financing for education) does the principle of equality cause her pain rather than gratification.

Craig Cabot, the patrician judge of chapter two, is our final exemplar in the socializing domain. As our instinct for symmetry would urge, he is wealthy, egalitarian, and essentially contented.

In his upper-class childhood, Craig "always seemed to have whatever I wanted." He is the only interview subject to mention the rationing of World War II; as his sole experience of shortage, he remembers it. Now he is "damn well-off" because of his own income, his inheritance, and his wife's wealth. As a result, even though Craig tries to imagine Maria's and Vincent's frustration in the face of constant scarcity, he cannot quite empathize with something so foreign to his own experience.

For example, Craig uses two methods to resolve his daughters' squabbling over toys. At first, he urges them to share because, as he tells them, " 'When all is said and done, you are closer than any two human beings in the world,' and 'Even if you don't get along with each other, you must be able to rely on each other, to be fair with one another.' " He intends to foster fellowship, sharing, nurturance, and intimacy—the psychological elements of norms of strict equality and need. But often, he concedes, "We buy the same thing twice. When the older one is dancing all over the place with that thing [a new skateboard], the other one wants it. So fortunately I can—maybe it isn't so fortunate, now that you think about it—but in any event, it's certainly the easier way for me to get two. Maybe it would be better if I made them share one." Equality has shifted from sharing existing goods to providing two identical sets of goods, which is possible, of course, only with an abundance of resources. Craig worries that such lavish treatment inhibits sharing and makes the girls "miss out on a lot—and I guess this is a good deal my fault—because it comes to them very easily. I can't think of anything that they have to work for or want for a long period of time. That, to me, is not a good situation." But it seems silly to deny them pleasures and advantages that he can so obviously afford; after all, "Who am I going to kid by keeping them from having it?"

Craig's wealth also permits him, to his embarrassment, to avoid the difficult choices "which I assume a lot of families have": "We don't have the decision, 'Should we eat out Saturday night or use the money to buy clothes?' We have budget problems, like Aristotle Onassis and everyone else down has. But we don't have (pause) I don't mean to make that sound like we are so much different or better off than anybody else. The economic facts of life are that I *am*, to a large extent [better off than most people]." Some choices, of course, cannot be avoided even with unlimited resources, and major decisions "are essentially joint" between him and his wife. His description of their "discussions" suggests a cold and uncommunicative marriage, but there is no hint of hierarchy. Most of the time, "we just assume things are going to be a certain way, and they are to a large extent. There are no church-state issues."

Craig first endorses competition among students as "the nature of pretty much all our enterprises." Whatever goal children set for themselves, "They're going to have competition [all] along the line. It would therefore appear that the more practice they had in competition, the more apt they would be [to learn how to be] successful." But, like that of Phillip Santaguida, Craig's glib certainty fades upon further consideration, and he finally insists that competition must be circumscribed by fair decision rules: "Be no good for either one of them for Hilary, who's the younger one, to have to compete with Susie on the same level. You have to deal with competition with your children along the same lines of fair play that business or government has to deal with competition generally in society. There have to be rules, there has to be a structure." Otherwise, just "put[ting] people in a ring and say[ing], 'Okay, winner take all' " will create "disaster."

But even structured competition has no place in a classroom. Instead, schools should be "flexible enough to allow the gifted student to move along," as well as to help the needy student. Like Anne, Craig resists choosing between upwardly and downwardly redistributive versions of a need norm: "Okay, you have one dollar to spend — where are you going to put it? I don't know. Whichever way you jump, you're wrong. The better way to do it is say, 'Let's rethink our priorities on the budget and instead of spending it on something else and only having one dollar for education, let's have two dollars and do it.' I don't mean to criticize the question, I'm just saying it's a dilemma." When forced to choose, however, he favors "the deprived child," with "the prayer that the gifted child will compensate better."

Craig gives two reasons for choosing the egalitarian alternative. First, a community is obliged to mitigate the pain of its worst-off members. Without special help, the needy child "is going to become progressively disadvantaged as time goes on. Time is not on the child's side. That could have grave effects," such as "anxiety, guilt, sibling rivalry," and rebellion. Second, and conversely, a community is obliged to maximize all its members' chances for success and happiness: "A child should not, by virtue of the dumb luck of living in one geographical area, be handicapped or have greater opportunity because of that. You have to do whatever you can to give everybody a fair shot at a happy life. I would lean toward subsidizing [needy] people or institutions to effect that kind of equality. Gifted individuals are better able to take care of themselves."

Craig does not shrink from the implications of this argument. Not only does it risk "blow[ing] a Nobel Prize winner," but also "it doesn't help me very much because it would pull down the average, and I'm in a better than average school situation." But he would sacrifice his relative advantage to satisfy his "overactive gland that gives me a lot of concern for people who are lonely or suffering or deprived." Craig attributes this "overactive gland" partly to his privileged background: "I'm far more liberal than my father is because I've been able to afford it better than he could. It's an easy thing for a person with a lot of money to say, 'Let's not discriminate against poor Tom because he has a black face.' Because it's no skin off your behind to say that. But the guy who is fighting for a job and has no other reason than that Tom has a black face to get him behind him and get ahead of him, may search for that reason. So talk is pretty cheap." But Craig insists that he would "feel the same way had I had those experiences [of the poor laborer]," and he chastises himself for not doing "a damn thing about it. Frankly, I don't feel like changing my life and working as a lawyer in a poverty office. What I do is give interviews and expound my views." He has, in fact, reformed one state's juvenile code, and he carefully teaches his children "that there's a lot of injustice, inequality of treatment—I make opportunities to bring things like this up."

It is, of course, unclear how actively Craig would support a redistributive political movement, but one cannot doubt the sincerity of his egalitarian beliefs. He moves freely among norms of strict equality, need, and investments because he sees them all simply as variants of an overriding principle of equality. The fact of equal human worth and the obligation it imposes on socializing agencies to seek equal well-being for all—these principles matter more than any specific normative claim. Thus Craig feels conflicts neither among norms, as some of the other rich do, nor between norms and resources, as some of the poor do. He is, therefore, both contented and deeply principled; he avoids complacency only through an acute awareness of his luck, a desire that others share it, and guilt that he has not done more to bridge the gap between them and him.

Conclusion

We can draw several interim conclusions. First and most important, both rich and poor respondents generally start from a principle of equality to make distributive judgments about the socializing domain. Despite exceptions and hesitations—points to which I shall return—most respondents choose some norm that fosters prima facie equality when considering home, school, and community. These eight respondents are more articulate than, but not different from, the other twenty interview subjects. In short, except for a few people most of the time, and most of the people a few times, both rich and poor respondents share a commitment to a principle of equality in the socializing domain.

With that point clear, we can move on to the caveats and shadings also revealed by this analysis. First, respondents vary in the specific egalitarian norms they use in the socializing domain. They prefer strict equality and need in the home, need and investments in the schools, and egalitarian procedures in the community. In all three settings, they rely on a norm of results to keep themselves or others from being "too soft." Let us briefly consider each of these variants on the principle of equality.

Parental and marital love has both extensive and intensive dimensions; that is, parents want to show that they love all of their children equally, and that they love them enough to sacrifice for them. Spouses want equality with their marriage partner and want each to be willing to sacrifice for the other. In short, strict equality and need predominate in family relations. An example of equality is provided by Michael McFarland, an earnest assembly line worker, who tries at Christmastime always to have "two the same — same color and all — of the toys" for his two children. Occasionally, the urge for strict equality dominates even at the expense of a more needy child. David Fine, a successful and very self-confident architect, has a dyslexic daughter, Sara, for whom an exclusive private school was recommended. "So since we love both of our girls equally, we applied for *both* of them. And of course Laura got in and Sara didn't." Some parents foster strict equality for psychological rather than philosophical reasons, that is, they hope it will alleviate envy among their children. Judith Baum, a sophisticated child psychologist, deliberately had her three children as close together as possible, so that "you wouldn't have the sibling rivalry, which I thought must be a dreadful thing. So they were kind of all of a piece. Went to bed and got up at the same time, and ate the same foods, and were all treated somewhat equally. We never had sibling rivalry."

Examples also abound of parental eagerness to respond to children's needs, whether they be physical necessities or intense desires. Staying home from work or a social event to care for a sick child is so obviously right that they seldom devote more than a few words to saying so. Poor parents work overtime to buy a coveted toy for Christmas or to pay for a school field trip; rich parents proudly describe their son's new guitar or seriously discuss the extra help they give to daughters with math anxiety. Poor respondents' confessions that they cannot afford to gratify their children's — or their spouses' — needs were among the most poignant moments of the interviews.

Most respondents leaven this focus on equality with discipline, an occasional insistence that their children produce results in order to be rewarded. Some assign daily chores; others pay allowances in direct proportion to school grades or tasks accomplished; many worry about "spoiling" their children. Similarly, although they seek equality with their spouses and are willing to sacrifice for them, married respondents occasionally insist that their partner "produce." One of Mary Lou Trask's explanations for the slow disintegration of her marriage is the fact that "my husband at one time helped good in the house, but he's kind of gotten away from that now. Ya, it does get very annoying sometimes 'cause he's not too motivated about things."

When they discuss schools, the focus shifts slightly toward the differentiating principle; respondents rely on norms of need and investment, and almost never seek strict equality among students. Some use the norm of need to urge redistribution upward, to provide resources to children with special abilities. For example, David Fine argues that "gifted children may require as much or more time as children with learning disabilities." But most want teachers and school budgeters to help the slowest students the most—a classic use of Rawls' difference principle.

Investments and education are linked in two ways. First, students who work hardest, pay most attention, and are most responsive to their teachers may not require the most help, but do deserve the greatest rewards. Second, education itself is viewed as an investment in the community and the future; therefore becoming educated merits compensation. The relation shifts from investing in the educational process to education as an investment in the social process. For example, Amy Campbell, a wealthy and underemployed lab assistant, remembers her father's claim that " 'Wealth didn't amount to a whole lot, but if you had an education, it was something you never lost.' " During the Depression, "he always was able to do work that interested him even though the times weren't good, because he had an education." She urges her daughters to pursue professions, so that they will be "happier and be prepared."

Strict equality is important in the school setting only as a counter to competition, which most people reject. Mary Lou Trask, a pieceworker in a dress factory, is horrified by the idea of all students receiving the same grades (strict equality), but urges children to share homework, because "in doing with others, you learn to associate with others, and you learn to accept these for what they are." Once again, a norm of results surfaces sometimes as a check against being "too easy on the kids," especially with regard to promotions from one grade to another. Both rich and poor oppose social promotions or promotions based on the child's emotional need to progress. Educational advancement is too closely tied to career success to be ruled by a principle of equality; at this point, the socializing domain blends with the differentiating economic domain.

Finally, respondents generally express the principle of equality in the neighborhood or in their social philosophies through a desire for procedural equality and the elimination of ascriptive differences. They often sound like echoes of Tawney — seeking fellowship, trust, and mutual respect through an equal division of resources. Sometimes, however, a need norm is perverted from a right into charity, and responding to needs becomes benevolent, not just. For example, Wendy Tonnina, a young saleswoman in a local store, gives discarded clothes "to churches and other things — sometimes almost new. Every year I'll change from summer to winter clothes, and if I didn't wear something all last winter, and I know it's going to sit there again, I'll give it away, rather than throw it out. So I do help people." Not only donors see responding to neighbors' needs as charity; so do some recipients. Ruth Sennett, who is seriously disabled with cancer and lives on $3,000 a year, describes again and again visits from her former coworkers: "They've been very nice to me, the girls. They brought me food and coffee, and they fixed the lunch and then they cleaned up, very good. Very nice, yes. I can't believe it, that they're so good to me." A norm of results appears in discussions of the local community mostly as a demand that local politicians achieve what they've promised — or get out of office.

Thus under the umbrella of a principle of prima facie equality in the socializing domain, respondents pick and choose their norms to fit particular situations.

The second caveat to the general conclusion so far is that, although respondents are similarly egalitarian, they are not similarly happy about it. Egalitarianism is sometimes associated with contentment and sometimes with sorrow. Support for equality does not always *cause* contentment or sorrow, since occasionally the poor are egalitarian because they think equality might alleviate their distress. But if we cannot infer a simple causal relation, we can at least conclude that the rich resemble the poor in the variety of their emotions about their normative judgments.

This finding seems to imply that it does not matter how much money one has, since one can be rich and unhappy or poor and happy. But such a conclusion would be only superficially true. Looking closely at these people, we find that the *quality* of the unhappiness of rich and poor differs in two ways. First, the poor vary mainly in the degree to which they are able to act on the principle of equality within their economic constraints. If they can do so, they are content; if not, they are bitter and unhappy. The rich have fewer external constraints. Therefore their internal conflicts play a larger role; that is, they vary mainly in the degree to which they integrate different distributive principles. If the rich sustain their belief in equality in the face of undesirable consequences, they are content; if they vacillate between the principles of equality and differentiation, they are bitter and unhappy.

If this generalization holds true for other people, it leads to an interesting argument for greater equalization of wealth. The search for freedom from external constraints — negative freedom[4] — resonates through American political history. Whether explicitly or not, Americans have always preferred to wrestle with internal demons rather than external despots; after all, the Puritans, Founding Fathers, abolitionists, and suffragists, among others, all exemplify Americans' insistence on being free from even a benevolent authority outside themselves. Thus the unhappiness that comes from having to face the consequences of one's own beliefs seems "more free" and more desirable than the unhappiness that comes from not being permitted to act on one's beliefs. Poverty does not permit the luxury of normative conflict and thus inhibits a person's moral autonomy.

Second, and more simply, the topics that make the rich and the poor unhappy are very different. Vincent is worried about tonight's dinner and next month's heat; Ernest is upset that his son married someone whose religion he does not approve of. Maria hurts for her grandchildren because they cannot afford to complete vocational high school; Barbara hurts for her children because all their classmates returned from spring vacation with a Caribbean tan, whereas they had to stay home.

These differences do not mean that Barbara's and Ernest's pain is felt less deeply than Vincent's or Maria's. But they do mean that we, as political thinkers and actors, can make judgments about whose pain should first be assuaged. If we agree that food and education are more important than in-laws and vacations, we are on our way to deciding that it is more important to alleviate the pain of the poor than that of the rich. This judgment leads to the same conclusion as the one above regarding freedom, but it is judgment, not fact. Strictly speaking, my main conclusion thus far is narrower — that rich and poor agree in using a principle of equality in the socializing domain.

5 The Economic Domain and the Principle of Differentiation

Respondents follow the same pattern in their beliefs about the economy as they followed in their beliefs about the socializing domain: they agree on a principle of justice, but vary in the satisfaction they derive from that principle and in the specific norms they use to implement it. But in this case, they agree on a principle of differentiation, not of equality. Both rich and poor use the same principle; the very people who were egalitarians before are now differentiators. These two facts suggest that normative differences depend less on social class or individual ideology than on the domain of life being addressed.

Let us examine these abstract claims as they appear in the concrete details of daily life for our eight representative respondents.

Differentiation, Bitterness, and the Poor

If the poor are unhappy about the absence of equality in the socializing domain, we might expect them also to be unhappy about the absence of economic equality. Some are, as we will see later. But most poor respondents do not seek economic equality; therefore they are not distressed at its lack. Instead, they seek *fair* differences in income; they are unhappy not because differences exist, but because so many existing differences seem unjust.

Maria Pulaski exemplifies the poor person's acceptance of the principle of economic differentiation combined with dismay over its implementation. She has spent most of her adult life doing "domestic work." Although she claims at first to "love it," she talks later about her exhaustion, aching legs, and envy of people with other jobs. Her main complaint, however, is that she receives too little pay and too few benefits for the work she does, a complaint based on a norm of results. Heavy cleaning deserves five dollars an hour, but "they hate to give you that money. It's not fair. You do your work right, you should get paid accordingly." Her explanation for employers' stinginess is a humiliating one: "They think they're giving you something, that you have to work, you *need* the work. They feel maybe they're better than I am." Maria can retaliate only by applying the norm of results in reverse, so that she does just the work that she is paid to do. "If they're good to me, I'm good to them. I'll do the windows. But if they don't pay me the money that I want, I don't do them."

But the same norm of results that causes her anger also prevents Maria from begrudging even a stingy employer her wealth: "Well, she's a professor, she's making her money, she's working hard at it." Others "must have worked for it in order to have all that money. Or maybe somebody that gets a very good education goes right into the job. Sure, they deserve it."

Her use here of a norm of investments—hard work and education merit reward—is much more differentiating than her use of the same norm in the socializing domain, for two reasons. First, she insists that hardworking janitors deserve more than lazy ones, but even lazy doctors deserve more than both. Janitors deserve perhaps $7000, doctors over $50,000. Once Maria wonders if executives deserve their "$60,000" annual salary: "I don't think they do all that [much] work, do you? Sit at their desk—they got it easy." But she suppresses that thought immediately: "Well, maybe it *is* a lot of work. Maybe they have a lot of writing to do, or they have to make sure things go right. So maybe they *are* deserving of it."

Second, she argues that only producing something of value really merits reward; hard work is valuable solely for its results. Payment by piecework is fair because it accurately rewards differences in productivity: "If you want to work hard, you'll get your money, and if you don't, well, you don't." The minimum day rate is low, "but if you're not putting the work out," it is fair. She knows that assembly line work is boring, but to her that fact simply means that one should become educated enough to change jobs, not that assembly workers deserve greater compensation.

But believing firmly in a norm of results is a far cry from believing that wealth always corresponds to productivity. Maria knows that some of the rich did not earn their wealth. Some are rich simply because "they might have *been* rich"; after all, "Where money is, money goes." Others inherit, and still others get "a break, luck—marry the boss's daughter." She also knows that all of the rich are not virtuous; she describes in detail the marital and alcoholic problems of her employers. Furthermore, she knows that her husband's demotion and severe pay cut were due not to personal failure, but to the 1974 recession: "It's just [that] the work wasn't there." Less personally, she knows that "sometimes even a college graduate tries so hard and they can't even get a job. Jobs aren't available." Promotions do not always go to "the one that works very, very hard"; sometimes "somebody else comes in that's well off, they get the job."

Each of these situations "isn't fair. If you worked hard at it, why not get it [the promotion]?" Albeit defensively, Maria insists that her rich employers are not "*better* than me. Because they're rich, they probably *think* they're better than me. But I think I'm just as equal as they are." And she is deeply discouraged about her own and her children's future. Despite her constant work, "It's a struggle. If I buy clothes, then we don't eat. And I wouldn't dare make a bill. Can't afford it. And the way things are going now, I doubt it'll [ever] be any better." Prospects for the next generation are no better; her son has tried to start a house-painting business three times, "But the money, he's bringing it in, but then it's going out. Try hard and try hard, and you don't make any money. It all goes out." But regardless of all this evidence that a norm of results is often inoperative, Maria never suggests even after the interviewer's probing that the accumulation of wealth should be in any way curtailed.

Similarly, Maria uses a norm of results to evaluate poverty despite her own arguments against its validity. She points out that not all the poor deserve their fate: "Some *can't* work. Maybe they have a problem, it could be the economy, some aren't making that much money. $140 a week—you can't live on that. So they have no choice. They go on welfare." She also describes ascriptive discrimination. In what she clearly sees as a heretical statement, she leans forward to whisper that blacks "must have had a reason for" rioting during the 1960s: "Don't forget, they were really pushed around from the beginning. I shouldn't even say this, but this is confidential. They *were* [pushed around]." But still, Maria claims that many people are poor because either "they don't want to work," or they "make the money and drink it all up. They don't care about the kids or the clothes. Just have a bottle on that table all the time."

And despite her reliance on a need norm in the socializing domain, she rejects any need arguments in the economy. Blacks should be hired only according to seniority and qualifications; affirmative action is as unacceptable as racism. Employers have no obligation to aid employees in emergencies or with chronic high expenses: "You have six children, I have none? Well, if I'm working hard at it, I think I deserve it." Promotions and layoffs should depend on hard work, education, seniority, and productivity — not on need, equality, or egalitarian random procedures.

Maria is in a bind. She *knows* that she works as hard as she can, that she hasn't enough money, that her employers underpay her, that many people deserve neither their wealth nor their poverty, and that her descendents seem destined to relive her frustrations. But she *believes* that the rich should keep their wealth, that a hardworking cleaner deserves less than a lazy executive, that work and education are supposed to bring upward mobility, and that wages should not reflect need or promote equality. She tries to subsume her knowledge of economic injustice under her differentiating economic beliefs. The result is discouragement, helplessness, and confusion.

Distress takes many forms. Maria is unhappy, but she is passive and resigned. Vincent Sartori is just as disappointed about discrepancies between his differentiating economic beliefs and actual economic differences, but he is angry and violent. For example, he earned good wages in one job, but found the dangerous working conditions, speedup pressures, and disparities between workers' and bosses' pay intolerable. The "huge gigantic driers," which "will take your skin right off" if "you just *tap* them," put him in the hospital for a week once; and the foreman constantly "used to hop on me, yellin' and gripin' and bitchin'." The situation was made even less tolerable by Vincent's conviction that the foreman really cared only for his own comfort, not for productivity. When the work goes smoothly, "The foreman can be up in the locker room playing cards. Hey, but when the machine breaks, he gets mad. 'Cause [then] he's gotta get out there and make sure you guys are doing it right, and *he* doesn't like to sweat."

Vincent resisted the speedup, " 'cause every time I try to keep up with them I would end up having an accident. I said, 'Well, to hell with this.' I'm not gonna wind up losing an eye or a finger. I just did it *my* way." His way started with vehement, if incoherent, protests: " 'Hey, this is America, isn't it? I'm not an animal or a machine. What's good for that guy is good for me, too.' Equal. That's the way I figure it." But his way did not end with protests: "I got mad, I threw the knife at the guy. I said,

'Well, if you can do it fucking better, you get *your* ass down there and do it!' " He was fired soon thereafter.

One moral that Vincent draws from this story is that productive workers deserve more pay and respect and better working conditions in comparison with people who merely hold high positions. Bosses are too highly paid because "a foreman—what does he do? He's got a white shirt—big deal. He's in his office. It's the *worker* that's actually breaking his back. So why doesn't the owner say, 'Why should I pay this foreman so much for sitting on his ass, when *these* guys are the ones that are really giving me the production?' But who am I? I can't change the system." But despite all of this buildup, Vincent does not argue that workers should make just as much as foremen. At this point, his norm of results works against more equality. Once he calms down, he decides that "I could be 100 percent wrong by saying the manager ain't nothing but a jerk. Actually, the guy could have burdens as far as paperwork, and getting orders, and getting certain production out." And besides, "You got a lot of workers, some might goof off, or who's a heavy drinker? You gotta make sure he's not drinking on the job." Thus managers do something that workers cannot and so deserve more pay. Productivity merits more than title, but productivity defined as responsibility deserves more than productivity defined as output of goods. Vincent concludes that $50, instead of (as he perceives it) the current $100, is the proper discrepancy in pay for ranks in a factory.

Unlike Maria, Vincent uses a norm of investment to determine fair wages within one rank; therefore he rejects the productivity focus of piecework. Everyone with the same job deserves the same pay because "this one will do a little more than this one, and yet this one is still doing his best that he can do. You can't knock the guy for not putting out as much production as the next guy. Because everyone is not alike." But like Maria, he rejects need and strict equality as criteria for pay, promotions, or layoffs. Despite the fact that he limps from a childhood accident, he insists that handicapped workers should be paid only for the hours they work and that factories have no moral obligation to hire them.

Vincent continues to rely mainly on a norm of results to determine fair incomes for various professions outside the factory and continues to find the world wanting in this regard. Women "should make more. You're working in an office, same thing with a guy, but a guy will make more money. Not that I'm sticking up for women's lib, but hey, a woman *works*." Emergency room doctors who work hard "to try and save you" deserve their high incomes. Bank tellers who do "a lotta paperwork and figuring" deserve more in comparison with bank owners, who are "up in your big office sittin' down." Some professionals earn too much for the work they do: when he is arrested, "you go up to the lawyer, you pay him $200. He goes up and sees the prosecutor, works out a deal before you get in front of a judge. *There's* the lawyer's pay. They keep me from going to jail, but it's an easy racket they got, easy racket. How much work do they have to do? They gotta talk, make deals." If Vincent's preferred pay scales were implemented, they would often make incomes more equal. But his preferences rest on a desire for rightful differentiation, not for equal pay.

Moving away from wages for specific occupations and into questions of general wealth and poverty, Vincent retains his anger over unfair differences as well as his enthusiasm for fair differences. He condemns those who get rich by exploiting misfortune: "Doctors, lawyers, bondsmen — they *like* to see you get in trouble. They're buying so many properties and things, and where are they making it from? *You.* You gotta keep going to a bank and borrowing the money. You sign your whole life away." Furthermore, he is angry that the rich get unfair "breaks," which help them become richer. His example here is legal: "With their money, they get to know the right people, then the right people get to know the better people. Before you know, you're over at the judge's house, you say, 'Hey, Tony, I got a nephew, his case is coming up in a couple of months. Remember his name,'" and he pantomimes a judge recognizing someone and dismissing the case from court. But "if *I* go out and have a fight, the law's arresting youse — breach of the peace! It's not fair."

But once again, all of this anger does not generate a demand for leveling. Vincent deeply admires those who "*became* rich. If a person keeps his mind to it, and works and works, and he's banking it, hey, good luck to him! That's good." He despairs over his own failure: "I wish to hell I could do it. I always said for years, 'I wanna get rich, I wanna get rich.' But then, phew! My mind doesn't have the strong will. I say, 'Well, I'm *gonna* do it.' Only the next day's different." He believes that willpower is as essential as hard work to success; he has done plenty of work, but woefully lacks the will.

Considering the low end of the economic scale, Vincent does not condemn all the poor, but describes the welfare system as "a gigantic rip-off. It's hurting the person that really *does* need it." He has vivid, detailed stories about recipients who "just want to keep their booze, cars, and that's it" — and no such stories about the deserving poor.

He has several reasons for condemning welfare cheats. First, he is outraged at lazy people who take advantage of both the needy and the taxpayer. Second, he thinks most welfare cheats are blacks, who demand too much from guiltridden white liberals. They "*had* a rough life," but "they're not riding in the back of buses no more [or] eatin' in a special restaurant. They got what they want. That's it—end it." Moreover, black demands threaten his job prospects; alcoholic blacks, dangerous on a shop floor, were still hired over more qualified whites by "threatening to file for discrimination." Finally, he is deeply frightened by rock-bottom poverty. Asked about "people on welfare," his first response is, "I would never, *never* want to go on welfare. I hope not, anyhow." Because Vincent fears that his debts and volatility will overwhelm him, he struggles somehow to distinguish himself from the hopelessly poor. He therefore cannot permit himself Maria's insight that circumstances may keep people poor despite their best efforts; he must believe that effort eventually succeeds.

Caught between his poverty and his children, Vincent can think of only one way out—illegal gain. So far, he has limited himself to selling liquor and drugs illicitly while collecting unemployment. He sees no alternative: "If I did it the legal way, I might as well just close the door and put the lock on. I couldn't survive" the taxes and loss of benefits. Besides, his police record precludes a liquor license.

If his snack shop fails, "that's when you get disgusted and say, 'Well to hell with this. Can't make a buck the way you want to, might as well go out and commit a crime.' 'Cause I can't keep going through this all my life. I want to get *ahead* in this world." He thinks about crime "all the time. There's a couple of friends that I talked to yesterday for about forty-five minutes about doing a job, and it keeps coming into my mind. Jeez, that's almost $10,000 apiece. That's once in a great long shot that you make a hit like that." He has resisted so far because of his children: "That's what keeps me from a lot of things that I haven't been doing."

Vincent's readiness to discuss his proposed crime with a stranger running a tape recorder may indicate that he is not serious. But it may not. He is close to despair. Vincent believes that people have a right to become rich, preferably, but not necessarily, by legal means; yet exploitation and bad luck leave one barely a chance. Hard work, self-discipline, and productivity deserve reward, and Vincent maintains his precarious balance by grasping at this combination of norms of investments and results. But if just norms do not yield just outcomes, then one may be driven to crime.

Differentiation, Contentment, and the Poor

Not all poor respondents complain of a gap beween actual economic differences and fair economic differentiation. Some see little or no gap;

others see a gap, but do not let it disturb them. But regardless of their perceptions and emotions, the same people who seek equality in the socializing domain support differentiation in the economy.

Pamela McLean illustrates best how poor respondents can be happy with a distributive system that leaves them near the bottom. Her only complaint about her secretarial job is its low pay. She earns $2.75 an hour (in 1976 dollars); the other secretary, Ann, earns $3.10; and the "boss," Vinnie, earns about $3.60. These differences are fair, says Pamela, because Vinnie must "make sure the job gets done. She has the headache of it all," and Ann "takes all Vinnie's slough-off stuff. She has to be a little more on the ball [than I do]." For example, Ann runs the mimeo machine, whereas Pamela's job is purely "menial. I'm not using my brain, I'm just using my fingers." Once Pamela questions basing wages on such minute distinctions and comments that "after all, each of us is spending the same amount of *time* at the job." But she immediately rejects this opening for an equality norm; her wages are "a fair thing."

Pamela judges other salaries by a mix of investments and results criteria. Professors deserve high pay because "they studied a lot longer to get where they are. Especially [with] the cost of a college education. And it must not be easy to stay ahead of some of the fast-thinking students that they have. Plus that's more of a twenty-four-hours-a-day job than what I'm doing. I'm all for rewarding people financially for the more effort or time that they've put into something. Anybody who specializes in something should be compensated for it." In rapid succession, she invokes compensation, skill, responsibility, effort, and training as justifications for a large reward. But if these criteria clash instead of concurring, productivity supersedes effort in her eyes. If a hardworking, but clumsy, worker "was costing me [the employer], then I might just have to tell her, 'I'm sorry, I like you and all, but you're not able to put out the amount of work I need to have done, and so I have to fire you.' "

Like Vincent, Pamela sometimes uses a norm of results to castigate the undeserving rich and bolster deserving workers. Nursing home managers "take a big rake-off of the top" while the "staff is doing terrible degrading-type work. Where's the justice in that?" When managers make too much, workers "who are really down there sweatin' it out, making the product" make too little. But despite the redistributive implications of these views, Pamela rejects explicitly egalitarian arguments. The needs of large families are irrelevant for deciding wages: "If they both work as hard, the gal without the big family is just as tired at the end of the day." So are the needs of the handicapped: "It's not their fault that they're handicapped — and yet it's not my [the employer's] fault either." And Pamela applauds profit-making. After all, "Why have a business if you aren't going to reap something? It's expected that you should live well."

Earlier we saw Pamela's insistence that she never notices differences among people, but when pressed, she shows the most detailed awareness of economic distinctions of any respondent. In an unconscious parody of academic analyses, she identifies seven classes: (1) "the filthy rich, over $200,000, that own big business"; (2) a "lower filthy rich," who earn over $50,000; (3) an "upper class" of "most professional people," who earn over $20,000; (4) the "upper middle class, who have all the basics, buy many of the luxuries, but not all," and who earn between $15,000 and $25,000; (5) the "lower middle class, who are squeaking by very nicely really, pretty much get all the basics, but their luxuries come very slowly and not too often," and who earn $8-15,000; (6) the "upper lower class, living in fairly nice homes, probably mortgaged to the hilt, but at least they do have adequate housing," earning $3-8,000; and finally (7) the "poverty people — that's the people who are on welfare and really just barely squeaking through," without adequate housing, who earn under $3,000. Groups 6 and 7 "are not the brightest people. And I'm not sure whether, because they aren't the brightest people that's why they're in that class, or if because they're in that class they just don't shine. It's probably the first reason, though." Groups 1, 2, and sometimes 3 "use a lot of words that sometimes you don't understand, and you wonder if they do too. The richer they get, the bigger the words, and the less understandable they become." Pamela is obviously aware of subtle differences in income, style, and ability, and she understands the interaction between current position and future prospects. Her egalitarianism among friends, therefore, results from deliberately ignoring, not ignorance of, class distinctions.

Pamela applies a wry, but sincere, ascriptive norm to the "filthy rich." Although "somebody got to be rich," she is glad it is not she. Wealth entails too many responsibilities and too much "facade. Couldn't dare go uptown with my hair in rollers because other people would say, 'look it — Mrs. Got-rocks with her hair in rollers!' And [now] if I want to run uptown in rollers, I can do it, who cares? It's just me. And I like that feeling." She cannot tell if the rich really "have an air about them," or if "I *feel* they have an air about them. I'm not sure how much is genuinely them, and how much is me in awe [of] their position as, quote, 'position.' " But even if their exalted status is only imputed, Pamela still maintains that the rich "have a responsibility to be good-citizen-type people. I don't want to think of the rich as being bums. I want them to be nice and stylish, not fashionable, but I don't want them to look like a bunch of beatniks, unclean, and weirdos. I don't think Nelson Rockefeller should sit out in his front yard in his lawnchair with a beer. He wouldn't look good." Furthermore, the filthy rich "have a certain responsibility because of their richness to share their talent, to use their knowledge and talents to solve problems in the world."

Pamela knows that many of the rich are "selfish, bored, divorced fourteen times, have no purpose to their life." She also knows that although some have "good business heads," most are "born rich" or "in the right place at the right time." But for almost the only time, Pamela's emotions dominate her reason; she retains her ascriptive awe even when she knows that its objects do not warrant it.

Pamela regrets the persistence not of the upper-upper class, but of "poverty people." She sees poverty as the result of three factors, none the fault of the poor. First, inheritance: "Poor just goes on and on. The poor are poor because their families were poor and their families before them. The same as the rich stay rich, family-wise, the poor stay poor, family-wise." Second, environment: "They're a victim of circumstances sometimes, because they're born into this, and the kids grow up not knowing that there is a better life somewhere else. And unfortunately, the schools aren't any help." Finally, psychology: "They think they're poor forever, the majority. They've been beaten down so many times that they just don't care to try." Even those who have "blown the chance they've had" cannot be blamed: "How did they get on drinking and drugs? It's part of their environment, which is poverty. Many people drink and take drugs to escape the situations that they're in, and an unhappy poverty level would be a good reason." Thus she emphatically denies that poverty is anyone's just deserts.

This conclusion implies to Pamela a responsibility to help the poor, but she knows that "being poor and accepting help is hard." Many mothers at the well-baby clinic at which she volunteers "probably wish I'd go fly a kite. I'm all happy and bubbly and tell them, 'What a wonderful child!' and they're worrying about how they're going to feed that kid any supper tonight. And they think, 'Who in the heck is she?' And I just want to crawl in a hole somewhere. I sometimes feel like I'm trying to impress them with my *goodness*, even though I'm *not*." This empathy makes Pamela fear that classes cannot help conflicting: "Even *trying* to get on a level with the poor not only makes conflict for them but [also] for me. Those people need help, but I just don't know how to give it without feeling like I'm offending them." At this point, Pamela almost despairs; the poor do not deserve their poverty, but ascriptive class differences make a response to need almost impossible. For once, all norms seem to combine to produce a hopeless situation.

But she does not despair for long. Setting aside the problem of the very poor, Pamela argues that mobility makes remaining economic differences just. People should not be "assigned to" a class; "if people don't like their particular circumstances," there should be "something that they can change to. I would hate for us all to be the same and just vegetate in that one area." Even failures can recover: "I can't think of anybody rich, or middle class, or even in the $6000 area, really going down with the poor and staying there. They know that if they struggle and try, they can escape being poor." Thus the tragedy of persistent poverty is less the lack of goods than the fact that "the poor don't know that they can get out."

Here is the real difference between Vincent and Maria, on the one hand, and Pamela, on the other. Her belief that education, "drive," and "personality" will succeed is firm and unquestioned, whereas theirs is desperate and uncertain. Pamela is so sure that most people can advance "a little ways" that she can accept the fact that "then it's very difficult to go a whole lot further." That is all right; only the inability to go anywhere is tragic.

Pamela may feel both more confident and less constrained by limits than Vincent and Maria mainly because she is less poor. But the constraints are still there. Her husband, Pete, is in a "dying trade"; their savings account will not survive another layoff; Pamela refuses even to think about college tuition or retirement. Nevertheless, she demonstrates one possible response to economic constraints — ignore them. She focuses instead on her satisfactions and her conviction that, with the glaring exception of the chronically poor, people can control their own fate. Therefore she is "content to be right where I am," sorry for the poor, cynical about the well-off, awed by the very rich, and optimistic for her children. If the world is just, then economic differentiation is fair, and most actual differences are good.

Differentiation, Indifference, and the Poor

Yet another emotional reaction of the poor to economic differences is indifference; that is, some of the poor know of the gap between the top and bottom of the income scale, but they refuse to judge it. That refusal does not mean that they express no views on economic distributions. Most do hold distributive norms and differentiating ones at that. But they apply these norms only to settings that seem at least potentially controllable, such as their own workplace; for apparently uncontrollable phenomena like social class, they see principles of justice as irrelevant. What is, must be — or at least there is nothing one can do to change it. Therefore why waste time and emotions judging its fairness? In short, some of the poor use a principle of differentiation on particular economic issues, but seek to avoid any distributive judgments on a large economic scale.

Phillip Santaguida epitomizes such a stance. He learned early to accept what he could not affect. Before becoming a door-to-door salesman, he changed jobs often, not by choice, but because "jobs ran out, got laid off, there were strikes. Never changed for better pays, I didn't. There was no such thing as changing. You *stood* on a job. You liked your job, you got used to it." Concern about working conditions, job satisfaction, or even pay was a luxury he could not afford.

Phillip is willing to make distributive judgments about wages in familiar occupations. In these cases, he vacillates between norms of investments and results, sometimes combining them, sometimes opposing them, and sometimes ignoring one or the other. His company's executives deserve high salaries because "they have more headaches than the regular worker. They must bring homework home." Here effort and productivity coincide. But some people in high positions do not work hard enough to merit their rewards. Unskilled bricklayers, who earn three dollars an hour, are "really underpaid towards what skilled bricklayers get," about nine dollars an hour. This ratio of wages is "mixed up. They're getting, not twice as much, but *three* times as much." Here one must balance high position and greater productivity *against* effort in order to determine a fair wage.

Phillip sometimes considers only effort: "Prostitutes, pimps make more than they deserve for the work they do, the time they spend. A nice, honest woman working at a sewing machine all day long earns about $15 a day. Prostitutes go out and earn it in ten minutes. So they're being overpaid." Politicians are too: "Getting, say, a salary of $20,000, then you have graft, favors — maybe $50,000. So that makes them $70,000. A man that does what they do, with all their secretaries and everybody else doing their work for them, they don't deserve it." Note that he objects not to graft or immorality, but only to the disproportion between effort and reward.

Finally, Phillip sometimes considers only results. If an assembly line worker tries harder than another, but "is not producing the same, he shouldn't get paid the same." Workers with different family expenses should "get paid the same. They do the same kind of work. Let him [with the large family] go someplace else — get more money." The government, not the employer, should "compensate" handicapped workers or aid workers in emergencies.

All of this does not resemble the generous, even self-sacrificing, egalitarian of chapter four. Nor does it resemble the cynical social Darwinist of chapter two. Indeed, Phillip becomes a Spencerian only when he surveys the broad economic structure. Pay differences in the workplace are desirable and can easily be made just. But extremes of wealth and poverty are necessary, understandable, and not wrong — nor are they desirable or just. They are simply inevitable results of an inevitable process by which people get what they can and give what they must. Only if social Darwinism, stripped of all its claims for progress and the betterment of the human race, can still be called a distributive norm does Phillip's view of the economy become a theory of justice. Otherwise, it is simply a theory of human activity, which he will neither praise nor condemn. Let us examine these views.

Phillip believes that the wealthy have deliberately created the American class structure. In the 1950s, the "medium class" began "getting richer" and merging with the "rich class," so that soon "there was gonna be only the rich and the poor." But "the rich man manipulated it on purpose — inflation. The money that that man saved, that he was starting to get rich with, wasn't worth much anymore." The wealthy were successful; Phillip argues that classes are now moving further apart, and the medium class is having more trouble than ever before simply staying in place.

Nevertheless, the existence of the rich "doesn't bother me a bit. You have a king and a queen — they get money for doing nothing. They were born in it. So, Howard Hughes is just like being a king." The wealthy are simply a fact of life — no more subject to control or criticism than royalty are.

Like royalty, some wealthy Americans inherit their money, but most "manipulate and steal. 'Cause if he was that honest, he could never make that kind of money. You're dishonest someplace — that's how you get the big money." Furthermore, inequalities cumulate: "Because you're poor, you don't have the chance. The rich men — they have the better opportunities. Money buys almost everything, money's at the top of the list all of the time."

But even dishonesty and unequal opportunites, despite the fact that they are more easily controlled than inheritance, do not move Phillip to seek justice: "No, I'm pretty open-minded about all these kind of things. [It] doesn't sound right, but that's the way it's gotta be." After all, why worry about what he cannot change: "I know I don't like it. But I don't let it bother me."

Phillip is no more complimentary about the "medium" class with which he identifies. Its members "work hard trying to get ahead," since they must "pay through the nose for everything." This does not imply that the harder one works, the richer one will become; rather, the less money one has, the harder one must work to get any more. "A rich man don't have to work hard. What does he work, one hour a day? He makes his own hours. But the medium has to take maybe two jobs, or work twelve hours, six days." This extra work also does not imply more virtue; members of the middle class are just as dishonest, "but they haven't got much power, enough money, to manipulate much." Besides, their goals are not virtuous; all they are working for is "more money. Money is the root of all evil." No one is exempt from "striving for more, more, more. The priest isn't ever satisfied with his collection offering. [He spends] every week wondering, 'What can I do *this* week to get more collection?' People are bitching, 'They got no money.' Three TVs, stereo, deep freeze, power mowers—everybody's never satisfied."

But just as he accepts the ruthlessness of the wealthy, Phillip sees middle-class greed as inevitable, legitimate, and even pitiable: "Me, I appreciate everything I got. I was brought up the hard way. We don't take things for granted. Today, no matter what you give a kid—see, *you're* in a different generation. You're in a tough generation, don't think it's easy for you. You *need* a lot more than I need. Today you need maybe eight pairs of shoes—we used to have one or two pairs." The price of "keep[ing] up to that " is "you gotta hustle and hustle and never stop." But still, people should be left alone to work too hard for the wrong things and even to manipulate others. It is simply unfortunate that the middle class is less lucky, smart, or dishonest than the rich, so that it trades more "heartaches" for less reward.

Phillip distinguishes between two kinds of poor. Some have opted out of the hedonic treadmill: "Rich man gotta get up and worry about his next dollar. Poor man, he stays in bed. The guy got nothing, he don't care what the neighbors got as long as he's got his TV and bottle of beer." Phillip neither condemns nor seeks to help these "ne'er-do-wells"; they are simply not part of his community.

He worries deeply, however, about the other kind of poor people—the majority who "have a man that's a drunkard, a gambler. Sometimes they're left without a man, or they have too many children they can't support with the money they make." They have not chosen, and therefore do not deserve, their fate. Abruptly abandoning the law of the jungle, Phillip gives a long, impassioned speech about our duty to pity and help the blameless poor:

> You go in a store, if he wants twelve cents for a can of beans today, tomorrow he wants fourteen, by the end of next week, eighteen. He's changing 7500 items every day. It's a madhouse! *I* can pay two

cents more. How about the lady [who] has four kids, she has to have *four* cans of beans, she can't afford *one* can? What we're talking about now is the essential that they need. They *have* to have food. Jennifer, someday go in the store, watch how many people look things over, and handle them, and don't buy them. Know what that means? They can't afford it. I get so that I get depressed, so I won't do it [go shopping]. See, that's what breaks your heart with poor people.

Here Phillip resembles Pamela and differs from Vincent: since the very poor do not threaten him economically or emotionally, he can afford to feel sorry for them. This is the only point at which Phillip too comes close to despair. He can live comfortably with the fact that the rich and the middle class do not merit their position. But the poor also do not merit their position, and this knowledge is almost intolerable. Again like Pamela, however, Phillip has few solutions for such a deep tragedy.

Phillip again dons his Spencerian armor to explain mobility. It depends on luck, ruthlessness, unequal resources and opportunities, tenacity, and, very seldom, skill. Once again he neither applauds nor condemns this process: "Everybody is trying to make it. Very few people get the breaks, the luck. That's life." But as we saw when he refused to castigate the wealthy, this indifference is a deliberate choice. Although he will not fight it, Phillip declines to participate in the process by which fellow workers are promoted: "They don't care whose feet they stepped on or how they did it, they wanted to become foreman. I could have done the same thing, but I'm not built like that. I don't want to step on anybody's toes. I'd rather be working and be happy at it, not be foreman and [hear] everybody say, 'He's no good.' That's hard, to push people around."

Phillip knows that he does not particularly deserve his economic constraints, but he prefers living with them to railing against them. Although "if I said I didn't like money I'd be crazy," he does not "want to get rich any more. I worked all these years and I didn't get rich — now I make the best of a bad bargain. I make myself satisfied." The law of nature determines distributions, and if its outcomes are not fair, then justice does not exist. There are exceptions to this rule — poverty, specific occupations, and Phillip's own family and actions, all of which fall under different norms. But Phillip cannot change the world; therefore he generally shrugs his shoulders and ignores things that anger or frighten Vincent and Maria.

Thus although the reactions of the poor to economic differences vary from helplessness to anger, contentment, or deliberate indifference, they agree in supporting economic differentiation. Except for anguish about the deeply poor, they ignore in the economic domain the egalitarian norms they rely on in the socializing domain. In short, their principle of economic justice leads them to support a system — or at least an ideal version of the system — that does relatively little to support them in return.

Differentiation, Bitterness, and the Rich

One might expect the surprises in this chapter to be over once we have discussed support by the poor for economic differentiation. That is basically correct; we are not surprised to find that the rich also support economic differentiation. But a close examination of emotions felt by the rich does yield unexpected results. Many of the rich are as distressed or angry as the poor are about discrepancies between ideal and actual economic differences. Even though they benefit from unequal distributions, they fear that others benefit much more and unfairly so. Even more strikingly, they are sometimes ambivalent about the justice of differentiation itself and feel uneasy about their own success and others' failure.

Barbara Azlinsky mixes support for economic differentiation, bitterness over actual economic differences, and occasional flashes of egalitarianism, which she does not know what to do with. Neither she nor her husband, Ian, she feels, are properly appreciated and rewarded at work: "I've been overlooked as far as advancement. It bothers me. They could have found a spot for me somewhere." Ian was just "bumped" from his job through "a dirty deal" in which his "sincerity" and loyalty, instead of yielding rewards, made him a safe target for political maneuvering. Barbara concludes bitterly from these experiences that doing one's job well brings neither appreciation — "It's ridiculous to give your life to something for thirty years and not even get a wristwatch" — nor financial reward — "I had more in the bank when I first got married than now. And that's upsetting. [It's] the unfairness of being back at the same level." A norm of results does not work as it should.

Barbara also uses a norm of results to decide who in other occupations is over- or underpaid. At one point she defines it as social contribution and uses it to promote more equality: "Teachers should get a greater salary. They are molding everything, they are spreading their knowledge, more so than doctors or lawyers. You're teaching the next generation their values, and they're just always looked down upon." But most often, she uses it to differentiate among people. Those who do not produce, whatever their job, are overpaid. Watching coworkers "who try to get away with everything, you wonder *why they are there*. It's just like a housekeeper staying in the bathroom for an hour, and you know darned well she's hiding from her boss. They want to get paid for something they're not doing. I resent that sort of thing." Entertainers are also overpaid: "To think that Muhammed Ali is getting millions! Our society is sick when it comes to that." Her examples of others' pay, like her own, all illustrate her belief that a norm of results should, but seldom does, obtain.

Unlike the poor respondents, however, Barbara does not believe that most professionals are overpaid and blue-collar workers underpaid, for two reasons. First, the former are intrinsically more valuable than the latter — an argument verging on an ascriptive norm: "I've worked, I've gone to school for my professional status, I'm entitled to get more than they [garbage collectors]. They may have a stronger back, but I have a better brain, and I'm a better person." If someone "ceases to enjoy" assembly line work, he or she should seek a new job or more training. For the others, after all "there *are* some people that *like* the time clock, they don't think to plan or anything."

Second, wealth should and sometimes does follow accomplishment. Business executives "got there fighting with their brain and wit, and they *deserve* it. Someone that's developed land or done things on their own, they're entitled to profit." A norm of results even justifies inheritance because if a legatee "isn't intelligent or have that drive, he will lose the business." Retaining one's inheritance is evidence that one has the ability to do so; therefore one deserves it to begin with.

Thus far Barbara seems upset over failures to apply a norm of results properly, but also sure when and how it should be applied; however, the picture is not yet complete. She frequently concludes a strong argument for differentiation with a contradictory argument invoking an egalitarian norm. Thus, to take the points made above in order, she finishes her diatribe against her own and Ian's employers by saying, "But it's what you put into it, I guess." After castigating garbage collectors for greed, she adds that, nevertheless, she pities them because "I had a goal, I had something to do, which they don't." After praising business executives, she decides that many executive salaries are not "fair. I just wonder what he does, if it's just the title or the name. You could have things rolling along without someone being in charge, too."

Barbara's dual confusion, between the justice of differentiation and unjust differences, and between differentiation and equality, come to a head in her discussion of the very wealthy. She cannot decide whether to criticize them, praise them, or both. On the one hand, the very rich are not necessarily moral or deserving, since some simply "had it through the generations." But on the other hand, she "admires" the many who *are* "self-made" and "intelligent," who show "self-perseverance," and who are "opportunists." Despite her norm of results, she cannot decide if the *"nouveau* rich" [*sic*] are more praiseworthy than the inheritors, since the former are less philanthropic. But even the generosity of the old rich seems to be calculated: "You don't [know] whether they're doing it for their own mark upon this world or not." At best, their generosity comes easy, since "they are not busy working for the money that their greatgrandfather did. Therefore they can sit back and philosophize. [If] you don't have to worry about not going to work, you can think how you can better the world." Thus self-made millionaires are admirable, but miserly; inheritors are generous, but not for admirable reasons.

Finally, however, Barbara succumbs to ascriptive awe. Society benefits from the existence of the very rich, since "some people have as a goal, 'Why can't I be as rich as Rockefeller?' " She does not invite wealthy neighbors to her home "perhaps [because] I have such an inferiority complex with the very wealthy and influential that I am ashamed of my house, compared to their house, and their signed pieces, and sculptures, and everything." Pamela and Barbara define *rich* differently, but their ascriptive respect is similar.

Barbara is less ambivalent about, and therefore harder on, the poor. The poor are solely responsible for their position, and poverty, unlike wealth, has no redeeming social value. She is "annoyed at the lower income because if they can't get a job here, they could go someplace else and look for another job, rather than stay here and collect unemployment." Even though the availability of jobs "doesn't show in the country's statistics," nevertheless employment "all depends on your pride. Like a cleaning woman — if you want money, you will do that. You have to compromise."

If jobs can be found, then people are poor because they are lazy and prideful. Even so, they lack the right kind of pride. In her working-class childhood, the women would "sweep out their house and continue down the steps, and the sidewalks would be clean. If there was something in the street, they would just go out and clear it away. Everyone felt responsible and there was a pride." But "that disappeared" when "the blacks came in and didn't do much. So we saw the neighborhood deteriorate so."

Finally, the poor are wasteful and destructive: "The only way my husband and I got *here* was saving and doing without. I have seen a lot of waste that I wouldn't have tolerated if I were the mother. Like biting into an apple and throwing it out. I would cut it away and put it in the refrigerator, so that someone else would eat it. And that's just one little 'if' thing."

Barbara condemns the poor so strongly because she wants equally strongly to believe that upward mobility depends on "an individual's drive." But as before, Barbara worries that her prescription for justice does not work in reality. After all, to become rich "you need money to invest, play around with. We had the opportunity, but we were afraid to take out a second mortgage. And the person that *did* do what we were thinking of doing got a lot of money in it. But they *had* money, and that's where the rich get richer." At one point, in fact, she worries that "the American dream is no longer in existence." She immediately counters this fear with several rags-to-riches stories, but the fear that effort and skill count for less than luck, ruthlessness, and prior holdings remains.

Barbara will not even discuss downward mobility, except to attribute it solely to personal failings. Luck is irrelevant: "There has to be another reason. I mean, there *has* to be a reason."

This insistence that "there *has* to be a reason" for success and failure encapsulates Barbara's normative view of the economy. She endorses differentiation in holdings; she wants desperately to believe that actual differences are just. All too often, however, wealth results from "survival of the fittest" or luck, not from "free enterprise." This frightens and angers her, since it makes her own unsatisfactory bank account seem even more insecure and unfair. In the socializing domain, Barbara is torn between "humanitarianism" and a bitter perception that "it doesn't pay to be a good Joe." In the economic domain, she is torn between a norm of results and actual economic outcomes. Thus in the former domain, her conflict lies in the tension between equality and its undesirable consequences, whereas in the latter domain, her conflict lies in the gap between just norms and unjust realities. But she remains disappointed, angry, sometimes hostile to the interviewer, and often so confused as to be incoherent.

Differentiation, Contentment, and the Rich

Most of the rich do not feel, as Barbara does, that their well-being is precarious and their efforts largely unrewarded. Instead, they are pleased with their position, unquestioning in their support of economic differentiation, and only rarely troubled by evidence that some make too little and others too much.

Ernest Berkowitz is one such contented wealthy respondent; he shows none of the ambivalence and anguish in the economic domain that he did in the socializing domain. He is, however, still reluctant to discuss certain issues—this time his hitherto unquestioned economic and social assumptions: "You're asking me specific questions, and yet I don't think that I've had enough exposure to this area of questioning. In other words, how do I know?" He often ignores or reinterprets questions, especially if they point to a contradiction that he cannot resolve.

But Ernest clearly conveys some views, such as how much he loves his business. He grumbles that, as owner, "you're supposed to know everything that goes on." But he is not complaining: "Follow[ing] everything in the store from the smallest to the largest detail is just one of the jobs." He is comfortably paternalistic toward his employees. At $6000 a year (in 1976 dollars), his "girls" are "just average wage earners. Presumably they have a husband that provides the main source of income." Their few abilities and simple job justify low wages: "A salesperson is a salesperson. How good can they be? If they're going to be *that* good, they've got to be more than a salesperson." He is annoyed that his employees expect an annual raise: "There isn't any place for them to advance, and there isn't any incentive for me to think that 'Boy, they did a great job, so now I'm going to pay them much more!' 'Cause it's the *same* type of job every year." Because his employees cannot become more productive after a certain point, he feels he has no obligation to pay them more.

Upon reflection, this harshness makes Ernest uneasy: "The problem is, the employee doesn't have (and I don't know how you could fix this) recourse as to the fact that they *are* doing the job well, [therefore] why aren't they being compensated more for it?" He can suggest no solution to the dilemma—"I don't know, it's a complicated thing"—and veers into a demand that the government stem inflation.

Ernest also worries about, but does not try to resolve, two other employee problems. First, they are not "protected enough for the future. Because suppose this woman that's working in my office for twenty to twenty-five years is *not* married? What benefit does she get when she gets all through, other than her Social Security program, which is not enough?" Nevertheless, he has no pension plan, since "there's nothing the government says I *have* to do." Insecurity about the future is unfortunate, but not unjust; therefore he feels sorry, but not apologetic.

The second problem stems directly from the first. A seventy-year-old widowed employee "wanted to work, and she was quite able to, but I wanted to break in younger people, and she wasn't going to be around forever. I just had no choice, and I had to be *tough* about it. So I kept cutting down on her time" until she "wasn't allowed to work" anymore. He urged her to "join a senior citizen group. She would be a *natural* for that." But inexplicably, "she just doesn't want to"; she preferred to work. Ernest speaks long and eloquently about the "tough situation" of the elderly, and he proudly describes his grandfather's insistence on working full-time until age eighty-five. After all, "Keeping active is what keeps you going." He vaguely realizes that he reacts differently to an unwanted employee than to his grandfather, but he sees no injustice in it. He is, again, sorry but not apologetic, and concludes, "So I don't know, there's no answer for that. I can't, you know . . ."

In his own business, then, Ernest mixes norms of results, ascription, need, and procedures. His employees must produce and defer to their employer's wishes; he, in turn, must reward them as he thinks fair and be concerned about their needs. Within those boundaries, as long as he follows the rules of the game for honest but profit-minded businessmen, the effects of his actions on his employees are irrelevant to any discussion of justice. They are playing in the same game as he is, and they must accept its consequences. Their problems warrant pity, but not redress.

Employees other than his own are even more subject to an ascriptive norm. A coal miner earns too little, but simply raising wages "would make him have a *lot* of money that he might not know what to do with." A better alternative is to "retire him at fifty-five instead of sixty-five. Because his life span's going to be shorter anyway. And at *that* time give him money. If he pisses it away, then that's the end of him — you can't do anything about that angle." Executives and professionals, on the other hand, can be trusted with their full salaries, which should depend on their value to their company. The prescription is that of his own business — value depends on accomplishments — and he continues to assume without question that sales executives accomplish more than salesclerks.

If greater equality would benefit employers as well as employees, Ernest supports it. Thus the government should improve the educational system, for if public schools are good enough, employees will not need to send their children to private schools and therefore will not need higher salaries. Similarly, employers should hire the handicapped, especially when hiring a handicapped person would free highly skilled employees' more valuable time. But where an egalitarian norm cannot serve differentiating ends, it must be dropped, however regretfully. He is glad that "in school there is *some* credit given for pure effort," and he wonders if "they could do something" about rewarding effort in industry. But "you're trying to tie it into monetary [considerations], and that's not easy." Again he has no suggestions — "This area that you're into today is a toughy" — and does not pursue the subject.

Ernest explains upward mobility by means of two procedural norms. The first is a random event — "timing. The person in the right place at the right time can accomplish something, and [that is, even if] he didn't have nearly the ability as the other guy who *wasn't* in the right place at the right time." The second is a Hobbesian willingness to "take advantage of a situation when it's presented." Ruthless competition and the differentiation it produces lie outside the realm of moral judgment. "There always will be movers in this world of ours. It isn't moral value or whether he's entitled to it or not—I don't think that's a big part of it." He worries that "many people are stymied by not having enough money to do something," but once again he offers no solution: "You don't just hand out money to somebody, just because someone wants to get ahead." Thus faith in mobility, which is so essential to Barbara, Vincent, and Pamela, is not a keystone of Ernest's beliefs about economic justice. He would like all people to have equal opportunity, but they do not, and random or amoral factors matter more anyway in achieving success. It may be that his lesser emphasis on mobility corresponds to his greater emphasis on ascription, that is, that opportunity and status are alternative justifications for material differentiation in the minds of respondents as well as in Western political theory. Whatever the case in general, Ernest in particular is not too concerned about the problems of mobility.

In fact, Ernest is not too concerned about very many of the problems of economic justice that he points out. Unlike other respondents, he does not seek advancement; he is "comfortable, not lacking anything, satisfied with my status." Nor does he understand why envy "is at all levels. You're asking the wrong guy, because I am not a striver. I'm an acceptor." And yet, he knows that "strivers—that's what this society produces." Just as employees earning $3 an hour envy those with $3.50, so "if someone is in Fort Lauderdale where the yachts go up to $100,000, he can't move up to Palm Beach where the yachts *start* at $150,000." He also knows that striving and envy generate a struggle of all against all, which overrides other normative claims. On a large scale, "the world is a selfish world. Little business wants to become big business, and big business wants to become *bigger*. And who's to stop them? And if they're big to begin with, *now* look what you're up against." On a small scale, the struggle leads to ruthlessness with aged employees, insecurity for all employees, and rewards that do not always reflect productivity or effort. Ernest regrets these hardships and other gaps between norms and outcomes, but feels no responsibility for alleviating even those he causes. Compassion is not obligation, and justice is not equality.

Like Ernest, Anne Kaufman mixes norms of results, ascription, and procedure within a general principle of economic differentiation. Also like him, she has few qualms about the justice of her principle and few doubts that it is generally carried out in society. Certainly her norms of results and ascription are carried out in her own liquor distributorship. Her main criterion for wages is simple: "Any job should be paid in proper proportion to what is performed." Like Ernest, she rejects the claim that every year "you automatically always have to give a raise whether the person's entitled to it or not." And also like him, she gives a norm of results a distinctly seigneurial tone. Even "with jobs so hard to get, some people don't show much conscience or concern about doing the job, to *keep* the job. Then every once in a while, you find a nice young fella, [whose] father worked for us many years ago in our original business, [and] who's anxious to apply himself. He's interested in the customer and their welfare. And he's rewarded properly because you really appreciate somebody that *will do their job*." The ideal employee is one who is part of the traditional family labor force, who "marries a nice girl," and who is productive.

Norms of results and ascription also reinforce each other in Anne's justification of low incomes for "dirty work." She does not "minimize" unskilled labor, since "I would not want to make it my regular lifetime occupation," and she worries that manual workers "don't earn enough to be inspired to work harder to produce more to get more." But still, "Some people just never can rise above that particular level mentally, physically, or whatever it takes to leave that humdrum existence. I can't see a man who cleans a bathroom get the same pay as a doctor with skill." The unskilled laborer deserves compassion and help, but not the income of a skilled professional.

The compassion of an ascriptive norm sometimes outweighs the discipline of a norm of results when Anne is confronted by claims of effort or need. For "nice" workers, "Sometimes you appreciate their sincerity and their attempts, and if they're working at their ability, you reward it." Furthermore, the Kaufmans have "rescued employees many times, and I can't say that it was always appreciated." Anne responds to still another type of need by hiring handicapped workers and giving them "the benefit of the difference" in wages so gracefully that they are not forced to feel grateful or pitiable. Nevertheless, their pay level depends upon their accomplishment. In addition to precluding "a lot of disgrumblement [sic]" among fellow workers, that strict rule simply reflects life's harshness: "You have to develop *some* sort of a chill. I don't mean to be indifferent, but you can't be submissive to every sympathetic feeling, because you really end up being stepped on very often and not being able to do your *own* job and help the person who *needs* the extra help." Again like Ernest, Anne slides here from a norm of results to a norm of unbridled competition. Even if some outcomes of a just process are unfortunate, everyone benefits in the long run by accepting them as inevitable and finally fair.

Anne loses her cool, yet compassionate, stance toward workers only when she discusses trade unions. Even though they ended "sweatshop conditions," which without their "monitoring system would come back again in certain places," they do vastly more harm than good in her eyes. They are corrupt, hypocritical, selfish, and prone to "resort to some pretty strong-arm stuff, I *know*. Threatening stuff." The NLRB (National Labor Relations Board) "doesn't care *how* they spit in the face of a businessman." Anne's animosity stems from her belief that unions systematically seek to destroy her world by demanding more for all workers than they deserve. They threaten both norms of ascription and results, and she attacks back.

For one thing, Anne argues, union organizers disrupt the orderly hierarchy of a workplace. She was shocked when a "troublemaker" decided "that he's gonna have a union [among her employees]. He was a wife-beater, he stole, wrecked a truck, drank away his pay. When he was in debt, we financed him, okay? Short-lived appreciation. And this is *his* background — no quality in this man, is there? You're gonna put *him* against *me*, when I've been responsible all my life? No way." A challenge to her fairness and authority by a man with "no quality" is intolerable.

For another thing, unions violate a norm of results by denying an owner a fair profit, even at the cost of destroying the business itself. For example, Anne's cousin "just *gave up* [his business]. He said, 'I can't hassle it anymore. Every time there's a new round of union talks, I give in, because it's that or close my shop.' And that year he closed his shop, put forty people out of work. He didn't want it. They wouldn't give him any peace. It's *greed*." She does not see that the union might consider an employer who can retire at will in New York City wealthy enough to raise workers' pay. They asked for more than they deserved, and that is unjust.

Anne is too intelligent and clear-sighted to blame all industrial evils on unions; she sees large corporations as just as greedy, ruthless, and impersonal. But the virulence of her attack on unions is astonishing in the face of her normally calm sophistication and suggests the depth of her commitment to the principle of differentiation in the economy.

Anne makes clearer ascriptive distinctions among classes than do most other respondents: "Of course in this country, the way it is supposed to be, everybody is born equal. But I don't really believe that's true. The *concept* and the idealism is fine, but we aren't all the same. We're born into different areas, homes, attitudes. We're shaped by different influences, so we *don't* end up the same." She identifies three social classes. The rich "consider themselves better, untouchable. Whereas there is discrimination against minority groups, nobody would dare touch white Anglo-Saxon Protestants. It wouldn't occur to me to say, 'I have to come to your home or your club,' 'cause I don't belong there. And they wouldn't accept me anyway." The rich are often lazy and probably have inherited rather than earned their wealth, but if they "put it [their money] to good use, contribute to the arts and to helping underprivileged people, it's fine with me. I don't begrudge it to them." In this case, then, ascription overrides results. The wealthy are a class, culture, and even race apart, with unquestioned high status and distinctive good works to perform.

Anne separates herself even more sharply from the poor: "There's times that I find myself cringing at how people behave. I see people who live a completely different life in their social mores, morals, attitudes toward their children. They'd be satisfied to live in a dirty, slovenly situation. *I* wouldn't — if that makes me in another social class, yes I am, in that respect. Our values are different. If that's what *they're* satisfied with, that's their privilege, but I really think there *are* social stratas." Just as the wealthy appear "snobby" to her, so she is "a snob" to the poor. But she is "simply appalled" at the ways in which "they make their own disaster." She does not want to blame the poor for their conditions, but after all, "That landlord didn't punch out those windows or break the door. It's too bad if you have to live in less desirable conditions, so why make it worse?" She therefore feels almost forced against her will to hold the poor responsible for their own misery.

Anne goes through this cycle of incredulous and unwilling, but angry, condemnation several times. After elaborate and shocked anecdotes showing the vulgarity, ugliness, and irresponsibility of lower-class life, she concludes, "Why do I have to accept that? Are we all one class? At the risk of being called a snob, I don't have to associate with people like that."

At this point, Anne seems to explain poverty solely through ascription and results. The poor are a different race (her stories are always about blacks), with an inferior culture and world view; they are also lazy and unproductive. But her intelligence and sense of fairness finally produce a more subtle, empathic view of poverty. For example, after castigating their gaudy, but unkempt, clothes, Anne reflects on poor people's "very miserable circumstances" and lack of "hope of ever getting out of it": "And so they have to get their personal satisfaction 'cause they're still people just as you and I are. Bright colors, outlandish designs, that's their outlet. The pink Cadillac syndrome—people living in perfectly rotten housing, but they own a very expensive car. That is their personal feeling of accomplishment." Asked how people become poor, she answers simply, "Oh, it's so sad, if you're born into it, you can't always get out of it." The apparent stupidity and laziness of blacks are often due to "malnourishment," "the evils of the welfare system," or "lack of proper training." It is even possible that "our society deliberately keeps some people down by unemployment and very low wages" (a sentence from the written questionnaire), although "I don't know of anything that *I* do to keep people down, using myself [as an example]. Do you have a specific?" She once heard a black minister say, " 'To be poor is to be almost a nonperson. To be black and poor *is* you're a nonperson. People don't give you any consideration,' " and this idea was a revelation to her. Despite its threat to her principle of economic differentiation, she struggles to evaluate it fairly: "That's true in a lot of respects, but I wouldn't say necessarily altogether. I could not accept it in full." The balance between high standards and indulgence that she shows in the socializing domain returns in her final explanation of class distinctions: "It's a human tendency to shy away from these things that are uncomfortable. And there *is* a need for everybody to feel a little bit better than the next guy or certainly to protect ourselves from feeling *less* in comparison to someone that's better than we. So you have, in ethnic groups and the levels [that is, classes] of societies, 'They spoil the neighborhood.' They don't want other groups to move in 'cause they'd change it or change their values. And they *do* very often."

Like Pamela and Phillip, Anne finds her endorsement of economic differentiation severely shaken when she contemplates the poor. Also like them, she falls back on a shaky insistence that, despite much evidence to the contrary, upward mobility is still possible. Even though "the Horatio Alger story doesn't always apply anymore, there *are* new avenues. It's a case of being a go-getter, [being] more aggressive to *find* the opportunity to do more. Not everything is finished." But in a final parallel to Pamela and Phillip, Anne herself rejects the quest for "more things": "I've mellowed. I've tasted so many bitter pills that having the comfortable things I *do* have, and health, are more important to me than having more money than I could spend. It wouldn't do me any good. I don't want to sound [like] Pollyanna, but I really can exempt myself from greed."

Thus Anne, with one crucial exception, endorses both the justice of economic differentiation and actual distributions of economic goods. Norms of results, ascription, and occasionally procedures usually reinforce, but sometimes offset, each other in her eyes. The dilemma of poverty shakes, but does not destroy, her basic contentment; she concludes that since "we're surrounded by evils, we have to appreciate the goods."

Differentiation, Unease, and the Rich

Finally, some of the rich support economic differentiation, but only uneasily. They are torn between a principle of equality and a principle of differentiation; they verge on one of the alternative patterns discussed in chapter seven. Their ambivalence, combined with their acute awareness of their own high status, makes them embarrassed and defensive about wealth, and even leads them to toy with the idea of fundamental economic changes. But they find major change as hard to think about as the poor do, and they have much less incentive to do so. Therefore they fall back into accepting economic differentiation while worrying about whether both the principle and its implementation are fair.

Craig Cabot demonstrates this form of ambivalence about economic differentiation. The picture is complicated in his case, however, by his distinction between economic matters, about which he says little, and justice, about which he can barely be silenced. Justice for Craig is a legal principle — "flexibility, the humanity of the law. So justice is done when the rules of law are interpreted with common sense, reason, experience, and a sense of fairness." Distributions are a matter of economic choice; therefore "there really isn't any such thing as economic justice. The expression *economic justice* is jamming together two sometimes conflicting concepts. Because what's just isn't necessarily economic, and what's economic is very often not just." For example, an "enlightened despot" might respond to "poor Mrs. X, who just takes her eye off the road and gets clobbered and ends up a paraplegic," by saying, " 'Well, we're all human. Poor Mrs. X, we have to take care of her.' " That is "a perfectly legitimate and reasonable thing to do," but "it isn't justice, so don't do it in the name of justice. You're taking from all and giving it to a few, for economic reasons. But there's nothing *just* about it, if justice is fairness. Because you're transposing the victim. The victim is the person whom you are taking the money away from to give it to this lady who, really [it] was her own fault."

Separating justice from economic need in this fashion was vital when Craig was a trial lawyer. As counsel for a defendant employer, "I felt terrible" about a plaintiff's injuries, but "I invariably overcame that. Because invariably the people were overreaching, malingering. Then I'd say, 'Well, screw you. You're trying to screw the system.' The system of justice is of really deep significance to me, and if they try to undermine that system, that is enough for me to go after widows and children and maimed and retarded." Legal justice dominates economic need in Craig's normative hierarchy; therefore he can, without qualms, defend bosses against workers. He can also consider many economic questions dispassionately, since they skirt what matters most to him.

Craig supports economic differentiation firmly but with clear limits: "There should be a level beneath which people should not be allowed to drop. I *don't* feel the same way with saying that there should be a ceiling above which people should not be allowed to achieve." Within those bounds, fair distributions depend on a fair market process: "If society needs certain work or services performed, society will have to pay for those services on a supply/demand thing. My general reaction to all these questions [about fair wages for particular jobs] is not so much reward, but supply and demand."

Thus Craig endorses the acquisition of great wealth through the market. A thriving corporation "must make good business sense, so it's legitimate to that extent." A claim of class conflict is not "accurate. The fact that a businessman makes money from his employees does not diminish the fact that the employees make a living because of the opportunity to work that the businessman has provided. If some guy gets himself into a situation, through luck or skill, and he can set up that kind of a thing—terrific. 'Good luck to you!'"

Craig would like egalitarian norms to carry some weight in the market process, but he does not know how to incorporate them. For example, a need norm is "very appealing from a moral point of view. People who work for a long period of time, under hard working conditions, shouldn't be cut off like dead timber at the end of their prime productive years." Yet market processes have priority: "How you go about doing that, I don't know. I don't believe you could legislate it. Can the government make up for it in other ways, without interfering with the free market? I don't know, really." Similarly, his "sympathies go toward" underpaid service workers: "It's indecent that a singer can make thousands of dollars on an appearance, and a teacher can never make that much in a year." But he doubts that "it would be good to just change the social-economic picture of this country to such an extent that you could do anything about it." The principle of equality should be used to smooth off the rough edges of the market, but how and how much, Craig cannot say.

Craig refuses to "think in terms of classes. Those are useful distinctions only for the purpose of planning." But even this limited use is vague. When asked to explain further, he shrugs, "What *do* you have to plan? (laugh) It seems to me economists are running around finding out [all] kinds of things that involve what people are doing. I wish I knew more about economics, but I . . ." But like Pamela, he cherishes his ignorance: "If you start thinking in terms of class structures, if that becomes institutionalized, then it's a very damaging thing."

The law, as well as the economy, has "no class bias that I've ever perceived." If anything, tax laws "discriminate against the rich man because they're graduated against him." Zoning laws also "protect people against the abuses that vast money can generate"; they favor "the little guy, the person who's trying to preserve the integrity of his property against the big developer who's going to come in and try to destroy it." Craig ignores arguments that zoning laws are also a barrier set up by wealthy whites against the poor and blacks, and that tax law in practice bears little resemblance to tax law on the books. He sees the law as a neutral or even egalitarian framework for an economic system — not as a bulwark for the differentiated status quo.

Craig's only ascriptive argument is invoked when he discusses white-collar crime. In his eyes, punishment should rehabilitate, not merely punish; therefore white-collar crime requires lesser sentences than violent crime. He is not "bothered a hell of a lot" that an embezzler of $30,000 is not jailed, while a professional thief who takes $1,000 is jailed for thirty years, "because the mechanical, state-imposed punishment is secondary to the punishment that has already been exacted upon the [former] person. The loss of prestige, family, position in society, the ridicule and humiliation are very acute in a white-collar situation." Craig assumes here that lower-class society, and therefore lower-class criminals, have so little sense of morality, family responsibility, and social pressure that they will not respond to moral suasion as a middle- or upper-class criminal will.[1]

Again like Pamela, however, Craig is not nearly as oblivious to economic differences as he claims to be. He knows that the administration of law has a class bias: "A law against loitering is an economic law. A man with five bucks isn't loitering. A fella with twelve cents — he's loitering. Alcohol abuse, sexual crimes, lascivious carriage — parading around in a way which is not compatible with our Puritan ethic — have some uneven philosophy in terms of racial or minority [administation]."

Most notable, however, is Craig's extraordinary sensitivity to the plight of poor blacks in a white middle-class legal system. Like Phillip, he is moved to give a long, impassioned speech at the thought of this terrible consequence of economic differentiation. A typical jury "will do better by a middle-class defendant than by a minority," because

the minority criminal defendant is going to be panicked. He won't have any ease in the courtroom, everybody will be hostile to him, his own lawyer will be distinct from him. *All* the court personnel will—the judge, jurors, prosecutor. He's sitting in there naked and alone. He's less articulate than everybody else. Combine that with [the fact that] he's got more to lose in terms of his job. His family may have pressures economically, which are putting domestic pressures on. He will not have the peer pressures that the middle-class fella will, but he will have all the rest of it, which will make him nervous, *more* inarticulate, *more* panicked, and *more* likely to be guilty in the eyes of the jury. He won't deal with the jurors in such a way as will engender in them any confidence in his credibility.

That is all from an outsider's point of view. From the jury's viewpoint, "If I'm trying to convince you of something, and I'm talking to you, and I'm looking at you, and I'm not sweating and stammering and looking away, you're more apt to believe what I'm saying. So to whatever extent they are prejudiced, that's going to be fueled by his anxieties." In addition, the defendant's own lawyer is more of a problem than a solution. No matter how hard the attorney tries, he is still a public defender, and it just "isn't the same thing, no matter what you do, as representing a friend, or a colleague, or somebody in the same social-economic community."

This dismal situation cannot be ameliorated: "It's a matter of human nature. You're not going to be able to do anything about the fella's anxiety. You could convince him all day long, send him to *law school,* and he still will come away feeling trapped." An attorney can try to ease the tension and "infuse some aggression into him" to "get him over the anxiety and fear," but the only real solution is worse than the problem. "The villain in this whole thing is the disparity of classes. The obvious remedy is to equalize, which is no virtue. This argument would go out the window if everybody were essentially the same." But that is unacceptable to Craig, as we saw in chapter two.

Thus Craig is not simply a patrician who, from his exalted heights, ignores all distinctions below. He believes that market procedures create fair economic differences, and he is blind to class biases in the law, but his caveats are almost as important as his principles. Need and social contribution play an important role in economic policy, even if not in legal justice. And most important, his deep morality and vivid empathy for the losers in his beloved legal system prevent his wholehearted endorsement of economic differentiation.

Conclusion

The single most important conclusion here is that most respondents, both rich and poor, endorse differentiation in the economic domain. We now cannot conclude that the dog doesn't bark simply because it is muzzled; that is, we can no longer argue that the poor really do seek economic equality, but are silenced by fear or the absence of a chance to express their secret views. There are crucial caveats, to be explored in later chapters, to the claim that the poor support economic differentiation, but the caveats are not "They are prevented by external force or lack of opportunity from expressing their true, egalitarian views." That argument is too simple.

That the rich support economic differentiation needs little comment, although here too caveats giving shape to that skeletal conclusion will be examined later. The main point at this stage is that variation among respondents depends not upon income, sex, political ideology, occupation, or education, but upon the domain of life that they are addressing.

With the main conclusion clear, we can move to qualifications. The first addresses variation in differentiating norms used in specific settings. Respondents use primarily a norm of results and sometimes norms of investment, ascription, or procedure in the workplace; they use results and ascription to evaluate the wealthy; they use a contradictory mix of investments and competitive procedures to explain mobility; they show no consistent pattern in viewing the class structure; and they use a contradictory mix of ascription and circumstance to evaluate poverty. Let us briefly consider each of these statements.

First, respondents insist that productivity should dominate in decisions about fair wages. Even those who argue forcefully that need, effort, or strict equality should be used in the socializing domain reject such claims in the economic domain. Rich and poor differ, however, in the effect they would generate by using this norm and in the other norms they use to modify it.

On the one hand, the poor often combine a norm of results with an investment norm, and often argue that if productivity were truly rewarded, this would create *more* equal incomes. All four representative poor respondents made these claims, as do others. For example, Sandra Wilson, a nursery school aide, mixes investment and results criteria to argue that aides should be paid more and principals less. Her argument has several steps. First, the aides do everything the teachers do except give grades, and yet teachers are paid more. Their higher position is immaterial: "People should be paid on the basis of their work, not their title." Second, the principal is overpaid because "he doesn't *do* much. He comes around maybe once or twice a month, and he gets a report, and he leaves, and that's it." Finally, the superintendent deserves even more than he earns because "he works very hard, he's been to school for eight years, and he has an awful lot of responsibility." This last phrase holds the key to Sandra's basic belief: "People should be paid for their responsibility." Her real complaint is that teachers are not more responsible for the children they "produce" than the aides are, and that principals are less responsible than either. Thus both investment and results norms mandate higher wages for hardworking, productive aides and lower wages for lazy, unproductive principals. But equality per se is not Sandra's goal; the highest-paid worker, the superintendent, deserves even more than he now earns, "because of all the headaches he has."

On the other hand, wealthy respondents often combine a norm of results with ascriptive or procedural norms, and often argue that if productivity were truly rewarded, this would create *less* equal incomes. Each representative rich respondent made such arguments, as do others. For example, David Fine, the wealthy architect, is angry that construction workers "are making too goddamn much money. I could teach you to be an iron worker in about two weeks. That's the level of the skill. And these guys are making $18 an hour! When some clod can make $25,000 a year as an iron worker or a carpenter, there's something wrong. Particularly since, well, what does an assistant professor make?" He concludes that "people should get paid according to what they accomplish"; the poor would agree with that sentiment but would infer different consequences from it.

Second, respondents mix norms of ascription and results when they evaluate the rich. All believe that some of the rich have not earned their wealth, but none claim that violators of a norm of results should therefore give up their holdings. In fact, many feel it necessary to argue the reverse—that someone who achieves a high position is nevertheless just as good as someone who started there. Ruth Sennett's misconstruction of an interview question illustrates this curious phenomenon. I asked a question intending to discover if she thought that those who work their way up the corporate ladder deserve a greater reward for their achievement than does the president's son born into the same position. In answer, she insisted that *even* the upwardly mobile deserve equal pay for equal work: "If he got there, he's the same as the one that was rich. He should get paid the same, like the rich one." The norm of results is turned on its head in this way because an ascriptive norm intervenes. Ruth starts with an assumption that those born in high positions deserve more than those who achieve them, so that an ascriptive norm becomes the baseline against which a norm of results has to contend.

Even some wealthy respondents use ascriptive as well as results criteria when they discuss those who are wealthier. Their perspective differs from that of the poor respondents, of course; to the poor, anyone making over $50,000 is very rich, whereas to the rich, $50,000 is a middle-class income. But the differentiating norms remain the same.

Third, my respondents are not at all sure that America really is the land of equal opportunity. They all want to believe that upward mobility is possible for those with drive, talent, and ambition, but they are dubious. Too often, the lives of the poor have resembled Peter Schmidt's. As a teenager, he wanted a college education, "But there wasn't too much money around, and somehow or other, when I really needed the big money behind me, it wasn't there." He took a job in a hardware store, because "without higher education, I couldn't think of going into too many other things, you see." Peter does not expect things to be different for his children, since he still cannot afford for them to study instead of work.

Even the rich who pride themselves on their own upward mobility fear that it will be less possible for their children. David Fine, for example, whose enthusiasm for the market system is almost boundless, finds limits here. He criticizes public works jobs for welfare recipients because they give the worker no incentives to achieve: "If it comes from private enterprise, at least the guy has a feeling that he has an opportunity of working his way up." But when asked if that feeling has a realistic basis, he responds simply, "No." Since no one has a solution to this problem, most conversations on the subject of mobility end as abruptly as the one just quoted.

Fourth, there is no clear pattern to respondents' definitions of, and explanations for, the class structure. Some resemble Pamela in the intricacy of their distinctions; some resemble Anne in the richness of their explanations. But others resemble Maria, who defines the "poor class" as "when they have nothing," the middle class as "not that well-off, but not that bad either," and the upper class as those who "have all the money and [are] able to do things and not have to worry about going into the store." Some are sure that the United States has classes; others are sure that it does not. I found only one general, and unsurprising, response: almost all define themselves as members of the middle class, no matter how poor or rich they are.

Finally, the subject of poverty invariably raises the most intense and painful comments of any subject in the economic domain. Many respondents abandon their principle of differentiation at this point, since they do not believe that the poor are responsible for their fate. The sympathy of poor respondents for the poorer is often more informed and more personal, but the sympathy of rich respondents is just as deep and more touched with guilt. As with mobility, few can suggest any solutions to the problem of poverty that they would be willing to live with; therefore conversations on the subject tend to trail off into helpless grimaces.

But the complexity of the subject of poverty does not end there. Running through the deep sympathy and distress about objectionable circumstances is often a thread of ascriptive blame. Some claim vaguely that "there always has to be a working, laboring class"; therefore we must simply learn to live with that fact. Others are more obviously racist, although they usually try to hide their prejudice from themselves and the interviewer. But conversation makes it clear that many poor as well as rich respondents see the very poor as members of an alien race, culture, and style of life, which they neither understand nor approve of. After all, as Jean Gilmore explained, "We always feel more comfortable with our own type people in our own heritage."

Only one respondent is cheerfully and explicitly racist. Isaac Cohen, the businessman described in chapter two, defines his wife's family as "nigger rich." He explains the term in a broad imitation of black English: "If you suddenly come into big money, the first thing you do—the family don't have nothin' to eat—but you go and buy yourself a flashy suit and a big Cadillac, with big wide, wide white sidewalls, and you put on the flash. And then suddenly there ain't nothin' left!" He explains that the laziness induced by being on the dole becomes hereditary. "If you don't use your brain and think and reason, you lose the *ability* to think and reason. This is going to become a genetic thing, from generation to generation." It is "unfortunate" and not their fault, but blacks are especially prone to inherit the inability to achieve: "I don't employ a black. I haven't found one that I felt was worthy of my trust." Even Isaac finds racism and its economic consequences "terrible," but "the facts of life and the economic facts of business are such that" he feels compelled to perpetuate them in his own business and social relations.

Thus, under the umbrella term *principle of differentiation*, we find subtle variations in the norms used for particular elements of the economic domain. We also find, under the umbrella phrase *support for economic differentiation*, subtle variations in the emotions associated with that support. Specifically, we find four main reactions: contentment, bitterness, apathy, and unease.

Some respondents are enthusiastic about differentiation: not only does the economy distinguish among people, but it should also be praised and bolstered for so doing. Both rich and poor hold this view. People who are contented with the economic domain as it is share several characteristics. They see little divergence between the prescriptions of a particular differentiating norm and actual holdings. Despite specific injustices, the general pattern is fair. They are also satisfied with their own lot in life. The satisfied poor know their economic constraints, but refuse to let constraints dominate their world view. The satisfied rich know that they have everything they need and many things they want; they refuse to covet goods outside the range that they can attain. Contented respondents also perceive a sharp difference between their own satisfaction and the endless striving of others. They may admire or pity strivers, but they are profoundly thankful that they themselves are not so acquisitive. Finally, contented respondents are profoundly sympathetic toward the poor and deeply disturbed about this deficiency in an otherwise good society. Poverty is the only subject about which they lose all equanimity.

Some respondents support economic differentiation, but still express bitterness when they think about it. Just as contentment may seem surprising in the poor, so bitterness seems surprising in the rich—but both phenomena occur. The unhappy respondents also share some characteristics. All are upset over the great divergence they perceive between just differentiation and actual differences. All believe that they have not been rewarded as they deserve. The poor in this group feel severe economic constraints, sometimes to the point of not being sure that they can feed their families. The rich are not severely constrained, but their visions of where they should be or what they might have leave them frustrated. Finally, the bitter respondents are the strongest critics of the poor, combining occasional sympathy with frequent attributions of laziness, immorality, or racially-based ineptitude.

Some respondents support differentiation only because it seems inevitable. The marketplace perhaps should not distinguish so sharply among people, but it does, and we can do nothing about it. For these people, the economy is a force of nature. Its worst effects should be mitigated and its best effects encouraged, but fundamentally, it will do as it chooses. We can only acquiesce with good grace. For example, Michael McFarland sees inheritance of wealth as "a thing that has to be, but I don't think it is fair." Similarly, he "feel[s] sorry for" the poor, but "I don't think we're *unfair* to poor people. There's really nothing you can do with them."

Some respondents are uneasy about their support for differentiation. Their principle of differentiation is vulnerable to egalitarian claims, and they can neither combine two irreconcilable principles nor give one up in favor of the other. They tend to maintain their belief in economic differentiation, but hedge it about with qualifications and mention of mitigating circumstances. A good example of this ambivalence is Timothy Saunders's discussion of fair incomes. He is a gentle, thoughtful bank teller, who "starts with a feeling that there is too much discrepancy between what people make and what they do." But he continues: "For a lot of people, economic competition seems to enable them to accomplish what they want to accomplish. Sometimes in so doing, not only do they help themselves, but they do help others, perhaps in spite of themselves. So I'm not even thinking to myself that we should abolish the free enterprise system that we have, so long as we do a little better on welfare." Since the market transforms private vices into public virtues, we must accept the by-products of this alchemy with good grace and ameliorative measures. As Timothy implies, the uneasy differentiators are likely to be extremely sympathetic toward the poor and to distinguish sharply between "good" (that is, earned) wealth and "bad" (that is, unearned) wealth.

Finally, a few respondents cannot be said either to support or oppose economic differentiation, because they simply cannot imagine an economic system different from the one they know. Consider this exchange, which follows Vicky Pateman's description of the custodial ranks in the school where she is a dishwasher:

JH: Is it a good thing to keep the differences between these ranks of jobs, or would you rather see those differences become less important?

VP: I don't quite get what you mean there. In other words, to know the difference between heavy custodian and light?

JH: Yes, Should we keep those differences clear or not?

VP: Well, yes, because the pay is different.

JH: Why *should* the pay be different for different ranks?

VP: The difference is according to your title.

Finally, asked how she would decide incomes for everyone in her school if she were starting from scratch, Vicky says, "Well, I'd find out from my union book. It gives you the wages, and then you add up the hours they work." This is normative support only in the sense that absence of color is a color.

What are we to make of all this? At a minimum, we can give no simple description of the dog that doesn't bark. It is not being forcibly prevented from barking, and in some sense it is quiet by choice. But the substance of and emotions attached to that choice vary widely. Most people most of the time want productivity to be rewarded, but that desire can lead them to seek either upward or downward redistribution. Sometimes they want the nonproductive to be rewarded, and that desire too can lead them to seek either upward or downward redistribution. The emotions they bring to these wants range from enthusiasm to desperation to indifference.

We should not forget, amidst all of this complexity, that the poor do differ from the rich. It is one thing for a person to be contented with his lot because he resolutely ignores his two-digit savings account; it is another thing to be contented because he has everything he wants. It is one thing for a person to be bitter because she cannot pay her bills; it is another thing to be bitter because she cannot buy expensive birthday presents. It does not deny or denigrate the pain of the rich to argue that the pain of the poor is more serious. If that is the case, we can legitimately decide that the needs and desires of the poor deserve a greater response than those of the rich. But as before, that is only a judgment and must be kept distinct from the empirical conclusion that both rich and poor support differentiation in the economic domain.

6 The Political Domain and the Principle of Equality

When respondents consider political issues, they generally return to a principle of equality in making distributive judgments. They do not, however, shift from economic differentiation to political equality as abruptly as they had switched from equality in the socializing domain to economic differentiation. Instead, as the issue discussed changes from political influence over economic distributions to purely political distributions and rights, respondents move from somewhat differentiating to strongly egalitarian norms.

Just as in the other two domains, respondents vary in their choice of particular norms, their emotional responses to their own beliefs, and their ambivalence about their views.

Equality, Bitterness, and the Poor

Some poor respondents find no joy in their political beliefs because of both external constraints and internal conflicts. Externally, they believe that the government treats them unfairly compared to others, whether these be the rich, blacks, or some other group. Internally, they are distressed at their inability to reconcile their differentiating economic beliefs with their egalitarian political beliefs. Thus, although external constraints were mainly responsible for distress among the poor in the socializing and economic domains, both external and internal contradictions lead to unhappiness in the political domain.

Once again, Maria Pulaski and Vincent Sartori best exemplify how distributive norms can induce frustration. Maria's political views range from differentiation through uncertainty to vehement egalitarianism; she is ultimately dismayed at her own unorthodox and apparently hopeless desire for change. She begins by claiming that the government should protect private property, but she also wants the government to limit the harm that property rights can inflict on the poor. Thus it would be "impossible" and "unfair" for tenants to take over a building owned by even a completely irresponsible landlord, but tenant strikes to "force" essential repairs should be legal. Neighborhoods may not expropriate price-gouging stores, but the government should "force storeowners to lower the prices." Even applying the right of eminent domain is "terrible" for people who "have had it [their property] for so many years," but a fair price and an important community need might dominate private rights. Maria here seeks, and generally finds, a careful balance between the differentiating right of property and the egalitarian claims of consumers and the community in general. Furthermore, she expects the government to find and maintain a similar balance.

Maria tips the balance toward equality when discussing taxation. She does not know how much tax she and her husband pay, but she knows it is too much, especially since her work provides her no benefits. More generally, she says that the poor pay too much in taxes because the rich pay too little. For one thing, the rich cheat; they "deduct every little thing" from their taxes, and when "they give 10 they'll say 20." She does not know how to deduct, and her husband refuses to, for fear of "getting into trouble." Second and more fundamentally, the whole tax structure should be changed. Those who earn less than $15,000 should pay nothing; people making $15,000 should not "pay too much"; people making $30,000-$40,000 "should pay a little more, if they're making more"; and "if they're making a *whole* lot, take more from them." With these changes, "Then the one that makes the less shouldn't [that is, wouldn't have to] pay as much. Why should they have to pay more? The rich would still have a lot of money."

With more tax revenue, the government could enact a long list of social welfare policies to "help the poor." It should eliminate college tuition, increase Social Security payments, guarantee job training and jobs with a livable income, and provide national health insurance. After all, "What happens when he [her husband] retires? Sure, you have the Medicare, but Medicare doesn't pay for everything. They have that [health insurance] in Europe, so why not here?" Maria would even pay higher taxes for these services "if they weren't too, too high. Sure, why not? To go into a hospital, you walk out and you have a bill of a couple of thousand dollars. So it's better to pay a little more taxes now and get that service."

Maria fears, however, that the government's commitment to help the needy is not as great as her own. Because the rich use their money to "control the government and benefit more," politicians give only lip service to solving problems like inflation, which "the middle class people, and the poor, we suffer by. But the rich, no problem"—so no solution. Even worse, the government deliberately exacerbates the "terrible" problem of rising food prices: "They store all that sugar and potatoes and then throw it in the ocean! I can't see this. We need all this here. I don't think they should push all the prices up like that." Similarly, the government does too much to bail out failing industries: "They wouldn't help the poor—why should they help the rich?"

This suspicion of malfeasance in high places leaves her feeling helpless, confused, and "really mad. When they make their speeches, they promise you everything. Then when the time comes, they back out. Well, they *should* be able to do something. Why shouldn't they? Can't they? Or could they? I think they should be able to do something, but what, I don't know." Citizen protest sounds like a good idea, but experience tells her that it is futile. City residents' recent protest of rising electricity rates "didn't work out. What can they do? Have their meetings and whatnot; they can't do anything. Prices are just going up, that's it, you have to pay."

Helping the poor differs, both politically and normatively, from taking resources away from the wealthy. Most Americans at least pay lip service to alleviating poverty, but fewer express the more egalitarian demand that this be done by reducing the holdings of the rich. We have seen that Maria wants more government aid to the poor and less aid to the rich. Sometimes, despite her support for private property, she goes a step further to support policies that help the poor at the expense of the rich. In my terminology, she moves from a norm of need to a norm of strict equality. She is cautious at these times: perhaps "I'm wrong, I'm saying too much I'm not supposed to be saying." But still, if she could allocate tax money, she would "share it with the people! Take it from the rich, give it to the poor. That's how I feel about it. I'm honest, right?"

Maria is, more than anything else, confused about the nature of political rights, power, and representation; but these subjects do provoke her anger at the government's unequal treatment of its citizens. For example, too many people who can hire "a good lawyer get away with a lot when they go to court. Whether they have money or not, they should get the same thing like we would get if we went to court."

And yet Maria retreats from equality when confronted with the question of equalizing holdings. She recognizes dimly that material, as distinguished from political, equality challenges her principle of marketplace differentiation; therefore she alternates between rejection and endorsement of redistribution, ending uncertainly with the latter. Let us examine those changes.

Maria consistently supports a guaranteed minimum income great enough to "live moderately, like everybody else, and don't have to worry about everything." But a maximum income is different. She first flatly rejects it, since "if you're a doctor, you deserve more. I'm only cleaning house." Later, she speculates as to how society would change if incomes were equal: "I don't know. I never really looked into that. Close to the same would be a good idea. No, I don't know. I don't really go for that. If you're working hard for something, and you're making a little more money, I believe in that. But maybe it *is* a good idea. Really. And then I wonder, 'Well, is it or isn't it?' " And so on. Still later, she decides that with more equality, "maybe things would be easy for all of us. If we all made good money, it would be great. But that'll never happen. If it does, it's a miracle." She concludes finally, "Good, fine, sure, I'd love it [an income of $12,000 for all]. And not have to worry about anything, just pay your bills? That would be great."

How can all of this be explained? On the one hand, Maria opposes current inequalities in the allocation of benefits and burdens by the federal government. It should respond more to the poor, less to the rich, and equally in the legal system. These egalitarian beliefs do not conflict directly with Maria's principle of economic differentiation; therefore she can assert them confidently. Here she is angry only because they are not carried out.

But responding to needs and ensuring political equality differ from equalizing incomes, and Maria either defiantly supports or, more often, resists taking this step. She does "not believe in this equal, all equal." But she also fears the implications of an attempt to think through this conflict between domains. In utopia, "We could all live normally and not have to worry about money or anything. And have a good life, you know, not have to struggle like this." But, as we saw in chapter two, for "things to get better," we would have to "change the government — no, I shouldn't say that!" She "should not" say such things, she should not even think them, because they are radically different from everything she has ever heard. And besides, "that'll never happen" unless there is a "miracle."

Maria is dismayed by her apparently unorthodox, hopeless impulse toward change. She has no idea how to implement it or even how to begin thinking about it. As soon as she tries, she confronts her norms of marketplace differentiation and her assumption of their inevitability. Finally she gives up, left with bitter and inchoate sentiments that she can neither integrate nor forget.

Vincent Sartori avoids Maria's constraints on "acceptable" thought, but he is even more constrained by pessimism and cynicism. He has little trouble in reconciling conflicting claims of right and need when he discusses the property rights of landlords, exploitative shopkeepers, and communities. But his views on taxation are more complicated and finally founder on his political cynicism. He bases his initial opposition to inheritance taxes on a norm of results: "If I'm working and I'm banking my money, I'm planning for *their* [his children's] future. So hey, if I turn around and pass away, they got every right in the world to get what I worked for." But wealth acquired illegally or immorally does not carry the same right of inheritance. Nevertheless, it still should be inheritable, because "if they lose it, who's gonna wind up with it? The government. Who the hell else is it gonna go to? That's why I say, it's all just one big piece of pie, and more than three-fourths of it is the government." By this point, his argument has shifted ground. All private inheritance is not equally just; it is merely preferable to the only alternative he can imagine — the black hole of government waste and corruption. In fact, if resources from estate taxes came back to the community in wages, housing, or schools, instead of going to the politicians, Vincent "would 100 percent agree with it [higher inheritance taxes]."

Vincent's views on income taxes are similarly tangled. He starts with a norm of need; taxes should ideally be strongly progressive because of the diminishing marginal utility of money: "Hey, $8-$9,000 — that's *marvelous* if I can make that. But if I gotta turn around and pay a good amount of tax . . . But *you're* making $70,000 a year, you live in luxury. So even if you're paying $2-$3,000 a year in taxes, it ain't gonna be no big loss. You got a beautiful home, your kids are well dressed, you got food in your refrigerator. It's not gonna hurt you to pay the difference on what we want to knock off of the lower class." But Vincent's argument gets sidetracked because he is angrier about absolute levels of taxation than about its relative inequities. Taxes are so high only because politicians simply pocket tax revenues. The government claims to be in debt, then collects taxes, "and then $40,000 into your savings account, $10,000 to the community, another $80,000 to your secret savings box. That's how it is today."

Vincent's mistrust is partly due to ignorance. He knows about taxes, but he is completely unaware of government services and expenses. Therefore he has no choice but to believe that tax money is "stashed aside" by corrupt politicians:

vs: Like the court system, parking meters, toll stations — you're bringing in a good bit of money at the end of a day. Where does that money go to?

jh: Maybe the toll money goes to maintain the roads, and the parking meter money goes to . . .

vs: Well then, where's the person's *taxes* go to? I gotta pay a quarter to go into West Haven. *And* I'm paying taxes out of my pay. Where's all *that* money go to? It's going somewhere. Maybe to Switzerland in one of those safety-deposit boxes.

If the government will not spend its revenues from inheritance and income taxes in the interests of the people, then it has no right to collect them. Thus Vincent prefers no taxation at all (a highly differentiating view) to progressive taxation (an egalitarian view) because of his total distrust of the federal government. It would be misleading to characterize him here as either egalitarian or differentiating. He is merely disgusted and confused.

Vincent wants to believe that a strong leader could restore government rectitude. After all, things have not always been this bad: "I don't have it word for word, [but] like Lincoln said, in those days 'The government was *for* the people,' and all that. The government today is just the government for the *government*." Politicians as recently as John Kennedy have been "damn good. He wasn't like some of these presidents you get now, sneaks and crooks. Don't forget, Kennedy wasn't accepting no pay. He was only getting a dollar. Most of it was going to charity." Vincent wonders if the Kennedy case is generalizable, if we should elect only millionaires to the presidency because they can afford to "take the job mostly to do things for the people." But, he reflects, most of the rich "don't really give a damn about the people," so a poor president who "knows what it's like to be poor" might be better. Yet "he might say, 'Well, hey, *I'm* getting this money. To hell with the poor people now.'" Ascriptive criteria for leaders produce only a stalemate.

With that path to a good leader blocked, Vincent falls back on individual personalities. He deeply mourned Robert Kennedy, a man "doing mostly what he could for the people." Chappaquidick "ruined" Ted Kennedy; an admired senator is in trouble over "campaign funds and everything"; even Spiro Agnew, whom he admired for "telling the press right to their face," is "a little sneak too." He trusted George Wallace because "he's not like these other guys—'Well, I'm gonna do *this* for you, I'm gonna do *that* for you.' And never do it." But he too is no longer a viable candidate—leaving Vincent with no hope for the government or for distributive justice.

More generally, Vincent is sure of what Maria suspects, namely, that the government is inextricably tied up with big business. "They just want to suck them [the voters] in and get elected, and then start making deals with these big companies." Government aid to large businesses such as Lockheed is a "crock of shit. Where's their money going? Spending too much on golf? Or buying too many real estate properties? You got hundreds of millions to give to companies, but yet you can't give a hundred million to a community to have everything remodeled and live the way you're supposed to live."

Despite his earlier support for economic differentiation, Vincent consistently endorses political action to equalize holdings. One "right of Americans" should be "an easier way of making a living. And that's up to the government." He has "never even thought about" redistributing income, but upon reflection, he decides that "*something* has to be changed. Well, they don't really need that much of an income anyhow, the big businesses." He is vague on specifics, but decides that, except for welfare chiselers, "It should be just equal. Where a working man gets a fairly decent pay, [so that] if he goes out and spends one hundred dollars on groceries, he's still got a few dollars more if he wants to take his kids out somewheres to a movie. I mean, why make millions while the other person's only making a couple of thousand?" He used to oppose communism because "they don't have the freedom like we do, living like a robot," but if a communist society permitted free speech, "Maybe it wouldn't be so bad. There's a lot of times you say in the bar, 'Hey, the way this country's going, whew! Maybe it should become communism.' "

In utopia, everyone would have "enough where you're making a buck, you got groceries and a bank book, I got a house, you got a house, big front lawn, clean." But class conflict and entrenched, cumulative inequalities will forever prevent the arrival of utopia: "A lot of low classes are jealous because of the upper ones. And the upper ones, they won't give a flying shit for you anyhow. They *got their* money."

Only one thing could reverse this dismal scene—grass roots political democracy with equal power for all. Vincent is thrilled that a person who he thinks is from the government is asking his opinions—"I could talk like this all day"—but he suggests an improvement: "It would be nice if we went down to the stadium and put up thousands of chairs and just sat there with the public and talked. It's difficult for you because you're going from house to house, and you get *this* person's vision of what it is and this one. But if everyone was together in one big group, and they hear this person coming up with something better than what they're saying, then their minds could get more formed, and they'd say, 'Hey, *this* is what we should start demanding,' and 'Let's start protesting *this*.' " United citizens could also have political clout. If the whole community went "forward to City Hall, the mayor's gonna start worrying, and he's gonna be making a call to the governor. Then it's not only the city, you got the whole *state*. And then it starts going up the government, and *that's* when the [federal] government will start saying, 'Well, hey, we gotta start doing something, because the people are starting to get *wise*.' " In this fashion, political malfeasance and inequity could "easily, *easily*, be ended."

Why does Vincent not act on his convictions? He does not really know. He ignores neighborhood association meetings because so few people attend: "If you get a full house, I'll come. But there's no sense going if you get twenty people. What good is that gonna do?" His only explanation for such low attendance is that "when it comes down to the real nitty-gritty, they're afraid of something." Asked what, he shrugs helplessly, "Afraid of themselves, I guess. I don't know." But Vincent does not absolve himself of responsibility; in one of his tirades about the government, he stops midsentence and comments, "Actually, it's the people [who are at fault]. 'Cause *we're* the ones that put the guy in office."

Vincent is stymied. He is certain of only one thing, namely, that some people are so wrongly and wretchedly poor that "they'd be better off dead." But since he cannot pinpoint the blame for this tragedy, he cannot decide how to solve it. Sometimes he insists on personal responsibility: "Whatever I get in life, that's where I put myself, whether I'm the lower class, middle, upper, or what." In that context, he supports economic differentiation and wishes simply for more wealth. Sometimes he blames exploitative businessmen and corrupt politicians. In that context, he supports redistribution to end victimization of the poor. But governmental activity is part of the problem, not a solution; therefore he cannot turn to the government for redress. Thus he returns to a reliance on individuals and seeks full political equality and direct democracy. But he will not make the almost superhuman commitment needed for this transformation, nor will anyone else that he knows. He goes full circle, from personal responsibility to a realization of victimization and back to personal responsibility, but he finds no solution to his poverty and normative dilemma. He is bitter and frustrated; his only outlets are brawling in bars, throwing knives at foremen, planning a bank robbery, and making pathetic resolutions about his children's future. With little hope for either a better life in this society or a better society, he concludes on the written questionnaire, "Everything in stis [sic] country is falling apart."

Equality, Contentment, and the Poor

Some of the poor find their political egalitarianism not a burden but a source of gratification. They are neither torn by internal contradictions as is Maria nor embittered by corruption and injustice as is Vincent. Instead, they find ingenious ways to cover up or get around the contradictions between their differentiating economic beliefs and egalitarian political beliefs. Furthermore, rather than being disheartened by persistent inequalities, they are pleased with the extent of equality, encouraged about improvements from some point in the past, or hopeful about some point in the future. The contented poor seek the same goals as the embittered poor; the difference between them lies in the fact that some see the glass as half-empty and others as half-full.

Pamela McLean best exemplifies gratified egalitarianism that does not depend on naive optimism. In fact, the reverse is the case: her cheerful confidence permits her to recognize a wide variety of injustices and to incorporate a range of views into complex and nuanced arguments. For example, like most other respondents, she holds the differentiating view that the government should protect private property, but she can imagine some circumstances in which the "general needs of the country" should take precedence over property rights. If her house were robbed, "Who's going to pay for this damage? He's in jail, and he's going to pay society, but I'm still without my stereo, TV, I've got to have my floors and roof repaired. So the government should seize the belongings of the offender, sell them, and give the money to the offended, to help cover that." Thus property should sometimes be used to benefit those who deserve or need it most, rather than automatically remaining with its current possessor.

Pamela finds inheritance taxes "hogwash" and taxes on savings accounts "ridiculous," but she is egalitarian with regard to all other taxes. She justifies a progressive income tax through a desire to equalize sacrifice: "The poor certainly can't share what they don't have, and the next class needs to hang on to it to stay in their class, and the class above that is just barely getting started. So as you go up the scale, then there are the people who can afford to give a little bit back. The higher you go, the more they could give back." She agrees with Maria that not only is the tax structure insufficiently progressive, but also that the rich evade even their current tax burden. Rich people who "brag that they've found all these loopholes so that they have to pay nothing are pretty crummy Americans and are screwing the country. And when it comes down to it, it's *me* that they're really taking to the cleaners, 'cause *I'm* paying for *him*."

Despite these offenses to norms of need and strict equality, Pamela is "grudgingly willing" to pay taxes because "the money's got to come from somewhere. The programs they provide we can't do without." These programs are many and varied: "I get to live in the United States, I get an operating government, building of roads and parks, and bureaus and departments and red tape (laugh). I do provide a lot of jobs which are needed. I also get prisons and police, the FBI (laugh). Boy, I get a lot for $3000, don't I! Maybe I should sign up to pay more! No, I really do get a lot." Since she is aware of so many services, Pamela avoids Vincent's inevitable conclusion, given his premises, that tax revenues disappear into politicians' pockets.

Pamela agrees with Vincent and Maria that the government provides too many services to one group — the rich. Her explanation of political venality is, however, more sophisticated and sympathetic than theirs: "Why it happens is that it's probably going to cost the job of the politician who finally takes a stand against the rich. He will have to go to Lower Slobovia to live because they're going to sure as hell run him out of here. So nobody really wants to stir up that whole mess." She insists, however, that the Watergate scandal and increased voter sophistication spell the doom of politicians who are allied to wealthy interests: "You used to get elected through who you were or what kind of influence you had behind you. But the people have stood up and said, 'We're tired of voting for someone named Rockefeller 'cause his name is Rockefeller. We want to know what he's going to do. You have to offer us something.' [So] we see a different breed of politician now, one who does really want to listen." Pamela mocks politicians who "scurry to become pure in a big hurry," but she clearly approves of the shift from ascriptive to results criteria — and thus to a slightly more egalitarian way of choosing officeholders.

Pamela is more aware than most other poor respondents of the American creed that "all men have the same basic rights. God didn't love one person more than another just 'cause he made one Hungarian and one Polish." She is pleased, if a bit caustic, about the fact that the United States appears finally to be taking this form of equality seriously: "People are falling all over their feet to make sure they don't offend, in any way, a minority group. So that now we are all pretty much equal. I don't think the people stand for *not* being treated equal anymore. People have decided that 'If we don't like it, we can change it. All we've got to do is start yelling.' "

This new insistence on rights has two effects, in Pamela's eyes, one negative and one positive. On the one hand, ever-expanding rights run counter to other rights, leading to intractable conflicts. Through affirmative action policies, we "may be discriminating against the white person and actually stepping on their rights, to give the rights to someone else." More personally, the "right to advertise an abortion clinic on a big billboard [violates] my right to go for a ride and not have my children practicing their reading on abortion billboards and then having me explain what abortion is! Why should I be forced to explain this to my nine-year-old, who is not ready at all to grasp this?" She has no solution to these dilemmas, other than to "just let some of my feelings be known" and to wish "everybody's rights and mine agreed."

On the other hand, the new citizen militancy offsets the stranglehold of the rich on politics. Increasingly, politicians "are afraid to even let their name be associated with big business." Citizens now need only to "let their voices be known. The dumbest thing we can ever do is vote for all these guys, send them off, and never tell them again what we think." Rights are now equally distributed, but they carry corresponding obligations; we cannot criticize inequality of power if we do not accept equality of responsibility.

Because Pamela sees the government as benevolent and competent, and getting more so, she is enthusiastic about social welfare programs, within limits. Her guiding rule is: "I want people to be able to reach it [success], and everybody should be helping everybody get there, as many as can. But I don't think you should guarantee anything for anybody." Of course, Pamela blurs this distinction between opportunity and results as much as everyone else, but generally she uses it to seek extensive, but not exhaustive, redistribution in kind.

For example, Pamela wants federal aid to education and national health insurance, but she also wants to retain private schools and hospitals in order to give incentives to work one's way out of the public facilities. She wants guaranteed jobs, but not "makework," which is wasteful and degrading: "I don't think anybody should expect, just because you're a welfare recipient, for you to go out and collect garbage." But welfare without work wastes taxpayers' money and is just as degrading; most welfare recipients "are resentful of the fact that they don't work."

Up to this point, Pamela has balanced her norms of results and need, but the question of a guaranteed annual income upsets this balance. On the one hand, guarantees breed an attitude of " 'You *owe* it to me, give it to me now.' It's too easy. *Somebody* has to earn it to give it to these people, and why not they themselves?" But on the other hand, for "people that are *really, really* hurting, we have to go to them and find out, 'Why didn't you use the opportunity we gave you? What is the problem, and how can we help you?' Something else needs to be done for that group," and perhaps a guaranteed income is ultimately necessary.

Pamela's ambivalence about providing incomes for the deeply poor foreshadows her uncertainty about equalizing incomes. She initially rejects it, for three reasons. First, equality is not attainable because "a lot of people" would object. The rich would have "no one to look down on and say, 'Well, I'm a lot better-off than so-and-so.' " The poor would have "no one to look *up* to, 'Well, I'd like to get to where she is.' " The middle class would complain that " 'We could all buy the same things, and then where would "average" go?' If everybody was at the same place, then my same place would maybe be at the bottom of the ladder now, because everyone below me had been raised to me."

Second, if somehow we overcame these objections and attained equality, it would not last. "It would be nice if we did" have equal holdings, but "the American way of life wouldn't allow it to be that way [for long], unfortunately. Some guy with a smart brain is going to come along and ruin the whole thing because he's got a better mousetrap, and away we're all going to go again."

Third, if somehow we overcame both of these practical obstacles, we would face a moral problem. Equality would drain away ambition — "We'd just kind of percolate" — and destroy our moral fiber. Asked about the argument that people could stop worrying about money and focus on other things, she answers: "Yeah, right. But what would they think about? That's what scares me. If they thought only helping-each-other things, that'd be fine. But I can only see that this utter contentment just breeds a lethargic condition that prevents our minds from going on to reach these unknown goals. You've got to have some kind of incentive, and for most people, the incentive is money. Unfortunately."

Strong objections to redistribution — but at second glance, somewhat shaky ones. Pamela is sorry that equality seems unattainable, and she sees none of her objections as relevant to herself or her family and friends. She does not covet wealth; she refuses to make social comparisons; she does not rely on relative gratification for self-esteem or on relative deprivation for motivation; she would not sink into lethargy and corruption with financial security. What is more, she knows that her rules of human nature do not fit her own case; discussing ambition, she interjects, "I don't suppose *I* had that ambition, though, and I'm surviving without it." She also does not believe that her friends are any more materially motivated than she is. At one point, she muses, "If we were all the same, equal, all the same, . . . hmm. It might be fun." But her fears about all the people whom she does not know make her conclude that the certain risks of equality outweigh its possible benefits.

Pamela tries to resolve this disjunction between her norms of differentiation and equality through a curious definitional sleight of hand. She rejects "equality," but proposes that incomes should vary by no more than $10,000. Minimum wage and tax legislation should narrow "this terrible $15,000 to $40,000 break" between worker and employer. Pamela is unaware that this is an extremely egalitarian proposal; she sees it as a compromise between total equality and great differentiation.

In fact, Pamela's utopia may be an egalitarian's ideal community. Its members are independent but cooperative, solicitous of the needy but respectful of others' autonomy, productive but noncompetitive, equal but not identical. The perfect society is "everybody living in accord, going about their own business and having separate interests, but that hopefully these interests all mesh nicely, they aren't bumping into each other and conflicting. We're all living very peacefully in this society where everybody has enough to eat, everybody is doing their own thing."

Pamela is not a "Mrs. Goody-two-shoes"; she worries about apathetic citizens, immoral politicians, money-grubbing children, the desperate poor, the heedless rich, and her own precarious finances. But she is gratified by answering the needs of her children, satisfied with the justice of (most) economic differences, and hopeful about increasing the political equality of all citizens. Only on the questions of poverty and redistribution do her subtle realism and sense of humor fail her. She is deeply distressed by poverty and would like more egalitarian policies, but she will not reject economic differentiation. As a result, although she knows her own foolishness, she concludes wistfully that "it *would* be nice if everybody was a little bit above average."

Equality, Indifference, and the Poor

A final emotional response by the poor to their own political egalitarianism is indifference, a refusal to feel either gratified or frustrated. These people would prefer more political equality, but they will not go out on a limb with great hopes. Therefore they express egalitarian preferences, but expect never to see them realized, and insist that it does not really matter anyway. They generally deal with the disjunctions between their economic and political beliefs by ignoring them altogether.

Phillip Santaguida is such a resigned egalitarian. He holds strong beliefs about political justice, but he refuses to become emotionally involved in those beliefs.

Phillip first takes the differentiating stance that property rights are sacrosanct. Even the claim of eminent domain, which most respondents grudgingly accept, is "wrong. He bought that property, it's *his* property. I don't care if they want to put a hospital there. Go pick some other spot. Start a new town. Don't take my land." Besides, the government does not play fair: federal officials "want to take my land, but they don't want another country to come and take *their* land." Inheritance taxes should be low; his father "worked pretty hard for that money. It doesn't belong to nobody but me." Unearned millions have the same status as hard-earned thousands; like most other respondents, Phillip simply extrapolates from his own situation and denies that dramatic changes in scale should affect his judgments. After all, "It's the beauty of being part of the U.S. — what's yours is yours. The government just don't come over and take it. That's why we got America."

Like Vincent, however, Phillip would retract this hard-line differentiation if the government would "share" its acquisitions with the people. His argument has several steps. First, private property is simply a loan from the government, which receives its interest in taxes. Second, "The people *are* the government. So we pay [taxes] into the government just like I paid it to my mother and father." Property and taxes are simply loans of a common good from one group of citizens to another, just as money and possessions in a family are used exclusively by some, but really belong to all. The real problem, then, is not that the government claims a share of goods through taxes, but that it does not trade fairly: "My Uncle Sam doesn't give me very much return for the amount of taxes we pay to him. They got enough smart guys up there [who] know how to share it between themselves. If they would share it a little bit more to the people, they would get it back eventually anyways." Phillip's argument resembles Vincent's, without the bitterness and with a dose of political theory. Phillip is egalitarian here in two ways — in his claim that private property is merely a loan from the common stock and in his desire that the benefits of tax revenues be distributed more broadly.

Despite the government's malfeasance, Phillip seeks higher taxes on the rich, who bribe politicians to evade taxation and thereby "steal from *me.*" Unlike most other poor respondents, however, he prefers proportional to progressive taxation, for several reasons. First, it would reward and stimulate productivity: "Why should I pay 30 percent, and some [that is, the poor] pay 10 if they don't want to hustle and earn money? [As things are now], I wouldn't try for a raise, because the government's going to put me in a different category and take more out of my pay." Second, a clear, simple proportional tax would decrease the likelihood that the rich could evade their share; since they now "pay practically nothing, it would be good if they *did* pay 30 percent like I am." Thus Phillip here combines a differentiating norm of results between workers and the lazy poor with strict equality between workers and the dishonest rich. He concludes, triumphantly, that with an enforced proportional tax rate of 30 percent, "think of the money that the government would take in!"

Phillip has so many suggestions for spending these new revenues that "years ago, when anybody talked like this, they were [called] 'communist.' " First of all, "Today in America, there shouldn't be *any* poor people." Even food stamps are inadequate; "People gotta have money to buy the stamps. Those real poor people, they can't even buy stamps." He blames the insufficiency of antipoverty programs on politicians' callousness: "They can talk about it, write about it, but they don't have the experience of being hungry. Talk is awful cheap if a man's got money. Politicians got plenty of money."

Second, social programs should benefit all citizens, not just aid the neediest. "They don't have enough schools, prisons, playgrounds, housing projects, the government. Haven't got enough trade schools," convalescent homes, or public transportation. Phillip does not simply seek a cornucopia of gifts; he argues that many of these projects will provide jobs, more tax money, and substitutes for less desirable forms of aid: "There's about ten openings and eighty teachers looking for that. That means there's no work. That's the government's fault. Why don't they build more schools? [Then] the classrooms wouldn't be crowded, the kids would get a better education, they'd have people building the schools, maintaining the schools, the teachers — all making money [instead of collecting unemployment]." Since social programs would benefit both the people and the treasury, Phillip can explain their absence only through politicians' laziness: "If you've got a nice job, getting all this big, big money, you're going to worry about school teachers?"

Phillip makes one stipulation, however: the government must provide loans but not handouts, guaranteed jobs but not a guaranteed income. His arguments resemble Pamela's: handouts are humiliating and morally dangerous to recipients;[1] jobs provide pride and skills to their holders;

taxpayers deserve some return for their money; and inflation is an inevitable concomitant of pay without productivity. He would even pay higher taxes for a jobs program, since "if they give you a return for your tax, people don't mind paying the tax."

Phillip is as cynical about politicians as Vincent is, although he views them with resignation rather than outrage. He tells long stories of political chicanery, whose moral is always "as many dollars they get, that's people they're obligated to." Because politicians and businessmen need each other, they form an unholy alliance in which the former "can pass the bill, and he [the latter] gets a feather in his hat." But unlike Vincent, Phillip does not blame individuals or seek a leader to change the system. "It couldn't run differently. You take one out and you put another one in — he's in the machine. They're going to run you. You can't break it down. You'll be out of a job fast." Also unlike Vincent, Phillip is not outraged at dishonesty per se; he is only annoyed that when a politician "takes a trip, I pay through the nose."

Given his cynicism, Phillip is surprisingly sanguine about purely political rights. He insists that only one-third of the politicians are dishonest and that Watergate proved that "the people were stronger than they [politicians] were. Justice came in the end." After all, by definition, the government "can't be too powerful because the government is the people." But his pessimism does not disappear for long. We have "justice [only] for the rich, not for everybody. There's supposed to be justice for all, [but] a lot of the laws were made for certain people. If you're lucky enough to have a lot of money, laws can be broken very easily *within* the law." Furthermore, discrimination persists — in his youth against Italians, later against blacks, now perhaps against whites. Such privileges for the rich and penalties for ascriptive groups offend him because they deny our innate equality — again, a surprisingly idealistic stand: "I met all kinds of people. They may be richer than me, have a better position. They're not better than me. They're all human. I don't consider you better than me because you had an education. You might be a big professor, but if you get stuck with a flat tire and you don't know how to fix it — how could you be better than me? Now I could go out and fix that flat tire — I'm smarter than you now." After all, "We are all born equal; the Lord gave us two hands, two feet, and a brain if you will use it."

At this point, Phillip reaches an impasse. A democracy is supposed to treat all citizens equally, but economic differences interfere with equality. And yet the government cannot, perhaps should not, interfere with the dog-eat-dog marketplace. Phillip's discussion of redistribution, therefore, is an attempt to resolve this dilemma.

Phillip gives three reasons for opposing equalization. First, guaranteed equal incomes would destroy the free enterprise system, which "keeps the U.S. going. Nobody would want any dangerous job. Nobody would want to work on Sunday. Who's gonna mow the lawn for the rich?" Second, and more profoundly, human nature includes an immutable urge to dominate; if the government tried to enforce equality, this urge could no longer be channeled into the relatively safe stream of capitalism. Instead, people would, as we saw in chapter two, by necessity become "cannibals, stealing from each other and killing each other. Money is the root of all evil. You just don't wave your wand and change things. It'll always be that way." Phillip convincingly argues that he would not participate in this rat race, and he has resisted all temptations to "step on other people's heads" — but everyone else would. Third, an inegalitarian class structure is part of "human nature. There has to be all classes of people. Doesn't sound right, but that's the way it's gotta be." This ascriptive norm is logically incompatible with the Hobbesian war just described, and both partly contradict the norm of results described first, but that matters little. What does matter is that Phillip combines three norms into a powerful picture of economic and social differentiation, with which his egalitarian political beliefs cannot compete. Thus he concludes, "It's just a mere dream, everybody have the same thing, just a foolish dream."

Yet Phillip hates greedy storekeepers, rich tax evaders, exploitative landlords and lawyers, and he is deeply pained by victims of poverty and discrimination and by a supposed democracy that ignores them. High incomes are not all that desirable anyway: "Anybody could live with $50,000 very comfortable. Anybody that makes more money than they'll ever be able to spend don't deserve that kind of money. They don't need it. They're only taking most of it from the average working man."

Thus like Pamela, Phillip turns to sleight-of-hand resolutions for an unresolvable dilemma. The government should let a businessman "make all he wants, but *tax* him. He can keep making millions — let him pay tax on it." For doctors, the government should limit "not what they could *earn*, but what they should *charge*. Let the man earn, but not charge the working man." Finally, the government should freeze prices, but not wages — thus curtailing profits and permitting the poor and middle class to get ahead.

Phillip's logic is faulty, but his impulse is clear. Somehow the government should see to it that none suffer because others gain, that not only are all people created equal, but also that they remain equal — and it should do these things without violating human nature, free enterprise, and natural forces. He searches for ways to achieve essentially incompatible goals — and not surprisingly meets with little success.

But Phillip generally responds to his normative dilemma by ignoring it. That the values of family and polity do not hold in the economy is too bad, but inevitable and immutable. Therefore Phillip seeks happiness at home, detaches himself from injustice and misery, and refuses seriously to consider alternatives. Redistribution is impossible and undesirable – or rather, undesirable *because* impossible. His psychological self-protection extends to a refusal even to speculate about his own or the nation's ideal future: "I just hope for the future. That's the only way I could put it. You live on hope."

Equality, Discontent, and the Wealthy

If normative judgments directly reflected self-interest, narrowly defined as preferring more goods to fewer, then the poor would be consistently more egalitarian than the rich in the economic and political domains. We have seen, however, that the poor do not, in fact, seek economic equality; their principle of economic differentiation keeps them from pursuing downward redistribution. Tensions in their normative judgments center around the question of whether their self-interest and political values will dominate their economic values.

If the norms of the poor do not always follow narrow self-interest, then we might expect the rich also to ignore self-interest on occasion. That is indeed the case: the rich support more political equality than their material self-interest would dictate. Tensions within their normative judgments center around the question of whether their self-interest and economic values will dominate their political values. Some of the rich are adept at reconciling or suppressing these tensions; others are not.

Barbara Azlinsky and Ernest Berkowitz represent those who have difficulty reconciling their norms with one another and with the real world. We have seen how Ernest is distressed by normative conflicts in the socializing domain and how Barbara is angered by conflicts between her economic beliefs and actual economic practices. We see now that both are unhappy about discrepancies between political beliefs and practices, and between economic and political beliefs.

Barbara generally "believes in private enterprise, private property, private different things." For example, slum landlords are not exploiters, but "basically good human beings trying to keep their homes in good condition" in the face of people who "don't have thought for other people's property." But community rights can dominate private rights in special cases. Telephone and utility companies "should be state-owned, because there's no competition"; in the absence of a free market, the dangers of private exploitation are so great that public control is preferable. Hardly a strong communitarian sentiment, but Barbara is at least willing to consider circumstances in which community needs might supersede private rights.

Barbara uses the same set of arguments to evaluate taxes. In general, property rights should not be violated; therefore the salaried middle class "shouldn't be taxed so heavily." But private rights should not be permitted to become exploitative: "It's a crime that the government doesn't do anything about those loopholes," which help the rich and hurt everyone else. A neighboring politician has a home "triple this in value" because he evades taxes that she pays, and "it gets me mad." Unlike Vincent, she does not think the solution to tax inequities is a drastic reduction in the tax level; after all, without taxes "how would the government survive? Someone's got to support it. It just had to grow." Thus Barbara resembles many of the poor; the burden of proof lies on those who would curtail property rights, with the exception of taxation. Taxes are problematic not because they confiscate private holdings, but because the confiscation is not sufficiently egalitarian.

Although Barbara scorns the many social programs that "don't work," she supports guaranteed jobs and extensive job training, and thinks that "poverty should come first" on the policy agenda. Social Security should redistribute downward: "I resent the elderly that are millionaires that are getting a Social Security check, like someone who doesn't have any [money in the bank]." Tuition subsidies would "help the intellectual person," who "in turn [would] help others. You're part of society — everybody has to do something to help society." Loans to medical students who later practice in rural areas "are *terrific*. Doctors learn something, some of the pain makes them humble." Because the expenses of a severe illness can "bleed a young couple that really should have a lot of living to do," we need national health insurance. Barbara stops short, however, of a demand for universal free medical care: "As far as free medical, it's *ideal*, but I wouldn't say it's a *right*. You talk about socialistic, you have to realize: What does that entail? Who's gonna pay? Someone has to pay. The doctors will not give a free clinic. It's give and take, and you have to theorize on how things are going to be decided, which I'm not good at."

As this quotation suggests, Barbara cannot reach a conclusion about other social policies. We saw her ambivalence about food stamps in chapter two. Similarly, she first rejects a guaranteed annual income because "it is not good" for people to "get something for nothing and just expect to get more and more." Yet, she muses, "a certain necessity *does* apply. Well, maybe I *would* support a minimum income. It would be nice." But finally, "sometimes I wonder if it would be fair" to those who have succeeded on their own. She can deny neither the claims of the needy nor her norms of investments and results. Her ambivalence leaves her — and sometimes the interviewer — confused and immobilized. She concludes only, "The theory is fine. A lot of theories are fine, but if I'm on the other side of the fence, I don't like it."

On purely political goods, Barbara has no ambivalence. She believes that the government should, and usually does, promote equality of all citizens; here, for perhaps the only time, using a principle of equality brings her contentment. The government effectively "curbs big business, like [that is, with] the monopoly laws, which is good," and it is "getting more aware of" the need to close off tax loopholes. "Underdogs," who "are not organized, they're too ill or too poor to get to Washington," may "need someone who can get to Washington and lobby" for them. But even for them, the congressional system may already have a solution at hand. "The representatives of the town know what's going on in their own district. If there's poverty, or starvation, or unemployment, they should know. Otherwise they shouldn't be the representative." The courts generally treat equally all who pass through them, although "down south in Mississippi, it doesn't seem as though they're fair to blacks." Finally, she proudly recites the rights of all Americans, which together ensure "the dignity of being free to do what you want to do." Thus most citizens now enjoy equal power, representation, legal justice, and freedom, and the government has systematic ways to redress the balance for those with too much or too little.

Barbara's political egalitarianism does not extend as far as redistributing holdings, for several reasons, some already mentioned: "it's not good" for people "to get something for nothing," and equal incomes would "homogenize the country." There is also the problem of incentives; middle-class Swedes "have lost their drive to do more because of the taxes," and "the majority" would here too. Finally, she has a purely normative objection: "I don't think everyone's born equal, so I can't see that philosophy [of redistribution]."

But again Barbara is uncertain. She knows that the incentive question is not simple; even with equal incomes, "a few will strive more, beyond what the government goal is, for self-acknowledgment or the reward of the country." And she observed other things on her trip to Sweden besides the middle-class loss of incentives: "Life seems very happy in Scandinavian nations, and everyone has enough. They have their little boat or summer weekend cottage. Their medical bills are taken care of, their education. It's interesting."

This double message about redistribution has two bases. First, Barbara no longer believes, as she once did, that effort and virtue lead to achievements and rewards. As a result, she cannot decide whether the nation should abandon the goal of proportional justice or strive even harder to reach it. If the former, then we should redistribute in order to eliminate insecurity for the middle classes and insufficiency for the poor. If the latter, then we must insist that everyone work and struggle as Barbara has had to do.

Second, Barbara sharply separates the ideal from the real world. A Scandinavian welfare state is only an impossible dream in a large nation. "Idealistically," a member of Congress should represent both his constituency and the public interest; realistically, "he can't do both." "The *philosophy* of democracy is a very good thing," but often the "good-looking" candidate wins, and anyhow, "Something can be done faster by a small group [rather than] the mass." Thus a "socialistic system is just like the Congress. In theory it sounds good, but it doesn't exist realistically."

Barbara realizes that this discrepancy between real and ideal confounds her distributive judgments: "See, my theories seem to clash with a lot of thoughts. Idealistic is one thing, being realistic is another. And I can't find any solutions." She cannot tell, and neither can the interviewer, whether her ambivalence stems from a deep normative conflict or a masking of self-interest with liberal clichés. She knows that her hesitance about equality results partly from the implications of redistribution for her own position: "The thing is, you put yourself in the situation. If you are a welfare recipient, of course you want taxis, you want things. But I'm paying for my own food and my own taxi, and I resent it." If "you place yourself in this [her own] position," you oppose redistribution, but "okay, place yourself on the other side of the fence, and you say yes." She will not oppose her economic self-interest. But she also describes utopia as giving people "the freedom and the happiness of doing what they want to do and not worrying about the bills." Probably she herself does not know what she "really" believes in; rather, she holds a variety of beliefs as strong as they are contradictory.

Barbara's bitterness, unlike that of the poor respondents, stems more from psychological than material roots. She cannot reject her "humanitarian" upbringing, with its concern for the poor and for the long-suffering middle class, but she cannot bring herself to endorse policies that would destroy her hard-won superiority. She is surrounded by evidence that people — whether family, neighbors, bosses, employees, the poor, or the rich — are exploitative and self-serving, not just and honorable. The ideal world would have more equality, but the real world should not even try to promote it. Barbara is too honest, or too well socialized, to dismiss her humanitarianism, but she is too insecure and bitter to embrace it fully. She alternates between "realism" and "idealism" and remains the most confused and unstable of all the respondents.

Like Barbara Azlinsky, Ernest Berkowitz holds egalitarian ideals but accepts, even supports, great differences in the actual world. But unlike her, he avoids bitter disorientation and preserves a somewhat defensive emotional distance from his own beliefs.

Ernest upholds property rights as "part and parcel of having your own choice about anything or everything you want to do." But because he sees private property as a means to freedom, not an end in itself, he will consider more egalitarian routes to the same goal. Practicality, not morality, should determine the extent of property rights. For example, nationalizing the oil companies is a plausible means of "seeing to it that prices don't get out of sight." He regrets that President Nixon's program of wage-price controls was abandoned just when "the people were getting adjusted to it. It wasn't a great hardship. Nothing was accomplished — could have been." Rent control and tenant strikes are fair means to equalize power between renters and landlords — and this from a landlord. In deciding where a new highway should be built, "If you have a choice of knocking off twelve houses in the way or knocking off eighty-two homes, you should knock off the twelve." Ernest is, in sum, less protective of differentiating property rights than many of the poor, and his egalitarianism sometimes dominates his economic self-interest.

Ernest has similar views on taxes. He only mildly opposes even "confiscatory" inheritance taxes: "That's a very complicated legal structure. I wouldn't know how to approach that. If the thing was built up, I don't see where it should *all* be taken away." A greater concern is that "very briefly, I don't think the rich are taxed enough." Although his definition of "the rich" differs from that of poor respondents, his objections to the tax structure and actual tax incidence are identical to theirs. First, the rich cheat: An IRS (Internal Revenue Service) audit of his taxes might yield $350, but with an audit of a "multimillionaire, they could get half a million out of them." Second, even if the laws are enforced, the millionaire pays no more than the small businessman: "*That's* the inequity made possible through tax laws that were made up by the people who had the money to begin with." Ernest's argument for progressive taxes is a textbook-clear example of a norm of need based on an assumption of diminishing marginal utility of income: "Suppose the guy down the bottom of the ladder had $50 more a year. It's a small amount of money, but it's *important* to the guy with the extra 50 bucks. So the guy up at the top, he wouldn't do without anything. What's he gonna do — fire one of his fourteen maids or something?"

But Ernest knows that his protests will have little effect: "This is a rich country [that is, country for the rich], and it's not going to change, because you can't change those laws. The poor people aren't strong enough to change laws. [The rich evader] doesn't get grabbed, because those tax laws are protecting him. He's using that [set of laws] to get, to keep his funds. And that's the biggest problem that you've got in this country, which I don't think can be changed." Ernest is struggling here to express and protest a deeply circular inequality. The rich set up a tax structure to benefit and protect themselves; they then use the money thus generated to gain enough political power to pass laws giving them more benefits and greater protection. Ideally, this system should be abolished; practically, it appears impregnable.

The egalitarianism of this view is striking when one realizes that Ernest has no complaint on his own behalf. Middle-class protest about a tax squeeze is "overdone." If "the middle income is benefiting from what's in the middle [such as "better schools or recreation areas for the kids"], then they have to take care of it." He is "only paying my share of taxes"; thus his support for progressive taxes is not a disguised claim that he, as one of the "poor," is overtaxed. Instead, it is a normative claim that the government should respond to economic needs.

Ernest endorses a variety of new social programs. Some, such as jobs for the handicapped or aid for workers in an emergency, are desirable because they would relieve employers of pressure. Other proposals are not motivated by self-interest. Schools with ghetto students need more federal aid, and we need nationalized health care "because the setup of this country for taking care of older people is not in good shape." Ernest would curtail programs for the bankrupt rich; helping Lockheed or New York City is simply "bailing out a situation that developed because of incompetency. It's the old story of getting your house in order before you fix them up." Those with resources should be judged by a norm of results; those without should be helped through a norm of need.

Ernest does eventually set limits on his desires for redistribution. First, the government should not directly redistribute wealth: "I'm in effect almost saying, 'Take from the rich and give to the poor,' but not quite. You're not supposed to *give*, that's what I'm trying to say. [But] tax the rich in such a way that the poor get helped by it." Second, after the government guarantees jobs, if anyone refuses to work, "then don't pay 'em," and let their children go hungry "if necessary." Such harshness might be "beneficial to all of us [because] you wouldn't have all these people lining up that I'm paying for, without producing." Ernest grudgingly concedes that he would not let children starve, but if their parents were sufficiently lazy, he would come close.

Finally, he responds to the idea of setting an upper limit on incomes with "No such thing! Socialism, communism is the first reaction I get. Depriving the democratic way." He first uses a norm of results to explain his opposition: "You really defeat the American approach, if somebody wakes up someday with an idea, and it makes him into being worth ten million dollars, for you to tell him that no matter how well that idea works, he is only going to be able to be worth one million with it. It doesn't make sense to me." He follows that normative claim with an empirical one: "The minute you set limitations on things, in the next minute somebody's figuring out how to get around it. That's the way the country is made." But Ernest immediately denies the absolute truth of these claims; some people invent for "the idea of the thing," not the money, and not everyone would try to evade the income limits. After all, "I'm not a striver. I'm an acceptor."

A surprising number of respondents claim that other people would not permit equality to work, even though they themselves might welcome it. The irony of this view, of course, is that if everyone assumes others to be avaricious, the (perhaps false) assumption becomes a self-fulfilling prophecy, since everyone then endorses social institutions that induce avarice. Ernest himself resists a guaranteed income for exactly this reason. Even setting aside concerns of productivity and laziness, a guaranteed income is unworkable because "the big hue and cry of the country [is] about why the blacks haven't picked themselves up from the ground and really gotten somewhere. People are saying, 'If you give them money, the *less* they're going to want to work.' " He does not know "if it's true, but a lot of people *think* that it is. So if you turn around and give everybody a certain minimum, you're going to *increase* this kind of talk." In other words, whites' belief that blacks will not work if guaranteed an income is reason not to give them that income because it would reinforce (probably wrong) racist assumptions. In quick succession then, Ernest rejects income equality, gives two reasons why, rejects his reasons, then insists that another equally mistaken reason makes income guarantees impossible.

He muddies the water further by distinguishing an unattainable egalitarian ideal world from a necessarily differentiated real world. Like Barbara's distinction, his has two interpretations, neither of which we can accept definitively. The split between ideal equality and real differentiation may conveniently assuage one's conscience during the pursuit of one's self-interest. Or it may permit an uneasy truce with an inevitably unjust society. One who holds the latter view might even be willing to give up material advantages if he or she thought equality could be realized. The interviews suggest that the first interpretation best explains Barbara's ambivalence, and the second explains Ernest's. Let us examine the evidence in his case.

Ernest has "always considered myself a liberal person." He abandoned his father's Republicanism for the Democratic Party, voted for George McGovern, and worries about the cumulative effects of political and economic inequalities. "There's never enough money directed toward education" because teachers lack political clout; "the poor can't organize"; even Ralph Nader is ineffective, because he has only "a limited amount of money to work with"; John Kennedy "*bought*" that White House." In short, "*Money governs politics.* Big business or cartels run the country. They're so strong that they don't even have to worry when they send a lobbyist up to Washington if he's going to get the job done or not. It's already done before he gets there."

The most important point about this unholy alliance, says Ernest, is that no one can control it, and therefore we should not even try: "That's this world of ours. Whether we have a Democratic or a Republican president, no matter what you or I want to do, we are under control of world politics, big business. It's been going on for years, and it's going to continue to go on. Everything is absolutely controlled, and you and I as nice clean-living American citizens, we have nothing to say about it." Utopia would have few cumulative inequalities: "The guy at the top is going to have enough," but also "nobody is going to starve to death," and society would "take care of people when you get older, when you get to the level where you no longer are going to produce." A society of "everyone living in peace and harmony" would be "ideal, fantastic"—but once again, "I *don't* mean that that's the thing we should strive for. It can't be done." We are simply wasting our time with such a vision, because "in order to accomplish these things, you've got to strive toward them. Well, who's going to be doing the striving? Is the guy at the top going to strive to make things easier for the guys at the bottom?" Ernest does not want to discourage youthful idealism—"I don't think you can fight it, but I'm older, you're young. Okay, if you feel you can, more power to you" —but he will not share it. The search for justice is for the young and optimistic. He is neither: "I find it difficult to fight it, and I'm complacent about it at this stage of life, okay? People get lazy."

Ernest's "complacency" is not real contentment; it is a refusal to care deeply about his own ambivalence. He is painfully torn between equality and ascription in his family life, and that is enough normative conflict for him. The economic domain is not problematic: good business practices may harm innocent employees, but they are just and inevitable, as well as profitable. The political domain could be another source of distress. He "wouldn't mind if we moved more in a socialist direction, that'd be fine." But equality would jeopardize his economic beliefs and interests, threaten the American way of life, require a major effort for its achievement — and maybe would not work. He has enough normative dilemmas to deal with; therefore he turns almost in relief to an insistence that equality will never be obtained and thus is not worth considering.

Equality, Indifference and the Wealthy

All wealthy respondents do not feel torn between self-interest and equality. A few simply oppose political equality; those we will discuss in chapter seven. Others do not so much oppose equality as seek other goals that have the incidental effect of muffling egalitarian claims. Political differentiation may follow from the pursuit of some other value; these people are simply indifferent about whether it does or not.

Anne Kaufman exemplifies those for whom circumstances and other focuses, not norms, dictate indifference toward differentiation. She feels trapped between the demands of the poor and the selfishness of the rich, and she fears that the middle class — her greatest concern — is being squeezed out. Therefore she often supports differentiation because she rejects claims that, in the name of equality, would benefit the top or bottom at the expense of the middle.

For example, in considering rent control, Anne worries about landlords as much as tenants: "There has to be some better system, not equality. I wouldn't want to be paying the rents people are paying for places that really aren't worth anywhere *near* it. But on the other hand, if a man has to supply heat to a building, the costs are exorbitant today. It has *no* relationship to when this rent control was established." Similarly, although tenant strikes "may be the most forceful way to get a point across" to irresponsible landlords, one must remember that tenants can be "revengeful," destructive, and unreasonable. She seeks a balance between these competing interests, such as prohibiting tenant takeovers but encouraging legal action against exploitative landlords.

Anne seeks the same balance between competing claims for policies of taxation. Some deductions are valuable. Charitable deductions promote philanthropy; equipment and inventory depreciations are essential because "if you keep punishing the average businessman, then you've defeated the purpose, because he can't conduct a successful business and in turn can't hire people to get the jobs that business generates." But others are not; too often big businesses "abuse" a "legitimate original intention through subterfuge, disguising, and hiding, [and they] get away with more than they should." As a result, "inequities have built up, the poorer guy has to pay too much," and for "the middle man in small business, the proportion is much too high." Thus she seeks to aid the poor, help the middle class to aid itself, and control big business without destroying it. In the process, she invokes norms of need, results, and investments.

Anne opposes the substitution of a progressive state income tax for Connecticut's current regressive, high sales tax. And yet, the nation's biggest problem is "pretty well up front and center—our poor people, poor and aged. That's a great, great importance. I don't like the way it's being handled, and I wish I knew how to do better. So many inequalities."

She has thought carefully about possible solutions. Urban renewal, for example, is not one. Redevelopment in her home town "was the worst mess! It took over ten years, and they destroyed the city in the process of rebuilding it." It bred "a lot of dishonesty," benefited only private construction firms, and severely harmed small businesses and the poor because "nobody could wait around that long while they tore things down or left things empty." Another wrong solution to poverty is national health insurance, despite the "prohibitive costs" and "so much waste" of the private health care system: "From what I hear in England, there's not the best care, and there's abuses of it. Where something comes free, people will stand in line."

Anne is, however, enthusiastic about proposals for some social programs, especially those that combine need and investment norms. We must help the elderly poor, who are "reduced to eat[ing] animal food, which is horrible to think about. How demeaning and undignified!" She also "approve[s] of less expensive education beyond high school for everybody," including college, career training, or vocational schools. Although affirmative action seems like "reverse racism," she points out that "the blacks all these years had the same complaint—that the white kept the preference." She doesn't "know how to equate" the conflicting claims of blacks and whites, but she does know that "we better accept more blacks into the work force on an upper echelon. Otherwise you're going to perpetuate the welfare problem, if they don't get jobs." She is most enthusiastic about projects modeled on the Peace Corps to "*help* the underprivileged [by] those who *do* have the know-how, the education." These projects, combined with a well-run program of guaranteed jobs, would benefit both taxpayers and welfare recipients—again a balance of egalitarian and differentiating norms in an effort to protect the middle class as well as help the poor.

But Anne's enthusiasm about even those programs she endorses is tempered with pessimism; here she resembles Vincent and Phillip. "If less of the money went to graft and into greedy hands, there'd be more funds available for those various things." She is "glad that [welfare] is there for those who need it," but disturbed that "our welfare system has become *absolutely terrible.* So many frauds are perpetrated, and people have learned how to use the system to their own advantage, [so] they don't want change." The "welfare mess" is not the fault of recipients: "welfare is designed partly to buy off" potential rebels; it "pyramids one regulation on the other"; and it "promotes a kind of sloth." We could correct these "pyramided mistakes" only by "erasing what we've done and start[ing] all over again. And I wonder who's going to be able to get a program like *that.*"

Anne would even pay higher taxes for programs to help the poor, especially the deserving poor. But she would do so only if the programs would be effective, and "that's where it gets lost! No corruption and with more efficiency, and it doesn't seem to *happen.*" She knows that objections such as hers are often excuses for preserving inequities, and she sympathizes with blacks who are angry that we are "*very slow* about the improvements that should be made." But still, "It can't be done overnight. And I don't mean that [as] a retreat from responsibility, to say, 'If we hold them off, we won't have to do it.' To get the mechanics of a lot of things going does take time. That's an inefficiency in big government."

Like her skepticism about social programs, Anne's opposition to equalizing holdings is more pragmatic than normative. She would like "more equalizing, but I don't think I could accept an across-the-board kind of system," for several reasons. First, people would have no incentive to "give more than they think they can get away with." Second, equality is unattainable: "In communist countries, isn't it all supposed to be equal? I don't believe it is. The upper echelon of people, there's differences there." Third, and most important, is simple self-interest: "Well, it may sound shallow, here I'm sitting in a comfortable home, but it's what we worked for. I could have lived with less. I *did* live with less, one room with a galley kitchen. It isn't that it can't be done, but it seems almost hypocritical to be saying that I would be satisfied with equality of things. If I lived in a country that had that political system, my thinking might be oriented toward accepting [it], but now, no. I couldn't, I wouldn't *want* to, accept it." And yet, Anne worries about people who "just couldn't do any better than they did. I would like to see them protected and not suffer for it.

There may be a lot to [the Swedish social welfare system]. The old person lives a comfortable existence. It has to be easier to know your medical expenses are going to be cared for." Since "if I had less I could live with it," the question of redistribution leaves her uncharacteristically hesitant: "I don't know, that's a sensitive thing. It's both emotional *and* business. Am I right in this? It's hard to say specifically. I couldn't."

Anne is neither a strong egalitarian nor a confirmed believer in differentiation. Unlike Barbara and Ernest, she does not retreat to a vision of ideal, but unattainable, equality as a way of accepting real differentiation. Instead, she remains ambivalent about the real world and concludes with a weak and uncertain differentiating stance.

As Anne points out, however, recent changes in her political thinking make her much more willing to entertain unconventional ideas than she used to be. She began the series of interviews by announcing that "at the outset, I might have been a conservative person, but with maturity, instead of getting *more* conservative, I [have] opened myself up more." Her son's countercultural "dissatisfaction" during the 1960s shook her severely, and she emerged from this "very difficult time" changed in several ways. First, she is more "flexible. I don't judge other people as much by *my* standards as I [once] might have. It's expecting too much that everybody has to be the same. I wouldn't want it that way, 'cause I'm not necessarily right about everything."

Second, she is now more "critical." She used to "look up to political institutions and respect them. I wouldn't have dared say 'No' or assert myself. I figured I wouldn't be following the law or the socially accepted way to do a thing. If that's the way it was, that's the way it had to be." But now, "I'm disenchanted. I might be more willing to challenge it." For example, she now believes that because "political bosses control a lot of the voting and thinking and whether things can get done or not," the poor and "the quiet, unassuming, law-abiding middle class [do] not have enough to say." Similarly, "I used to think they [the police] were above the criticism that they've been subjected to. Unfortunately, they've been exposed to not be as (pause). There's power again. Private army, privileged class, privileged few, and they're in a position to wield power. And I wasn't even *surprised* when I heard of the things that were done intimidating people. I'm *sorry* it happened, but I wasn't surprised." Anne is too "timid" to take direct political action, and she hardly expresses a coherent radical ideology, but she no longer believes that "you have to do what the laws are or what you was [sic] told you were supposed to do."

Thus her son's experiences and her own honesty in facing complex, even unpleasant, new facts have made Anne both more cynical and more

egalitarian in the past decade. She resists speculation about utopia because it is "very unrealistic." But she does wish that everyone's "lot would
be a comfortable one, a good one. 'Perfect' is different [for everyone]. But
if you can wake up every day with good health and know you're gonna
have your meals, and clothes on your back, and you could earn a living,"
that would be a good start. Anne is one of the most definitive and least
defensive of the respondents, but the question of redistribution leaves
even her torn between the possible virtues of equality and the proven virtues of differentiation.

Equality, Commitment, and the Wealthy

Finally, a few wealthy respondents are so committed to political equality
that they would be willing to work against their own economic self-interest to promote redistribution. No one in my sample was acting on his or
her beliefs about distributive justice, but several knew that if they did,
they would be far to the left of mainstream American political action.

Craig Cabot best exemplifies the wealthy respondents who remain
within the dominant pattern of figure 3, but push it to its limits. His extraordinary verbal dexterity, legal sophistication, and moral earnestness
sometimes preclude direct answers to questions—and always preclude
brevity. For example, he can justify a community takeover of an exploitative store "emotionally. But as a lawyer, I can't make any legal argument for it. Because once you start down that road, you're opening up a
horrible precedent." He then details the dangers "if people are allowed to
react emotionally and do what they want to do by changing the law," cit-
ing such examples as evicting a black merchant in a WASP (white Anglo-
Saxon Protestant) neighborhood and shutting down massage parlors in a
"hysterically" puritanical New England town. He concludes that it would
be impossible to write a law to permit community confiscation of oppressive institutions but prohibit the takeover of merely nonconformist ones.
Any attempt at such a *general* law "would be a disaster"; therefore any
particular confiscation, no matter its merits, is unjustifiable.

Similarly, claims of eminent domain are not to be judged by who is
benefited or harmed; they are always legitimate because "in a jurispru-
dential way, when you buy property you know you always have that
risk." Civil disobedience, no matter how unjust the law it protests, is "an-
archistic" and very risky because "taken to its logical conclusion, [it leads
you to] say 'No laws are any good' or 'No authority is any good!' " Thus
Craig's judgments about political justice have little to do with the sanctity of property or the redistributive result of any action. Rather, fair actions are those that follow correct legal procedures.

Because he sees taxes as a matter of economic policy, not a matter of legal justice, and because he talks enthusiastically about the latter but only reluctantly about the former, he is almost silent on the question of taxation. He suggests only that a good tax structure should "tax *all* income" and foster "good public policy." Thus, for example, tax deductions that stimulate a businessman to expand are "good for the people he employs, for him, and for the people who need the building." But tax deductions that merely enrich the rich are "where we run into trouble." He supports progressive taxation and deductions that workers can use, but beyond that, "I just am at sea with this whole damn thing."

Craig has more to say, all of it egalitarian, about the outlines of a good social welfare policy. Just as schools, if forced to choose, should help the slowest students even if "you blow a Nobel Prize winner," so should society help its neediest citizens even at the expense of the well-off. Society has the responsibility "to do whatever you can to give everybody a fair shot at a happy life." There is always the risk that "you might lose out on an extraordinary talent," but social justice requires that we run that risk. "The extraordinary talent is mostly a benefit to himself. I would rather take care of, or make things equal for, the disadvantaged person."

Another broad rule for Craig is that although nationalization of industries is inefficient and oppressive, "The public does have the right, within the framework of a capitalistic society, to make certain regulations so that a few people can't monopolize the economy. There's just so much space and land, and these materials cannot be manipulated for the sole purpose of the profit of a few." He recommends few specific regulations because his economic knowledge is too thin, but his policy preferences are clearly egalitarian.

Craig does specify one policy — government provision of jobs and incomes. Inflation is a "terrible thief," but unemployment is worse, an "agonizing problem" and "devastating social crisis." He argues here for an inverted need norm; the government must equalize hardships. "Inflation spreads the risk more evenly. A middle-class family who finds its buying power shrinking isn't at a crisis level that an unemployed person is." Even more serious than the financial crisis is the threat to the "emotional stability" of the unemployed, since most people would "rather work than be paid off." Thus assuring jobs is preferable to assuring "handouts."

Craig carries this argument further, thereby making it considerably more radical. If people cannot or will not work, or if society benefits from permitting them to stay at home, then they should be guaranteed an income high enough to enable a family to live with reasonable dignity. His answer to the often-expressed fear that people will have no incentive to work if guaranteed a living wage is to treat the lazy as ill: "Our society does not think twice about the justification of taking care of sick people, disabled people, emotionally handicapped people. I don't think you have to stretch it too far to conclude that a person who just doesn't want to work is a handicapped person. A person who is that far out of the main-stream — everyone else needs this for feelings of fulfillment or an ego-trip, or whatever — is emotionally handicapped." Thus a guaranteed income simply extends a policy of guaranteed jobs, but does not substitute for it.

Craig argues that he is not simply being a "bleeding-heart do-gooder" here. Society must protect itself from malingerers just as it does from other criminals. After all, nothing "we've talked about up to this point would suggest that we could have a society which did not need either an army or a police department." Just as the creation of banks calls forth bank robbers, then police to restrain them, so guaranteeing incomes would create shirkers and institutional responses such as a civilian draft. But eventually, he abandons caution: "Even if that whole rationale is out, assuming that what I just said is pure gibberish, what's your option? To allow a person to die in the streets? And then what are you going to do about that person's dependents? I don't think there should be any stipulations for that [a guaranteed income], any more than there's a stipulation for your right to have a healthy body."

As the quotation above suggests, Craig has another reason for a strong need norm besides his concern for "the victims." It is concern for "the family unit, [which] to me is the glue that civilizes any society. Economic crisis within a family is going to shatter that glue. It is not in the best interest of our society to allow that family to break up for those mechanical reasons." To pursue a classic conservative goal, Craig comes close to radical egalitarianism.

He realizes the financial implications of a high income floor: "The wealthy are going to be paying more than the middle. So it *will* be a cost" to him and his class. But the cost is fair: it's "the price that the wealthy pay for living in a society which has made possible their wealth." He does not worry that "millionaire Z is going to be paying hundreds of thousands of dollars to support this system. You're going to deter his energy? I say 'Too bad.' "

"If you push it too far," however, redistribution will be counter-productive: "You'll destroy the incentive of the individual who is trying to make his life better. You would be destroying the basis of the free enterprise system." Therefore we must not impose a limit on the money a person can earn or possess: "Let them go as far as they can go, as long as they're not, you know, tearing the legs off alligators."

Craig supports the free enterprise system and thus opposes complete equalization for several reasons described earlier. First, equalization leads to bureaucratic control, a cure worse than the disease. Second, he is not sure that equality, which is uncomfortably similar to identity, is completely desirable. Third, the effort needed to equalize would destroy the very social structure it is intended to save: "It's part of the strength of this republic that we've solved those issues 200 years ago, and we are fairly middle of the road. [Now] it's a question of: how are you going to manage that middle of the road? We don't want to have church/state problems, we don't want to have one class against the other kind of class, we don't want to outlaw unions, we don't want to do those kind of rupturing things. So what we want to do is manage an economy."

Government's role in "managing the economy" is crucial, but must be limited. It should "give us a fair shot at whatever our definition of happiness is, [and] monitor the laws to protect us. To be sure that those people who are in a powerful position, with resources and clout, have got to respond to the public need." Even this limited role requires "the government to be big—everything else has gotten big too. There are more people going to school—we need more school specialists. The health field is expanding—we need money for research. I don't have confidence in the private sector doing all those things." Nevertheless, as James Madison would point out, we must worry about "the tricky part of it, the balance of power between too much and too little governmental oversight. If you order your society so closely, you're having a public control rather than a private control, which I said I didn't want to get into."

Craig relies once more on fair procedures and legal justice to achieve this balance. First, "There is an escape valve in the courts, which are totally independent. And that protects us. We have a super arrangement." Second, when new action is needed, "It's a question of drafting laws which will allow it to happen," rather than relying on a politician's discretion. Third, even though some people "wield a ton of influence, there are laws to regulate lobbyists, [and] the amount of money a person can donate to a politician. [We also have] freedom of information laws, ventilation by the press." Finally, "Any citizen who can read and wants to take the time can make a good decision for himself among the two [candidates for an office]. I abhor the notion that there should be a select group [making decisions], and I don't think that'll ever happen here."

Thus Craig seeks a polity that avoids both differentiating laissez-faire capitalism and egalitarian social control. Utopia would no longer require such careful balancing of freedom and equality. "Everybody could get whatever they reasonably needed, and everyone had to give whatever they reasonably could. It wouldn't be guided by the profit motive at all." It would be "hard to find an evil in that"; the only problem is that "I don't believe that that can ever happen." All we can hope for in the real world "is to have a society where people have the opportunity to expand, to make for themselves a happy, useful life, without the opportunity to do that at someone else's expense."

Craig comes close to, but stops short of, complete egalitarianism. In the process, he integrates the three domains more than any other respondent we have seen so far. Government must provide full equality of opportunity to allow citizens to operate freely in the economy and lovingly in the home. That prescription implies four things: careful early training by example and precept to teach children to respect the rights and dignity of others, to care for the needy, and to fulfill social responsibilities; a very high floor of material resources, in order to fulfill norms of equality and need as well as to provide real opportunities for productivity; a strong legal system and the use of just procedures by the government to regulate the boundaries within which the market may operate; and no limits on market success or incomes generated therefrom. In his view, we need enough political redistribution of wealth to shape, but not to destroy, economic differentiation.

Conclusion

I draw three conclusions from this chapter. First and foremost, both rich and poor respondents are generally egalitarian in the political domain. They want political and civil rights to be distributed equally to all citizens. They want tax and social welfare policies mainly to take from the rich and give to the poor and middle classes. Their vision of utopia always includes more equality, whatever else it contains. Combining this conclusion with those of chapters four and five demonstrates that the three domains of life, not economic class or personal ideology, best explain how distributive beliefs range from egalitarian to differentiated.

Second, respondents vary systematically in the particular egalitarian norms they use to evaluate specific political issues. Let us examine several such issues: views of private property, desirable tax policy, social and welfare policies, political and civil rights, governmental redistribution of wealth, and utopia.

At first glance, private property appears sacrosanct to most interview subjects: they automatically reject suggestions that property rights ought to come second to community needs. Thus for example, although Mary Lou Trask thinks a tenant strike "doesn't hurt and maybe you can get something," a tenant takeover is "never" fair. "If it ever gets to that point where you've tried the other things, and it doesn't work, the only thing I can see is you just go find another place, that's all." Even the government's right of eminent domain, a principle solidly grounded in American constitutional history, is eyed dubiously by many respondents. As Mary Lou puts it, "It seems in a way that you're stepping on the individual's rights." The automatic association of private property with individual rights is, of course, a fundamental tenet of American political thought, and it is hardly surprising that no one endorses private takeovers or is enthusiastic about public takeovers, whatever the justice of the cause. Differentiation with regard to property seems as solid as a norm can be.

When pushed a bit further, however, many respondents do accept at least the possibility that community needs might take precedence over individual rights. We have seen Pamela McLean's and Vincent Sartori's beliefs that if the proceeds were to be distributed for the good of all, properties unjustly acquired, used, or transferred might legitimately be confiscated by the government. Mary Lou Trask similarly leaves a door open to egalitarian claims in her discussion of eminent domain. She describes a friend who, despite being "relocated [into] a much more bigger and beautiful home now than they had," is still very unhappy about being forced to move. Nevertheless, "There's times when it has to be done. If you [the government] treat them right, like you understand their problem, one person's rights has to become less than what is better for the majority of people." Thus respondents concede that property rights can be superseded if several conditions are met. Only the government, not private citizens, may act in the name of the community; the property must in fact be used to benefit all citizens; and the government must follow proper procedures. With these qualifications, even the most confirmed differentiator yields to more egalitarian claimants.

Respondents also begin from a principle of differentiation in discussing tax policy, but they abandon it much more quickly here than they do for property rights. All would like to pay lower taxes, but most recognize that tax revenues are essential for government programs that they support. They even claim to be willing to pay more if they could be sure that their extra payments would be used efficiently for specific policies. Thus Amy Campbell initially endorses a guaranteed annual income instead of AFDC because it "would save money by get[ting] rid of the padding, social workers, administration." But even if it required higher taxes, "We'd still do it. Oh, of course. You've got to try — it's awful the way they [welfare recipients] live." She would prefer lower to higher taxes, but she also prefers higher taxes and good programs to lower taxes and poor programs.

Respondents see taxes on inheritance or wealth as unfair, both because they tax property more than once and because they apparently preclude saving for the future of one's children. Michael McFarland, for example, argues that "it's wrong, taking away money from somebody that has earned it. You pay taxes all your life on the money you earn, and then when you pass away and you leave some money to your relatives, you gotta take *more* money out of it. It seems like tax on top of tax." He sees the Rockefeller inheritance as only quantitatively larger, not qualitatively different, from his own. Rockefeller heirs should be able to inherit "all their nice places 'cause I think they'd like to keep it in the family, pass things right down the line. Like if my parents ever passed away, and say there was $10,000 to be inherited, I should be able to inherit $10,000, not $8000 or less."

And yet most respondents are incensed that income taxes are not more progressive. Still discussing the Rockefellers, Michael says, "They're making so much money off the country they ought to pay, same as the poor people have to pay." Like most respondents, Michael identifies two ways in which the rich evade their fair share of taxes. First, "The higher brackets have all kinds of loopholes. We don't have the brains, or the lawyers, or the know-how to avoid paying it, and they do." Second, the tax structure itself is insufficiently progressive: "Ten percent could seem a lot to poorer people, but 10 percent to richer people would be just a drop in the bucket. The more money you take out of the country, the more money you should throw back into the country."

Even the wealthy seek a more progressive tax structure, although they often use a different standard to define "the rich" than the poor use. Judith Baum, who "belong[s] to what is usually referred to as an intellectual elite," is "all for a really graduated ability to pay. And one pays — *not* the kind of thing where you buy fake businesses, and you incorporate yourself as an individual in order to manipulate, get the tax write-offs." Her language is more sophisticated than Michael's vague reference to "stocks and bonds," but they use the same norms of need between, and strict equality within, income classes to evaluate income taxes.

With regard to welfare and social policies, respondents no longer begin by thinking about private property; hence they start out and remain egalitarian. They overwhelmingly support national health insurance, although some also want a private medical option. They endorse tuition subsidies, housing subsidies, higher Social Security payments, and so on. They most firmly support a guaranteed jobs program using both public and private sectors, and they at least claim that they would be willing to pay higher taxes to ensure its success.

Those who dislike their own jobs or who view human nature pessimistically see a jobs program as a way to force people to work, rather than permitting them to receive a handout. It would also give taxpayers some return for their money. Sandra Wilson, for example, who is deeply dissatisfied with her pay and working conditions, does not "know as you can guarantee anything," but still thinks a government jobs program "would be a good idea. There's a lot of public works jobs that could be taken care of that way. I mean, I *work* for my money! Why should somebody who sits home seven days a week get $4000 just for doing that?"

In contrast, respondents who like their jobs or who view human nature optimistically see a jobs program as a way to permit people to be productive and to retain self-esteem, rather than forcing them to accept a handout. Timothy Saunders, for example, worries that unemployment creates "a loss of vitality, or nerve, or direction, or something like that." After all, "There are enough potholes and dilapidated buildings and unused farmland, that we are wasting people's talents and physical resources. So if they can't [find work] through private enterprise, then government should do it." Whether for punitive or sympathetic reasons, then, virtually all respondents include guaranteed jobs in their policy recommendations.

With the exception of tax loopholes, respondents are much less aware of social policies that redistribute within one class or upward than of policies that redistribute downward. No pattern is discernible in either their awareness or level of support for upwardly redistributive programs. The highly educated and egalitarian Craig Cabot can think of no law that favors the rich, whereas the poorly educated and less egalitarian Phillip Santaguida describes how the rich and the politicians together create inflation to keep the rest of the country poor. Some support federal aid to ailing industries because it helps workers or because everyone deserves help in time of need. Others oppose such aid because it forces the poor to subsidize the rich. But generally respondents are unaware of the existence, or even the possibility, of upwardly redistributive policies.

Respondents are unambiguously egalitarian in the realm of pure political or civil rights. All can list at least a few "basic rights," although some lists might not be recognizable to the Founding Fathers. All insist that whatever our rights are, everyone should share them equally. Similarly, at least at a high level of abstraction, most respondents argue strongly for democracy, although Ruth Sennett praises the fact that "we do what the president says. He rules the country, like you have dictators in South America." Much more common is Amy Campbell's description of the right to vote as "something very important. I always do vote. When it comes right down to the wire, I go out even if it is ten minutes to [the polls' closing time], even if my car is locked in the garage. 'Cause [if I didn't], I'd feel like 'This is awful. What if I didn't *have* this right?' "

People do not believe that their vote actually determines the government's actions; with the demise of political machines, Amy says, "now it's your big business coming in with their interests, their money and clout. It's on a much larger scale, and it's scarier." She has no more of a solution to special interest and big business control than did Ernest Berkowitz earlier. As she puts it, "Well, you feel helpless, don't you? You *have* to. If you don't, you're a dummy." But this lack of equality in decision-making signifies to Amy only that equal rights have not yet been fully achieved, not that they do not or should not exist.

Equality of rights means so much to these respondents partly because they see it as a direct consequence of inherent human equality, the issue on which they take the strongest egalitarian stand. The first opinion that Vicky Pateman dares to voice is that "We're all created equal, and there shouldn't be any differences in [that is, because of] our creed, our color. God put us on this earth for a reason. And if you're white, you're white; if you're black, you're black. There shouldn't be no difference whatsoever." Others are more sophisticated: of course there are differences, but they should not matter politically. In Jean Gilmore's terms, "Men are not created equal. They have different intelligence; they're born into different situations. What it [the phrase 'All men are created equal'] basically means, of course, is whether you're white or black or rich or poor, you should have your equal say, your equal education, be treated equally. That's what they mean. Do I agree with that? Yes, of course."

Of course, "being treated equally" means very different things to different people. As political scientists and activists have known for years, respondents do not always mean in concrete situations what they claim to mean in abstract terms. Vicky Pateman opposes affirmative action policies; Jean Gilmore lists characteristics of "people who are not equal to me." Nevertheless, respondents firmly and consistently use the norm of strict equality in discussing rights and human worth.

People may slip in their allegiance to equality as they move from abstract rights to specific circumstances, but at least they begin with consistent convictions about rights. That is not the case for redistribution of wealth or incomes. It is extraordinarily difficult to decide whether a respondent "really" supports redistribution or not—and that may be the most important finding on this subject. Respondents cannot make up their minds because redistribution pulls them in equal, but opposite, directions. Viewed as an economic issue, it is wrong because it violates the principle of differentiation. Viewed as a political issue, it may be right because it satisfies the principle of equality. Wholehearted endorsement of redistribution would require both that people overcome the disjunction between economy and polity, *and* that they choose equality over differentiation.

Much of American political thought is dedicated to the proposition that economy and polity should be kept separate; it would be astonishing if these respondents did not concur. And yet they will not reject the claims of equality. Therefore they waffle. They claim that economic equality would be fine for themselves and their friends, but would not work for everyone else. They claim that equality would be fine for a while, but that it would never last. They support it, but with exceptions as large as the rules. Or they oppose it, but seek upper limits on wealth, lower limits on poverty, or both. Some refuse to think about it. And a few literally cannot imagine it: their ability to make connections between thoughts simply short-circuits at the idea of deliberate political control of the economy. Thus most respondents certainly do not support the redistribution of wealth, but they also do not exactly oppose it. They do both and therefore neither.

The most startling finding of this chapter is the respondents' visions of an egalitarian utopia. Even Barbara Azlinsky and Anne Kaufman, who do not really seek or expect greater equality, believe that in an ideal society, all people would have "the freedom and happiness to do what they wanted to do" or "a comfortable life, a good one." According to conventional wisdom, Americans do not want equality of condition, only an equal chance to become unequal. True, most respondents are of two minds about redistribution, but this is *not* to say that all they really want is the opportunity to live better than others. Ideally, they would like a society with at least a comfortable middle-class life for all, and perhaps without great discrepancies of wealth, status, or power.

Let us briefly examine the utopian visions of several other respondents. Consider Steven Vistacco, who earned "about $2000" in 1975 as a sometimes-employed plumber's helper. His wife works part-time, so they "manage to do decently well," although "you get a little disgusted, because the more you make, the more your product goes up. There doesn't seem to be any solution to it." Steven is less upset about incomes and prices, however, than about pervasive prejudice and competition. "There's a problem: Who hates this race? Who hates that race? The Arabs and Jews, we're constantly going over history, wars renew themselves because of jealousy and hatred." Economic warfare is just as bad: "There's a sort of middle between the poor and the rich, but the way things are going with the prices and pay scales, it seems like they're trying to get you. It seems like they'll *eliminate* the middle class. Nothing's stabilized. It seems like a never-ending battle." For Steven, in an ideal society: "You could help one another and be more respectful of people regardless of their nationality or race. Be in harmony with everybody and have good employment. [It would] be good for everybody, so everybody would be happy, content. One wouldn't be jealous of this one or jealous of that one, fighting, keeping up with the Joneses, [saying] 'You're better than me,' [or] 'I've got a better house.' " Consider, more briefly, other views of utopia from poor respondents:

> Okay, [suppose] I am president. We disassemble those missiles and all that crap, have a big Bicentennial melting pot. That would be a heck of a lot of money for improving things. Life is short, and it's cruel enough anyway — why not put some good experiences and good health care, good books, and good teachers, and nice yards and houses for people and pets. I just hope, by changing the priorities and the normal tone, that the scales would be changed somewhat.   (Timothy Saunders)

> No poor. Everybody with the money for a few of the *nice* little things in life, you know, the little extras. No war. That would be terrific.   (Sandra Wilson)

> You go in certain sections, the houses are nice. You go in another section, the houses are bad. You go in another section, they're worse. So you pick the better part. Maybe the whole world should be like the better part.   (Ruth Sennett)

> If you could have anything you wanted, to have money. There's a lot of things you can't have because you probably haven't got the money for it.   (Vicky Pateman)

Each person embellishes his or her utopia with good health, travel, a loving family, no crime, and other values. But each begins with universal material well-being and absence of divisive, corrosive differences in wealth.[2]

Most of the rich have a similar vision of universal suburbia, even when they attempt to deny it. Judith Baum, the sophisticated and very voluble child psychologist, believes that we could not "legislate" equality of condition "without turning the whole society into [being] so strictly controlled I wouldn't want it. That's throwing out the baby with the bath water." In addition, "freedom of choice" and "options" are more important than any income guarantee. "With them, that person can always, well, can *sometimes* — if he wants things badly enough — do other things" to earn money, such as get a second job. "Most of us follow certain paths which, given the opportunity to do it all over again, we'd do *exactly* the same thing." So the government should not equalize incomes; with enough freedom of action, people will end up where they choose to be. Nevertheless, "A utopia would obviously be free of disease and poverty. There is an amount of nutrition that everybody can have. We can, by practicing restraint, and R & D [research and development], and a whole bunch of other things, live on a finite planet with finite resources, *if* we're willing to give up certain things. [If] we recognize limitations and struggle for constant improvement for everyone and allow for as much individual liberty as can be exercised without hurting the mass — yes, that's my utopia."

Next, consider David Fine, the exuberantly successful and aggressively intelligent architect, who glories in his entrepreneurial abilities and self-made wealth. He believes that "altruism and philanthropy and brotherhood are motivated by self-interest, because it makes us all feel better to be philanthropic and to help others." He has no illusions about his own deep involvement in a model low-income housing project: "Anybody who tells you they're doing things for other people is not telling you the complete truth. Because you always do something for yourself, and if other people benefit, well, then that makes it even better. But I get a tremendous kick out of it." He "philosophically agree[s] that there should be a better distribution of the wealth," but "I sure as hell would feel awful if my estate went to the government," and "I don't believe in socialism, because the government is not capable of running things efficiently." Finally, he is "a *very* competitive person. I don't like to lose." And yet even with his love of competition, assertion of self-interest, and pride in possessions, David's vision of utopia is fundamentally egalitarian. The best possible future "would be the health and welfare of society. See, I feel that *my* quality of life has already been augmented, whereas I can look at society in general and feel that *their* quality of life should be augmented. Physical and mental health, opportunities to get an education, in general I think there are other things to augment the quality of life." Finally, consider the other wealthy respondents' views of utopia:

> Peace, everyone working or having enough to live on and having what they want out of life. Everyone in the world having enough food. And freedom to look for new horizons, new frontiers, such as space, and everyone being able to do what they would like to do. That's utopia. (Jean Gilmore)

That's *one* thing I think is terribly important — communication. People don't understand each other, and they're immediately frightened. If we had one language all over the world, boy, that sure would help, wouldn't it? Maybe we would let people follow their natural inclination rather than set rules on people. It would be *lovely*.   (Amy Campbell)

The worst utopia is the popular classic, retiring [that is, retirement]. That to me is a *disaster*. But in utopia God made a paradise, a place where people could be creative, or truthful, or busy, accomplishing something during the day in their own image or with their hands. You don't find busy people making trouble. In retiring, they sleep without pills, they're anxious to get up in the morning, they're ready. That's utopia.   (Isaac Cohen)

The rich have more idiosyncratic visions than the poor; they focus on the quality of life rather than on material goods. As Isaac Cohen says, "I'm not talking about money. Money is just survival. To me, money is unimportant, and comforts are important, real, tangible."

This difference brings to mind a recurring theme. The fact that the poor feel more material constraints than the rich is not in itself surprising, but it has important normative implications. The poor are more often torn between distributive norms and material limits: if they have nothing to distribute, how can they operate according to a norm of need, or any other? The rich are more often torn between conflicting distributive norms; they take for granted that they can carry out their choice once they make it. The same considerations appear in designing utopias. With two exceptions, the poor seek a society in which everyone is wealthy enough to be able to choose among distributive norms, to pursue their interests, and to think about freedom and the good life. The rich assume that everyone will have this degree of wealth; they therefore focus directly on choices, interests, freedom, and the good life. Their visions assume a fairly high standard of living for everyone in the community, regardless of class, sex, productivity, virtue, need, competitive urge, or any other differentiating criterion. Basically, then, these too are egalitarian visions.

Finally, variations occur, not only in the particular norms used for particular issues, but in respondents' emotional reactions to their own distributive beliefs and to a world that is sometimes unfair.

Some are bitter or angry over their inability to reconcile their economic and political beliefs. This disjunction between equality and differentiation becomes particularly problematic when they consider the plight of the very poor, or when they are impelled to think about redistribution. Some (and they may be the same people) are bitter or angry less about internal conflicts than about external failures. Too often, they find, the polity is unable or unwilling to implement the egalitarian policies it endorses. This reaction occurs especially when they consider tax policies and political rights and authority. More poor than rich find political egalitarianism a source of distress rather than of gratification, and the poor tend to be more deeply distressed.

Some respondents, however, find a principle of equality in the political domain to be a source of gratification. They see not persistent inequality, but great and growing equality. They are pleased with past achievements, optimistic about future policies, and relatively satisfied with their current situation. They are also able either to ignore the disjunction between economic and political beliefs or to "solve" it with a verbal trick or two.

A few respondents refuse to feel either gratified or distressed about their political beliefs. They defend themselves against the dangerous emotions of either hope or despair by insisting that one cannot fight existing injustices, or that one must pick one's battle and ignore the rest of the war. Curiously, the two respondents who best exemplify this view, Anne Kaufman and Phillip Santaguida, are contented in at least one of the other two domains. It is as though they recognize, consciously or not, that strong political norms will cause them grief, and they simply do not want to deal with the emotional consequences of conviction.

A few other respondents are sufficiently committed to political equality, and sufficiently convinced that it does not now exist, that they express willingness to take action on its behalf. Craig Cabot best exemplifies this emotional stance; he is in the curious position of endorsing the dominant pattern of beliefs so strongly that he almost rejects the existing society, which fails to carry out its own promises. At times, he is "more papish than the Pope."

Thus the third part of the dominant pattern of beliefs is not simple. Support for equality is weak in discussions of property rights, but grows stronger as the resource to be distributed shifts to social policies, pure political rights and authority, and finally utopia. The question of redistribution is simply unresolvable within this pattern. Partly because of the disjunction between economic and political beliefs, emotions related to political norms range from dismay to joy to indifference to rebellion. We should note once more that although the emotion may be the same for rich and poor, its basis and moral force may well be different. It would not be correct to conclude that if only the poor would become more optimistic and trusting, distributive problems would go away. It is correct to conclude that, despite having less tangible reasons for doing so, the poor sometimes feel as happy as the rich, and the rich sometimes feel as unhappy as the poor when they consider political equality.

7 Alternative Patterns of Belief

Despite variations in particular norms used, belief in their use, and satisfaction derived from their use, most respondents follow the normative pattern outlined in figure 3. The fact that they seek equality in two domains and differentiation in a third should not be viewed as inconsistent in the sense of being "incompatible, incoherent, or illogical."[1] The term *inconsistency* commonly implies that one *ought* to be consistent, to maintain identical beliefs across a wide range of circumstances.[2] Consistency is often an unexamined virtue in liberal thinking. If one wants conscientiously to object to killing Vietnamese, one must also conscientiously object to killing Nazis; if a political science department wants to hire a Marxist, it must also be willing to hire a Fascist. Our precepts of due process, equal opportunity, equal protection under the law, and one person-one vote all assume that just and moral governance requires consistency.

Yet consistency may not always be a virtue or the highest form of moral reasoning. In some circumstances, it may impel blind adherence to rules, a refusal to recognize that situations differ and "correct" conduct should differ accordingly. Civil disobedience, even violence, may perhaps be justified in opposing a senseless, brutal war, but not in opposing school desegregation. Senator McGovern argued that military "protection" of Israelis in 1979 may be justified even if military "protection" of Vietnamese in 1963 was not. Men and women, or blacks and whites, may be different in ways relevant to particular circumstances and perhaps should be treated differently under those circumstances.[3]

Of course, relativist arguments are extraordinarily slippery and dangerous; liberals have good reasons to be wary of them. I cannot provide rules for deciding when consistency is or is not a virtue. My point is narrower; I wish merely to argue that consistency should not automatically be assumed to be the most moral or sophisticated stance. Disjunctions that follow an intelligible pattern may be the most subtle response to a highly complex world. The respondents discussed so far use a variety of norms that sometimes contradict one another; they do not use norms randomly or inconsequentially.

This chapter, however, examines those few respondents who *do* try to be consistent across domains. Three rely on differentiating norms of results, ascription, and market processes; three rely on egalitarian norms of strict equality, need, and investment. The former group endorses competition or hierarchy; the latter group seeks downward redistribution of wealth.[4] And just as we saw earlier, they differ in the specific norms they emphasize and in their emotional responses to their own norms.

Differentiators among the Poor — Sally White

The Socializing Domain   Sally White, who was introduced in chapter two, is twenty-seven years old, divorced, cheerful, self-confident, very talkative, unemployed, and deeply in debt. She attributes her family's middle-class status to the fact that "our whole family has always been workers," and she is determined to teach her seven-year-old son, Ken, that "if you really want something you have to work for it." His allowance is "chore-based": he earns toys by accumulating points on assigned tasks. Even when he is not anxious to earn something, Sally tells him, " 'You have to do this tonight. I don't care if you want to play a game. This is your responsibility.' " It would be hard to imagine a more deliberate effort to instill a norm of results.

Sally wants adults to stay out of children's arguments: "I always try to build up independence, where kids have to learn how to handle the situation between each other." She comes close here to a prescription for survival of the fittest, softened slightly to accommodate a young child. She also teaches her son the value of privacy and property rights: "I've always believed in sharing, but if there's a kid who is very destructive, I say, 'If you don't want somebody to touch it, just don't bring it out now. Play with it when you're alone.' " Sharing and cooperation are valuable, but possessions are more so. In all of these ways, Sally is more differentiating than most parents are with their children.

Again unlike most respondents, Sally wants schools to focus on gifted children. She is furiously voluble about Ken's school system, which "spends 99 percent of the time with the slow learners and completely overlooks the intelligent children. My son's been very badly abused. He's bored, craves attention. They're totally ignoring him and wasting him. And here's a child that at three years old knew the name of every dinosaur there was!" Sally's belief here may depend more on her own situation than on a general principle, but she does broaden her concern to address all children. She proposes that students be tested, grouped by ability (not age), and then rewarded by need and effort. Such a system would lead to the greatest productivity among all students.

As her prescription for schools suggests, Sally is not unidimensional. She has "very miscellaneous thoughts" about competition among children because "sometimes the child that's losing will just completely fall back because they give up." Children that "work *full steam* and still cannot do it should not get an F"; they should be grouped with others of their ability, so that they do not constantly fail. She is much more enthusiastic about creativity and independence than about correct answers; however even in these cases, achievement is her goal. Competition is bad because it stifles motivation among losers; creativity and independence are good because they promote future accomplishments. Thus all aspects of Sally's daily life are structured either directly or indirectly by a norm of results.

The Economy   After holding six jobs in nine years, mostly in small companies that have folded, Sally is now unemployed. She is, however, discouraged neither about the success rate of small businesses nor about her own career prospects. She "was always paid fairly for what I was doing"; her jobs gave her "lots of good experience"; and her budding business as an efficiency consultant, although not yet successful, will blossom as soon as she can "contact the people, get established."

Sally believes that wages should depend on a combination of norms of results and ascription. Assembly line workers deserve low pay because they are "mostly people that couldn't do anything else." Futhermore, for them "it's not a dull, boring little job — they enjoy doing it, or obviously they wouldn't *be* doing it. They sit there, and they're just thinking about these little things — they really don't have too many thoughts about too much. Usually in an assembly room, they have a very happy little atmosphere." Supervisors, however, deserve high pay because their work "is very taxing. They're responsible to see that those twenty people get out this work. One person goofs up—that person doesn't get yelled at, he's [the supervisor] the one that gets it. It's an ulcer job." But even if managers inherit the business and "spend the morning at the golf course, the afternoon at the bar," they still should be able to keep their money. "Maybe it's not really fair, but really, it's *their* business. They own it, and if that's the way they want to run it, that's up to them."

Sally also combines norms of results and ascription to justify great wealth. Most wealthy people are "pushers," "very brilliant," and "have human feeling 'cause they've been down." Some inherit, however; they "don't appreciate it," are "greedy," and "don't have any human concern at all." But even the undeserving rich must be left alone; as we saw in chapter two, wealthy individuals give us role models, and property rights are sacrosanct.

Sally explains poverty as learned laziness. The poor learn that the government will "just hand them things, not make them do anything to get it," and they do not learn the joys of middle-class diligence because "they have never *been* up. They just don't have the faith that they're going to be." They "get married at sixteen, have 200 kids right away," "start drinking and lose a job," lack "a strong character," or accept the low wages of unskilled labor to avoid "the aggravation or the worries" of the ambitious. She rejects the possibility that better jobs may simply not exist, or that most welfare recipients cannot work. After all, "If you were told you had to work to get this check, you'd do it. 'Cause you're not going to want to see your family starve. And it's as simple as that."

Sally sounds harsher at this point than she really is because these comments do not reflect her faith that the world is really just. For those who do "get into a working frame of mind" and "keep pushing," the opportunity to advance is "unlimited. You can do whatever you want to do, if you go out and *do* it. It's just people get too lazy to do it, and then they blame it on this or that, you know, 'I'm black so I can't get ahead.' And that's not true. Each person makes their own life." Government programs have eliminated all structural barriers to mobility, so that "ambition," "creative talent," "courage," "faith in your own ability"—not race, class, the state of the economy, or luck—can now determine success.

In sum, Sally's differentiating norms are optimistic and humanistic in her own eyes. "In the long run, it equals out. People that are morally unethical get it in the end. Just look at gangsters—they end up getting shot to death, right?" Conversely, so long as the virtuous are "a little bit aggressive," they "get their rewards." In the end, "Somehow things seem to fall into place."

The Polity Sally's political views extend her economic views: the government's main role is to protect and enhance market processes. It should always bolster property rights: rent control and tenant strikes are wrong; health and safety standards must not interfere with a landlord's control; taxes should not penalize those who succeed in the market. Thus, tax shelters that others complain about so vociferously (she rejects the phrase "tax loopholes") are fair: "I don't think the government's really *giving* them to you, if you're smart enough to figure out how to build up a tax shelter. They're fair because you really *did* lose the money. [When] I buy a car for business, and it depreciates $1000, then I really did lose that $1000." She is the only poor respondent for whom tax evasion by the rich is a mild annoyance, not a deep frustration. After all, "Anybody tries to get off paying taxes. Really. If you can think of a way. It just seems like you're paying so much anyways." She rejects inheritance taxes and state income taxes in favor of regressive, but voluntary, taxes such as lotteries and sales tax.

But, although "I grumble, complain" about taxes, Sally does not endorse a minimal night watchman type of government: "Deep underneath, you have a feeling that you contributed to something, that the money is going to worthwhile places, things that *have* to be done." In fact, rather than reductions in government programs, she proposes many additions. Some favor business. She supports federal aid to ailing industries, since she assumes that such aid would not be given unless it is economically sound: "They have all those smart people up there that are not just going to throw away money because they like the corporation. I'm sure they weigh it out." But some of her proposals would redistribute downward. She seeks environmental and consumer protection, and aid so that the poor will be "put into the level where they can contribute." Thus she endorses "free child care, free medical benefits, more job opportunities, more training skill centers," voluntary national health insurance – all to help people become "educated and taught a job, so they can go out and earn money." Once they have the first job, preferably in private industry but if necessary in a public works program, they will "build up their feelings within themselves of contributing and being something. And then they're going to want to move on." Neither the current welfare system nor a guaranteed annual income gives this "motivation," and therefore both are equally misguided. Sally would pay more taxes to support job-producing programs, even though she resents all taxes for maintenance programs.

Thus Sally is not a nineteenth-century laissez-faire capitalist, but a modern welfare state capitalist. She seeks differentiation for its own sake no more than she seeks material equality. Her goal is equality of opportunity, in which "everybody starts out the same, and it is what you make of yourself that is your end result." The polity has two responsibilities in the pursuit of this goal. First, "If people fall, their friends and the government should help them pick up and start over"—thus a wide variety of social programs, especially for the poor. Second, the polity must provide the political counterpart to equal economic opportunity, that is, equal freedom—to express one's views, defend oneself, influence politicians, live as one wants. Just as Sally believes that the economic world is ultimately just, so too she is pleased about Americans' political freedom. Neither agencies nor courts favor wealthy, white, or well-educated citizens. Voter influence over political decisions is "really beginning to equal out," and "everyone has an equal say [in elections]. If things don't get done, it's because they [the people] don't go out and do it. The power is with the people." The freedom to have abortions, live openly as a homosexual, use drugs, dress idiosyncratically—all of these social rights are great and growing, in Sally's eyes. Finally, class and race discrimination is coming to an end in electoral politics because for politicians, as for businessmen, ignoring blacks, women, and the articulate poor is not in their self-interest. Thus, although no ethnic group had "a bed of roses in the beginning," all are able to "work themselves up. Maybe we're more advanced because we started before the blacks, but it's finally happened [for them]. And it'll happen for the Chicanos too." In all of these arenas of political life, Sally sees and applauds individual freedom of action; equality is desirable in politics only as the equal right to do what one wants.

Not surprisingly, Sally rejects material equalization as an "infringe[ment] on my freedom. I don't need them to provide for me. And I don't want to *pay* them to provide for me. That's too much power." Not only would more equality threaten freedom, but it would also destroy the unique value of the United States: "The whole American ideal has always been, here you can really strike it [rich] if you want to. If you took that away, you'd stop thinking." Eventually, "it *would all* fall apart. Everybody would be lumped in one class. It'd be like Russia. Pretty soon, then, we wouldn't have the churches or anything else." In sum, too much equality "would kill your spirit. It would kill mine anyways."

Thus Sally both demands that people be held accountable for what they do, regardless of their circumstances, and assumes that the resources are always available for people to do what they want to do. She sees differentiating norms as both stern and encouraging; she is both rigid and humanistic. In her own life, "Things are at their worst, career-wise, love-wise, whatever," but Sally "still feels very happy with myself. I still have my choices to make. I just have a very strong sense of independence, and I have to work it out on my own." Thus Sally's principle of differentiation is, finally, an insistence that all people accept responsibility for their lives, as she has for hers.

Wealthy Differentiators — Eleanor Fox

Eleanor Fox is Craig Cabot's counterpart in status, charm, and elegance, but they could not be more different in their distributive judgments. She is a seventy-year-old widow, is descended from a long line of aristocratic Yankees, and lives in a restored manor on twenty-five acres of land. Her norms seem only slightly influenced by the twentieth century; she combines strong ascriptive views with modesty, intelligence, independence, and a sharp sense of humor.

Socializing Domain   Eleanor endorses a norm of results for punishment and reward of children: "I don't believe in sparing the rod, in that if the child doesn't behave, they can be spanked." Requiring her rather "spoiled" children to do chores for their allowances "would have been much better for them," partly because training children in certain skills "broadens them."

As this last phrase implies, however, Eleanor uses an ascriptive norm more than a norm of results. For example, Eleanor and her husband usually "made decisions together," but marital equality has its limits: "A friend of mine just depends upon her husband to do everything for her, even scrub the floor or clean the stove. Why, I wouldn't *dream* of having my husband scrub the floor or clean the stove. I'd do that myself. And why shouldn't a woman? If she's a housewife, that's her job. Her husband's working. And her husband *has* been working, [if] he's retired."

Similarly, Eleanor wants schools to be run according to criteria of results, competitive procedures, and, especially, ascription. Accomplishments should determine grades — "I don't see any other way of grading them, excepting what they're capable of doing" — and punishments — "The teacher should be allowed to correct the young people and use a ruler on their hand." Teamwork teaches students to "learn from each other" and "get along well together," but competition is even more valuable, since it "stimulates them into wanting to improve their ways both in athletics and in studies."

But ascriptive issues matter more than discipline or achievement in Eleanor's evaluation of a school. She worries that her grandson's Montessori school is too lax, but "you can't really go to public school down there [in New York City]. You might be two or three in a whole class, the white ones. Not that the white or black makes too much difference — the black children, they're darling. But, I don't know, there's something so that they don't get on together the same way. Maybe they don't grasp things as fast."

She cried when her daughter danced with a black student at a high school dance. "I said, 'You couldn't, Vicky, you couldn't.' I couldn't conceive of her allowing a black person to put his arm around her or get that close." She reports proudly, however, that she has since "broadened out more. I have even *kissed* a black person, man."

Thus Eleanor relies exclusively on a principle of differentiation in the socializing domain. Her only lapse — the "spoiling" of her children — she now regrets.

The Economy Eleanor relies just as heavily on differentiating norms in the economic domain. The only example she can give of possible underpayment is low and decreasing dividends to stockholders: "I resent the fact that the workmen are resentful, because they say, 'The companies are making a tremendous profit, and they should share it with them!' I can't see it that way. Because if the businesses were making a tremendous profit, the dividends were [that is, would be] going up and up, and you were [that is, would be] getting money, equalizing with the labor going up. But they haven't done that in a long time. It's been really quite hard." Businessmen deserve much higher salaries than workmen, for two reasons. First, "It takes a tremendous amount of knowledge to run a business. None of the laborers would be able to do it. They've got to have people that know more than other people. And in order to do it [that is, attract them to your business], you should pay them." But this orientation toward a norm of results and the market is only a brief digression from her more important consideration — again, an ascriptive norm: "You feel sorry for the people who are not getting everything you're getting, [but] you just can't have a country without labor, without different classes in it. You've got to have a laboring class with less pay. You're going communistic if you do [try to eliminate wide differences in pay], and I don't think it's possible. And when you get communistic, it lasts for how long? Then the country goes to pieces." After all, a nation "cannot *live* without people who are willing to collect the garbage."

Like Sally, Eleanor explains poverty through a vague attribution of laziness, which is "part of their personality and probably home life. Same as with a crime, I think that that's inborn." She has more to say about wealth, which people acquire and retain only through "brains and know-how to handle their affairs." But like Ruth Sennett, she feels that the upwardly mobile have shakier claims to wealth than do those who inherit and therefore need more defense. Speaking of the nouveau riche, she feels compelled to say, "It's their *right* that they should have an opportunity to take advantage of it [their new position]. I don't resent it at all." After all, society benefits from the existence of the rich. Asked how, she responds, "Of course, I always loved kings and queens. The English still worship their kings and queens."

As all of this suggests, Eleanor is an unabashed advocate of class, racial, and sexual distinctions. The upper class "really knows quite a lot," and the middle class, in which she includes herself, "knows more" than members of the working class do. "And whereas I'm very fond of some of them, I wish that they knew a little bit more about some things, particularly if they try to say things in one way, and I know perfectly well they're another way." Knowledge, she says, is a good way to measure class because "people get to be smart from generation after generation of the way they're brought up. Maybe a great-great-great-grandfather wasn't very smart, but he got smarter, then the next generation got smarter," and so on, until individual merit shades into inherited position, just as Bagehot said it would.

Eleanor's racism also stems from this blurring of norms of results and ascription. Black inferiority is "inherited. After all, they did come from a hot country where everybody in the heat of the day will take a nap. You just don't have the ambition to do anything in that terrible heat. And having for generations lived there, they are just plain lazy from the environment. It lasts on." Eleanor recognizes that "so many poor *white* trash are *worse* than some of the blacks," and that some blacks are "down-cast, just trodden upon"; she struggles to overcome her own prejudice. But still, "They've got to get their education slower, start at a lower level. *If* they can do it, *fine*, I have no objections whatsoever to a colored person taking a job alongside of a white."

Finally, Eleanor is "not a suffragette at all," for three reasons that also mix norms of results and ascription. First, married women are "taking so many jobs that put other men, other families completely out [of work]." Second, women are less fit for certain jobs, such as driving limousines: "A man, generally speaking, is a better driver. [Also] is she going to be capable of lifting those heavy suitcases way up on top of that limousine?" But, once again, an ascriptive claim underlies these pragmatic arguments: "I don't see any sense in woman equality anyway. A woman was born to raise her children." As with her view of blacks, Eleanor knows that she is out of step with most people she respects, and that her own experiences do not support all her beliefs. She has had *"very* good" women doctors; her sister-in-law is "a *beautiful* driver"; she prides herself on her ability to build furniture, shingle roofs, and manage complex financial affairs. But still, "I just don't want a woman doing things like being ministers."

Thus Eleanor combines norms of results and ascription in the economic domain, so that she assumes that merit depends on class, race, or sex. She knows that her own experiences often contradict her beliefs and that her views are now outmoded, but she remains unusually illiberal, or at least unusually candid.

The Polity   Eleanor's few political observations are mostly differentiating, and she is more aware of middle- and upper-class problems than of lower-class ones. For example, she opposes rent controls because "I feel sorry for the landlords. Everything's gone up for them, and how can they be squeezed into not letting them increase the rents? Absolutely ridiculous." Inheritance taxes are "awful, because it's in the family, and the family has a perfect right to hand it down to their children if they want to." Arguments about motivating parents or providing for children are superfluous; simple possession is enough. If only to demonstrate, however, that no one is entirely predictable, Eleanor is "on the fence" about the right of eminent domain. It's "heartbreaking to see roads go through property," but still "they've got to find someplace to put these roads." In this case, at least, community needs dominate individual property rights.

Although she accepts taxes as a necessary evil, Eleanor describes the nation's worst problem as "the tremendous spending. It is terrible, going up and up and up, and I don't see how they can expect to get out of debt when they keep giving more monies to people who demand it for this and that." She has few ideas for new programs because "I don't think there's anything left"; her only suggestion is a mandatory public jobs program. Too many of the nonworking poor "are just plain lazy, and it's dreadful the amount of welfare that's given for people sitting around doing nothing. If they're given money, they should report to work."

Eleanor, like Sally, wholeheartedly endorses equality defined as equal political freedom, and she is pleased with its level in the United States. No group has too little influence, except "big businesses which are really held back" by requirements "to hire people who are not equipped mentally" and "conservation and all that." She "can't conceive" of members of Congress "paying any attention to anyone except the people that they represent. They should do it, so I just figure they *do* do it." The courts are too lenient, but they favor no groups unfairly. Surprisingly, she worries at one point that "if you're born into a family that has gotten something, you have an advantage," but generally she is pleased with the political equality she sees in the United States.

Also like Sally, Eleanor's main goal is freedom — "the biggest thing there is" in America. "Everything you do, it goes back to the freedom that you have to do what you want." But she fears that "the poorer people are demanding such tremendous things, which do away with your class. As soon as you do that, you get into your communists, and there just isn't any reason to use your brains or do anything." In the 1950s, she thought Joseph McCarthy "was crazy," but in retrospect, "He was *right*. The place is full of communists doing their best to get this country back down."

It is astonishing, in view of all of this, how mild are Eleanor's objections to equalizing income when the subject is divorced from communism. Although initially the rich "might quit their jobs," boredom would bring them back to work. Although initially the poor might "squander" their new wealth, they "will gradually learn" financial responsibility. She denies Sally's main objection: "I don't think it [equality] *would* be dull. Everyone would be doing different things, 'cause everyone's so different." Equality would reduce useless competition to "keep up with the Jones." Finally, and most surprisingly, utopia "would be everyone living on the same level and doing their jobs, and everyone happy. This is so ridiculous — all those people scrapping with each other and can't agree." Equality is impossible, not undesirable: "If everyone was peaceful and happy, why, might as well abolish the monetary system. People were happy when they used to exchange things, give a barrel of beer for a barrel of flour. There wasn't the jealousy of people having so much money. [One could] just do the things that would appeal to you. No, if the world could get along, then all this argument and trouble over money — after all, most of the troubles boil down to that — why would anyone object?"

How can we explain this reversal? Eleanor has none of Barbara Azlinsky's liberal guilt; her ascriptive norms are out of step with "the modern world," but she is not ashamed of or defensive about them. Nor does she share Vincent Sartori's desire for equality combined with fear of government; she trusts politicians to "do their very best." Rather, she has an atavistic classical or medieval view of equality as "an intimation of ultimate perfection but not an appropriate standard for existing society, . . . because economic, political, and cultural circumstances combine to make inequality seem a synonym for order and natural necessity." Equality is "the ideal order either of a remote and irrevocable past, or of those exceptional individuals capable of extraordinary wisdom, asceticism, and virtue."[5] Eleanor describes just such a past and such a class; she is neither a Platonist nor a medieval mystic, but echoes of these thoughts persist in hers.

Wealthy Differentiators — Bernard Bloomfield

To Bernard Bloomfield, ascriptive criteria are obstacles to be conquered, not pillars of a stable social structure. One basis for his disagreement with Eleanor is obvious: she descends from a long line of Yankee aristocrats, whereas Bernard's parents were poor immigrant Russian Jews. In 1976, he was fifty-three years old, earning $80,000 a year, and extremely proud of the distance he had come.

Socializing Domain   Bernard's impoverished childhood gave him an intense desire "to get beyond just working with tools in a shop such as my father had. I didn't like the environment of that type of person, I wanted a higher level of living." This was less a material drive — "The money didn't bother me at all. That really had no influence" — than a social one — "It was important that I would be associated with people with more intellect and intelligence than what came with the typical construction worker. That was the biggest motivation I had." Bernard is as sensitive as Eleanor to class and status, but he views them as subjects of individual choice, not immutable forces to which one must adjust.

Bernard strives to give his children the same drive. He taught them not to "cop out. Once they commit themselves [to a decision], they have to go through with it." He taught his son the work ethic by cutting off his allowance after his Bar Mitzvah. He "became very upset" until Bernard told him " 'where you can earn your money. You come with me down to the lab on Saturdays and in the summertime, and that's where you'll get paid. As long as you're home, this is what you're going to do.' " Even though his daughters "were the responsibility of their mother, as far as what they had and didn't have to do," they too had to earn all spending money for college, so that they would learn "some values in terms of how you spend your money, and where you get it, and what it's worth."

Bernard wants schools also to prepare students for the hard life ahead. Grading systems should teach students to "learn to face it as it really is. If you are not an A student, there's nothing wrong with it, but you should know. Because it's the bottom line; and it's preparation for your adult life. If you need $18,000 a year to support your family, and you make $15,000, there is no sense in covering it up. The sooner you know it, the better off you are." Bernard judges all teaching techniques by their likely effect on future productivity. Children should learn to work together because "there's hardly any profession of work that doesn't require cooperation with other people." Competition for its own sake is misguided: "It's not that important for me to be better than my friend. The motivation is [that is, should be] to create objectives that are important for *me* to work towards." Thus he prefers the egalitarian norm of cooperation to the differentiating norm of competition because the former increases productivity and the latter does not.

Bernard's insistence on achievement is not, in his eyes, hardheartedness. When he was a child, after every report card students and their parents lined up in front of the teacher, who "just read off all the things that you did wrong, and all the grades that you got. And then you got belted in front of everybody." This system "served the purpose, so that you worked. There was that conscientious effort to get past the point where you're not going to be belted or shamed." Modern permissiveness is simply an indication that "parents don't *care* with a lot of these kids." Harshness is not an end in itself; loving parents and caring teachers should use strict discipline to help children succeed as adults.

The Economy   Bernard left a promising corporate job in his youth because "I want to have control over what I do. If I've accomplished certain things, I'm entitled to that benefit." These two sentences encapsulate his economic values: people are responsible for their actions, and they deserve the full measure of reward or penalty for what they achieve or fail to achieve.

Thus Bernard sees unions as inherently unjust because they force some workers to receive less and permit others to receive more than they merit. Salaries should be negotiated individually. Only if they fail to get education or training, or if they lack commitment, are unorganized workers vulnerable to employers' greater resources and options.[6] A good worker can always find a job at a fair wage.

Wages as well as employment should depend on achievements. Training, seniority, and effort are irrelevant unless they are "responsible for more productivity." Insistence even on cost-of-living raises rebounds against employees, because after a secretary works up to a salary of $175 a week, Bernard fires her and hires someone new at $140. "Now the one for $175, she has to go accept a job for $125 and loses her seniority." A norm of results sometimes shades into a war of all against all: productivity can be the only criterion in determining layoffs "because I still have competition. It's survival for me. My customers don't buy from me because I'm in greater need of a profit than my competitor. So the rules should be the same for everyone, without trying to appear cold and heartless."

Bernard is not unidimensional, however. Schooling must be available to all; only then can workers be penalized for lacking in education. Teachers are underpaid, and doctors are overpaid "even to the point of sinful." He would pay higher taxes to aid needy, deserving workers. Even though so much charity "might not be right," he adds defensively, "Still, I don't think I could live with myself if I knew [of] a house where people were starving and [the] father was willing to work."

Bernard abandons this softness when discussing wealth and poverty. He "admires" the rich "for their courage, foresight, and accomplishing certain endeavors of such sizeable proportions to propel them into the elevations that they stand in." But those who inherit money must "utilize their time constructively" to earn his respect. A wealthy playboy is "disgusting," whereas Bernard's son has "worked to qualify and justify to sit in the driver's seat. [So] he won't really inherit the business, he's sort of been fitted to it."

In fact, the proper use of wealth is itself a burden that merits reward: "Everybody working for me needs me as a leader in order to preserve their jobs." Even worse, the possibility of losing great wealth is so frightening that "there's a risk of doing permanent physical damage to yourself as the custodian of this kind of money. So therefore there's a fee attached to it, and a person's entitled to the rewards if he can just successfully manage this money." At this point, the emphasis on productivity becomes completely circular: one is entitled to keep one's wealth as a reward for keeping one's wealth.

Bernard explains most poverty as "complacency or laziness," but there are important exceptions. For example, blacks have physical disadvantages that Jews lack: "I could change my name, have some facial surgery done, and say I was anything that I had to be in order to get a job. They couldn't do that." Others "just follow the same pattern [as their parents] because they don't know any different, and there's nobody to yank them out of it and expose them to the real world." For these people, "Society has the responsibility for upgrading the minimum standard of living" to provide "a starting kit." But we must beware of too much aid, because "we still need those people to go pick in the tobacco fields."

How can Bernard move so quickly from harshness to concern and back to harshness? As with Sally White, the idea of equal opportunity provides an answer. Bernard wants to ensure all people a fair chance to advance; he does not care if some people muff their chance and become menial laborers. With a few exceptions, "In this country, the opportunities are there for those that are aggressive and demonstrate the ability. What made this country grow and *will make* this country grow is the fact that there's no door closed to you." Even apparent structural obstacles can be incentives: "For example, going into chemistry *wasn't* necessarily a *good* decision, [because] Jewish people didn't get jobs in industry. [But] where somebody else might look at it as a barrier, it really wasn't, because if you know the other guy is going to get the job before you, and you've got any ambition, you know you've got to be better than he is. So then it becomes a built-in advantage that you're not even aware of, but just out of survival you work harder." Once all people are given an equal "starting kit," they are on their own. They control their accomplishments, which should control their rewards.

The Polity   Bernard is unique among respondents in claiming that "I could care less whether I pay another $2000 of taxes or $10,000, as long as it's not 100 percent. I don't care, because so what?" This apparently anomalous view makes sense in light of his drive toward achievement and status rather than material rewards. His goals are clear: "creating jobs and being responsible for so many families," making his own family "proud of what I'm doing," and "the satisfaction of being able to make the business happen." He does not value money as an end in itself; he values it, instead, as an indicator of degrees of success or failure.

But Bernard is not completely indifferent to taxation and property rights. Tax incentives—not "tax loopholes"—stimulate the economy and entice exceptional people into difficult jobs. High inheritance taxes are unjust and unwise: "Why should I work all my life and run the risk that three idiots that got jobs out of patronage are going to decide whether my daughter is going to get my money? No way. Before I'll do that, I'll stop working. The country can't grow that way." Tenant strikes "can't be justified"; even if a landlord "wants to abandon a building, that's his privilege. If a person is in financial distress, he must seek relief, or his physical well-being will be damaged, and there's nothing that's worth that, right? So he's going bankrupt in the most expedient way he knows. He's entitled to it." Thus, although Bernard does not care deeply about his own taxes and property, he does care that property rights be upheld and that tax levels encourage and reward success.

With a few exceptions, Bernard wants social programs abolished. A few are valuable: we need national health insurance "because the medical field *just don't stop* at any point" and regulation of utilities because they "just kick the whole economy off balance and raise havoc with everybody's budget." But beyond that, "I have some pretty firm opinions of free lunches." Unemployment compensation should only "give you temporary support while a total effort is made on your part to find another means of endeavor." The workweek is too short. Students should pay college tuition because "anything you get free is worth nothing." People have no right to guaranteed housing, food, or environmental quality; all they have is "a right to have an opportunity to be deserving and earn this." Free lunches are just as wrong for the rich as for the poor. Federal subsidies simply make favored industries flabby and deny others equal opportunity. Even though unbridled competition "means certain people getting hurt," that is "part of the casualties of war. You just have to pay that price."

Like Sally and Eleanor, Bernard bases his political views on his passionate attachment to individual liberty. He echoes James Madison in one concern about social programs: "If you gave government all the power you would like to see 'em have so they could move swiftly [on desirable policies], then if it got into the wrong hands of too many Nixons, it would be destroying too many people." His other concern is more philosophical: "If you want total security, then you have to give up your independence. If you want the government to support you and do for you, then there's no way you're going to have anything to say anymore. They're going to be saying everything and doing everything."

Bernard fears that a trend toward choosing security over freedom has already begun, because politicians "cater to their [welfare recipients'] whims in order to solicit their voting support." Like left-wing critics and William Graham Sumner, he castigates the helping professions which "thrive on having the have-nots support them while they try to get something from the haves to give to the have-nots." But his solutions differ from those of the leftists and even from Sumner's. To stop the "very dangerous" trend toward dependency among welfare recipients and special interest groups alike, he suggests giving taxpayers a weighted vote, so that citizens with the greatest investment in the nation's economic stability and freedom would have the loudest voice in decision-making. After all, "If I was paying the bills, they're not going to give everything away." He simply dismisses the idea of equalizing incomes as a blatant violation of both individual liberty and distributive norms of productivity.

If Eleanor harks back to Plato and St. Augustine, Bernard recalls the social Darwinists. His utopia would make only fragmentary, nonpolitical changes; he would like "just to take illness away and just say, 'You live to a certain point, and then you drop dead' without suffering. You go to a certain point and, like your car, she just stop running." More change would only be for the worse: "We're living in the greatest country in the world. It's proven. So we can't change the basics."

Like the other differentiators, Bernard mixes harshness and idealism. Authorities must discipline subordinates for their own sake; achievers must win and nonachievers lose; sometimes the world is a jungle; individual freedom to get ahead is the greatest value. Such a system may be harsh, but through it, in the long run justice will prevail, and everyone who survives will be better-off.

Consistent differentiators share several characteristics. Above all else, they seek individual liberty, defined as negative freedom. They feel few if any of the internal conflicts among norms that respondents who follow the dominant pattern of beliefs feel so strongly. But they are not unidimensional fanatics. They all hold opinions that contradict their dominant views; they are aware of these divergences; and they do not feel compelled to eliminate them in the interest of total consistency. None feel any of the tension about redistribution that all the followers of the dominant pattern feel, because none feel a disjunction between economic and political values.

Differentiators also differ among themselves. Sally emphasizes results with a tinge of ascription; Eleanor emphasizes ascription with a tinge of results; Bernard emphasizes results and social Darwinist competition and vehemently rejects ascription. Eleanor favors fixed and largely closed classes; Sally seeks equal opportunity to advance through government action; Bernard seeks equal opportunity to advance through government inaction. Sally began and remains poor; Eleanor began and remains rich; Bernard began poor and has become rich.

I have too few respondents to be able to identify why these particular people hold an alternative rather than the dominant set of norms. I can, however, compare their arguments to those of egalitarians and followers of the three-part pattern in order to illuminate the range and implications of distributive views. But that task comes later; first, we must examine the egalitarians.

Egalitarians among the Poor — Salvador Tivolli

A few respondents use a principle of equality to evaluate all three domains of life. Consider Salvador Tivolli, who is sixty years old and lives with his second wife in a house she inherited. In 1976 she earned $7000 a year as a clerk; he received $3800 in disability pay for an accident that left him with a permanently frozen hip joint and constant pain. On this money, they are "just meeting ends, just clear it every week." His pension seems so ludicrous that, for the only time during the entire interview, he is bereft of words: "I only get $320 a month. I worked forty years. I paid a lot of money in that Social Security. Forty years is a long time." Worst of all, however, is his "disgust" that his disability leaves him "hanging around without any work to do."

Socializing Domain   Salvador learned from his father that working at a job takes precedence over everything else; Salvador quit school after six years because "we couldn't do the homework, 'cause my father used to give us work to do at night." This hard work kept Salvador and his twelve siblings from going on welfare, but his lack of education caused one of his biggest disappointments — his inability to join the police force. "I took the written [test]. Couldn't make it. It hurts, you know." He cannot understand why students drop out: "They got a good chance to get a good education, and they don't care. I say to them, 'You're gonna be like me someday. I wanted to *be* something. I couldn't be it because my father wouldn't give me an education.'" Like Maria, Salvador has learned through experience that hard work does not substitute for education in efforts to get ahead.

He shows the same ambivalence — acceptance of a norm of investments combined with distress at its consequences — in discussing his former wife and children. After his children were born, he and his wife "never got along. For twenty-seven years, I slept one place, she slept another place." He rejected divorce because "I wanted to make sure my children were old enough when I left this house. A lot of people, they walk out when their kids are six months old. I can't see that, the childrens gotta suffer. Let her go out, do anything she wants — at least I know I'm bringing food home to my kids." He will "never forget the day my son turned twenty-one. I said, 'This is it. Give me my clothes.' Out I went." He accepted the responsibility implicit in an investment norm, but he received few if any rewards from it and rejected it as soon as he could.

Salvador has no ambivalence about a norm of investment in schools. He laughs at the very thought, but if by some miracle he were a teacher with slow, but hardworking, students, "I would give 'em good [grades]. If they tried, they deserve it." Sports should not be competitive; instead, "if the kid [isn't] doing right, there should be correction on that, 'cause the girl or the boy that wants to play, he's trying hard to get in."

Thus in the socializing domain, Salvador relies mainly on a norm of investments. He does not always like the results of insisting upon personal responsibility and hard work, but his allegiance to the norm provides a solid, realistic base for the egalitarianism he displays in the other domains. No one hearing him describe his childhood, his disability, and his marriage could suspect him of softhearted romanticism.

The Economy   Salvador is much more eloquent about economic issues. He talks long and lovingly of his thirty years in a plant making cardboard cartons. First as a worker and later as a foreman, he strove to develop a sense of community among his workers, for three reasons. The first was personal inclination: his greatest asset, he feels, is his ability to "get along with everybody. That's what I do, make friends." But second, by treating his workers as equals, "I got more work out of my men. They always worked 100 percent for me." After their morning orders, "I never bothered them," except that "unlike all the other foremens, I used to eat lunch with all of 'em, change my clothes, take showers with'em and everything. I had my own office up there, but I wouldn't [use it]." If the supervisor, too, would "mingle in with the men, he'd be better off. They'll work for him more." Finally, Salvador seeks fellowship among workers because the factory *is* their community: "*We made* that plant. It was like a home to me over there. I loved it. When it closed down, it broke my heart. 'Cause we started from scratch over there."

Salvador believes more strongly in workers' rights, collective identity, and the equal worth of all people than any other respondent. Workers, for example, could more easily take managerial positions than vice versa. Managers "couldn't last eight hours on an assembly line," but workers could easily manage, since "they got the girls to do the paperwork for you, they got the foremens to produce the work for you, all you do is sit down." In fact, workers are worth more to a company than supervisors. For one thing, most managers "don't know nothing about production," since they got their job through "knowing somebody." For another, the manager's entire worth depends on his employees: "If the workers didn't produce, what could the manager do? They'd [the "top brass"] get rid of him, 'cause he's not producing." He gleefully describes how his shift once, in fact, used a slowdown to "get rid of" a harsh and stingy foreman. Thus workers should choose foremen, make production decisions, and earn more in comparison to managers.

Salvador does not demand equal pay; a supervisor who "is responsible," knows his business, works hard, and treats his workers well deserves high pay. But Salvador can think of only one supervisor in thirty years who deserved his salary. Usually the manager "takes money out of *his* [the worker's] pocket. He wouldn't be in business if he wasn't taking out of his pocket. They gotta make a profit." Salvador here is unconsciously discovering Marx: managers' pay and company profit both depend on expropriating the surplus value of workers' labor.

All workers should be paid the same except for maintenance men, who have a "dirtier job," and press operators, who have "a rough job." Neither seniority, education, nor productivity merit higher pay. Piecework is both "the ruination of production," because it rewards hurried and sloppy work, and unjust, because it penalizes one worker for a breakdown in another part of the interdependent productive process. Thus equal wages among workers, like equal status, are both fairer and more efficient than differentiation.

What little Salvador says about the wealthy is uncomplimentary. "The wife'll say, 'Well, I worked hard today,' and here she's got a maid doing her work," and the husband is worse: "People like that gotta have something on the side to make money. They get rich that far — they ain't gonna make it by working. I ain't seen anybody made worth a millionaire by working. They invested, yea, but they invested something on the side too, that people don't even know [about]." The only paths to wealth other than dishonesty are luck, disciplined betting on the horses, and moonlighting, which makes "a guy of sixty-two look ninety." Salvador does not regret his failure to follow any of these paths, because he does not envy the rich. "Money *turns* you"; when former friends "get up there, they don't even bother with you. Never call you, come out to the house. They think they're the Joneses or something. Who needs friends like that?" Contrast this attitude with Vincent Sartori's: he hates the rich because he envies them, whereas Salvador dislikes the rich enough to reject them. "I hope I don't become a millionaire if it gonna turn me. I'd rather live the way I'm living now. Friends is worth more than money is worth to me."

The poor, in contrast, "get along better. They ain't got nothing, but they'll offer you coffee, whatever they got. They got a big heart, they're good." Salvador's explanation of poverty and welfare is more complex than his explanation of wealth. Some welfare recipients "can't help it. Either husbands run out on 'em, or they got in trouble, got three or four kids, she can't work." But he is more often, and more eloquently, critical of the many welfare poor who "don't wanna work, all they want is welfare." He describes young healthy women or old healthy men receiving Medicare, husbands secretly living with families on AFDC, filthy and drunken parents raising their children in hungry squalor. "The government should get an investigation around here, all over, go house to house," to check for fraud, filth, and child abuse.

Salvador's surprising criticism of the poor stems from his work ethic and sense of responsibility. He has nothing but contempt for welfare cheats and irresponsible parents; he has nothing but sympathy for the unemployed, disabled, or working poor. Welfare recipients who refuse even unappealing or ill-paid work should be "punished. Say 'Take the job, or you don't get no more checks.' " Welfare and unemployment pay-ments (he does not distinguish clearly between the two) should be kept lower than the minimum wage to encourage work, except for money ear-marked specifically for needy children. But for "the ones that need it, I'm 100 percent," and he worries that their payments are too low.

Salvador's greatest economic concern is the scarcity of work for the poor and working class. He was unemployed for three years after a lay-off, even though he would "take anything." He tells as many stories of desperate job-hunters as of shirkers, and he finally erupts in anger: "There's no work around, and everything's going up, that's what burns me up! That's what really hurts. How can people live? There's *no work* around." In these circumstances, the old rules of deserving what you earn are simply a mockery, and he insists that either the rules or the circum-stances must be changed.

Salvador's economic egalitarianism is not dogmatic. Some jobs de-serve high pay; some poor people deserve their fate. But factories and so-cieties ought to be communities in which people respect each other, work their hardest, accept their responsibilities, and receive about the same re-wards. More than any other respondent, Salvador seeks Tawney's vision of fellowship through greater equality of income, authority, and status for all community members.

The Polity   Salvador pursues the same themes in the polity, and they again lead him to seek downward redistribution. For example, inheri-tance taxes should be high in order to teach the work ethic to the rich. "Leave 'em enough to get by, [but] let 'em see what a dollar is. [A million-aire's son] don't know what it is to work. All he does is sit down and get in trouble." Furthermore, we need extensive social programs, such as lower college "intermission" [that is, tuition] and "special training schools for even the slow"; we should "import" the British plan for national health insurance. A guaranteed annual income is "a damn good idea. We should have them rights." Even if "they want [to add] a few dollars on taxes, sure, I'd agree with that. At least you know it's going for some good cause."

But the "most problem that we got now" is combined unemployment and inflation. His first policy recommendation is by now familiar: "Spend money to try to create some *jobs*." A mandatory jobs program would both reduce welfare exploitation and "open jobs for people that wanna work. I wish *I* could work. I always worked hard in all my life. You hang around the house, you go crazy. That's rough." This echo of

Craig Cabot gives us an important clue to understanding variations in respondents' egalitarianism. If work violates people's innate wish to do nothing, then the government must motivate people to earn a living through differentiated monetary rewards and fear of starvation. But if work is a right, a means to self-fulfillment, then the government should enable all people to earn a satisfactory living, not demean them through welfare and enforced laziness or through wealth and learned laziness.

If the government does not provide jobs and does permit another Great Depression to occur, "there'd be awful riots, for Christ's sake. I'd support them. A whole gang will go up and burn the White House down. You work all your life to get a home, and then all of a sudden [a] depression comes and you can't afford to pay your taxes, and then you lose everything — boy, that's heartbreaking. Sure, I'd burn the place down. They'd have to kill me. I think a lot of people would do it too." Salvador is no wild-eyed revolutionary; he laughs as he says this. But he does say it. Even a communist state might be preferable to the "rough" future that he now envisions. A Russian coworker described collective farms and concluded, " 'As long as they give me the seed to plant, I don't mind it. They take a quarter of whatever you got, but,' he says, 'you have plenty of food on the table.' " This makes good sense to Salvador: "Well, they make a living, that's all that counts. That's why you're on this earth, to make a living, right? Not to worry about no food on the table." He is "not ashamed" that he voted for a communist aldermanic candidate, since "she had a very good idea. But people don't realize that. They hear that word *communist*, they get scared. It ain't as bad as they think it is."

It is not at all clear how far Salvador would be willing to act on these beliefs. Asked what a "radical" is, he insists, "I don't think it's nice. I don't care *how bad* of an enemy you got, you just *ignore* him, I would never call him radical like that." He prefers legal redress or simply moving to tenant or community takeovers of exploitative landlords and grocery store owners. But, in the final analysis, if the landlord or store owner "can't run the right prices, the community should take over the store," and the government should "give the apartment to the tenants." Similarly, if in the final analysis our society leaves people unemployed and broke, then a communist state is "a *good* idea."

Salvador's support for limits on incomes — "Cut 'em all down. Be better off" — exemplifies this potential radicalism. Again, he seeks community through equality: if we were "all one class people, one wouldn't be showing off to the other one. This one here can't say, 'What does he make? What does the other guy make?' It'd be better one flat rate." With monetary competition minimized, "All the people [might] get together. People ain't pulling together now. Like a ball team—they don't pull together, they're gonna lose the *game*. Same thing."

Salvador wants political, as well as economic, equality, but he sees politicians, who "got their hand in the pie someplace" and "wanna be big wheels," as no better than businessmen. Politicians too often respond to special interest groups at the expense of the general public. Minorities—"The black, they get what they want. Don't let anybody kid you. They'll go up and march in front of Washington, they get something"—are as favored as the rich. "Businessmen always have more to say than anybody else. His friends [the president's] he'll listen to. The outsider, he won't listen to." Ordinary citizens are ignored: "Like, when you write to the president, you wanna hear something? His *secretary* answers the letters for him!"[7]

The courts treat people even less equally and therefore less justly. Watergate criminals "shoulda got a stiff penalty [and] no parole." But "If you don't know nobody, you ain't got justice. Some poor kid can go in there, and he'll get six months; some kid well-off whose father's a lawyer, he'll get probation." Finally, judges are "scared of the blacks," to whom they give "too much of a break." He concludes his survey of the courts by saying, "They call that justice? I don't call that justice."

Salvador does not base his desires for political and economic equality on an assumption that all men are created equal; the famous phrase "means that everybody's built the *same*, created the *same*, which ain't." He does base his desires on a belief in equal human worth: "I never put myself better than anybody else," and "I don't think anybody's better than me." Even if "they have more money than me, as far as friends, I'm better than them." Utopia would recognize and respond to equal human worth; there would be "no wars, plenty of work. That way nobody will be on welfare. They'd get along good. Sure, because no one would say, 'Oh, Jesus, he's on welfare, and I'm supporting him!' Also you can't say, 'Well, he's making more than me.' We're all making the same now. We all have the same." But Salvador has no hopes for achieving his wishes: the rich will "never, never change," and the government will "never do anything." But a clearer egalitarian vision would be hard to find. Those who live up to their obligations deserve respect, friendship, and help; fellowship among peers is both more enjoyable and more productive than competition in a hierarchy. Shirkers should be taught the joys of contribution, whether by denying the rich their inheritance or the poor their welfare check. Work is honorable; workers are the most valuable members of society. Most striking, Salvador rejects the easy route of postponing his egalitarian demands and judgments until some ideal future; he uses them to measure his own behavior and that of his bosses, fellow citizens, and political leaders. As a result, he subjects American society to a critique much more radical than he realizes.

Egalitarians among the Poor — Rod Thompson

Rod Thompson, who was introduced in chapter two, is as intelligent as he is inarticulate. His egalitarianism has a different flavor from Salvador's; he cares less about the virtues of community than about its pleasures. Life is there for enjoyment, and equality seems the best route to happiness for all.

Socializing Domain   For Rod, equality begins at home. Parents must treat all their children "on the same level. You can't give [to] one, some to another one, and leave the other one off in the corner." Parents should also teach children to share because "it's really important to have friends, so you give people just a little added incentive to like you. So you share with them a little more, and you do without for a while." After all, most conflicts over goods are due to "jealousy, not that you really need the thing." If good relations matter more than "the thing" itself, then any resolution to conflict is more important than the nature of that resolution. Thus Rod cheerfully yields to his friends' suggestions because he does not really care what they do, as long as they do it together. On those few occasions when he and his girlfriend disagree with their "hang-out gang," they "just go your separate ways and do it. There's no big problem like that."

Easygoing accommodation characterized most Thompson family decisions when Rod was growing up. Sometimes difficult decisions were simply avoided — "A piece of pie left? You had your usual arguments about it, and it just went back into the refrigerator" — or decided by ascription — "Big brother beat up on medium-sized brother, 'til little brother got what he wanted." But most often, "we all sat down and decided where we would go and what we'd like to do. There were no major hassles." His family still shares work with more concern for smooth and quiet accomplishment than for fairness or proper rewards: "There's no set thing to do. Everybody knows that there are certain things to do; who's ever around to do them can do them."

The complement to this apparently effortless cooperation is the fact that family members "like to make their own decisions and do what they think is right." Rod cherishes his independence: he will do without new clothes or rock concert tickets rather than ask his parents for money. The

Thompson family, then, exemplifies fellowship rather than identity. Its members are cooperative, but independent, peers, not tightly-knit nurturers and dependents. In simplest terms, Rod was taught to foster equality more than respond to need.

But Rod is not egalitarian only because sharing goods and chores is easier than fighting about them. He has a tougher streak. He praises competition because it makes "you set your standards higher than the week before." He praises his parochial high school for teaching him that "discipline" is "real important. It was a hard adjustment, but it was all right. It works." Furthermore, his relaxed manner is a conscious, and sometimes difficult, choice. When his father tells him what to do "after four years of [his] doing the same thing every day," he forces himself to "just grit my teeth and mutter under my breath. It doesn't do any good to tell him off. It'll only get both of us mad for longer than we'd be [if he says nothing]." He refuses to show anger because "I wouldn't give anybody the privilege of getting me mad. Just a prideful thing." Instead, he tries to "get away, go to your room" and lose his temper in private.

Thus Rod's casual egalitarianism is not casually derived. Because "you always want everybody to like you," he tries "to make the wrong a right" by swallowing anger, sharing goods, abdicating decisions, and shouldering extra work. He avoids Maria's feeling of martyrdom to family, since he lacks her economic constraints and personal sacrifices. Thus he is cheerful rather than embittered, relaxed rather than resigned. But like her, he deliberately chooses to make life easier for those he cares about.

The Economy   Since Rod lacks Salvador's rich work experience, his discussion of the economy is thinner and more abstract. Nevertheless, he combines criteria of effort and social contribution to determine fair wages. Thus, for example, community college teachers are underpaid in comparison to Ivy League professors. The latter are "superqualified, but they're not actually teaching, they're more like supervising," since their smart students learn mainly on their own. But "it's really a lot tougher to get it through to" less willing or less intelligent students; therefore teachers of lower status deserve more pay. He advises me to tell my professors that they are overpaid and should return some of their salaries—then warns me that "it won't work." But his point is no joke; if job status and social contribution do not coincide, the latter should dominate and reduce income inequality.

Regardless of how salaries are set, "no way" should any job be much more lucrative than any other: "They just don't need it. There's no reason for that. There can't be that much of a difference in value." Rod's explanation of large pay differentials is a tangled, but intelligible, theory of exploitation of workers' surplus value: "Whoever pays the salaries are benefiting more from the people they're paying than the people that they're paying are benefiting from them. So that's the only reason why they did it [that is, hire and pay workers]." As we saw in chapter two, justice would lead to incomes between $20,000 and $40,000: "Better yet, you could have everybody make the same thing."

Rod's feelings range from outrage to cynicism to pity when he thinks about the wealthy. The very rich are "disgusting." Some inherit, some "just lucked out," some are dishonest — but none worked their way up. By the time they are wealthy, "they probably don't actually work [at all]. People below them do all the work. They just walk in, 'So long, good job, fellas. I'm paying you well to do this. You're paying me well, too.' Go off to the golf course, change their clothes five times a day, go to cocktail parties."

Rod moves from anger to amusement when he shifts from the Rockefellers to the upper middle class — moving, in his words, from four Mercedes Benzes to three. Some of the moderately rich did work for their wealth and should be permitted to keep it. But note the cynicism in this description of a well-heeled party: "House was enormous, kegs of Heineken — his *own* kegs. Probably got a new lawn put in [after the party]. Probably Astro-turf. Big huge German shepherds guarding the place, probably had bodyguards running around in their swimming trunks trying to be secret. I got the impression that the [his friend's] father was born forty with two rich kids, a nice tall stately wife, and they were just placed there like that. Not like they got in trouble when they were kids and stole ice cream from a truck. They always *owned* the ice cream trucks."

Rod is neither awed by nor envious of the rich, for several reasons. First, "They're never happy. They got four or five wives. They always run down to Mexico to get their quickie divorces, then ten minutes later the same guy's doing the marriage for them. That seems to take the joy out of it." Second, they are deprived of the chance to succeed in their own right: "A lot of the things that make happiness are tough, but when it all works out, it is worthwhile. [The middle class] can tell people that they did it on their own, and they get a special pride out of that. They like that more than marrying into your wife's inheritance." Finally, and most important, ascriptive snobbery is offensive. His rich friend's father "talked and laughed with us," but when his wife or other adults appeared, he "had to have class, present an image. You're placing yourself on a pedestal, you want to be noticed. You're saying, 'Look at my car, and my outfits.' " The middle class, in contrast, does not "parade around. Down to earth and natural and talk actually what you feel." Rod, too, is "content getting not lost in society, but being more a part of it than being set away from it." Thus, like Salvador and unlike Vincent, Rod can avoid the intense ambivalence of both hatred and envy of the rich.

Rod is much vaguer about the causes and consequences of poverty. Some "are lazy, don't care." Even with more money, "they might not know how to live, go out and spend it stupidly, and when it's all run out, they go right back to laying around drinking their six-packs." But others "might have conceded defeat, just living out their strength" because they cannot find jobs, and "don't know how to function in our society." Still others "are probably *more* hardworking than the rest of us 'cause they're trying to get what they've never had and they see other people have." They are still poor only because "they never even had a chance to be successful. Their ancestors never had a chance." Rod does not sort these explanations and evaluations into clear groups, but he does reverse normal racial stereotypes. Poor whites "are mostly stupid. They don't know their chance when they see it." But most poor blacks "never actually had a chance, there's a lot of things going against them." Like Salvador, Rod sympathizes with structural poverty, but feels contempt for the merely "stupid" poor.

With that exception, Rod consistently seeks social and economic, as well as interpersonal, equality. He rejects ascriptive claims, uses a norm of results defined as social contribution, and mainly relies on an inarticulate assumption of the equal worth of all people.

The Polity   Rod endorses more progressive taxation because he assumes the diminishing marginal utility of money, and because tax loopholes such as charitable deductions simply permit the rich to "present that they're doing something good, when actually they're evading paying more money." Taxation per se is not problematic because "taxes are for the whole, the good, concerned with everybody. Everybody complains about 'em, but they don't realize that the different kind of benefits is what they're getting back." He cites welfare, unemployment compensation, and medical care as benefits of taxation. Only defense expenditures are excessive: "Why do they need to blow up Russia four times? Only hit it once." Redirecting defense expenditures could solve our biggest problem, unemployment, through a jobs program that would both "force" people to "stop living off the government" and satisfy those who "would like to start workin' again."

But the best federal policy would be redistributing wealth downward. As we saw in chapter two, his argument is utilitarian, not based on rights. Regardless of desert, "Guys making astronomical prices, they could cut down to help out the little people. Rockefeller could give a million dollars and not blink an eye. That would help out a few people."

Rod recognizes weaknesses in his views and conducts complex arguments about them with himself. Some hardworking executives do deserve high salaries. We cannot simply confiscate even undeserved holdings. Most seriously, "Some people would be doing everything, and others won't be doing anything, but still making $20,000. You can't do that." The problem is motivation: "You always gotta need some sort of goal to reach. And it just happens that it always seems to be money."

But the incentive problem is not insuperable. For one thing, "If you really liked your job, you'd do it 'cause you want to, not 'cause you have to." Boring jobs should therefore be made more interesting, and he suggests several ways to do that. But most important, even boring work is better than none. "Running around like a nut" at work makes eight hours seem 'like two hours. It wasn't fun — I guess when you look back at it, it *was* [fun]. I just can't imagine collecting unemployment, sleep your eight hours, the other sixteen just sit around doing nothing." Surely, he concludes, others would also want to work after they had had their fill of laziness.

Rod also has a nonutilitarian reason for equalizing incomes. Less competition would make society "better. Most people who are making the same income stick together, go to the same things, function the same way. So if everybody did it [that is, made the same income], hopefully that would happen." Furthermore, if people could not make more money, "you'd have to find other things to do." Thus society would become more diverse, not less, with equality of incomes.

Rod is convinced, however, that we will never create such a society; the rich "band together" against change and, if threatened, would "ruin the people in office, get somebody else in to lower their taxes." Worse yet, the destructive culture of poverty could be eliminated only by taking "a little kid away from his parents when he was first born." And even that may not be soon enough: "Usually if the health of the parents aren't that good, the kid may have brain damage or something like that, so he can't function successfully." Rod concludes helplessly, "I don't want to sound like you should get rid of them or throw 'em in a big furnace," but he can think of no other solution to the apparently permanent effects of poverty.

After running into a dead end on economic change, Rod turns to the subject of political change. "A select few" politicians should not make all decisions, because "they're not that worldly that they have the answer to everything all over the place." Instead, "The individual people [who] live in the actual situation, [and who] really are concerned about housing or food, know the best way to go about doing it." But pessimism again prevails: policy making is "so distant from you that you know you actually don't have any control over it. Just one group is running everything. They're just making you feel like you had something to do with it, letting you work." Rod cannot identify this "one group," but he can spell out the vicious cycle of implications of his analysis. Because "nobody's gonna listen to me," and because "you have other things that are of concern to you, you're just passive about it, don't let your projects be known." We should try to reverse this decline, because after all, "When all them [citizens] pool together, they really *do* count," but he has no suggestions for how to begin. Rod lacks Vincent's clear vision of everyone gathering, conferring, and marching off to confront the mayor, but they share an instinctive, frustrated populism.

Rod's only solution to these economic and political stalemates is to "wipe out society completely and start all over again, with a perfect male and female. I'd be the perfect male, and we'd work from there." He turns serious, however, and continues: "You'd have all your same factories, but people being happy doing what they're doing. Just people hardworking, they get their jobs done, they don't make things worse for other people." For those "that don't want to do nothing, or aren't happy in what they're doing," there is always Hitler's Final Solution, as we saw in chapter two. This is too extreme — "You don't *burn* 'em, I suppose" — but "maybe put all the renegades, all the bad people, on a reservation in their own little world, and let them try to function."

How does a humorous, easygoing egalitarian conclude that the path to the good society goes through elimination of "bad people?" There are several answers. First, the argument should not be taken too seriously: Rod is joking and trying to enliven the conversation. Second, beneath his relaxed amusement is considerable despair. The United States may be moving toward the worst possible society, of "misfits always trying to get by without doing nothin', by using people, stealing their ideas, their money. Progress never seems to work out, we always mess up. The bad seems to always dominate, where it can really hurt the majority." From this perspective, incarcerating evil people may be our only chance for staving off disaster for all.

But most important, absolutism is Rod's temporary escape from the world's terrible complexity. He can counter any argument he makes and then counter that, until he feels helpless to conclude anything. Sometimes he simply evades, usually he chooses the more egalitarian solution, and occasionally he reaches for an absolutist certainty. Consider his discussion of a confiscatory inheritance tax: (1) "Probably shouldn't be one. It's his money, he can do what he wants"; (2) "But if they're not going to distribute it to charity, and they don't need it, they *should* have inheritance tax"; (3) "Maybe a business, he could leave *that* to whoever he wants, but the leftover money, you could distribute *that*"; and (4) "You can't just take his money. I'm a little confused here. I think that's a dumb answer." This is not simply verbiage. In the next sentence, Rod realizes that his confusion comes partly from conflating the desirable and the necessary. He continues: (5) "It would really take a complete different society to straighten out everything. You can't just say, 'He's got a million dollars, he only needs $50,000,' so you take the rest of it"; (6) "It wouldn't be a bad idea. It'd be a good idea. You can't do it, there's too many people around. But if you had your ideal society, that would be the way I would do it"; (7) "I'm going around in circles here. Some people maybe don't deserve it, so why should they get it?" and finally (8) "You can't just kill 'em off in front of a firing squad." It is at this point of complete blockage that Rod begins to argue that "maybe you should wipe out society and start all over again."

Rod is stuck. He is neither a latent Nazi nor a random generator of ideas. Rather, he is too intelligent, too untrained, and too isolated from other political cultures for his own good. He can always see several sides to any argument; he does not know how to weigh and order them; and he lacks access to a political ideology that would help him think through his unconventional beliefs. He will not give up his principle of equality, but he cannot reconcile it with the differentiated real world. Without a political movement to show him how equality might be reached without intolerable insult to justice and practicality, Rod cannot think his way out of his political and philosophical tangle. He concludes only that, "They should change the world but they can't. None of this stuff that we've been talking about is possible." He will therefore continue to focus on "things around you, so that you don't think about it much."

Wealthy Egalitarians—Bruce Abbott

Bruce Abbott blurs the lines between domains more than any other respondent, for two reasons. As a school psychologist, he sees schools as both socializing agency and workplace, and as a thinker he resists distinctions between economy and polity. He judges all domains of life according to a single principle of justice. His normative pattern may be simple, but it is not at all simplistic. He has thought more about distributive justice than any other respondent, and his answers to most questions are complex and sophisticated.

The Socializing Domain With a wealthy minister for a father, Bruce grew up with "a very strong sense of being privileged." This background induces deep humility sometimes—"I got rewarded overly much. That's made me humble"—and a sense of superiority at other times. This superiority in turn vacillates between a compassionate sense of noblesse oblige to aid the needy and an authoritarian insistence that everyone meet his standards of virtue and desert.

These complex emotions and their complex normative counterparts are exemplified by Bruce's work history. He left a lucrative, prestigious job as a psychologist at a small college to work in an inner-city public school in response to his belief that he must earn his privileged status by aiding poor blacks. At first, he was proud of his success in sending many students to white-dominated private schools or colleges. But "when blacks became very angry, it was very difficult for me. There were hard years. So you wondered whether you were doing the right [thing]." Eventually he decided that "the role of a white in dealing with race relations might be to work with the attitudes of white kids," so he transferred to a mostly white suburban school. Through this sequence of jobs, Bruce moved from humility to paternalism to confusion and anger to withdrawal from the front line of race relations—all in a search for justice and his role in promoting it.

Bruce's family norms are simpler; he pursues a principle of equality through a mix of egalitarian norms. His children all had chores, allowances, and privileges, but he felt no "strong compulsion" to provide "oversimplistic" identical treatment. Instead, "we tended to do it a little bit more individualistically, when a kid was *ready* for the bike." Educational expenses also were determined by need: "We tried to help each kid to do what came up for them to do that would be meaningful. In that sense, we treated them equally, but in terms of dollars and cents, no. So our sense of fairness comes out—where the kid's at and where the need is, as opposed to some set formula."

Family decision-making is more strictly equal. He and his wife share household chores and most major decisions. For other issues, Hilda uses his suggestions in budgeting household money; he buys the new car that she wants, "So who's making the decisions, in a lot of ways?" He likes mountains, and she prefers the beach; therefore vacations were spent half in mountain climbing and half in beachcombing.

Bruce is most voluble about justice in the schools. His grading philosophy, for example, has changed with his career changes. In college, teachers should be "hard, demanding, [the student] had to be superior to get an A. Kids that would work like hell and still not answer the question on the final exam, boy! Down would come their grade. Sympathy, yeah, but still, 'This is what you earned — this is what you get.' " He later abandoned such a strict norm of results in favor of "tell[ing] teachers to use grades or anything they can to encourage youth." He gives two reasons. First, even in college, "I became more understanding for kids who are naturally at the bottom of the heap, but who worked like hell." Second, reinforcing this norm of investments was a realization of the overwhelming needs of ghetto students: "Grading became ways to support you. I asked teachers to bend over backward to give you an assignment that you could succeed in, so they could give you an A. So that you would believe next time that you might, so that at least you would *try*. And if you didn't get A, B, or C, then the teachers gave you a plus and said, 'Please complete or do over again.' Never show them an F. 'Cause they've seen so damn many of those, they don't want to deal with them any more. They *can't* deal with [them]. They quit, they won't try." Finally, in his suburban school, he mixes norms of results, investment, and need according to the particular student. Only slow or "turned off" students should be graded solely by effort or need; schools should be "tougher" with the "best kids. Sometimes the teacher needs to say, 'Jesus, you can do a lot better than this sloppy job.' "

As the previous sentence suggests, Bruce, like Rod Thompson, stiffens his egalitarian "softness," in this case by resisting students who see that he "is friendly with people, and constantly come around and expect favors." To such students he does not "usually jump up and down and yell about it. I just say, 'If you're going to cut class, you lose credit.' " He insists on this rule because "kids don't have a sense of responsibility. You've got to define it. I don't want to be rigid, but I don't want to be exploited."

Personal humility, respect for others, responsiveness to need, encouragement of effort, a clear sense of right and wrong, and acute sensitivity to exploitation — this combination is the key to Bruce's views on the economy and polity, as well as the socializing domain. Justice at home and especially in schools is a microcosm of justice at large.

The Economy and Polity   As we saw in chapter two, Bruce has thought long and hard about "who deserves to be poor in rich America." He concludes that incomes should be limited to "enough to live well" — about $50,000 — for several reasons. First, no people are so much more valuable to society than everyone else that they deserve vastly greater rewards;

his old college classmates may be "very successful, very wealthy," but they are "not more talented, or work harder, or make harder decisions than some of mine." Second, "Our society is horribly wasteful. We're *very* expensive for the world to support," and only lower incomes will significantly lower consumption. Third, "The discipline of not having too much is of value in a person's life. I don't want to be able to go out for dinner every night. I don't have the right, nor do I want that right."[8] Finally, wealth corrupts its holder; most of the rich are "wasteful," "spoiled," "profane," "pathetic," and "don't care enough."

Bruce shares Rod's prescriptions for solving the incentive problem if incomes were equalized. Some people are not motivated by money and would work hard in order to "improve society." But others would need "re-education" to wean them away from selfish, mercenary goals. This re-education would not only permit income equality to work, but also would teach people to be more concerned about the general social welfare — a subject whose deep importance to Bruce we will see below. Thus if limiting incomes would require a change in people's motivation, that is a further reason to limit incomes, not an argument against it. This point gives us the first hint of Bruce's authoritarian streak.

Under the $50,000 limit, Bruce would use criteria of "skill, contribution, risk, effort," and the job's appeal to determine exact pay levels. But he focuses most on the question of which needs do or do not merit social response. Some do not: "If I had four children, I'm responsible for four children. If that means I don't get to take my wife on a twenty-fifth anniversary [vacation], that's the way it is." But others do: "If you've got sick children, I don't think it's a very humane society that says that's up to the individual father and mother to handle." He decides finally that needs that one brings on oneself do not deserve social support; those that one could not control, do.

As this careful boundary-setting implies, Bruce rejects Craig's call for help for all the needy. In fact, as we saw earlier, he argues that a person who "does not value working or making wealth" deserves "respect for his desire to not contribute" and "help to find meaning and value in his life" — but no social resources. This argument holds whether the noncontributor is an upper-class dropout or an alienated slum-dweller. Bruce has deep empathy with the poor and understands that welfare recipients "don't feel that they're taking advantage" because they see welfare "as natural, in the sense that 'Mother always got it, and I love Mother, she's done a hell of a lot for me. And there's no way that what Mother has done since I can remember, which is live off the state, is degrading, because my mother is as good a mother as any there is.' So those kids haven't been conditioned as you, as I am. They don't even really understand that other people *con-demn* them in some ways. They may not have known anything different than that. Therefore it's normal, not a failure." Because our society creates such welfare dependency, it should expend great amounts of resources and energy to help the poor escape it. But in the final analysis, if the person is "not going to contribute anything to other people, and he doesn't mind being poor, I guess we'll let him be poor."

Bruce gives two reasons for this sternness. First, "People exploit one another, and there's a time where you're just a goddamn bleeding-heart liberal. You just have to say, 'Cut it out, don't give me all that crap, you're not going to kid me anymore.' " Second, "Individual fulfillment is vitally important, but there's also a social dimension in one's existence, and therefore as a member of society, you are expected to contribute in a social way."

Bruce expands on the theme of social responsibility when he discusses other government programs besides income redistribution. He does not "really mind paying" taxes, because they provide for the collective good: "A lot of things that would make American life better need to be accomplished socially rather than individually." Examples are national parks and crime-fighting through poverty programs rather than the use of private guards. In fact, he would like even broader government control to prevent this generation of Americans from "wastefully, expensively" using up all the world's natural resources, thereby depriving other nations and our own descendants of their rightful share. In short, "We have to increasingly recognize that there's certain disciplines and restraints and that I've just got to give up things for the public good. So the 'Do your own thing' is one of those things that we've got to start educating people *isn't* the highest goal and isn't always the best. Do the *public* thing. It's got to become more important." At this point, Bruce moves to a position that many Americans would see as unacceptably repressive.[9] It is "wrong" that "tolerance has become almost an absolute among people. It would be a better society if we would limit the sale of stuff [such as pornography] that *hurts* social value. I believe in freedom, but a lot of that's a bunch of baloney." Government should act as a "positive social agency" by restricting activities such as gambling and mindless television shows that "allow people to fritter away their time." We must even ask, "Why should people have life supports for months, at tremendous cost, when you don't have the most elementary medicine in other parts of the world? I don't find that easy to live with. Some handicapped people should not live." He is, finally, as thoroughgoing a utilitarian as Rod: both would sacrifice a few individuals to enhance the lives of all others.

But whereas Rod wants the people who are directly affected to make distributive political decisions, Bruce takes the opposite course. Individuals will sacrifice to achieve the good of all only under the direction of a strong leader — and democracy may not be able to produce such a leader. At a local level, teachers should not elect principals, because "you end up with favoritism, politicking, not the best people." Nor should teachers make substantive decisions, because they are "very self-centered, get on their own bandwagon, and blow their horn, and don't look at anybody else at all." In fact, schools need less democracy, not more: "This participatory leadership sounds a hell of a lot better than it is. We really need principals who can manage the thing as you might organize a factory." Once good leaders emerge and "explain their decisions carefully and fully," teachers should "make the best of it, not bitch."

On the national level, we must encourage leaders to "stride out of their own needs to reach for power and influence." Democracy is a poor means of recruitment; campaigns force "superficiality" on candidates, and "the nature of their job," once they have been elected, forces them into "public relations" rather than good policy making. Nevertheless, we must hope for leaders who will "exercise independent judgment," and "tell people the truth about the way we live and ask them to make adjustments, to understand that there's some virtue in restraint and discipline." Bruce does feel some faint hope for the nation when he considers Jerry Brown and the 1960s generation, and he concludes that "our system stinks, but it probably is the best."

To stop at this point would do Bruce an injustice. He knows that "damn it, bureaucracies don't work either," and he steadfastly insists that "your greatest rights are the rights to do your own thing. If you want to work or bury yourself in music, you're free to. I have a very high personal priority for the right to make your own judgment, think critically." Thus he recognizes that too much focus on the social good is as bad as too little.

Some social programs, such as "greater equality through cash repayments," adult education, public television, and better political representation for Indians, the old, and children, enhance both individual rights and social responsibility. But all too often, these values conflict, and Bruce cannot choose between them. He insists, however, that the worst thing to do would be to "turn off to any problem that's complex." In an effort to avoid sacrificing either individual rights or the collective good, he offers a sleight of hand: perhaps we can redefine one of these concepts to make it compatible with the other. Private rights need not "have anything to do with standard of living or doing your own thing, as it's most often interpreted." Instead, it may mean "let[ting] me keep my dignity and identity as a thinking person" while working for the public good: "If I want to live decently, maybe I have to work in some job that has some value to others besides myself. I ought to be able to understand that as necessary. After that, though, don't make me say I like it. Don't make me say anything."

Bruce illustrates how egalitarian idealism can be both essential to and antithetical to freedom. On the one hand, people cannot be free in a society with great inequalities of wealth. The rich are lazy and corrupt; the poor are socialized to see dead-end dependency as natural and right; the middle class is competitive and complacent. People need respect, nurturance, material and symbolic rewards for effort, and material and symbolic aid in times of need in order to fulfill themselves and be truly free. All of this requires great downward redistribution, among other things. Bruce has acted on his egalitarian beliefs at considerable personal cost. And although "I'm not going to get up on a soap box and lead a revolution," he does muse that "probably I'll get involved somewhere along [the way] with" the Communist Party.

On the other hand, Bruce fears exploitation by the weak and would deny even a subsistence income to dropouts. In the pursuit of fulfillment for all, he comes close to endorsing censorship and the unplugging of kidney machines. He seeks a strong leader to educate and direct the populace, and he worries that a democracy will never produce one. His utopia appears to be a benevolent dictatorship with social and economic — but not political — equality, in which people may believe what they wish, as long as they also pursue the social good. It is a curiously illiberal notion.

Thus the consistent egalitarians, like the differentiators, are in many ways similar. They all want downward redistribution of wealth in the home, school, workplace, social structure, and polity. None are as singlemindedly devoted to individual freedom as are the differentiators. All use standards of equality not just as ideals, but also to measure the world as it is, and they all find it sadly wanting. None have any hope that the United States will ever reach their goals, but they are more resigned to that fact than either the differentiators or many followers of the dominant three-part pattern. All blame some, but not all, of the poor for their own fate, but none have any kind words for the rich.

The egalitarians also differ among themselves. Salvador is most concerned about creating a community of coequal workers; Rod is most interested in a group of friends; Bruce hopes for a corps of citizens dedicated to pursuing the public interest. Salvador seeks equality in decision-making among workers; Rod seeks equality in decision-making among citizens; Bruce seeks a boss at work and a leader in politics to save people from their own ignorance and selfishness. Rod and Salvador would set a minimum livable wage for all; Bruce would not. Bruce has a carefully elaborated political philosophy; Salvador has instincts honed by many years of experience and conversation; Rod has instincts that he cannot connect with one another or with his life experiences.

But their similarities outweigh their differences. All three respondents seek equality in all three domains of life; at last we have found some barking dogs. We can now compare people with different patterns of belief in order fully to understand why most poor Americans do not seek the downward redistribution of wealth.

Conclusion

The most obvious question about alternative patterns of distributive beliefs is: Where do they come from? What makes Eleanor Fox sound like a throwback to Plato? Where does Salvador Tivolli get his theory of surplus value? Why, in response to economic failure, does Sally White reaffirm her faith in capitalism, but Vincent Sartori make plans for a bank robbery? Why does Bruce Abbott's egalitarianism require people to contribute to society or starve, whereas Craig Cabot's egalitarianism requires only that people be human in order to receive a share of social goods? Why, in short, do some people follow the dominant pattern of equality-differentiation-equality, and others follow alternative patterns of complete differentiation or complete equality?

There is no easy answer to these questions. I found no obvious relationship between income, education, sex, ethnicity, religion, family background, parents' viewpoints, occupation, or any other descriptive characteristic and respondents' views. Both wealthy and poor seek to equalize across the board, or to differentiate across the board, or to equalize sometimes and differentiate at other times. In fact, the rich are more extreme than the poor in both directions. The wealthy differentiators more vehemently and single-mindedly support differentiation than do their poor counterparts, and the same holds true for the wealthy and poor among the egalitarians. Men as well as women seek equality, or differentiation. And so on. Perhaps a large sample could isolate trends and explanatory variables,[10] but a careful inspection of individual belief systems yielded no discernible patterns according to demographic criteria.

I can, however, suggest some patterns of differences among belief systems. First, despite conventional wisdom about working-class authoritarianism, the poor more often and more strongly support equality of political authority than do the rich. Vincent Sartori, Rod Thompson, Salvador Tivolli — all seek political and economic change through participatory democracy that forces political leaders to respond to citizens' demands. Compare them to Bruce Abbott, who seeks a benevolent dictator; Eleanor Fox, who would prefer rule by a white male aristocracy; and even Craig Cabot, who talks a lot about dignity and rights, but whose only comment on political reform is that more people should vote.

Second, the men tend to have stronger, more clearly etched views than the women. The most radical egalitarians are men; the most ruthless differentiators are men. The women, conversely, tend to be more aware of nuance and complexity, and tend to be both more ambivalent in their views and more diffident about them.

Third, those who see themselves as having been successful in their childhood tend to be egalitarian. Bruce Abbott, for example, says that being class president in high school and college "made me recognize that a lot of that is fake and unnecessary to achieve. If I had needs to succeed personally, I must have fulfilled them as a kid rather than as an adult." Because Rod Thompson was a local star on the softball field, he knows that competing and winning "are not the end of the world."

Fourth, those who have been upwardly mobile tend to be differentiators. Bernard Bloomfield best exemplifies this pride in one's own achievement and the demand that others follow the same path. But he is not the only one with this view — consider Barbara Azlinsky and Isaac Cohen. I can draw no conclusions about those who began and remained rich, for example Eleanor Fox and Craig Cabot, since their views are diametrically opposed.

There are other suggestions that patterns exist. Those who cherish friendship and have many friends tend to be egalitarian; those who seek to control themselves and their environment tend to be differentiators, and so on. But in-depth interviewing is not designed to yield broad statements about the kinds of people who hold one set of views rather than another — and this analysis has not done so. It is more fruitful to compare those who do, and do not, follow the dominant pattern of beliefs in another way, namely, to examine the nature and substance of belief systems and the virtues of consistency. This chapter, then, concludes with such an examination.

Some analysts of belief systems come down firmly on the side of consistency. A commitment to procedural consistency is a fundamental tenet of political liberalism. The equivalent psychological tenet is an assumption that sophisticated political thinkers have a "constrained" belief system. Their "ideas and attitudes . . . are bound together by some form of constraint or . . . functional interdependence," so that "given initial knowledge that an individual holds a specified attitude, [we would predict] that he holds certain further ideas and attitudes."[11] For example, an opponent of abortion should also oppose steeply progressive taxation, to be considered to have constrained or sophisticated beliefs; thus Pamela McLean would not be a constrained thinker. The impulse toward constraint appears to be deeply engrained: "The human mind, it seems, has a strong need for consistency and attitudes are generally changed in order to eliminate some inconsistency."[12] In his famous article on this subject, Philip Converse demonstrates that in 1956 only 17 percent of American voters were even marginally sophisticated. That is, only 17 percent used an ideological continuum such as liberalism-conservatism even "in a peripheral way . . . [and] did not . . . place much evaluative dependence upon it" or clearly understand it. Put another way, he finds that the average correlation coefficient among domestic issues for a mass sample in 1958 is only 0.23. From these data, Converse concludes that the vast majority of the American public is "remarkably innocent" of "any direct participation in [the] history of ideas and the behavior it shapes."[13]

The claim that most Americans hold inconsistent, nonideological, or even random attitudes has generated enough argument to keep an astonishing number of political science journals in business for years. Some scholars endorse or reinforce Converse's apparent denigration of the average person.[14] Some dispute him on methodological grounds.[15] Some question his findings[16] or argue that his fundamental assumptions presuppose his conclusions.[17] Still others accept Converse's results for the 1950s, but discern a trend toward greater constraint since then.[18]

But another, more fundamental, response is possible. One can argue that cognitive sophistication may not require consistency along a given ideological dimension. In fact, ideological consistency might even be a problem, not a virtue. Robert Abelson, for example, makes the "common observation" that "most of the worst inter- and intra-national conflicts of the world are greatly exacerbated by the human penchant for interposing oversimplified symbol systems between themselves and the external world."[19] Consistent, economical thinking may in this view simply be a poor substitute for the careful, reasoned ability to make distinctions that marks true cognitive sophistication. Perhaps people *should* behave differently in different circumstances or give different answers to different questions. Robert Lane states this position most forcefully: "Just as the person who is bound entirely by his ideology, so that experience does not have the power to change its elements, is an ideologue and unfree, so the person who governs all his policy recommendations by a single value is close to 'obsession' or borders on 'fixation' . . . The healthy person has multiple values and he finds them often in conflict; his health is revealed in his toleration of the conflict and the means he chooses to reconcile the conflict."[20]

Obviously, Converse and cognitive consistency psychologists do not advocate oversimplified, caricatured dogma; nor do Lane and Abelson recommend inconsistent or random nonattitudes. What is interesting about disputes over the value of consistency is the subtle middle ground. My interview data shed some light on two aspects of this debate: the relationship between consistency and sophistication of thinking, and the centrality of the liberal-conservative dimension in evaluating how much a person "participates in the history of ideas."

In reviewing the interview data, I find no obvious connection between normative consistency and cognitive sophistication. Some who follow the dominant three-part pattern have highly complex, carefully reasoned explanations for their disjunct beliefs; others do not. Some who always use differentiating or egalitarian norms have highly complex, carefully reasoned explanations for their single-mindedness; others do not. No one, for example, could be more sophisticated than Craig Cabot, and yet, from his vehement support of a guaranteed annual income, it might be difficult to predict his insistence that the law prosecute "poor little old ladies" who lie in court. And yet once one understands his distinction between justice and economics, these divergent beliefs fit into a perfectly coherent belief system. Similarly, one might not predict Phillip Santaguida's enthusiasm for social welfare policies from his insistence that class distinctions must be maintained. Yet both these views stem from an elaborate theory that distinguishes between evils that are necessary and must be accepted, and those that can, and therefore should, be mitigated. Once his theory is understood, his "unconstrained views" become "subtle distinctions."

Just as apparent inconsistency is not necessarily real confusion, so single-minded consistency need not imply obsession or fixation. Sally White, for example, believes wholeheartedly in rewarding all people from her seven-year-old son on up only for their achievement, but she encourages creativity and idiosyncrasy and opposes competition and conformity to roles. Bruce Abbott pursues a communitarian social vision, but he refuses to abandon the sometimes conflicting goal of individual freedom. Thus those who distinguish among domains, both rich and poor, are sometimes highly sophisticated thinkers, and those who pursue one principle, both rich and poor, are sometimes highly flexible.

Of course, we also have opposite examples — random or inconsistent distinctions and rigid ideologies. Ernest Berkowitz proudly describes his grandfather's insistence on working to age eighty-five, but he never connects this view to his employee's wish to keep working past age seventy. Vincent Sartori opposes the accumulation or retention of great wealth, but rejects any governmental tampering with private property. Differences such as these are not fine-tuned nuances; they are simply illogic or indecision. On the other side, ideology may disguise rigidity. Bernard Bloomfield sees his insistence that children be rewarded only for productivity and punished severely for misbehavior simply as training for successful adulthood. But he displays a clearly authoritarian strand. He had a harsh childhood at the hands of adults; why should other children escape the same fate now that he is an adult? Similarly, the humanistic, egalitarian Bruce Abbott sometimes comes ominously close to endorsing thought control, censorship, and euthanasia "for everyone's good."

We could also find examples of rigidity among the distinguishers, and inconsistencies among the single-minded. But it would be superfluous. The point is that both categories contain sophisticated, complex thinkers as well as inconsistent or obsessive thinkers. I have too few respondents to claim that one category contains more of a particular kind of thinker, but that is unnecessary for my main point. Judging by these data, it is simply incorrect to equate constraint — methodologically defined as the ability to predict one view by knowing another held by the same person — with cognitive sophistication. It may even be that the dominant three-part pattern is, in fact, a more subtle, complex response to the conflicting claims of varying norms and circumstances. After all, the philosophers described in chapter three seldom endorse one theory of justice to the exclusion of all others; why should we expect, or want, ordinary people to do so?

Converse also concludes that the lack of constraint among most Americans indicates that they do not participate in the history of ideas, except through a rote adoption of elite phrases or elite connections between issues. My data dispute this conclusion. Clearly the best-educated, such as Craig Cabot and Bruce Abbott, are the most comfortable with direct discussions of political philosophies; they would rank among Converse's ideologues or near-ideologues. Yet even Craig, with all his discussion of the social contract, natural versus manmade law, and social utility, only vaguely recognizes the names of John Locke, St. Augustine, and John Stuart Mill. More to the point, some of the less-educated and apparently unconstrained respondents use strands of identifiable political philosophies. Phillip Santaguida gives a coherent Marxist explanation of income differences, using concepts of the reserve army of the unemployed and surplus value. Rod Thompson explicitly rejects arguments based on Kantian desert in favor of those based on group utilitarianism and the diminishing marginal utility of money. Anne Kaufman, with only a vocational secondary education, gives a full account of interlocking obligations and privileges of each class within the total community, and then critiques her own argument from the perspective of the lower class. The fact that none of these people could identify the philosophers from whom their arguments derive does not negate their active participation in the history of ideas and in the behaviors prescribed by these ideas.

At the broadest level, this entire work is a demonstration of the strength of Anglo-American liberal political theory in ordinary people's distributive judgments. Respondents' distinctions between private and public, their individualistic view of the world, their perception of capitalism as the natural economic order, their beliefs that economic fairness differs from political and personal justice are all fundamental liberal tenets. If they lived in Aristotelian Athens, they would make radically different connections between wealth and politics, private and public life.[21] It is their very participation in the history of ideas that prevents the poor from seeing the economy in a way that would lead them to seek the redistribution of wealth. In sum, those distinctions that initially seem to reveal lack of constraint, and therefore lack of political ideology, are in fact evidence of the strength of political ideology in Americans' normative judgments.

These data also illuminate another issue in the belief system literature, namely, the centrality of the liberal-conservative dimension. We turn here to an examination of the substance — as distinguished from the level of cognitive sophistication — of respondents' political beliefs. Some scholars claim that disputes in such diverse realms as "law, mathematics, science, art, or child rearing" all "constitute a polarity extending from the extreme left through a middle-of-the-road position to the extreme right-wing position."[22] Most writers do not claim such a uniquely important role for a left-right continuum, but they clearly rely upon it.[23] Converse, for example, did not "require" that a person use a liberal-conservative continuum to be labeled an ideologue, but "it was almost the only dimension of the sort that appeared empirically."[24] For him, the liberal-conservative continuum is an "extremely efficient frame for the organization of many political observations," and he notes its extensive use in the "more ambitious treatments of politics in the mass media."[25] He concludes, therefore, that people who do not correctly distinguish liberalism from conservatism or aggregate their views according to this continuum are extremely unlikely to be ideologues or to have constrained belief systems.

Others, however, dispute the conceptual and empirical centrality of a simple liberal-conservative dimension. Milton Rokeach points out its conceptual flaws and proposes an alternative.[26] He uses a variety of data to show that most political positions are arrayed along two independent dimensions involving orientations toward freedom and equality. Even when Lloyd Free and Hadley Cantril use a liberal-conservative dimension, they find no direct relationship between operational values (concerning desired governmental activity) and ideological beliefs (concerning the proper role and nature of the government and socioeconomic system). Their respondents are generally much more conservative on the latter spectrum than on the former. They interpret these differences as evidence that Americans "pay lip service to [such] an amazing degree to stereotypes and shibboleths" that we are "almost schizoid."[27] But we need not accept their interpretation in order to learn from their findings. They may, for example, have found the same kind of patterning that I found, in which different domains evoke different normative evaluations. In that case, one could interpret their findings as evidence of ideological complexity and layering, not of mere irrationality. Regardless of the interpretation, however, they at least support the contention that a simple liberal-conservative continuum is insufficient to measure the political beliefs of Americans.

Richard Scammon and Ben Wattenberg discuss the emergence in the late 1960s of a new set of social issues involving crime, race, alienation, and concerns about drugs and sexual freedom. These issues, all related to "the more personally frightening aspects of disruptive social change," follow neither "a straight right/left or liberal/conservative" pattern. Instead, they form a new dimension separate from that of economic issues, and they had an important effect on election results during the past decade. Whatever their long-term importance, they provide another example of the failure of a simple liberal-conservative dimension to explain political attitudes or behaviors.[28]

Finally, on the one hand, James Stimson argues, in agreement with Converse, that the number of dimensions used to associate political issues *increases* as cognitive ability decreases.[29] On the other hand, George Marcus and colleagues find that the number of dimensions used to structure attitudes toward abstract political concepts *decreases* as cognitive ability decreases. Furthermore, they claim, the more dimensions used, the more sophisticated are the political beliefs.[30] Again, we are less interested in the results per se than in the fact that, whoever is correct, these writers show that many people do not always use a single liberal-conservative dimension to analyze politics.

We could easily find more claims about the conceptual or empirical insufficiency of a simple liberal-conservative dimension, and more suggested alternatives. But the point is clear: the very diversity of these claims and their forms of substantiation call the Tomkins-Converse thesis into question. Obviously people can, and do, use other dimensions or more than one liberal-conservative dimension. Thus the fact that most of Converse's sample could not distinguish liberals from conservatives or did not array their attitudes along a liberal-conservative line is not sufficient evidence to conclude that "the organization of more specific attitudes into wide-ranging belief systems is absent" for most Americans.[31] They may simply be using different substantive dimensions to organize their views.

There are methodological as well as substantive criticisms of Converse's assumption that the politically intelligent will use the same liberal-conservative dimension that he uses. Lane argues that the attempt to rank political beliefs along one dimension is "a mistake," because it "is based on the fallacious view that if some people see idea-elements properly clustering in a certain way, others should too. Such 'constraints' . . . refer to neither logic nor rationality," but only to the researcher's image of what seems obviously related or contradictory. But the researcher's cognitive map may not correspond to the subject's, and researchers must avoid confusing their preconceptions with logical relations.[32]

Walter Mischel makes the same point as Lane from the perspective of personality theory. Too often psychologists use ambiguous or vague measures, or assume similarity among test questions, among behavioral indicators, or between test questions and behaviors. They then interpret different responses by the same subject to "similar" stimuli as inconsistency, discrepancy between attitudes and behavior, or even neurosis. In fact, however, subjects may simply be responding to "hidden" distinctions in the questionnaire or experimental activities, or to environmental stimuli other than those evoked by the researcher. To expect identical responses to ambiguous or varying stimuli may be to substitute the observer's assumptions of similarity for the respondent's perception of relevant differences.[33]

Mischel concludes that "the existence of stimulus-free, highly generalized behavioral sets" — personality — is "unsupported by the data."[34] We need not accept such a sweeping conclusion nor enter into the psychological thicket of trait-state disputes, but there is a political moral here. Given competing claims for the "real" typology of beliefs, and given extensive evidence that what the researcher says may not be what the subject hears, there is no compelling reason to evaluate beliefs according to the subject's use of a liberal-conservative scale.

Not surprisingly, Converse has a response to these attacks on a single liberal-conservative dimension as an organizing device. He grants that the "broad-net approach" used by Lane (and this book) "can lay bare various organizing abstractions or generalizations" that a closed-ended survey cannot. After all, in-depth interviews seek to discover how people develop, use, and generalize whatever political perceptions they have, whereas surveys seek to discover opinions about a particular set of issues. Lane asks, "What are your views?" Converse asks, "Should the government do X or not-X?" No wonder, then, that Lane (and this author) discover personal patterns of organization that surveyors do not.[35]

But, Converse continues, many findings of the broad-net approach are irrelevant to both policymakers and researchers, either because the topics discussed are not on political or research agendas, or because "the respondents lack linking information or overarching perspectives" that are needed to deal with topics that *are* on these agendas. If the "various organizing abstractions" discovered through the broad-net approach "are entirely idiosyncratic or at least oblique to the most common shorthands at the upper levels of the communication system, and if the respondents do not even understand the conventional shorthand," then the abstractions are useless to anyone except their holder.[36] They cannot be communicated to policymakers and researchers in usable (that is, generalizable) form, they will be misinterpreted even if they are heard, and they provide no guidelines for determining what most people would choose on a particular issue.

Fair enough. If everyone has a unique world view, set of normative judgments, and policy recommendations, then researchers cannot understand and catalogue them and policymakers cannot consider them in making decisions. But that, of course, is not the case, as volumes of socialization studies, surveys, and political culture studies attest. We certainly do not all see eye-to-eye, but a claim of complete idiosyncrasy is a straw man and surely not what Converse intends.

Even if we agree, however, that the political beliefs of most Americans are "more or less" similar, we have not yet shown that they are similar enough to be generalizable by researchers or usable by policymakers. This is the point at which my research makes its contribution. We know from Converse and others that a simple liberal-conservative dimension does not provide a pattern for belief systems once we move beyond well-socialized elites who get their cues from the "ambitious" media. But we have alternative suggestions for generalizable systems of beliefs, such as those cited above and my own. Most of my respondents, rich and poor, educated and not, use the three-part pattern of socializing egalitarianism, economic differentiation, and political egalitarianism to evaluate distributive questions. Thus they are neither liberal nor conservative, but they are very far from having purely idiosyncratic, nongeneralizable, noncommunicable beliefs.

If further research replicates my findings, then perhaps we will be able to conclude that the problem of communication lies with the myopic elites, not the ignorant masses. Perhaps it is time for academics, journalists, and policymakers to stop trying to place all issues and all people along a single liberal-conservative dimension if most people do not use such a dimension. My respondents are liberal in two domains, conservative in a third; they follow a relatively simple, flexible, generalizable pattern. If others follow the same pattern, Converse's fears about idiosyncratic belief systems are groundless. In that case, why should we not stop expecting citizens to conform to elite standards of ideological consistency, and start expecting elites to change in response to ordinary citizens' patterns of belief?

8 Ambivalence

The Dominant Pattern and Ambivalance about It

I have thus far examined the range of distributive norms available to American citizens, shown that most respondents follow a pattern of equality-differentiation-equality in the three domains of life, and shown that a few are consistently egalitarian or differentiating.

But all of this is really only half of my argument. Interspersed throughout respondents' prescriptions for equality in the home or results in the workplace were hesitancy, contradictions, ambiguity. It is these shadings that made the analysis of the interviews so long and complex. It is easy to describe simple statements of position, even if it is not at all easy to analyze or explain them; survey researchers do an excellent job at this task. But given the opportunity, people do not make simple statements; they shade, modulate, deny, retract, or just grind to a halt in frustration. These manifestations of uncertainty are just as meaningful and interesting as the clear, definitive statements of a belief system. Hence my stressing their tentativeness as I delineated the dominant three-part pattern.

Yet it is not enough to say that people are seldom as certain of their opinions as their bald summary statements imply. We all know that and none more than survey researchers who must work around this fact. But here I can do what their data preclude, namely, treat ambivalence as a finding with the same status as the dominant substantive pattern and subject it to the same analysis. I wish to analyze it by seeking patterns of uncertainty, regularities among contradictions, explanations for frustration. Most important, I will show how recurrent types of ambivalence help to answer the original question of how rich and poor evaluate vast inequalities of wealth in a society that claims to be politically and socially egalitarian.

I use ambivalence as a generic term to indicate a wide range of views that modify the dominant three-part pattern of beliefs. Before examining its many forms, let us make clear what it is not.

Using different norms of justice in different domains is not ambivalence. Following the dominant three-part pattern does not make one an inconsistent egalitarian or a softhearted social Darwinist. To make that claim would be to fall into Philip Converse's trap, namely, to assert that people who do not always fall on the same end of a single continuum, regardless of the issue, are unconstrained or inconsistent. For some people, this very ability to keep domains of their life separate and to use different norms in each is psychologically and philosophically satisfying. Anne Kaufman, for example, both insists that people be held accountable for their actions and recognizes that people are not always responsible for their situations. She gives great weight to the former demand in her discussion of the market and therefore wants economic differences to reflect personal achievements. But she gives great weight to the latter recognition in her family life and policy recommendations, and therefore wants parents to aid their children and the government to remedy structural or random causes of poverty. By keeping the domains separate, she can balance norms that might paralyze her if they were forced into a direct confrontation.

Even conflicts between two norms within one domain need not lead to ambivalence, if the person is able to handle the conflict. For example, Pamela McLean's discussion of appropriate treatment of people with dependents demonstrates not ambivalence, but an awareness that one must choose between equally valid norms. Employers should not pay people with large families more than less needy employees, but they should lobby for tax exemptions for dependents in order to equalize the economic burdens of large and small families. These claims only "sound contradictory"; they are not really, because "actual salary for doing the same job is a little different than paying for the privilege of living in the U.S. And sometimes the people with less responsibility do have to carry the load a little more for those who are burdened with so many. [For] the privilege of earning the money and having the less responsibility involved, they [single taxpayers] pay a little bit more." Pamela's distinction between employers' moral obligations with regard to salary paid into a family and taxes paid out of it may seem silly to a strong proponent of a norm of need or results. But that is irrelevant; by finding and using a meaningful distinction, Pamela avoids either a confrontation or a stand-off between equally valid norms.

Most respondents, however, lack this happy ability to maintain and draw strength from distinctions among beliefs and domains. Most make the distinctions, but react to them with uncertainty and distress, not contentment and "health."[1]

Manifestations of Ambivalence

Manifestations of ambivalence vary. One is helplessness. Pamela Mc-Lean and Anne Kaufman are both uncharacteristically stymied and silenced by their inability to think of a solution to the problem of poverty. Ruth Sennett is similarly unable to devise a resolution to a normative problem. She lives on an annual pension of $3000, is grateful to her former employer for having paid her the minimum wage, and says she deserved no more. But redistribution would be "wonderful" because then she could pay her bills and "everyone would be equal." But she gets stuck when asked how we might reconcile her belief that people should be paid according to productivity and her desire that people be equal: "I don't know, what are they doing? I don't know what you mean. I can't answer you that. You go in certain sections, the houses are nice, you go in another section, they're worse. So you pick the better part. Maybe the whole world should be like the better part. That's impossible. When they throw down buildings, what do they do with all that stuff? Burn it? It's got to be someplace."

Sometimes ambivalence is manifested as anger. We have seen Vincent Sartori's frustration at not being able to figure out whom to blame for his poverty or where to turn for help. His only solution is getting into bar brawls, throwing knives at foremen, and making plans to rob a bank. Isaac Cohen is also angry, despite his wealth. He resents how easily wealth came to his WASP neighbors, without the extraordinary efforts that he and other poor immigrant Jews had to make. He resents government "pampering" of the rich through tax breaks, and he does not believe that any of the wealthy, including himself, really deserve to keep their money. But he also envies his neighbors, feels traces of ascriptive awe at "old money," and is "insecure by comparison." He deals with these contradictory impulses by isolating himself from and sometimes condemning his neighbors. "We do not seek their friendship. I am not interested in clubs. I cannot play the game." The very wealthy are "self-serving," "uncaring," "greedy sharks," who "swallow up little fishies" like himself and "destroy their [own] children." He describes the baleful influence, both physical and social, of the Rockefellers on their environment: "They destroy areas and then pick them up for a song. Taking over Saint Croix — one fertile valley on the island, and they own it. Is there any wonder there's a problem on Saint Croix? You can go on and on. All of the tax advantages that our drunken Rockefeller in Arkansas has — the rest of the country learned from what he was able to do [and are] now taking advantage of the loopholes that *his* people discovered. And *he's* nothing but a drunk." The Rockefellers, he concludes, are "bright, highly motivated, and ruthless." In his case, this mixture of envy, admiration, condemnation, and longing to belong finds expression in anger and bitterness.

A third manifestation of ambivalence is inconsistency. The clearest example is Rod Thompson's discussion of confiscatory inheritance taxes, described in chapter seven. Another example comes from Amy Campbell. She is "a little bit of a Marxist," sees the welfare system as "dehumanizing" and insufficient, and believes that a guaranteed income "would do away with a lot of problems we have in society." It might even "give a person a motivation to go back to work." But neither the employer, local community, nor federal government has any responsibility for helping workers with long-term needs or short-term emergencies. After all, the concept of need "brings in a variable that muddies the issue. You choose to have two cars and say, 'Oh, I need a little bit more money for gas or insurance.' What do you call need? It's in the eyes of the person who needs. No, you can't do that [supplement wages according to need]." As for emergencies, "Okay, if I'm a responsible person, I have insurance, don't I? It costs a whole lot of money every year, but that protects me." Society should help the needy, but need is undefinable, emergencies are a person's own responsibility, and no one is obliged to help anyone else. Her general claim and specific application of it are inconsistent.

A fourth and final manifestation of ambivalence is confusion, the dissolving into incoherence when attempting to express one's thoughts. Barbara Azlinsky provides the clearest example in her unedited answer to the question, "What role did luck play in your career?" "You know, being happy. As I said years ago when I first started working, and I think everybody was healthy and all that. Oh, I wouldn't say 'breaks' — I don't go by luck. Just feel that a lot of times, I mean, in business you gamble, and you do things, but we aren't business people, we aren't gamblers. But that's where you believe in Lady Luck and all that. But we just feel that if you've worked, then you should get. Well, that's, I think, why I'm a little upset." Barbara does not believe that luck should determine success, and she wants to believe in a norm of results. But she can attribute her own lack of success only to bad luck — which she does not believe in. So she is driven into a flurry of confused, incomplete, vague phrases.

The same thing happens to Ruth Sennett. For example, asked if any people are overpaid, she responds, "I don't know, dear. This is when I was young, my hair long. My husband died young. He had a heart condition. Well, you know, when you work in a shop, and if you get paid more than I do, then you have to fight for more. And then if you make the boss nervous, then she'll fire you. Like my sister was slow, and she [the boss] didn't give her a chance." These comments come after a long discussion of the difficulties of poverty, the greater desert of the rich, and the desirability of equality. Ruth cannot sort out these thoughts; therefore she retreats to non sequiturs.

But all of these examples are simply expressions of ambivalence, not explanations for it. The real task is twofold: to understand why normally intelligible, calm people sometimes become paralyzed, angry, inconsistent, or incoherent; and to examine the implications of these occasions for people's beliefs about distributive justice and the redistribution of wealth.

Normative versus Pragmatic Judgments

Analysis of the interviews reveals five types of ambivalence, which I shall examine in turn. First, ambivalence may occur when respondents attempt to evaluate some issues normatively and some pragmatically. After making this distinction, they may then question their placing specific items on one or the other side, or they may regret that certain subjects apparently cannot be evaluated normatively. This creates ambivalence: they feel torn between what ought to be and what apparently must be.

Simply choosing to view a question pragmatically or normatively may affect the substance of one's distributive decision but does not necessarily induce ambivalence. For Pamela McLean, the level of pay for dangerous work is a matter of market forces, not justice: "A propane driver shouldn't receive any more than a steel hauler. I mean, it's a truckload of something going somewhere. There is more risk, but nobody says you have to do that job if you don't want to — take an easier one.

Maybe the only way they could get people to do it *is* to offer them more money, but I don't think that should be a reward thing — that's a business problem." For Phillip Santaguida, the level of pay for dangerous work is a question of justice, not simply market forces: "Dangerous jobs should get more 'cause you're jeopardizing your life every time you take a dangerous job." Neither answer is hesitant or self-contradictory; neither person indicates ambivalence.

Ambivalence occurs when people vacillate and then try to resolve or ignore their indecision. Michael McFarland, for example, is paralyzed when trying to make normative choices because he perceives insuperable pragmatic obstacles. We *should* have truly equal opportunity: "If everybody started off on the same basis, come in [to the world] and they don't have no money, then nobody could have any complaints" about subsequent differences in income, since one's income would depend on "what you make of it." Michael's version of the good society is a classic statement of the American dream, but, as Garry Wills says, "The metaphor [of starting line fairness] is a mess."[2] Michael, although less articulately than Wills, makes the same point in his next breath: "Well, you need money to get through school, though. It would be very *tough*" to enforce equality of opportunity if some get an education and others cannot. He knows that equal opportunity does not, and may never, exist; therefore we cannot assume that people's holdings now, or ever will, accurately measure their worth. He cannot decide where to turn from there. Sometimes he tries to assume that "on the majority, most people end up where they deserve"; therefore current distributions are fair. At other points, he decides that real equality of opportunity is impossible; therefore we should "standardize" incomes, so that "everybody would be making about the same, and nobody would feel better off than the other person." Most of the time, he is simply stymied; the question of fair incomes is "a tough one." For Michael, normative choices must rest on pragmatic bases; when the bases are not there, he does not know what to do about his normative preferences.

Others deal with their ambivalence about what is and ought to be by refusing to think about desired ideals, perhaps even refusing to have any. Phillip Santaguida often does this. The world is full of "cannibals," whose nature would never permit equality; therefore the goal of "everybody have[ing] the same thing" is "just a foolish dream." Rather than working toward that dream, he "just hope[s] for the future." Amy Campbell even more explicitly seeks to avoid ambivalence by refusing to take seriously her own impractical dreams. At various points, she supports guaranteed incomes and jobs, steeply progressive taxation, and other social programs. But although Marxism is "a lovely theory," she will not discuss the question of equalizing incomes because "I don't think it works. They [China and Sweden] have the haves and the have-nots too. Maybe not as radically as we do, but they have them." Asked if we should work toward equality as an ideal, even if we know we will never reach it, she again answers, "I don't think it's possible. I remember reading Marx, and a lot of his ideas were just great. [But] Marxism doesn't work anywhere. Point me a finger where it works. It doesn't." Asked once more if equality is a desirable, even if unreachable, ideal, she insists once more, "I don't think it's possible. Don't you see what I'm saying? You're trying to get me out of reality, go floating on a magic carpet with you." She will discuss only "what is ideal in reality," in order to avoid tension between apparently immutable facts and evanescent values.

One could make the opposite choice. One could try to end ambivalence by beginning with a normative ideal and seeking to change the circumstances that block its attainment. This, of course, would be the strategy of a laissez-faire anarchist or redistributionist, and my sample contains no full-fledged examples of either. It does, however, have examples of people who seek to change the fact side of the fact-value discrepancy. Craig Cabot served several years on a governor's commission to reform laws concerning foster care. He expanded the commission's mandate, and left only after its purpose had been accomplished and it had degenerated into political squabbling. When faced with the problem of work incentives in an egalitarian society, both Rod Thompson and Bruce Abbott would try to change the structure of incentives rather than abandoning equality. Wendy Tonnina worries that "the people with all the money are in control. Money talks a lot in the government." As a result, "The small people, the working people have freedom [only] to a certain point. We can think what we want, but it's just—can we do anything about it?" But instead of giving up in despair, as Ernest Berkowitz does, she encourages her friends and fellow workers to "be tomorrow, more open-minded, to want better and more. They're not willing to sit back" any longer.

Of course, not only egalitarians want to change reality in order to approach an ideal more closely. Judith Baum wants to ban books illustrating two "extremely dangerous trends": the "terrible, terrible problem in this country of violence" and "this whole area of hopelessness." Children will not develop patriotism and the drive to succeed if they are constantly surrounded by evidence of social decay; therefore they should be denied books that lack "upbeat hope." Judith resists the word *censor-*

ship, but works actively to persuade librarians to take certain books off their shelves.

Thus far we have examined three strategies for dealing with tension between perceived pragmatic limits and an ideal vision. Some people simply live with tension without even trying to resolve it; others abandon the apparently hopeless ideal; still others seek changes in the constraining reality. Rod Thompson and Ernest Berkowitz follow yet another path in trying to deal with an apparent fact-value discrepancy; they insist on keeping the real and ideal worlds separate. If the two worlds are not juxtaposed, then one need not feel torn between their conflicting pulls. Rod's gyrations about an inheritance tax occur because the interview questions force him to consider real world limitations and ideal values simultaneously. He believes both that we cannot confiscate holdings and that people should not inherit fortunes. He sees no way of moving from the former necessary starting point to the latter desired outcome; therefore he twists uncomfortably between the two opposing forces until the interviewer permits him to change the subject.

Ernest Berkowitz also keeps normative ideals separate from everyday practice as much as he can. He is able to do so in the economic domain: he empathizes with workers' problems and wishes they did not exist, but he sees no reason to do good deeds that amount to poor business practice. He is, however, unable to do so in his family: when his son married a Gentile, Ernest became painfully aware that the ideal of religious tolerance was very different from the concrete fact of intermarriage.

Isaac Cohen shows the same split, although with less discomfort at the juxtaposition of ideal and real, in his discussion of fair incomes. Ideally, "once my kids are through with school, they're on their own." Children should not inherit their parents' wealth; the incomes of the wealthy cannot be "justified." People should be rewarded for "making a genuine contribution to society; my salary is totally unjustified by that standard, and I feel guilty about it." But he will not relinquish his holdings, disinherit his children, or stop searching for tax loopholes because "that's society. The name of the game is dollars. And I cannot . . ." Isaac claims that this discrepancy between values and pragmatism does not bother him, but he immediately begins a tirade against lawyers, who are "incapable bluffers" and thus *really* overpaid, and against "drones" and welfare cheats. Rod's confusion finds echoes in Isaac's bluster.

Both rich and poor feel this form of ambivalence, and both use the same four methods to combat it. But the combination of accepting apparently necessary differences and holding egalitarian values has profoundly different psychological effects on respondents' distributive views, depending on their wealth or poverty. For the wealthy, the gap between facts and values usually justifies personal inaction even in the face of an unfair status quo. They can see themselves as empathetic with the poor, even "socialistic," without feeling responsible to seek greater equality. This is not hypocrisy; they may sincerely wish things were otherwise, but because the market, or human nature, or political corruption are immutable forces, one would simply be whistling into the wind to endorse major changes. Maintaining tension between real world judgments of fact and utopian values permits them both to retain their privileged status and to condemn privilege.

But the gap between the existence of differences and the desire for more equality causes despair and frustration for the poor. They have a partial vision of how the world ought to be and how people ought to treat one another, but to act according to that vision would require that one be either a saint or a fool. They have no intention of being either, and they do not consider making the extraordinary effort that would be necessary to move the world from what it is to what it ought to be. Therefore their egalitarian values are limited to wistful visions of the ideal future or misplaced nostalgia for a golden past.

When the fact-value gap is reversed, so that respondents perceive great equality that belies their differentiating values, the psychology differs. The rich become strong and vocal opponents of the status quo, although they perceive their opposition to be futile. Only one poor respondent shows this pattern, and she is a rather defiant, confused opponent of the status quo. The first type of ambivalence, therefore, generally induces political inactivity, whether by providing an excuse for it or by setting up apparently insuperable barriers to change.

Normative versus Normative Judgments

A second type of ambivalence consists of unresolved conflicts among distributive norms within the same domain. Once a respondent chooses to consider an issue from a normative rather than a pragmatic stance, he or she must decide what norm is most appropriate. That decision is, of course, the subject of this book, and need not be recapitulated here. Furthermore, not all normative conflicts within one domain induce ambivalence. But some do, and we can identify circumstances in which ambivalence among norms, rather than careful balancing between them, is likely to occur.

Adjacent norms — those located beside each other in figure 4 — are least problematic, either for political philosophers or for my respondents. After all, Tawney did not sharply distinguish strict equality from need in his program for distributive justice in England.[3] Market liberalism is based on Locke's assumption that investments of work and virtue translate directly into results of productivity and social contribution. Racism and sexism seek justification in the claim that people with one ascriptive characteristic are more productive in certain ways than people without that characteristic.

Similarly, respondents slip back and forth between adjacent norms at some cost to philosophical rigor, but at little cost to psychological comfort. Maria Pulaski most often relies on a norm of need, but she makes equal divisions of the last piece of pie and household chores without worrying about this "inconsistency." Since Bernard Bloomfield assumes that boys can be expected to achieve more than girls, he demands accomplishments from his sons that he does not expect from his daughters — with no apparent unease about mixing norms of results and ascription. Isaac Cohen insists that hard work, even without great intelligence, yields achievement deserving rich rewards — and he cites himself as an example of the success possible through sheer effort. He is not bothered by this conflation of norms of investment and results or by the same mix in his equation of poverty with laziness.

But conflicts within one domain among more, and more dissimilar, norms can create great philosophical and psychological ambivalence — and can induce political paralysis. The standard debate in American politics between equal opportunity and equal results is, at base, a dispute between norms of strict equality and results. The conflict between a guaranteed annual income and a job requirement for welfare recipients reduces to a conflict between norms of need and productivity. Affirmative action dilemmas pit ascription, strict equality, procedures, and productivity against one another in complicated ways. Controversies over competency tests for high school graduation involve norms of investments, results, and ascription. As these examples suggest, many of our most intractable and politically volatile issues are fundamentally conflicts between two or more dissimilar distributive norms.

For my respondents also, simultaneously holding norms far from one another along the continuum of distributive principles creates ambivalence. Even Anne Kaufman, who is exceptionally adept at balancing competing values, is torn between her wish to gratify the needs of her rebellious son and her belief in maintaining high standards of performance even for him. Similarly, Pamela McLean juggles competing norms better than any other poor respondent, but she cannot even begin to reconcile free speech rights to publicize abortions with her parental responsibility to keep her young children innocent of knowledge about them.

Less adept respondents are even more distressed. Barbara Azlinsky is torn between humanitarianism and materialism; Ernest Berkowitz vacillates between equality and ascription. At one point, Michael McFarland endorses communism because the state would ensure everyone a job and the necessities of life. In that situation, "Anybody would be getting an equal shake. You'll still be working, but you wouldn't have no worries." And yet he regrets that unionization makes it "tough" for an employer to fire a lazy worker: "You just can't let 'em go unless you catch 'em really doing wrong. You're really tied down with them. Before they had the unions, if the guy didn't toe the line, he was let go. *Then* a person had to work." Now a union member can "slack off and push the work on the willing worker" with impunity. Michael cannot choose here among a norm of strict equality for necessities and jobs, a norm of results for the employer's sake, and a norm of investments for the workers' sake. As a result, he feels anxious, angry, and guilty—all at the same time.

Finally, David Fine vacillates between his love of competition and his belief that the meek should not be trampled upon. He learned "the importance of helping other people" through his mother's enthusiastic observance of Sabbath charity, and he "devotes around 25 percent of my time to do-good things." And yet, "The most important thing I learned from my father was to be competitive. I don't like to lose." He describes in loving detail his takeover of his father-in-law's business, mainly through being a good "bullshit artist." These conflicting norms of need and competition appear in his contradictory political recommendations. On the one hand, justice is "the fairness to consider an individual, understanding the individual in [the context of his] society, understanding the society. It's *fair* in this country to give some black kid who doesn't have any parents more understanding than somebody who knows [what] he's doing and is looking to steal blatantly." On the other hand, we must not interfere too much with market forces. Asked about exploitation of ghetto shoppers, he responds, "A man is entitled to sell groceries for whatever he wants to sell it at, and people are entitled to buy." David is not very disturbed by discrepancies between his policy recommendations based on need and those based on competition, because he does not take this whole exercise in normative evaluation very seriously. But he clearly expresses conflicts among norms within the same domain and just as clearly has no suggestions for resolving them.

Respondents generally have fewer strategies for alleviating conflict among norms than for alleviating conflict between a normative and a pragmatic approach to distributive questions. Most often, they leave the conflict among norms unresolved, and the degree of the resulting disturbance depends on their personality and the salience of that issue to them. Thus David Fine is not distressed even by tensions in his family — at least he does not let the interviewer see any distress — whereas Michael McFarland is deeply pained by the myriad conflicts he sees at his workplace and in the country in general.

Regardless of variations in distress caused by a conflict among norms, it always has the same political effect. People who feel torn between two views are unlikely to act forcefully to promote either; therefore by default, they end up "supporting" the status quo.[4] The only exception would be a leap to certainty on one side or the other, as Rod Thompson shows in briefly endorsing concentration camps for churlish workers.

Rich respondents are especially likely to be deeply affected by this form of ambivalence, as Barbara Azlinsky, Ernest Berkowitz, and Bruce Abbott demonstrate. This finding may, of course, be simply an artifact of a small sample, but the outlines of a pattern are clear. The poor are generally so preoccupied with external material constraints that they can seldom afford the luxury of normative conflict. Vincent Sartori has too little income to buy any presents for his children; why should he waste his time debating need versus achievement as a criterion for spending nonexistent money? Maria Pulaski knows only that she seems to pay a much greater share of her income in taxes than her wealthy employers do; why should she engage in debates over proportional versus progressive tax structures?

Only when one has enough money to have discretion in how to spend it is one confronted with difficult choices. Pamela McLean has an elaborate system for reconciling needs, effort, and chores accomplished in giving allowances to her children. When her husband works, the system is in effect; when he is laid off, there are no allowances and the system therefore is in abeyance. Ernest Berkowitz has the money to meet his payroll and the power to enforce his salary decisions; thus he can be subject to the contradictory pulls of ascription, need, and productivity in deciding how to allocate those resources. And as Craig Cabot points out, the poor are threatened by blacks who want jobs; only the rich can afford to debate the merits of affirmative action policies versus unregulated market processes.

This line of argument suggests systematic variation in the incidence of types of ambivalence. Material constraints induce the poor to focus on conflicts between the real and ideal worlds; lack of material constraints give the rich the opportunity to feel conflict among norms.

The Encroachment of Economic Values

The third form of ambivalence has a different nature from the first two, which involved conflicts between competing views of the world; the third involves the extension of one view of the world into inappropriate domains. People often permit market values, which are based on a principle of differentiation, to encroach on other domains. They neither intend this encroachment nor believe in it, but they still come to evaluate personal or political relationships according to criteria of productivity, efficiency, and competition.

Chapter three discussed how this phenomenon occurs. A society trying to maximize production should give resources to the most efficient producers, thereby increasing the total supply of goods and benefiting everyone. But the process is perverted: first, when efficient producers come to believe that they deserve large shares of goods as a reward for their services; and second, when the goal of increased productivity comes to dominate other, incompatible goals. "Inherent in economic rationality is a tendency for economic values to spread throughout a culture with the consequence that people come to be regarded primarily in terms of their economic utility."[5] Gratifying the needs of "useless" persons becomes an extravagance to be justified by charity or love—not an inherent right of all community members. Rewarding people for trying but failing becomes altruism to be justified as psychological encouragement—not a legitimate payment for fulfilling one's responsibility to do one's best. Finally, rewarding people equally, or equally within ascriptive categories, becomes hopeless idealism, anachronism, or irrationality. In short, norms of results and market procedures overwhelm all other norms, even in the socializing and political domains.

One could argue, as do Salvador Tivolli, Rod Thompson, and Bruce Abbott, that productivity should not be the dominant goal even in the economic domain. Or one could argue, as do Sally White and Bernard Bloomfield, that productivity should be the dominant goal in all domains of life. But these claims are substantive beliefs, not a form of ambivalence, and thus not our concern here. Ambivalence occurs when people are uneasy about blurring distinctions, when they believe that the domains ought to be kept separate, but nevertheless find themselves using market criteria in all areas of their life.

Let us see how some respondents express this type of ambivalence. Maria Pulaski almost always uses a norm of need to respond to her family, but at one point she insists that children "definitely" should do chores to receive allowances. Her teenage granddaughter is "very lazy"; when her mother gives her chores to do before going out, "She'll do it for a week. Then a week later, she's out — she's not doing anything. And I always interfere, tell her she shouldn't do that, keep her in the house. Let her do her work, *then* let her go out. They should have a chore to do." But her uncharacteristic sternness disturbs her, and she immediately amends it by insisting that older children should not have more work than young ones, that "it won't hurt" for boys to have the same chores as girls, and that all children should receive the same allowance for their chores. Thus even when Maria uses a norm of results in the family, she hedges it about with egalitarian rules, and her insistence that "sometimes it's necessary" is very defensive.

Pamela McLean uses a different strategy to incorporate the alien norm of results into her family values. Toys and goods are distributed equally, but when family finances permit, allowances are allocated by chores. Toys bought with those allowances are the only strictly private property in the family. Pamela explains her "earn as you go" program in exhaustive detail: "Sam mows the lawn and earns money. Carol, I paid her three dollars a week, but she earned it. She had to clear the table after supper, do all the dishes, load the dishwasher, and then she had to be available to help the rest of the time. But Sam decided he needed the extra money, so he'd do the job. Well, it went down to two dollars a week because all he does is the table and the dishes, and it takes a lot more pushing to get him at it than she. Keith carries back the garbage cans. He gets a quarter for that." As she continues describing her other daughter's chores, variations on these rules, and special projects to earn vacation money, she constantly emphasizes their exceptional nature. Pamela avoids Maria's defensiveness about a norm of results in the family by separating it sharply from her normal egalitarianism. She deals with her ambivalence not by modifying a norm of results according to an equality norm and vice versa, but by applying the alien norm only to carefully circumscribed situations.

The rich, as well as the poor, are ambivalent about their own use of economic norms in the socializing domain. Judith Baum had her three children as close together as possible in order to avoid "the sibling rivalry which I thought must surely be a dreadful thing." She vehemently opposes competition among children; she treated hers identically, and she taught them completely to share toys and friends. And yet she unconsciously conveys a deep commitment to norms of competition and results. She planned for her children's success literally before they were born: she tried to induce labor so that her oldest child would be born before January 1 and could therefore start school a year earlier than otherwise. She constantly compares their talents and praises them for skills and achievements. At first, her children responded to her unconscious message more than to her conscious one and became deeply competitive: "My younger two are not that friendly. He blames her for a lot of the things that developed with him in his teens. She picks on him. She tends to come on like a nag, with her older sister too." Later, they rejected their mother's drive for success, a rejection that Judith understands no better than their rejection of her equality norm. She explains the fact that "they were dropping in and out of college like yoyos" with only the weak excuse that "it was *the* thing in the sixties, anyway." All she could do at the time was "cling to the experts in child development" and take heart from the knowledge that "during the worst of it, she [her older daughter] still managed to buy the *New York Times* every Sunday." Judith cannot explain their rejection first of equality and then of achievement, because she is unaware that her own ambivalence calls forth confusion, rebellion, and further ambivalence from her children.

Tension also arises when respondents use economic norms of results and competition in the basically egalitarian political domain. Vincent Sartori cannot decide whether or not the government should guarantee incomes, because he cannot decide how much weight to give to the value of productivity. He believes that the rich are mostly undeserving and the poor are not usually to blame for their condition. He also strongly, if vaguely, envisions an egalitarian utopia. And yet he is angry at "welfare cheats" who refuse to work, and he advocates a strict means test and frequent checks by social workers on welfare recipients. Caught between his desire for equality and his knowledge of existing injustice, on the one hand, and his fear that a guaranteed income will benefit even shirkers, on the other, he remains ambivalent about policies to aid the poor.

Barbara Azlinsky's confusion over social welfare policies stems partly from the same set of contradictions. It would be "nice" to ensure everyone basic necessities, health care, and even a minimum income, but "sometimes I wonder if it's fair. When I think about how *we* skimped and saved and did without, I would like to see some other people do it." She vacillates again and again, depending on whether she is thinking of people as needy citizens or as unproductive workers. She comes to a firm resting point, as do most respondents, only on the question of guaranteed jobs. As she puts it, "Basically nobody wants a handout. Busy hands are nice, busy fingers."

This type of ambivalence helps to explain why so many people are enthusiastic about a jobs program. It is the only major policy that allows a norm of results to combine with all other norms instead of competing with them. Is the respondent torn between productivity and equality? Give everyone a job at a high level of income. Productivity and need? The neediest get the first or most lucrative jobs. Productivity and effort? Pay people according to the number of hours they work. Productivity and ascription? Grade jobs according to age, sex, marital or parental status. And so on. A guaranteed jobs program can simultaneously satisfy a norm of results and some, if not all, of the other valued norms.

Isaac Cohen permits market values to penetrate even further than Barbara does into the political domain, and he is even less able to devise a way of resolving the conflicts that result. He makes two contradictory arguments. First, "Our best minds are not governing us." If we made "a profession out of legislating, we would all be served. Take someone who doesn't have the educational background for understanding the social or business or international problems — this is courting disaster." Without "breed[ing] a ruling class," we should insist that candidates have at least a "minimum preparation." Here Isaac clearly calls for replacing political equality with political skill and hierarchy. But he will not carry his argument to its logical conclusion and claim that these professional legislators should always vote as their expertise dictates rather than as their constituents want. He begins to make such a claim: professional legislators could "get information in a given area and logically reason, 'What is good, not only for my constituency, but for everybody?' " Pork barrels and vote trading are "absolutely terrible. Make me sick to my stomach." But his basic belief in political equality does not permit him fully to endorse a Burkean trustee. He is incensed that the local congressman "couldn't care *less* what goes on in this constituency. He doesn't even live in the area anymore. His home here is an empty shell. He has no intention of coming back."

Isaac tries to resolve this contradiction between legislative efficiency and democracy by introducing a second argument using a norm of results. Here he distinguishes between rational, productive voters and ignorant, counterproductive ones. Whether a legislator should vote according to his district's wishes "depends on the constituency that he would represent." Unfortunately, "The average man on the street cannot reason as clearly as I. People don't read the newspapers — [they read] the local news or the sports news; they're just not interested in anything else." Such ignorant citizens should not be able to influence legislators; in fact, they should not even be allowed to vote. "They outvote me. *My* destiny rests on *their* vote? Something is wrong." He does not quite know where to go from there, however. He first advocates a poll tax, then a literacy test, then admits bafflement.

Isaac is caught by his own analogy. Workers must produce goods to deserve economic rewards; why should not citizens have to "produce" knowledge to deserve a vote and legislators have to "produce" skills to deserve an office? But he does not fully accept the analogy. He clearly expects me to oppose it, and at other points he himself argues for political equality. In short, he is ambivalent because he is unable to set clear limits on his own use of a norm of results, as well as on its consequences.

Finally, Jean Gilmore, who is a "Democrat, but a little on the socialist side," supports nationalization of utilities and health care, and praises the earned income tax credit as the first step toward a guaranteed income. She endorses an income floor because "I don't believe in people grubbing for food and a good place to live. I'm all for welfare if it's needed." Not only does she believe in it, she continues, but also "I do as much as I can to help. I feel I'm a very charitable person." She shifts here from justice to self-righteousness — from a claim that need deserves response to a claim that the poor are appropriate objects for charity. This shift occurs during a conversation in which Jean worries that some of the needy could work and therefore do not really deserve aid. At that point, she amends her endorsement of a guaranteed income; she would support it only "if you could separate the good from the bad. So they wouldn't have people claim it who could work." Those who can work deserve no help; at most, charity should prevent their starvation. She is "socialistic" only about the *deserving* needy. Thus combining a norm of need with considerations of productivity has the effect of constraining the former value until it loses its quality of justice. Jean is uneasy about this transformation, but she does not understand what has happened and therefore can neither combat nor accept it.

Thus ambivalence occurs when market norms are used in domains where they do not fully belong. Respondents do not really intend that such slippage occur, and they often become confused or defensive when alien norms distort their egalitarian personal and political views. Only when they discuss a program of guaranteed jobs are they unambiguously enthusiastic, since only then can a norm of results reinforce, not contradict, other norms.

Egalitarian Experiences versus Differentiating Beliefs

A fourth form of ambivalence addresses the relationship between beliefs derived from immediate, daily experiences and general, abstract beliefs. Social scientists have shown over and over that most Americans accept without much question certain liberal tenets: we are a free, individualistic nation with political and social equality; a market system is the best — perhaps the only — way to organize a modern economy; private property is sacrosanct; many of the rich deserve their wealth and the poor their poverty; big government is a dangerous threat to freedom; equality of opportunity is the best form of economic equality. Obviously, some people reject some of these tenets some of the time, but my analysis, as well as that of other researchers, demonstrates how strongly and how unconsciously most people accept most of them. People sometimes find, however, that events in their own lives do not fit comfortably into this world view. They know wealthy or poor people whose position is undeserved; they find that the liberty to vote for two equally undesirable candidates does not make them feel free; they are more constrained by employers' decisions than by federal laws or regulations; they find that equal opportunity means little to a teenage son who cannot find a job. In Antonio Gramsci's terms, the worker's "theoretical consciousness may be . . . opposed to his actions. We can almost say that he has two . . . consciousnesses . . . , one implicit in his actions which unites him with all his colleagues in the practical transformation of reality, and one superficially explicit or verbal which he has inherited from the past and which he accepts without criticism."[6] In my terms, people are ambivalent because they are torn between general differentiating beliefs that they have been taught and specific egalitarian beliefs that they derive from experience. As a result, they feel hesitant, confused, and anxious, and may appear to be inconsistent and nonideological.[7]

Many respondents demonstrate this type of ambivalence.[8] It explains the opposition to redistribution of Pamela McLean, Phillip Santaguida, and Ernest Berkowitz. Pamela, for example, does not rely on monetary incentives to make her work; she does not rely on others' poverty to feel gratified; and she would not sink into sloth and corruption if she acquired financial security. She does not know anyone, in fact, who displays these unpleasant traits. But she is convinced that "most people" are materialistic, competitive, and lethargic, so that redistribution is not feasible. Her general beliefs reinforce a differentiated status quo; her specific experiences refute it. She can neither escape her dominant world view nor wholly accept it; therefore she is left ambivalent about redistribution.

The rich, too, feel torn between general differentiating norms and particular egalitarian experiences. Ernest Berkowitz is not "a striver," and he would be happy to see a social democratic state. But he is convinced that most Americans would not permit it to survive, because everyone else appears to have an unlimited appetite for power and wealth.

Unlike those just described, Amy Campbell is extraordinarily aware of her own ambivalence. She is "a dumb romantic. Gee whiz, I never learn. I shouldn't, I know better in so many ways." As a teenager, she believed that World War II was the war to end all wars because "I saw young fellows who I went to high school [with] being killed, and I *had* to think that there was a *reason*. I had to justify losses of that kind in terms of some ideal." Even after many disillusionments, she still "go[es] back to being that kind of romantic. I do it for my own kind of coping measure. I have to feel that way." She knows that she deludes herself: "When I show myself the evidence [about "the American dream"], I know better. The only thing that makes you not too much of a moron is you're able to laugh at yourself occasionally and say, 'Now come on, you know better.'" Nevertheless, even if it does not exist, the American dream—"this goal, this thing that people set themselves on"—would be violated by income equality and government control of the economy. And despite her "annoyance" at her own naiveté and her knowledge of unfair inequalities, Amy clings to her belief in a world of fair differences: "In a gut feeling, I do have it, it's true. It's something that probably I got growing up, and you don't throw those things off easily. It keeps you from going crazy sometimes or from getting too angry about things." A clearer statement of this type of ambivalence would be hard to find.

Differentiating Experiences versus Egalitarian Beliefs

The interviews just discussed demonstrate the existence of one kind of "contradiction between one's intellectual affirmation and one's mode of conduct."[9] The opposite contradiction also exists; that is, some people have highly egalitarian general beliefs, but their daily experiences reinforce differentiating norms. Gramsci and his followers do not consider this form of ambivalence, but both survey and my interview evidence demonstrate its existence.[10]

All respondents who support an egalitarian utopia illustrate this form of ambivalence. They accept, even endorse, differentiation in their own workplace, but they think wistfully of economic equality in the distant future or past. Consider, in addition, Michael McFarland. On the one hand, he supports differentiation in his daily activities. His $10,000 income is "a fair wage"; his foreman's "brain power" merits extra pay; and shiftless workers are overpaid. He worries about spoiled children, law and order, and "lazy" welfare recipients—all concerns of a differentiator. A "radical" is someone "who, every time you would come up with a suggestion, he would be automatically against you." He defines communism just as negatively: "Russia. It just means you don't have all the freedoms. That you're run by the state."

On the other hand, as he continues his description of communism, Michael supports it more and more as a general ideal:

MM: The state would supply all the money for you. Everybody would be working for the state, there wouldn't really be no rich people in it.
JH: Would that be a good idea or not?
MM: It would be good. I don't know if you would make much money, but they [the state] take care of all your housing and your food and all the necessities. That would be good, if everybody is on kind of an equal level.

The more he thinks about it, the more enthusiastic he becomes. After all, "That's one of the problems [causing] people [to] get high blood pressure and things, it's worrying about where the next dollar's gonna come from. Worrying about paying bills, if I gotta go to the hospital." And yet when Michael returns to the more familiar ground of his job and taxes, he reverts to complaints about lazy workers and welfare rip-offs. He continues to vacillate between these two sets of beliefs and remains anxious, scared, and confused.

Or consider Wendy Tonnina, first on the subject of welfare. She "doesn't think there should have to be any poor people," but her specific recommendations for welfare reform are highly differentiating. She would support higher welfare payments "only if the poor wanted to be [helped]. I'm not going to sacrifice some of my pay that I went to work for, for someone who could care less." She resents welfare cheats and thinks recipients should "definitely be investigated better." Second, on work relations, Wendy excoriates big business for "just taking over the little people. It has them in the palm of their hands because the little people need the jobs. They're very selfish, and they're just out for all they can get. They can pay little people whatever they want because if they quit, they're goin' to get another little person to take their place. They just kinda run the world, you know." And yet she opposes affirmative action policies, not because they are unfair to whites, but because they give workers an excuse to "just sit back and feel oppressed. If someone's really lazy, it's easier to say, 'They won't hire me, I'm black' or 'Italian.' But if they really tried, they could get out of it." After all, no one "ever holds you down with their fist on your throat saying 'Stay there.' It's up to the individual to bring themself up." On both welfare reform and work relations, Wendy's general position is as egalitarian as her specific policy preferences are differentiating. As a result, she continually changes her mind about which distributive changes she endorses.

What are the political implications of these two final, mirror-image forms of ambivalence? Their main effect is to leave people in a state of political paralysis because they cannot think their way through their mixed beliefs to a definite perspective from which to act. Gramsci continues the passage on "two consciousnesses" quoted above by pointing out that the "superficial consciousness inherited from the past" has profound consequences: "It binds [its holder] to a certain social group, influences his moral behavior and the direction of his will . . . It can reach the point where the contradiction of his conscience will not permit any action, any decision, any choice, and produces a state of moral and political passivity."[11] Both types of ambivalence can have this effect. In the former, as Gramsci points out, people are too blinded by the differentiating world view they have been taught to jettison it when their own experiences teach them otherwise. In the latter, their vague egalitarian vision makes them uncomfortable in accepting the differentiating routines and assumptions of daily life. In both cases, as in the previous three types of ambivalence, they find it easier to live with, and to try to ignore, even distressing normative tensions than to undertake the enormous effort needed to resolve them.

Two Theses

From one perspective, my two main theses contradict each other. The first claims that the confusion of views presented in chapter two can be sorted into a discernible three-part pattern of equality-differentiation-equality. Respondents are not inconsistent and are not nonparticipants in the history of ideas; instead, they have coherent, intelligible, flexible, complex — if ultimately contradictory — beliefs grounded in solid philosophical traditions. The second thesis claims that respondents are profoundly ambivalent, caught up in a series of ambiguous, contradictory, blurred judgments. People are confused, and their confusion manifests itself in helplessness, anger, inconsistency, and incoherence.

Presented in such bald terms, the two theses seem to describe different interviews or different researchers' views of the same interviews. But the contradiction is more apparent than real; the real conclusion is that most people exhibit both the three-part pattern of beliefs *and* ambivalence about those beliefs. Some people, such as Pamela McLean and Anne Kaufman, hold beliefs that are predominantly clear and sharp — but even they express some ambivalence. Others, such as Vincent Sartori and Barbara Azlinsky, hold beliefs that are predominantly ambivalent and blurred — but even they express the dominant pattern much of the time.

The strength of in-depth interviewing is that it shows how both main theses can, and do, coexist. It shows that Schumpeter is correct in pointing out "the weakness of the rational processes he [the typical citizen] applies to politics and the absence of effective logical control over the results he arrives at."[12] It also shows that V. O. Key is correct in his "perverse and unorthodox argument . . . that voters are not fools, . . . [that] the American electorate [is] . . . moved by concern about central and relevant questions of public policy."[13] Both views are correct, but only partly so, because they ignore the other view. Analyses of American political beliefs must systematically examine both the pattern of citizens' principles of justice and the breaks in that pattern. This analysis has attempted that dual examination. My only remaining task is to analyze more fully the political implications of the combined patterns of belief and ambivalence.

9 Political Orientations: Why the Dog Doesn't Bark

My final task is to answer the nagging question "So what?" that lurks behind every scholar's work. Here, "So what?" means especially "What do citizens' norms of distributive justice imply about the politics of the downward redistribution of wealth?" Do citizens oppose it? Do they simply not support it? Do they seek more redistribution than opinion polls indicate? The answer is "Yes" to all three, plus more. This chapter examines that rather inconclusive answer and shows how the dominant three-part pattern, ambivalence, the emotional reactions of respondents to their own beliefs, and alternative patterns of belief all affect citizen opinions of redistribution. It provides several answers to the old question of why the dog doesn't bark and suggests what it does instead.

My argument here is most briefly presented in figure 5. The elements of this typology will each be examined in turn.

Patterns of Belief about Distributive Justice

Of the eight possible combinations of two principles and three domains of life, only three occur clearly in my sample — the dominant three-part pattern, consistent egalitarianism, and consistent differentiation. There is, however, one other possibility to consider, namely, holding no discernible pattern of beliefs. Cultural dropouts, unworldly artists,

Figure 5 Beliefs about distributive justice, responses to those beliefs, and political orientations.

Pattern of beliefs

		Dominant	Alternative
Response to pattern of beliefs	Active	Endorsement	Opposition
	Passive	Acquiescence	Indifference

religious mystics, or alienated ghetto residents may be unwilling to take a position on distributive justice. The very young or very old and the mentally or emotionally impaired may be unable to take any position. Since the absence of belief also has political implications, we end up with four patterns of belief to examine.

Response to Patterns of Belief

The other dimension of figure 5, a person's response to his or her pattern of beliefs, requires two points of explanation. First, one might interpret the term *response*, with its categories of "active" and "passive," as a behavioral dimension and thus view the typology as an interaction between attitudes and behaviors. That interpretation, however, is incorrect. The typology — indeed the book — does not directly address political action at all. It addresses only beliefs and respondents' feelings about their beliefs, not actions they might take as a result of their beliefs or feelings.

Second, the response to the pattern of beliefs contains both affective and cognitive elements. The affective element is the respondent's emotions about matters of distributive justice. We have seen emotions ranging from Pamela McLean's contentment to Vincent Sartori's bitterness to Ernest Berkowitz's resignation. The emotions have several sources: respondents' reactions to discrepancies or conjunctions between their beliefs and actual practice; reactions to the consequences of acting on or ignoring their own norms; varied ability to choose among norms within domains; varied ability to reconcile normative disjunctions between domains, and so on. Feelings change as a person moves through time or across domains of life. But all respondents react to their own beliefs, and these emotions propel them toward mental activity or mental passivity. Happiness and anger generate energy; resignation and confusion induce stasis.

The cognitive element of response to one's pattern of beliefs is ambivalence. Ambivalence takes five forms, focusing on either the relationships among norms, ties between norms and the outside world, or both. People who are highly ambivalent are likely to be politically static or passive. For example, Rod Thompson's inability to resolve the contradictions between his general belief in economic equality and his rejection of the specific policy of confiscating wealth leads him to abandon all political involvement even to the point of changing the subject of conversation. People who are seldom ambivalent, conversely, are likely to be politically energetic or active. They may be contented and eager to convince others that they too should be happy, as Pamela McLean is. Or they may be angry and tempted to lash out at the manifestations of injustice, as Isaac Cohen does. But the more certain people are of what they believe, the more actively they express and promote their views.[1]

Active emotions are often associated with low levels of ambivalence, but the association is not necessary or inevitable. One can react to great ambivalence either by becoming angry or by withdrawing; one can respond to clarity and certainty with either proselytizing conviction or complacence.[2] I will not try to generalize further about the likelihood of congruity between active emotions and low ambivalence or vice versa. I will also not try to predict which will predominate, if emotions and degrees of ambivalence conflict, in determining the level of activity of a person's response to his or her pattern of beliefs. Those matters may be entirely idiosyncratic or may show discernible patterns only with a large population of subjects.

In sum, people's responses to their own patterns of belief are composed of both affective and cognitive elements that induce either mental activity or mental passivity.

Combining these two dimensions, each with two possibilities, yields a four-cell table of political orientations—that is, four stances toward given economic and political distributions. Each orientation is one possible response to the question with which this chapter began, namely, "What do citizens' norms of distributive justice imply about the politics of the downward redistribution of wealth?" This question, in turn, is a less elegant, but more precise, reformulation of Sombart's question, "Why is there no socialism in the United States?"

Some people enthusiastically endorse the status quo; some passively acquiesce in it; some strongly oppose it; and some are simply indifferent to it. Let us consider the nature of evidence for and examples of each orientation, as well as its implications for redistribution.

Orientation No. 1: Endorsement of Given Distributions

Some people do not seek downward redistribution because they enthusiastically endorse the given distribution of wealth. They follow the dominant pattern of beliefs. They feel little ambivalence, or if they do feel it, they strive to overcome it by reaffirming their dominant beliefs. Their gratification takes the form of conviction, not quiet satisfaction; their uncertainty is expressed as an active search for answers, not as passive confusion. Thus their norms of distributive justice demonstrate a "wholesale internalization of dominant values and definitions."[3]

Analysts of varying ideological hues predictably differ in their explanations for why even those harmed by the status quo may endorse it. To Marxists this results from "the prestige (and therefore by the trust) accruing to the dominant group because of its position and function in the world of production."[4] Sociologists of knowledge describe how a particular world view "saturates the society . . . and constitutes the limit of common sense for most people under its sway . . . It is a whole body of practices and expectations, . . . our ordinary understanding of the nature of man and of his world . . . It constitutes a sense of absolute because experienced reality beyond which it is very difficult . . . to move."[5] Liberal political scientists emphasize the role of political socialization, "the learning process by which the political norms and behavior acceptable to an ongoing political system are transmitted from generation to generation . . . A well-functioning citizen . . . accepts (internalizes) society's . . . norms."[6] Liberal political philosophers emphasize America's deep-seated, even irrational commitment to Lockean values of individual rights, private property, limited government, and capitalism.[7] Political economists describe "the business molding of volitions" — the "sometimes nearly unilateral persuasion by business, governmental, and political leadership directed at ordinary citizens who do not themselves easily command, as leaders do, the services of printing and broadcasting."[8] There are yet other explanations of enthusiastic endorsement,[9] but the point by now is clear. For whatever reason, a significant proportion of Americans energetically support the political and economic status quo.

For our purposes, the most important feature of endorsement is the disjunction between differentiating economic norms and egalitarian political ones — a disjunction that causes people to reject the redistribution of wealth as normatively undesirable and economically impossible. Just as observers vary in the way they explain endorsement of the status quo, so also do they vary in their enthusiasm for its separation of the two domains. Pluralists praise the fact that Americans "ordinarily agree on a great many questions that in some countries have polarized the citizenry into antagonistic camps." Because of "this massive convergence of attitudes, political contests do not usually involve serious threats to the way of life of significant strata in the community."[10] And so the country remains stable enough to preserve the fragile flower of democracy.[11] Others decry this "moral framework which promotes the endorsement of existing inequality." Elites' ability to "define the reward system as morally just and desirable" and to "set the standards for what is considered to be objectively 'right' " in the economy, culture, speech-patterns, and politics deprives people of the chance to consider whether and how the electoral process should be used to control and shape the economy.[12] Others more vehemently condemn the parliamentary state for lulling the working class into a false belief in its political and social equality with other classes, thereby defusing any potential demand for economic equality.[13]

Thus what appeared initially to be a paradox — Why do Americans, who pride themselves on legal and political equality, accept so much economic inequality? — becomes perfectly intelligible and even essential in this view. Belief in the necessity and justice of economic differentiation permits political equality to exist; belief in the existence of political equality permits economic differentiation to persist. The disjunction is the very essence of Western liberalism.

In my sample, Pamela McLean and Anne Kaufman are the clearest endorsers. Both condemn some distributions, especially when they consider poverty, but both follow the dominant three-part pattern with little ambivalence and great enthusiasm. They seek justice, work hard to achieve it whenever they have any control, and see American society as fundamentally fair. Neither vehemently opposes redistribution of wealth, but on balance both prefer that the government stay out of the economic realm rather than merge domains and force a choice between principles of equality and differentiation.

Another endorser is Wendy Tonnina. Wendy dislikes huge corporations and sympathizes with the "little people" whom they employ and exploit. But she still believes that hierarchy within a firm is essential. Management, not workers, should pick supervisors because workers "might pick the girl they liked the most rather than who could do the best job." Management should also make production decisions "because there will be less hassles between the girls themselves" if they have no choice in their work assignments. Hierarchy is desirable for salaries as well as authority; paying all employees the same amount "would be ridiculous. You couldn't do that. I wouldn't do it. You can't punish the rich because we have poor people." Finally, she rejects government efforts to keep corporations from taking advantage of their workers "because it's someone's own company. You can't tell them they have to help somebody."

In the political domain, Wendy feels sorry for the poor, but blames them for lacking faith in the system: "It's bad for a poor person to grow [sic] their kids up thinking that this is the way it's going to be. They should grow them up like, 'Go out and get what we didn't get.' " Although politicians are often "babyish," she spends more time praising than blaming them, and she argues that "the government needs to be powerful because you have to have something as the head of society." For the country as a whole, "We're in pretty good shape"; for her children, when she has them, she hopes only that they will "be happy and relaxed."

In all these ways, ranging from private ambitions to work relations to political preferences, Wendy shows her support for the status quo. She has plenty of complaints, and many harsh words for bosses, political leaders, and corporate executives. But all of the problems she raises are small and correctable; more important, they all address leaders' failures to live according to the dominant three-part pattern of norms. She is often inconsistent, but seldom ambivalent; often worried, but seldom despairing. Wendy believes that too much differentiation is bad, but that more government intervention in the economy would be worse; therefore she is satisfied with existing trade-offs between free differentiation and mandated equality.

In sum, then, respondents who follow the dominant three-part pattern, who feel (or admit to) little ambivalence, and who are gratified by their beliefs and society's use of them, enthusiastically endorse the economic and political status quo. In their case, the dog does not bark because it is happily chewing a bone given to it by its loved and trusted master.

Orientation No. 2: Acquiescence in Given Distributions

The second political orientation is acquiescence. A person with this stance does not strongly endorse the given economic and political distributions; rather, he or she "complies because he perceives no realistic alternative."[14] People in this category, as in the first, hold the dominant three-part pattern of normative beliefs; however, whereas endorsers feel no ambivalence or seek to reduce it through reaffirming their beliefs, those who acquiesce feel strong ambivalence, which induces political paralysis. If people are in conflict about their beliefs, they will not work toward, or even propound, any large goal or clear pattern. By default, they end up "supporting" the status quo. Finally, this group is likely to feel helpless, bitter, resigned, or withdrawn when they consider their beliefs—all responses that induce mental passivity.

The most interesting question about acquiescence is: What fosters it? What leads people to live quietly with a set of beliefs that they do not fully endorse or whose real world consequences they sometimes condemn? Why do they not do something—whether changing their beliefs or changing the world?

First, since political and social institutions express the dominant world view, few forums exist to give disaffected citizens systematic alternatives. Societies create institutions and roles and thereby construct their own reality: "Commonsense knowledge is the knowledge I share with others in the normal, self-evident routines of everyday life . . . . Since the well-socialized individual 'knows' that his social world is a consistent whole, he will be constrained to explain both its functioning and malfunctioning in terms of this 'knowledge.' . . . Radical deviance from the institutional order appears as a departure from reality," to be explained as immorality, mental illness, or ignorance.[15] Thus even if people are uneasy about their own beliefs or the implications of their beliefs, they have nowhere to turn. Acquiescence "emerges not so much because the masses profoundly regard the social order as an expression of their aspirations as because they lack the conceptual tools, the 'clear theoretical consciousness,' which would enable them effectively to comprehend and act on their discontent."[16]

The role of institutions in promoting acquiescence explains the two types of ambivalence in which a person's abstract principles of justice are at odds with his or her concrete experiences. Rod Thompson, Michael McFarland, and Vincent Sartori do not want to abandon their egalitarian visions, but their experiences at school and work teach them that rewards go only to the person with the greatest ability or highest position. Michael seeks information about communism from a fellow worker in order to learn about an institution that might carry out his abstract egalitarianism, but the knowledge he gains is not reinforced; therefore it is scattered and distorted. Because Rod quit college and now sees only friends and customers, he has no idea where to turn to develop and deepen his redistributive impulses. Vincent would like to create a new institution—a political party of outraged citizens—but he has not the vaguest notion of how to do it or even how to find other people who might concur. Conversely, Isaac Cohen and Bernard Bloomfield hold differentiating visions that are belied by daily experiences. Isaac wishes that the ignorant and propertyless masses could not outvote well-educated and responsible elites, but he can find no party or group to give shape and direction to his vague desires. Bernard Bloomfield wants schools to prepare students for adulthood by punishment and a strict norm of results, but all schools that he knows of are too "soft," uncaring, or devoted to competition to implement his vision.

One consequence of ubiquitous institutional support for the status quo explains two other forms of ambivalence, namely, the encroachment of economic values on inappropriate domains, and the tension between apparent facts and values. Stable institutions with a long history, broad scope, and complex procedures become reified; they develop an aura of being "undeniable facts, . . . external [to the observer], persistent in their reality, whether he likes it or not."[17] Potentially malleable processes or behaviors become "facts of nature, results of cosmic laws . . . [Society] loses its comprehensibility as a human enterprise . . . The world of institutions appears to merge with the world of nature, . . . necessity and fate."[18]

The strongest version of this argument comes, not surprisingly, from the Marxists: "Although all aspects of social existence are in fact manifestations of fundamental relationships between *people*, . . . capitalist society gives the appearance that what is dominant is the relationship between *things* — money, prices, goods, . . . vote totals, written statutes and tables of statistics. All of these appear external to the individual . . . as 'given,' timeless, disembodied, static."[19] But one need not be a Marxist to point out how easy it is to perceive political and economic systems as objects, not processes.[20] After all, in a complex and interdependent world, it is extraordinarily difficult to determine who is responsible for what. As the factory worker Mike Lefevre queries Studs Terkel, "Who you gonna sock? You can't sock General Motors, you can't sock anybody in Washington, you can't sock a system . . . It isn't that the average working guy is dumb. He's tired, that's all."[21] Judges engaged in public interest litigation have the same difficulty in assigning responsibility, and therefore guilt, to individuals within complex institutions.[22] We all complain about bureaucracies being immovable objects or irresistible forces.

The result of this reification "is not simply mental misperception, but political paralysis."[23] If people cannot see "the human agency that is responsible for their exploitation," they also will not see "the possibility of the exercise of their capacity to make change."[24] Only arenas of life in which "practical action is immediately effective" seem worthy of attention and purposeful activity; people who try to change institutions "which seem totally beyond influence . . . appear as disequilibrated cranks whose dizziness leads them to attempt to halt the rotation of the earth."[25] Thus hedonism is not "psychic irrationality"; it is better understood as "an attempt to gain pleasure within a seemingly unalterable set of choices."[26] At worst, the belief that no one can control the world induces a belief that one cannot control even one's own actions. Individual roles may be reified as are institutions, so that people deny responsibility for their behavior: "I have no choice . . . [but] to act this way because of my position."[27] Or, as Phillip Santaguida says, "I have to like my hometown. Have no choice."

Reification of a given economic order underlies the type of ambivalence in which the norms of results and competitive procedures extend out of the economic domain and thereby distort other domains of life. Turning economic relations into "ghostly objectivity" does not stop with material goods. "It stamps its imprint upon the whole consciousness of man; his qualities and abilities are no longer an organic part of his personality, they are things which he can 'own' or 'dispose of' like the various objects of the external world." Once this process begins, all human relations are "subjected increasingly to this reifying process."[28] In my sample, Maria Pulaski, Judith Baum, and Pamela McLean all find themselves using differentiating criteria in domains that they generally reserve for egalitarian norms. All are uneasy about doing so, but none quite understands what she is doing or why.

Reification induces another form of ambivalence. Some respondents assume that the American economic order is a fact of life, regardless of its virtues or defects. Thus Phillip Santaguida assumes that it is "human nature" to be "cannibalistic"; Vincent Sartori assumes that politicians will always be corrupt; Ernest Berkowitz assumes that multinational corporations will continue to grow larger and more omnivorous. For these people, the search for justice is always constrained within the confines of the existing distributive system. Demands for radical redistribution would seem as silly to them as, if they knew of it, King Canute's order that the tides recede.

A second consequence of ubiquitous institutional support for the given order is not reification, but repression. If people somehow became able to see that processes and structures were once created and can therefore be changed or destroyed, they might acquiesce less in the given order. They might begin to develop alternative institutions, which existing ones would then repress or at least discourage, presumably because current structures benefit the groups that run them. "All the institutional mechanisms through which perception is shaped — the schools, the Church, the conventional political parties, the mass media, even the trade unions — in one way or another play into the hands of the ruling groups. The very framework for [the worker's] analysis of the existing system is fixed by the dominant vision of the world."[29] Even this list may not be long enough: there is evidence that the workplace,[30] the welfare system,[31] and even country music[32] repress alternative visions. None of my respondents showed evidence of having been repressed, and it is probably not a phenomenon that many people experience. But it always remains as an implied backup system if simple acquiescence or more profound reification does not suffice to maintain acceptance of the given order.

Another explanation of acquiescence in the given order focuses not on institutions at all, but on the indivdual psychology of confusion or "multiple consciousness." G. David Garson finds auto workers to be "full of ambiguity and overlays of consciousness. Different and seemingly contradictory orientations will be evoked depending upon the context." It is "an inherent characteristic of the present economic order" that workers are "bourgeois [and] . . . class-conscious, . . . both at the same time, for the same individuals."[33] Michael Mann sees a three-tiered confusion: people exhibit little correspondence among their egalitarian interpretations of concrete experiences, conservative political philosophy, and vague populist creeds.[34] Conceptual "disorganization" may be created by "conflicting interpretations of the application of certain values. There is agreement on the symbolic level of the value, but there is disagreement regarding its applicability to situations."[35] In addition, there is the simple fact that American society is enormously complex and interdependent, and requires people to have almost impossible amounts of information in order to make "informed" choices. Anyone who watches television news or reads a newspaper is bombarded with varying views, which may themselves be incoherent. It is little wonder that citizens feel confused enough to decide to leave well enough alone.

This explanation of acquiescence explains the final type of ambivalence, namely, contradictions among norms within one domain. Barbara Azlinsky is torn between norms of need and results; Phillip Santaguida vacillates between norms of social Darwinist competition and need. Many people feel pulled between two or more norms on particular issues, but Barbara's and Phillip's entire belief systems are based on this "multiple consciousness."

A final explanation of acquiescence is simply habit, "the enormous flywheel of society, its most precious conservative agent. It alone is what keeps us within the bounds of ordinance, and saves the children of fortune from the uprisings of the poor. It alone prevents the hardest and most repulsive walks of life from being deserted by those brought up to tread therein . . . It keeps different social strata from mixing."[36] The Declaration of Independence concurs: "All experience hath shown, that mankind are more disposed to suffer, while evils are sufferable, than to right themselves by abolishing the forms to which they are accustomed."[37]

There are at least three explanations for the force of habit. The first is biological: "The organic structure of man entails the formation of habit, for, whether we . . . are aware of it or not, every act effects a modification of attitude and set which directs future behavior. . . . Habit-forming . . . is a natural consequence of the helplessness of infancy."[38] The second is cognitive: "The influence of habit is decisive because all distinctively human action has to be learned, and the very heart, blood and sinews of learning is creation of habitudes. Habits bind us to orderly and established ways of action because they generate ease, skill and interest in things to which we have grown used, and because they instigate fear to walk in different ways . . . Habit does not preclude the use of thought, but it determines the channels within which it operates."[39] The third is emotional: an analysis of acquiescence based only on norms of justice "may be too cognitive, attitudinal . . . People like peace and quiet — radicalism is an uncomfortable state, to many people, of feeling hassled, and an outsider."[40]

Habit does not correspond to any particular form of ambivalence, but it does explain at least two types of comments by respondents. First, even when they hold rather radical ideas, people such as Michael McFarland and Salvador Tivolli recoil from the idea of radicalism. It implies to them violence, fanaticism, negativism, rejection of ordinary discourse and decency — putting oneself outside normal human society. If holding radical ideas means that one must abandon all normal thoughts and activities, no wonder so few people are willing to be "radicals."

Second, respondents sometimes give cliched, knee-jerk responses, but follow them with a more careful consideration that leads to different conclusions. Phillip Santaguida announces that he is the head of the house, then describes his egalitarian relationship with his wife. Vincent Sartori says of course many of the poor are needy, but describes only "rip-off artists." Maria Pulaski assumes that the rich deserve their wealth until she begins to think about particular wealthy employers. Jean Gilmore is "a little bit socialistic" until she thinks about all the virtues of capitalism.

Each of these examples demonstrates how strong habit of thought is until people are induced to examine carefully what they have just said to see if that is what they really mean. Casual conversation calls forth habitual responses that may not reflect the respondent's "real" belief. People may not even know their "real" beliefs until they are forced out of routine channels of thought in ways that challenge, but do not threaten, them.

I have paid such close attention to acquiescence in the dominant three-part pattern of norms because it characterizes so many respondents. Maria Pulaski, Phillip Santaguida, and Ernest Berkowitz, among others, are acquiescent. Phillip refuses to let great wealth and unequal opportunities "bother me. Otherwise I would be in the nuthouse." If he permits himself to get mad, "I keep getting madder and madder and *madder* at everybody around. It's no good. You've got to psych yourself." Therefore he now gets angry only at his golf game: "All this other stuff, I understand about it, I just step right over it. It don't bother me. I just hope for the future." Maria Pulaski says, "What can I do about the system? I can't tell the government." Vicky Pateman can suggest only one way to determine fair wages—look at the union's schedule of wages and multiply that by the number of hours a person works. A clearer example of reification would be hard to find. Finally, Ernest Berkowitz believes that multinational corporations are going to ruin our society, but "who's going to stop them?" Even the president is helpless: "Mr. Carter is going to be a real big hero and save the country millions of dollars in some kind of a program—but he's up against *billions*. Yea, so he carves a little notch or niche, and in eight years he will have done a little carving and gone down in history. He's not going to change it." With no chance of success, why bother even to try to change things?

The greater number of quotations here from poor respondents is not coincidence. The poor are more likely to acquiesce than the rich, perhaps because "only those actually sharing in societal power need develop consistent societal values."[41] Most social interactions are fragmented or superficial, and people need only to comply with specific role expectations for the interaction to be successful; how checkout clerks feel about their job is irrelevant to the grocery shopper.[42] Only when people approach "centers of power" does the smooth functioning of society require commitment to their roles and a consensus on beliefs. Passive acceptance is adequate for a factory worker or clerk; it is not for a teacher, psychologist, or judge. Furthermore, of course, the wealthy and powerful have more reason to endorse, not merely acquiesce in, their lot. Thus the beliefs of the poor can generally be ignored as long as they fulfill their roles. The beliefs of the rich matter more; therefore their socialization is more intense, and their incentives for endorsing economic differentiation are greater.

In sum, respondents may not seek the redistribution of wealth because they are not sure of what they want or if their wants could ever be satisfied. They accept the dominant three-part pattern of beliefs, but they are deeply ambivalent about it and caught in an emotional bind. They do not oppose redistribution as the endorsers do; they simply do not support it. But since not to decide is to decide, as Sartre says, they appear in public opinion polls and conventional wisdom as supporters of the status quo. In their case, the dog does not bark because it does not seem worth its while to waste its energy on an impregnable target or an indefinable unease.

Orientation No. 3: Opposition to Given Distributions

The third political orientation shown in figure 5 is opposition to the given distributions of economic and political goods. A person with this view rejects the dominant three-part pattern of norms in favor of an alternative pattern, probably either consistent egalitarianism or consistent differentiation. Opponents generally feel little ambivalence about their norms, and their emotions, whether passionate conviction or vehement anger, lead them energetically to expound their views.

Figure 5 is silent on the subject of whether to expect opposition from the left or the right of the dominant three-part pattern. Marxists expect egalitarian demands to emerge from the working class or that majority of the population with holdings below the mean. Contemporary political commentators point to differentiating demands emerging from subcultures of the elderly, ethnic groups, technocrats, fundamentalist Christians, upwardly mobile professionals, and single-interest groups. I cannot predict which group will be stronger at any moment; even Antonio Gramsci argued that turn-of-the-century unrest in Italy was as likely to produce repressive authoritarianism as socialist revolution.[43]

But the most interesting question about opposition is: Why is there so little of it in the United States? Why do most Americans enthusiastically endorse the dominant pattern of beliefs, or reluctantly acquiesce in it, or remain indifferent to it? Why, when they do seek change, is it usually piecemeal, ameliorative, and marginal?

I have room (and ambition) here to consider only a few points on this vast subject. Berger and Luckmann point out how difficult it is to question the "truth" of one's "knowledge" of the world.[44] Opposition requires new linguistic and conceptual tools. It is psychologically threatening because it challenges one's own history, the behavior of one's associates, and indeed "the order of the cosmos and the nature of man." It is socially risky, since if others do not accept one's deviant conception as true, opposition becomes isolated and futile. It is politically risky, since opposition implies a threat to existing authority and calls forth repression as soon as it spreads. Opposition does occur, since "all societies are [incomplete] constructions in the face of chaos," and "socialization [across generations] is never completely successful."[45] But its maintenance depends on a deviant group that can both provide psychological and conceptual reinforcement and solve the problem of power.

To overcome external obstacles, as well as internal problems of acquiescence, opponents must quickly develop a "mass political party based on the subordinate class," whether proletariat or born-again Christians. Only a large and well-organized mass party can introduce "a new set of political concepts and symbols" in order to "demonstrate the systematic nature of class inequality [or excess governmental meddling] and . . . reveal a connectedness between man's personal fate and the wider political order." Only such a party can provide the "major sources of political knowledge and information which would enable the subordinate class to make sense of their situation in radical terms."[46]

An opposition party has two requirements. First, "a human mass does not 'distinguish' itself . . . [and] become independent . . . without, in a broad sense, organizing itself; and there is no organization without organizers and leaders."[47] The problem with opposition leaders, assuming that they even exist, is that they come to enjoy their power and holdings, and they become coopted by their constant contacts with mainstream leaders. The problem of cooptation is old, unsolved, and just as problematic for the radical right as for the radical left. It provides an important explanation for the absence of long-term oppositional movements in the pluralistic, log-rolling political system of the United States. Once oppositional leaders "cease to present a radical, class-oriented meaning-system to their supporters, . . . such an outlook [will] . . . not persist of its own accord,"[48] for the reasons discussed above and in the previous section.

The other element necessary for effective opposition is a way of tying radical political ideas into daily life. A dominant world view is not simply imposed dogma, but an entire experience of life. Therefore, exposing an unaware, even if ambivalent, population to a new set of ideas — "that is, simply throwing out an analysis, no matter how correct" — will have little effect. Rather, "*There must be a process of class-wide rethinking*, conducted not in the abstract, but firmly in the context of everyday life."

This requires not only leaders, but also "a larger social stratum within the class which can facilitate the growth of consciousness, practically and intellectually."[49]

Pursuing this analysis would take me far afield from my subject into the realm of political parties, revolution, repression, and radical leadership — issues crucial to a theory of change, but not very relevant in the United States today. We have no mass radical party seeking total equality, complete differentiation, or any other distributive alternative dramatically unlike the status quo. Nevertheless, the sample does contain a few respondents who demonstrate both the tenacity and futility of individual opposition.

All the respondents who believe in alternative patterns of distributive norms, except Eleanor Fox, are opponents of the dominant value system. They express little ambivalence, and their emotions lead them to support their beliefs actively. This is not to say that all would join radical parties or attempt to overthrow the existing political structure even if such parties or movements were available to them. Bruce Abbott and Salvador Tivolli might; for the rest, it is simply too difficult to predict their behavior in a revolutionary situation.

Bruce Abbott has gone the furthest among wealthy respondents to live up to his own alternative creed and to convince others to adopt it. Bruce also has the most fully developed, coherent, consistent, radical world view. But other wealthy respondents are at least partial opponents. Bernard Bloomfield and Isaac Cohen both make arguments with radical implications when they urge the abandonment of drones and welfare cheats, and a reversion to nonliberal forms of political differentiation. Both apply differentiating precepts to their own lives, and both make at least sporadic attempts to convince others to adopt their position. Craig Cabot is a curious mix of endorser and opponent. He generally supports the dominant three-part pattern of beliefs, but his arguments about guaranteed incomes and work incentives imply significant changes in the political and economic domains. He has acted politically to promulgate his reform proposals. His views are sometimes oppositional; his demeanor and actions are impeccably conventional.

Among the poor respondents, Salvador Tivolli has the most fully developed alternative view and expresses the greatest willingness to engage in unconventional political action. He is intrigued by communism and voted for a communist aldermanic candidate because she had "good ideas." He claims that he would join a mob of dispossessed workers storming the White House if another major depression occurred. He thinks workers should run their own industries and make production, wage, and personnel decisions. Rod Thompson shares many of Salvador's egalitarian instincts, but lacking support from others, he is unable to sustain his unconventional perspectives or develop a coherent ideology. Sally White has taken the curious strategy of perceiving existing political institutions as fostering radically differentiating values. She can thereby strongly oppose the dominant value system, but not seek any major changes in the existing political order.

Finally, Vincent Sartori, although he is described as acquiescing in the dominant pattern of norms, is ripe for opposition. Unable to develop an alternative viewpoint on his own, he resorts to drinking, fighting, and fantasizing about robbing banks when his frustration with the given order becomes intolerable. But he has an almost instinctive belief in participatory democracy, a vehement desire for economic change and a lot of amorphous, undirected anger. He liked George Wallace as much as the Kennedys; there is no reason to believe that he would necessarily be an egalitarian radical. But he is a clear candidate for an oppositional party, if such a party were able to reach him in a manner he could understand and use.

In short, some Americans oppose the dominant system of values and react to their beliefs without ambivalence and with great energy. It is very difficult to generate and sustain a complete oppositional orientation on one's own, and none of my respondents do so. Developing an oppositional political movement that has a chance of significantly changing the given order is even more difficult. None of my respondents belong to such a movement, and there may be none for them to join. From this perspective, then, the dog does not bark because even if it did, no one would hear or heed it.

Orientation No. 4: Indifference to Given Distributions

The final political orientation shown in figure 5 is indifference to the given distribution of economic and political goods. A person with this view rejects the dominant pattern of norms in favor of some alternative set, most likely consistent egalitarianism or differentiation. But the alternative of holding no distributive views, or at least no systematic distributive views, is also important here. Those who are indifferent are emotionally passive, static, unconcerned about how their beliefs relate to others' beliefs or to actual distributions of social resources. In short, whereas opponents want to persuade others to accept their alternative beliefs, those who are indifferent "simply find a different way to live and wish to be left alone with it."[50] Opposition is a political orientation; indifference is a cultural or personal orientation (although it has political implications).

Indifference most often occurs in small cultures or societies set apart from their environment. Examples are religious cults, geographically or psychologically remote communes, artists' colonies, Synanon and other all-encompassing self-help groups, and residual ethnic or religious cultures, such as the Native Americans, the Amish, or Hasidic Jews. Alternative cultures can persist only in "areas of practice and meaning which . . . the dominant culture is unable . . . to recognize . . . [or willing to] overlook."[51] Such groups have strong internal solidarity coupled with little class consciousness or engagement with the broader society. In fact, parochial alternative communities may prevent the growth of class or community identification; the more strongly one identifies with an in-group, the more dangerous or alien the out-group — everyone else — appears to be. Such an attitude is not conducive to class solidarity.[52]

People with alternative viewpoints and life-styles may seek only to be left alone, but they face two threats. First, they are safe as long as they represent "areas of experience which [the dominant society is] willing to dispense with, which it[is] prepared to assign as the sphere of private or artistic life, . . . as being no particular business of society or the state." But if the dominant culture develops an "interest and a stake" in this area of life, "many new practices will be reached for, and if possible incorporated, or else extirpated with extraordinary vigour."[53] Consider the history of Native Americans. When their land became desirable to European settlers in the nineteenth century, they were "extirpated with extraordinary vigour." When their culture became exotic and romantic to twentieth-century whites, the whites moved in, developed "Indian" styles of clothing and ornament, and are now destroying through incorporation any distinctively native culture.[54]

Second, assuming they escape the threat of outside invasion, alternative viewpoints are safe only as long as their holders are prepared to resist the blandishments of the cultural mainstream. Consider how many Native Americans, or Amish, or Orthodox Jews have abandoned the culture of their childhood for the conveniences of the dominant American society.

This portrait of people indifferent to distributive issues needs two qualifications. First, members of alternative cultures may not react to threats by becoming acquiescent or enthusiastic supporters of the dominant pattern of beliefs. They may reject incorporation or extirpation, bind themselves more tightly to their fellows, and resist their attackers. They may even convince outsiders of the truth of their ways or ally with other unconventional groups to fight off threats. At that point, they move from passive indifference to active opposition. Second, one can be indifferent without associating with an alternative culture. An individual may simply drop out, refuse to consider any distributive questions, or even maintain a lonely alternative vision of the world.

None of my respondents are completely indifferent, although Eleanor Fox and Steven Vistacco come close. Eleanor is a person whose "experiences, meanings, and values . . . are . . . lived . . . on the basis of the residue—cultural as well as social—of some previous social formation."[55] She is an anomaly in modern American society, and she knows it. She relies almost totally on ascriptive norms: men are superior to women, whites to blacks, and elites to masses. Eleanor is not an opponent. She does not seek to persuade others of her views or to change the modern social structure that has left her behind. She feels little ambivalence, but mainly passive emotions; she wants only to be left alone to live out her life according to the values she learned as a child.

Steven Vistacco exemplifies another type of indifference—that of an accommodating, parochial worker.[56] He does not think either in terms of distributive justice or in terms of the domains of life used here. He focuses on his family, religion, heritage, and community—not on his work, the economy, the broader society, or politics. In his ideal society, people would be "equal to do things, to build, to live together in harmony and equal in their rights to do what's right for you and your fellow man. One against the other in the likeness of God." But he does not seek broad redistribution of social resources. Instead, he envisions a set of small, inward-looking interdependent communities: "Years ago in the seventeenth century when a man built a house, your neighbors got together and built one house, and then you helped your neighbor build his, and he helped *his* [neighbor]. People were more close then. You worked more in unison because you were dependent on them. You couldn't do it yourself because you didn't have the material. But yet too, you created more harmony within your group or community. More so than you are today." He does not particularly oppose a capitalist, liberal, open society, but he certainly does not accept its values as his own.

Thus some Americans do not support the redistribution of wealth because they do not care one way or the other. They may simply have given up any political involvement or even awareness; they may be exclusively concerned about an arena of life that does not involve distributive issues; they may belong to a group or culture that wishes only to be left alone. Alternative viewpoints that induce indifference toward distributive justice are hard to sustain individually and seriously threatened socially. Several of my respondents are partially indifferent, but none are fully separated from the world around them. In this case, then, the dog does not bark because it is preoccupied with doing something else, or doing nothing.

Conclusion

We have, then, four explanations for why the dog does not bark, or why poor Americans do not seek the downward redistribution of wealth. First, some people do not seek it because they do not want it. *Endorsers* support the dominant pattern of beliefs in American society, a pattern that calls for considerable equality at home and in the polity, but not in the economy. They believe in the classical liberal tradition, which sees government activity as, at worst, a threat to economic freedom and, at best, a supplement — but not a replacement — for it. They define political freedom as strict equality, but economic freedom as an equal chance to become unequal — that is, as differentiation. When forced by an importunate interviewer to face the fact that redistribution creates a conflict between their economic and their political values, they become uneasy and do not vehemently reject redistributive claims. But most of the time, they are not forced to face the question of redistribution; in fact, nothing in their normal environment gives them any incentive ever to consider it. Thus they can live quite easily with their normative disjunction. They may be ambivalent about some beliefs, and they may be unhappy about some consequences, notably poverty, of the American system of distribution. But their recommendation for resolving personal ambivalence and solving social problems is more of the same — more political equality combined with better capitalism.

Most people do not seek downward redistribution because they cannot imagine it or do not believe in its possibility. Those who *acquiesce* do not endorse the dominant pattern of beliefs in American society. They do not believe that capitalist differentiation will improve their own lives or the lives of their children and the deeply poor. They are painfully aware of the disjunction between economy and polity. But they perceive no other set of beliefs available to them and no way to resolve their disjunction; therefore they passively concur in the norms with which they were raised and which everyone else apparently holds. They are deeply ambivalent about their own beliefs and often deeply unhappy about the actual distributions they see. But people who acquiesce do not know what to do, and they do not feel politically effective; therefore they simply accept their lot and hope that somehow, someday, something will change.

A few do not seek redistribution because they strongly oppose it. *Differentiating opponents* reject even existing distributions as too egalitarian. They feel no unease about a disjunction between economic and political values because they feel no such disjunction. They unambivalently and happily support differentiation in all three domains of life; therefore downward redistribution holds no appeal for them at all.

A few people do not seek redistribution because they do not care one way or the other about it. Those who are *indifferent* ignore the whole question of distributive justice as it is posed here. They may simply have no opinion; they may use an entirely different set of norms or structure their lives according to an entirely different set of domains. They feel little ambivalence about their views and little desire to change the world to suit themselves. They just want to be left alone.

Finally, a few people do seek redistribution. *Egalitarian opponents* reject existing distributions as too differentiating. They feel no unease about a disjunction between economic and political values because they feel no such disjunction. They unambivalently and enthusiastically support equality in all three domains of life. They are the barking dogs.

The next task for social scientists is to determine how many and what kinds of people endorse, acquiesce, are differentiating opponents, indifferent, or egalitarian opponents. A survey would need to distinguish among kinds and degrees of nonsupport for redistribution of wealth. It should examine distributive beliefs in other domains of life besides the economic. It would also need to query distributive norms, ambivalence, and emotional reactions. Only after such a study is completed can we definitively pronounce on American beliefs about distributive justice.[57]

Policy Implications

It remains only to consider what this analysis suggests for political action in the future. Will the sleeping dog ever rise and bark? Will the poor ever demand redistribution? How will the rich respond if they do? Obviously, I cannot answer these questions, but I can now make some educated guesses.

First, and briefly, some short-term policy implications. Both rich and poor strongly endorse a program of guaranteed jobs. The philosophical reasons are clear: a jobs program resolves one widespread form of ambivalence, in which the economic norm of results seeps into the political domain. A jobs program permits, even encourages, combining a norm of results with any other norm; therefore it turns a contradiction into a complement.

Second, both rich and poor support much more equality than they realize, as long as it is couched in terms of need, investments, or results—anything except equality per se. Pamela McLean, for example, opposes the idea of equalizing incomes, but wants all the needy to be cared for, seeks a minimum wage of at least $10,000 a year, and thinks no one deserves more than $40,000 a year. If she is typical, the normative language in which a distributive policy is couched can greatly affect its support.

It is hardly news that many respondents mistrust government and politicians and think much tax money is wasted. But my analysis does suggest one important, eradicable reason why. Some do not realize the connection between taxes and services.[58] Vincent Sartori, for example, has no idea how the government spends its enormous revenues; therefore he is compelled to believe that corrupt politicians pocket them all. An educational program might increase support for and decrease mistrust of the government. After all, most people claim that they would willingly pay more taxes if they knew that specific social services would result from them.

Willingness to pay more taxes for specific services has two important caveats, however. First, almost everyone, rich and poor, is incensed that the very wealthy do not pay their fair share of taxes. They argue that loopholes are too large and that the tax structure itself is insufficiently progressive. Enforcing steeply progressive taxes at the very top of the income scale might add little to government coffers, but its symbolic value at lower levels would be enormous. Second, no one is enthusiastic about, and very few even accept, inheritance taxes. On this point, the sanctity of private property overwhelms the principle of equality in the political domain. Policymakers who seek revenues and support for government expenditures should not publicize inheritance taxes, even for the very wealthy.

Finally, perceptions and explanations of poverty apparently have changed since the 1950s. A comparison of my sample with Robert Lane's sample of male blue-collar workers in 1958, in their discussions of the nature, causes, and moral connotations of poverty,[59] shows that Great Society rhetoric has had an effect. Most of my respondents see poverty, at least for the majority of the poor, more as a result of bad luck or even structural biases than as the punishment for sin and laziness. Some people do make sharp distinctions between "good" and "bad" poor: the former do not deserve their fate and do deserve help, whereas the opposite is true for the latter. But the former category seems to be larger, in their view; and, on the whole, my respondents have much more sophisticated explanations of poverty than Lane's sample had.

More generally, what can we conclude? The dominant three-part pattern of beliefs mitigates against demands for downward redistribution, since it impels people away from a consideration of political control of the economy and away from the application of egalitarian norms to the marketplace. Some, however, reject this disjunction among domains in favor of demands for more equality or more differentiation. Even some of those who accept the dominant pattern are extremely ambivalent about it. Ambivalence may lead to attempts to reduce dissonance, to eliminate normative disjunctions among domains, and thus to support more equality or differentiation. But in most cases, ambivalence simply blurs the boundaries between domains, blurs the choice between equality and differentiation, diminishes faith in political action, and leads to political paralysis. We are left with an unstable balance between support for and rejection of the status quo.

Two things may happen with such a balance. We may continue as we are now, with little change in the status quo or in people's views of it. There are two reasons that we should expect more of the same. Respondents' very confusion and lack of coherent alternatives may be enough to maintain the existing system. After all, "uniformity of opinion on the grand issues" is not necessary to keep them out of political debate. To maintain the status quo, it is necessary only to "persuade citizens not to raise certain issues, not to make demands in politics on those issues." For example, corporations keep the question of public ownership of industry out of the political arena if they "persuade the citizen that the issue is not worth his energies, *or* that it is discouragingly complex, *or* that agitation on the issue is not likely to be successful, *or* that corporate autonomy is a good thing. Any one will do."[60] Thus almost any combination of norms, ambivalence, and emotions — as long as there are several such combinations — will keep the dog from barking. Some see redistribution as undesirable or even evil; some see it as unattainable; some cannot imagine it at all; some do not care; some cannot make up their minds. Putting all of these beliefs together yields, if not strong support for the status quo, at least no unified support for any alternative.[61]

A second reason that the unstable balance is likely to persist has to do with the nature of the dominant American world view. It is complex and flexible, has a long history and deep roots, and has withstood or absorbed great shocks and vehement opposition. It is "always a process, . . . not . . . a system or structure . . . It does not just passively exist . . . It [is] continually . . . renewed, recreated, defended, and modified."[62] More specifically, "Major social conflicts are transported *into* the cultural system where the hegemonic process frames them, form and content both, into compatibility with dominant systems of meaning. Alternative material is routinely *incorporated* . . . Occasionally oppositional material may succeed in being indigestible; that material is excluded . . . and returned to the cultural margins from which it came, while *elements* of it are incorporated into the dominant forms."[63] Consider, for example, the fate of the New Left of the 1960s. Some of its features—feminism, marijuana use, long hair, jeans and T-shirts, opposition to the Vietnam War and President Nixon—were absorbed into the dominant culture and lost their sting. Other features—the use of hallucinogenic drugs, ascetic communalism, violent revolt—could not be incorporated into the dominant culture, but have been neutralized as political forces by isolation and marginality. A similar process occurs with radical political demands. To advocate guaranteed jobs, incomes, or health insurance—or to advocate slashing taxes and welfare rolls—is politically respectable, even part of the mainstream. Stronger demands—to tax wealth or abolish Social Security—are relegated to "extremists" of the left or right. Thus the dominant world view is strengthened by its ability to bend enough, but not too far, with crosscurrents of wind. If these two arguments are correct, then the unstable balance of ambivalent support for the status quo is likely to persist.

There is, however, an alternative—the balance might be lost. After all, "Social phenomena are *constructions* produced . . . through human activity, . . . no society is . . . [a] symbolic universe."[64] Individual ambivalence reflects society's contradictions. For example, contradictions between social norms and apparent necessity correspond to one type of ambivalence. Racism and sexism are evil, but if there are no qualified blacks or women for a job, what is an employer to do? Special-interest domination of campaigns is undemocratic and wrong, but a member of Congress who remains pure and loses in an election cannot do anyone much good. Free enterprise is the best system, but if the Japanese government subsidizes Japanese steel mills, the United States government must do the same.

Normative contradictions in society correspond to another form of personal ambivalence. Liberalism urges people to work hard, but proposes that real satisfaction is to be found in leisure.[65] It affirms both individual rights and majority rule; it affirms democracy, but endorses strict hierarchy in the workplace, where most people spend most of their lives.[66] It affirms property rights, but insists that the community has a right to tax away some of one's holdings. Most importantly, it sometimes defines equality as equal outcomes, sometimes as equal opportunity, sometimes as compensatory inequality, and so on.

Contradictions between one's general beliefs and specific experiences correspond to still two other types of ambivalence. Theoretically, capitalism, in which private vices generate public virtues, is the most productive and efficient economic system possible. And yet we all know about free riders, money wasted through advertising and superficial style changes in products, planned obsolescence, simultaneous inflation and depression, total ineptitude in managing energy needs. In theory, our democratic republic is the most free and responsive political system possible. And yet we all know about entrenched special interests, gerrymandered electoral districts that avoid minority representation, laws that give symbolic rewards to the needy and material rewards to the wealthy, violent repression of dissent, bureaucracies immune to budget-cutters.

In response to these societal contradictions and strains, Gramscians claim that "bourgeois economic dominance, whether or not it faces serious challenge, has become outmoded: no longer is it capable of representing, or furthering, everyone's interests. Neither is it capable of commanding unequivocal allegiance from the non-elite. The potential for social disintegration is ever-present."[67] During "periods of social dislocation . . . one's experience does not 'stand the test of the future' . . . The accepted realities of the everyday world become subverted and the transformation of the class consciousness (and societal institutions) becomes a possibility."[68] Non-Marxists are sometimes equally apocalyptic: "The institutional order, like the order of individual biography, is continually threatened by the presence of realities that are meaningless in *its* terms . . . *All* social reality is precarious . . . The constant possibility of anomic terror is actualized whenever the legitimations that obscure the precariousness are threatened or collapse."[69] Former President Carter thinks the United States is experiencing a crisis of confidence.[70] My respondents sometimes barely control panic or explosive rage. How will people respond?

It would be wildly presumptuous to try to answer that question, and I shall not. I conclude merely by pointing out that the raw materials of opposition exist at least among some residents of one city. Many of the poor and a surprising number of the rich do not seek redistribution, but are so ambivalent about their own distributive beliefs that they do not oppose redistribution as much as they fail to support any system of distributive justice very fully. They sometimes seek equality; at other times, they seek differentiation; too often, they do not know what they want or even how to decide what the possibilities are.

Appendixes

Notes

Index

APPENDIX A

Demographic Characteristics of Respondents, 1976

Name (Spouse)	Occupation (Spouse)	Income (Spouse)	Age (Spouse)	Dependents	Ethnicity; Religion (Spouse)	Education (Spouse)	Residence
				Poor Respondents: Women			
Pamela McLean	Part-time secretary	$3000	38	4 children	Irish; Catholic	High school	Owns home, rents out one room
(Pete)	(Welder)	($3000)	(37)		(Scottish; none)	(High school)	
Vicky Pateman (widowed)	Dishwasher in school	$6000	60	None (2 adult children)	WASP; Presbyterian	11th grade	Rents apt.
Maria Pulaski	Part-time cleaning woman	$2000	55	6 grand-children; other relations	Polish; none	7th grade	Rents house
(Tom)	(Skilled laborer)	($7000?)	(55)		(Polish; Catholic)	(?)	

Ruth Sennett (widowed)	Disabled day worker	$3000 (SSI)	60	None (1 adult child)	WASP; none	7th grade	Rents apt. from brother downstairs
Wendy Tonnina (single)	Saleswoman in clothing store	$5000	20	None	Italian; non-practicing Catholic	High school, clerical course	Lives rent-free in parents' home
Mary Lou Trask (Sam)	Factory pieceworker (Factory foreman)	$4000 ($8000)	41 (43)	3 children	WASP; Lutheran (WASP; Lutheran)	High school (High school)	Rents house
Sally White (divorced)	Secretary	$6000	27	None (son lives with ex-husband)	WASP; none	High school	Rents apt.
Sandra Wilson (divorced)	Aide in nursery school	$7000	35	No children; 14 Chihuahuas	Irish; none	1 year of community college	Rents apt. from parents downstairs
Poor Respondents: Men							
Michael McFarland	Assembly line maintenance man	$10,000	45	2 children	Irish; Catholic	High school	Owns home
(Patricia)	(Housewife)	(None)	(45)		(Irish; Catholic)	(10th grade)	

Name (Spouse)	Occupation (Spouse)	Income (Spouse)	Age (Spouse)	Dependents	Ethnicity; Religion (Spouse)	Education (Spouse)	Residence
Phillip Santaguida	Salesman	$9000	68	None (2 adult children)	Italian; non-practicing Catholic	7th grade	Owns home; rents one floor to invalid cousin
(Marion)	(Part-time factory worker)	($2000)	(63)		(Italian; Catholic)	(7th grade)	
Vincent Sartori	Unskilled worker	$4000 (unemployment benefits)	35	2 children	Italian; non-practicing Catholic	10th grade	Rents apt.
(Val)	(Clerk)	($4000)	(35)		(?)	(?)	
Timothy Saunders	Bank teller	$10,000	27	3 children	WASP; none	B.A.	Owns home
(Sara)	(Housewife)	(None)	(27)		(WASP; none)	(B.A.)	
Peter Schmidt	Hardware store clerk	$6000	37	2 children	German; Presbyterian	12th grade	Rents house
(Tamara)	(Teacher)	($5800)	(36)		(Austrian; Presbyterian)	(B.A.)	

Name	Occupation	Income	Age	Household	Ethnicity; Religion	Education	Housing
Rod Thompson (single)	Assists father in corner store	$3000	19	None	WASP; none	1 year of community college	Lives rent-free in parents' home
Salvador Tivolli	Disabled factory foreman	$3800 (Social Security)	60	None (5 adult children)	Italian; non-practicing Catholic	6th grade	Owns home
(Valerie)	(Clerk)	($7000)	(58)		(Italian; Catholic)	(10th grade)	
Steven Vistacco	Plumber's helper	$2000	41	2 children	Italian; Catholic	High school	Rents home
(Lucy)	(Part-time saleswoman)	($4000)	(39)		(Italian; Catholic)	(High school)	
Wealthy Respondents: Women							
Barbara Azlinsky	Legal para-professional	$12,000	50	3 children	Polish; Jewish	B.A. & paralegal training	Owns home, several acres
(Ian)	(State civil servant)	($25,000)	(52)		(Polish; Jewish)	(B.A.)	
Judith Baum	Child psychologist	$10,000	53	Invalid father (3 adult children)	Hungarian; Jewish	M.A.	Owns home, several acres
(Jacob)	(Research chemist)	($34,000)	(63)		(German; Jewish)	(Ph.D.)	

Name (Spouse)	Occupation (Spouse)	Income (Spouse)	Age (Spouse)	Dependents	Ethnicity; Religion (Spouse)	Education (Spouse)	Residence
Amy Campbell (divorced)	Laboratory assistant	$10,000	50	None (3 adult children)	WASP; none	B.A.	Owns home, several acres
Eleanor Fox (widowed)	Housewife	$10,000 (investment income)	70	None (2 adult children)	WASP; Episcopalian	Finishing school	Owns home, 25 acres
Jean Gilmore	Housewife	None	48	1 child (2 adult children)	WASP; none	2 years of college	Owns home, several acres
(Bob)	(Contractor)	($45,000)	(53)		(WASP; Unitarian)	(High school tech. train.)	
Anne Kaufman	Housewife	None	55	None (2 adult children)	German; Jewish	High school	Owns home, several acres
(Charles)	(Liquor distributor)	($50,000)	(58)		(German; Jewish)	(Junior college)	

Wealthy Respondents: Men

Name (Spouse)	Occupation (Spouse)	Income (Spouse)	Age (Spouse)	Dependents	Ethnicity; Religion (Spouse)	Education (Spouse)	Residence
Bruce Abbott	School psychologist	$25,000	46	1 child (3 adult children)	WASP; none	B.A.	Owns home, several acres
(Hilda)	(Teacher)	($10,000)	(42)		(Swiss; none)	(B.A.)	

Name	Occupation	Income	Age	Children	Background	Education	Property
Ernest Berkowitz	Shoe store owner	$60,000	55	None (4 adult children)	Lithuanian; Jewish	B.A.	Owns home, several acres
(Frances)	(Part-time social worker)	($8000)	(51)		(Polish; Jewish)	(B.A.)	
Bernard Bloomfield	Chemical manufacturer	$80,000	53	None (3 adult children)	Russian; Jewish	B.S.	Owns home, several acres
(Judy)	(Housewife)	(None)	(49)		(Russian; Jewish)	(?)	
Craig Cabot	Judge	$85,000	37	2 children	WASP; none	J.D.	Owns home, several acres
(Elizabeth)	(Housewife)	? (family wealth)	(35)		(WASP; none)	(B.A.)	
Isaac Cohen	Clothing retailer	$70,000	48	1 child (2 adult children)	Russian; Jewish	1 year of college	Owns home, several acres
(Ellen)	(Housewife)	(None)	(47)		(Russian; Jewish)	(High school)	
David Fine	Architect	$90,000	50	None (2 adult children)	German; Jewish	B.A.	Owns home, several acres
(Anna)	(Writer & radio commentator)	($10,000)	(50)		(German; Jewish)	(B.A.)	

Interview Questions

The questions in this appendix provide an outline of the discussion topics during the interviews. In this sense, the questions began, but did not bind, the discussion. Some questions, for example, were not asked if the topic was covered in an earlier discussion. Other questions required probes and follow-ups to ensure that the respondent had fully discussed the topic. Finally, the questions were modified to make them appropriate for each respondent. For example, when the question was about children, if the children were all grown, I asked, "What did you try to teach . . ."; if the respondent had no children, I asked, "If you had children, what would you try to teach . . ."

I. Socializing Agencies
  A. Family and economic background
    1. How long have you lived in this town? What do you think of it as a place to live?
    2. Have you ever had any contact with Yale or people who work at Yale before? Has anyone in your family? Tell me about it. (Include how respondent felt about Yale connection.)
    3. Could you tell me something about your situation when you were growing up? For example, what kind of work did your father do?
    4. Did anyone else in your family work?
    5. How about your own family now—who are its members? What are their ages? education? occupations?
    6. How would you describe your family's financial situation when you were growing up? What were your home and neighborhood like?
    7. How about now—how would you describe your standard of living, home, and neighborhood? Is the area you are living in now the kind of neighborhood you want to continue living in?

  B. Moral guidance and children
    1. What were the main ways your parents helped you to grow up right?
    2. What are the important things you try to teach your children?
    3. Say your children are squabbling over a toy. How do you decide what is the fair way to end this fight?
    4. Say there is only one piece of pie left, and your children all want it. How do you decide who should get it? What do you want to teach them about dividing things up if everyone wants them?

5. What kinds of things do you like to teach your children about sharing with their friends? How about with people they don't know at all?

C. Education
1. How important is education in helping your children get along well in the world?
2. Do you approve of that?
3. How do you decide how much help to give your children with their homework? What did your parents do with you and your homework?
4. If you were a school teacher, and you had a class with ten smart children and ten not-so-smart children, how would you decide which ones to give the most time and attention to?
5. What do you think grades should be based on? What do you think promotions from one grade level to the next should be based on?
6. Some people feel that encouraging competition among children makes them work harder and do better; what do you think? How do you feel about cooperative work or teamwork among students?
7. Suppose that one of your children badly wanted to go to college, and you could afford it only by sacrificing some things for the rest of the family. What would you do?

D. Money and budgeting
1. How do you decide how much allowance to give your children? How was your allowance decided when you were young?
2. How does your family decide what to spend on food, clothing, a car? Do you think that is a fair process?
3. Suppose one person in your family really wants something special that will cost a lot of money. What do you do?
4. Say one of your children talks another into giving him (or her) his (or her) allowance; do you step in to stop it? Do you think that is fair?
5. Does anyone in your family ever feel especially privileged or under-privileged? When does that happen? What do you do about it?
6. Did you ever feel especially privileged or underprivileged when you were young?

E. Jobs and decision-making in the family
1. How do you decide who should do what kinds of jobs in your family? Do you have a fair division of labor?
2. Do you and your (wife, husband) work together on chores, or do you work separately? What did your parents do?
3. When your family has a big decision to make, say whether to take a vacation or not, how do you decide that? What did your family do when you were young?

4. How does your family decide what TV shows to watch? Did you think your family decided things fairly when you were a child?
5. What kinds of things do you punish your children for? How do you decide what punishment to give them?
6. How do you feel about your wife having a paying job outside your home? (OR) How does your husband feel about your having a paying job outside your home?
7. What kinds of decisions, if any, do your children make?

F. Health
1. If one of your children comes to breakfast on a school day and says he or she is sick, what do you do?
2. Do you or your (wife, husband) spend more time with a sick child than the healthy ones?

G. Friends
1. If you are with a group of friends, and some want to do one thing and some another, how do you decide what to do?
2. In a group of friends, do you find yourself acting as a leader? How do you feel about that? How do you react when other people act as leaders?

H. Ambitions for children
1. Is there anything in particular your children want to do when they are adults? What would you like them to do? Why?
2. Do you think they'll make it? (IF YES) Why? (IF NO) What *do* you think they're likely to do when they grow up?

I. Political socialization
1. Do you remember any of your political views when you were young? What were your parents' views? Does anyone in your family have very strong political views now? Do you and your (wife, husband) agree on political issues?
2. Can you think of anyone or any event that has strongly influenced your political views?

II. The Economy
A. Job history
1. Did you ever have any strong wish to go into a particular kind of work? (IF APPROPRIATE) Why do you think you didn't go into that kind of work?
2. Did your parents have any special ambitions for you? What do they think of your work now?
3. Can you tell me about your first job? How old were you? What was your pay? Why did you take the job? What do you think of the job now?

    4. Have you changed jobs or lines of work much? Why? Were you ever unemployed?

    5. Have you ever felt that any kind of unfair practices or discrimination kept you from getting a job you wanted? Do you know anyone who has been treated unfairly or discriminated against in a job?

    6. Did you ever feel that you had any special benefits or privileges that helped you get a job you wanted?

B. Present job

    1. What kinds of things do you do at work? How did you come to work as a (MENTIONED ABOVE)?

    2. What do you particularly like about your job? What do you dislike about it? If you could change any one thing, what would it be?

    3. Do you expect to stay in this job? What conditions might lead you to change it?

    4. If you could start over again, what kind of work would you try to get into? Why?

    5. Has your company ever done anything to you or anyone you know that you consider unfair? Has it ever given anyone a real boost who deserved it?

C. Wages — comparisons with self

    1. How about the amount of money you are making now — is that about the right amount for you or not? Why?
      (IF NO) How much more would you need to live comfortably?

    2. Does anyone else in your household earn money?
      (IF YES) Is the combination of your incomes enough to live on comfortably?

    3. What would you like most that your present income doesn't permit you to buy?

    4. How do you feel about your income now compared to five years ago — have you gotten a fair deal or not?

    5. How about the next five years — do you think your income will change much? Is that fair?

    6. How about when you retire — what will you live on then? Is that a fair return for your work?

    7. (IF NOT YET ASCERTAINED) How much money do you make now? How much does your (husband, wife) make? How much does (each working member of the household) make?

D. Wages — comparisons with others in workplace

    1. How would you compare your income to what other people like you make?
      What kinds of people are you thinking of?
      Is your income fair in comparison to theirs? Why?

    2. How much would you say your boss makes? How much would you

say the top management people make? How much would you say the
people at the bottom of the pay scale make?

3. Why do you think they make different amounts of money — for example, why does your boss make (MENTIONED ABOVE)?

4. Do you think it is fair that they make different amounts of money?
Why?
Do you think your own income is fair compared, say, to your boss's
income? Why?
(IF NO) Are there any good reasons for people to make different
amounts of money? Why are people paid unfair wages, do you
think?

5. Are there any people at work who get paid more than they deserve?
Are there any people at work who get paid less than they deserve?

6. Suppose you got to sit down and figure out what everyone in your
factory would get paid. How would you handle the following issues?
[FIND OUT ABOUT (a) value of specific positions, (b) upper and
lower limits, (c) strict equality, (d) placement of self, (e) special circumstances, and (f) reasons for distinctions among categories of
employees].

7. Can you imagine any situation where it would be a good thing for
everyone to get paid exactly the same amount?

E. Special circumstances and distinctions

1. Some people feel that people with more boring jobs, such as assembly
line work, should get paid more than people with interesting, varied
jobs, like managers. How do you feel about that?

2. Should people in dangerous jobs get paid more than people in safe
jobs? Should people with very hard physical labor get paid more than
people with light physical labor?

3. Now, think of somebody with about the same job as you. He or she
works just as hard, but isn't as skilled as you; so he or she gets less
done. Should his or her pay be the same as or different from your
pay?

4. How should someone who is very skilled, but doesn't work very
hard, get paid?

5. Would you feel any different if these people were very close friends of
yours?

6. Should two people who do about the same amount of work get paid
the same even if one has a big family and lots of expenses and the
other lives alone?

7. If workers have a sudden emergency, say their house burns or someone in the family has an accident, should the company help them
out? How? (IF YES) Is that the company's responsibility, or is it just a
nice thing to do?

8. How about people with handicaps or bad health? Should they be
paid for a full day's work or just for the hours they work, like every-

one else? Should anything special be done for them? Why?

9. How would you feel if someone you worked with suddenly won the lottery? What do you think he or she should do with the money? What would you do?

F. General social comparisons

1. Think for a minute about the pay scales for some jobs outside your workplace. How much do you think the following groups of people make? (a) doctors, (b) lawyers, (c) college professors, (d) bank presidents, (e) movie stars, (f) football players, (g) school teachers, (h) people who own their own small business, (i) unskilled workers, and (j) garbagemen.

2. (FOR ABOVE OCCUPATIONS) Why do (MENTIONED ABOVE) make (MENTIONED ABOVE) each year? Do you think that is a fair income?

3. How much do you personally think each of these people should be paid? Why?

4. Are there any types of jobs that we haven't talked about yet where people make more than they deserve?

5. Are there any types of jobs where people make less than they deserve?

6. If you got to figure out how much everybody would make in their jobs, apart from what they have now, how would you decide how much each person got? How important would the following be in deciding how much each person got? [FIND OUT ABOUT (a) upper limit, (b) lower limit, (c) need, (d) past treatment, (e) ascriptive traits, (f) skill, (g) hard work, (h) seniority, (i) character, (j) amount produced, and (k) value to humanity].

7. What would happen if everyone made closer to the same income, say between 10,000 and 20,000 dollars a year? What would our society look like? Would it be a good idea?

G. Power and authority in workplace

1. How do you feel about your boss?

2. How much say do you have over what gets done or the way things get done?

3. What do you do if you disagree with your boss?

4. Would you like anything to be different in your dealings with your boss?

5. In China, they sometimes send top management people into the factories for a year to learn what it's like to be a worker. Do you think that's a good idea?

6. How about sending workers into high-level management jobs to learn what it's like to be a boss — is that a good idea?

7. Would you like to be in charge of your factory or workplace?

H. Promotions and layoffs
    1. How do people get high-level jobs in your work? Is that fair?
    2. How do they decide who will get promoted? Is that a good system?
    3. How much do you care whether you get promoted?
    4. If you got to decide who would get promoted, how would you do it?
    5. How do they decide who will get laid off when that's necessary?
    6. How would you decide it?

I. Authority below and equal to respondent
    1. How do you get along with your fellow workers?
    2. Do you have any say over what other people do?
    (IF YES) What do you do if they disagree with you? Why are you the boss and not them? Is that fair?
    3. Are there any people who try to tell you what to do that you don't feel have any right to? What do you do in that kind of situation?
    4. Have you ever worked very closely with someone in a team effort, so that by the end you couldn't tell who had done what on the project? Did you like that? (IF NOT) Would you like to do that?
    How should pay be divided in that kind of situation?
    How should credit for the job be given?
    5. Do you work better by yourself or with others?
    6. Do you work better by competing with others or comparing yourself to them, or by sticking to yourself?
    7. What's the best way for a group of workers to solve problems that come up in their work?

J. Workers' participation
    1. Some people think that workers should choose their bosses, say by an election. Others think this would be a bad idea. How do you feel about that?
    2. Some people also think that workers should make some of the decisions that are now made by the management, such as setting production goals or deciding on working conditions. Others think that would be a bad idea. How do you feel about that?
    3. Should bosses pay more attention to what the workers think or what the management thinks when there is a problem on the floor of the factory?

K. Unions
    1. Do you belong to a union? (IF YES) How do you feel about it?
    2. Is there anything in particular that it has done to help or to hurt you? Is there anything else it should be doing to help you? Is there anything it should not be doing?
    3. Have you ever felt that unions were being too pushy with management?

4. Have you ever felt that the union leaders and management were sticking together and not looking out for the workers?

L. Other rewards
    1. Do you get enough fringe benefits, other than pay? Is there anyone at your work who gets too many or too few benefits?
    2. How about recognition for your work? Does anyone get too much recognition? Does anyone get too little recognition?
    3. Are your working conditions good enough? Does anyone have really bad working conditions?
    4. Do people at work spend a lot of free time with each other?
    5. Would you like it if people from all levels of your work spent more time with each other? Why?
    6. How do you feel when someone criticizes your company or its products?

M. Meaning of money
    1. What is the most important thing money can give you? What can't it give you?
    2. Some people feel that you can never have enough money; others think that you don't really need more than enough to live comfortably. How do you feel about that?
    3. If you had enough money to live comfortably without working, would you continue to work? (IF YES) Would you change jobs? (IF NO) What would you do? What do you think other people would do if they had enough money to live comfortably?
    4. What is the biggest satisfaction people can get out of their job?

N. Class structure
    1. Do you think of yourself as being in a social class? Which one?
    2. What other classes are there?
    3. How would you describe the people in the (MENTIONED ABOVE) classes? If everyone had the same income, would we still have these class differences? How important is education in separating classes?
    4. Say there are 1000 families in New Haven; how many would you say are in the (MENTIONED ABOVE) class?
    5. Do you think it's a good thing that we (have, don't have) different classes?
    6. What would society look like if we didn't have different classes?
    7. Some people say that classes will conflict with each other; others say that they can all get along and benefit each other. What do you think?
    8. Are there any classes that have special privileges? Do they deserve them? Are there any classes that have special problems? Is that fair?
    9. If we could do anything we wanted to change the class structure, is

there anything you'd like to do? What do you think will actually happen to classes over the next twenty years?

O. Mobility
1. You said you were in the (MENTIONED ABOVE) class, right? What class would you say your parents were in?(OR) Would you say you are better-off or worse-off than your parents? Does that seem fair to you?
2. How well-off do you think your children will be compared to you? How do you feel about that?
3. Do you think your own (class, position) will change much? Is that okay with you?
4. If you could be in any other class, which would you like to be in?
5. What are the things that cause people to move up in the world? to move down?
6. What kinds of things should make people move up? What kinds of things should make people move down?
7. In general, would you say that people end up pretty much where they deserve to be? Why?
8. Are there any groups that have a particularly easy time helping themselves? Is that fair?
9. Are there any groups that have a really hard time helping themselves? Is that fair?
10. Say we had a group of 100 children, and all their fathers were in the working class. By the time they were forty, how many of these children do you think would be in the (MENTIONED ABOVE) class? (REPEAT FOR EACH CLASS)
11. Now, say we had a group of 100 children, all of whose fathers were in the upper class. By the time *they* were forty, how many do you think would be in the (MENTIONED ABOVE) class? (REPEAT FOR EACH CLASS)

P. The rich
1. When you think of very rich people, like Nelson Rockefeller or Howard Hughes, how would you describe them? How do you feel about them?
2. How did they get to be as rich as they are?
3. Do they deserve to be that rich?
   Do you think they work harder than other people do?
   Do you think they are more moral than other people are?
   Do you think they are smarter than other people are?
4. Have you ever heard of the phrase, "The rich get richer . . . ?" (IF YES) What does it mean to you? (OR) Do rich people ever get breaks that the rest of us don't?
5. Are rich people any happier than the rest of us?
   Would you like to be that rich?

6. Do rich people have any special problems that other people don't have?

7. Do rich people have any responsibilities that are different from those of the rest of us? (IF YES) Do they usually live up to them?

8. Do you think there will always be very rich people in our country?

9. How do we benefit, if at all, from having rich people in the U.S.?

10. Some people say that income from inheritance is the reward for living a good life; others say that income from inheritance is unfair. What do you think?

11. Do people who inherit a lot of wealth have a right to do whatever they want with it, regardless of how well or badly other people are living?

12. Do people have a right to make as much money as they can and spend it however they want, no matter how it affects people outside their family?

13. Would we be better-off if there weren't any very rich people?

14. What would it be like if there weren't any very rich people? Should the government tax away the wealth of very rich people?

Q. The poor
1. When you think of very poor people, what kinds of things do you think of? How do you feel about them?

2. How did they come to be that poor?

3. Do poor people usually deserve to be poor?
   Do poor people work harder than most people?
   Are poor people more moral than most people?
   Are poor people smarter than most people?

4. Are poor people ever happier or better-off than most people? Do they ever get any special breaks that other people don't get?

5. Are some people or groups especially unfair to poor people?

6. Do you think we'll ever get rid of poverty? Would that be a good thing? Do the rest of us benefit at all from the fact that there are poor people?

III. The Polity
   A. Taxes
1. About how much income tax do you pay each year?

2. What's your best guess of how much someone who makes ($3,000, $15,000, $50,000, $500,000) a year is legally supposed to pay?

3. How much tax is a fair amount for you to pay?

4. Does the difference between what you actually pay and what you should pay matter to you much? How about someone who earns ($3,000, $15,000, $50,000, $500,000)—does the difference between what he or she actually pays and what he or she should pay matter very much to you?

5. Do you think the government should use tax laws to limit the amount

of money someone can inherit? Do you think the government should use tax laws to limit the amount someone can earn in a year? (IF YES) What should the limit be? Why? (IF NO) Should there be a limit on the amount of taxes any one person has to pay in a year?

6. Have you ever heard about some very rich people who pay almost no taxes? How do you suppose they do that? Do you think that is fair or not? How about very poor people—should they pay taxes or not?

7. Do you think it is a good idea for the government to help out big businesses that are in financial trouble? Should the government give tax breaks on certain business expenses?

8. In general, if you had to figure out how much tax people should pay, which of the following rules would you set up? [FIND OUT ABOUT (a) proportional vs. progressive, (b) income vs. total wealth, (c) admissible deductions vs. no deductions, and (d) other kinds of taxes, such as sales tax, property tax, etc.].

9. What kinds of things does the government spend tax money on? What kinds of things *should* government spend tax money on?

10. (IF NOT ANSWERED ABOVE)

    Does the government in Washington waste a lot of our tax money, or does it use tax money pretty well? Does the government in Washington spend tax money in ways that you approve of, or would you like to see some changes in government spending?

B. Personal experience and opinions

1. What would you say is the biggest problem facing the country? What should the government in Washington do about it, if anything? What shouldn't it do?

2. Would you say the government in Washington has made your life better? (IF YES) How?

3. Would you say the government in Washington has made your life *worse*? (IF YES) How?

4. Have you ever had a problem that you had to take to a government agency, such as a tax problem or a traffic violation? (IF YES) How were you treated? (IF NO) How would you expect to be treated if something like that happened?

5. Do you think you (got, would get) equal treatment with everyone else in that kind of situation?

6. Are there any kinds of people that you think would get especially good treatment? Are there any kinds of people that you think would get especially bad treatment?

7. In general, how do you feel about the way government agencies deal with people?

C. Power and influence

1. Do political leaders in Washington care much about the way people like you feel? Do local leaders care much about the way people like you feel?

2. Do political leaders try to do what's best for the whole country, or are they more concerned with other things? (IF LATTER) What are they concerned with?

3. Do you think officials in New Haven show favoritism in giving benefits to any groups of people? Do you think officials in Washington show favoritism in giving benefits to any groups of people?

4. Do the city officials pay enough attention to the needs of all people? Do the officials in Washington pay enough attention to the needs of all people?

5. Is the government in Washington too powerful? Not powerful enough?

D. Rights and equality in government

1. Which of the following are rights of Americans? (a) free speech, (b) religion, (c) movement, (d) the vote, and (e) carrying a gun. Should the government do anything to make sure we have the right to (MENTIONED ABOVE)? Do we have any other rights?

2. Do people demand any of the following even though they have no right to be given them? (a) food, (b) medical care, (c) housing, or (d) education? Are any of these things rights of Americans? Why?

3. Do the people in Congress represent everyone equally? Does the President represent everyone equally?

4. Should members of Congress focus on what their constituents want, or what the Congress thinks is best for the whole country?

5. Who really knows what is best for a person in the long run—the individual, or some of our leaders, or who? Do the people in Washington know better than others what is good for people in the country?

E. Government's role in the economy

1. Do you think the government should limit the amount of rent landlords can charge for apartments?

2. Should the government have fire and safety regulations for apartments, houses, and public buildings?

3. How do you feel about tenant strikes, when you hear of them or read about one in the paper? Have you ever been involved in one?

4. Should the government set a minimum wage? Should the government set a maximum wage?

5. Should the government make regulations where there are a few big companies in the same field of business—things like airfares, television programs, or gasoline prices?

6. Should the government be involved in consumer protection issues—things like regulating auto safety devices or foods and drugs?

7. Are there areas where the government makes laws or regulations that it should stay out of? Why?

8. Some people feel that the government must always protect private property; others feel that the government can sometimes take private property when it needs to do something badly enough—for example,

build an interstate highway or a new post office. How do you feel about that?

9. Sometimes people say that if a store in their neighborhood, say a grocery store, charges really high prices, that they have a right to take over the store and sell food to the neighborhood more cheaply, so that no one makes a high profit. How do you feel about that?

F. Direction of the national economy

1. Many people say our country as a whole is a lot richer now than it was at the turn of the century. Do you agree? Why do you suppose it is (so much richer, the same, poorer)?

2. Do you think the country is going to get richer in the next twenty years, or stay the same, or get poorer? Why? What effects do you think that will have?

3. When business booms in New Haven, who gets the benefit? How does it affect you personally?

4. When there is a recession, or businesses fail, who gets hurt? How are you affected?

5. What do you think might happen if we had another depression, such as in the 1930s?

6. Where do you think most of the profits from big business go?

G. Political labels

1. Generally speaking, do you usually think of yourself as a liberal, a conservative, or as something else? (IF LIBERAL OR CONSERVATIVE) Would you call yourself a strong (liberal, conservative)?
(IF OTHER) How would you describe your political views?

2. How would you say the liberals differ from the conservatives? Are there any ways in which they are the same?

3. Does the term "radical" mean anything to you in particular? Have you ever thought of yourself as a radical?

4. Some people talk about the "capitalist society" or "capitalism." Does this mean anything to you, or isn't it a phrase you use very much? Do you think this is a good way to organize a society? Why? How about the phrase "socialism"—does that mean anything in particular to you? Do you think this is a good way to organize society?

5. Should the government in Washington try out more new ideas, or is it better off sticking to existing ways of doing things? Why?

6. Do you think our problems in the U.S. can be corrected with a few reforms, or do we need bigger changes in the government and society? Why? (IF THE LATTER) What kind of changes do we need? Will they ever happen?

H. Role of citizens and politicians

1. What would you say a good citizen is?

2. Is it better for people like you to obey the law and respect authority,

or to learn when to disobey authorities and try to change laws? Why?

3. Do you ever feel that politics and the government are so complicated that you can't keep up with what's going on? How often do you feel that way?

4. When things really seem to be going wrong in the country, whose fault is it?

5. When you think of politicians, what do you think of? Why would someone go into politics?

6. Are there any politicians or people in government that you really admire? Who? Why? Are there any that you really dislike? Who? Why?

I. Welfare

1. What is the main reason that people go on welfare? When you think about people on welfare, what kinds of people come to your mind?

2. Have you or anyone in your family ever received welfare or relief payments? Did you try to seek help from anyone you knew first? (IF YES) How did you feel about it? What were the circumstances? How did you get off? (IF NO) How do you think you would feel if you received welfare payments? Would you prefer to seek help from someone you know first? Who?

3. Are there any groups or types of people who take advantage of the welfare system? Are any groups or people getting a raw deal?

4. Are any of the following kinds of welfare better or fairer than other kinds? (a) temporary aid in natural disasters, (b) aid for handicaps such as blindness, (c) food to mothers with young children and no support, (d) housing to mothers with young children and no support, and (e) aid to all families that don't have a decent standard of living. Would you be willing to support any of the (MENTIONED ABOVE)? Is help such as (MENTIONED ABOVE) a right or a charity? Should the aid for (MENTIONED ABOVE) be money or goods? Are (MENTIONED ABOVE) simply practical necessity or do the people have a right to these programs?

J. Redistribution in-kind

1. Now think about some of the things the government does with tax money to help different kinds of people, not just the very poor.
Does the government do enough, not enough, or too much for ordinary people with the following? (a) Social Security, (b) unemployment compensation, and (c) health care.

2. Would you be willing to pay more taxes to help pay for (MENTIONED ABOVE)?

3. Should the government set up more job training centers? (IF YES) Would you be willing to pay higher taxes to support them? Should the government provide more chances for people to go to college without having to pay tuition if they can't afford it? (IF YES) Would you be willing to pay higher taxes to support them? Why?

4. Are there any other kinds of programs that the government should set up? Are there any programs that we now have that ought to be shut down?

K. Redistribution
1. Should the government have the responsibility of making sure that everyone who can work is able to find a job, even if that means setting up public works programs? Why?
2. Should the government have the responsibility for making sure that every family has an income, even if no one in the family can work? Why? How strongly do you feel about that? (IF IN FAVOR) What should the minimum income be for a family of four people?
3. What would you think about the government changing the tax laws so that every family in America had just about the same income, no matter what kind of work its members do? Why? Do you feel very strongly about that?
4. If that program were set up, would most families be better-off than they are now? What would happen if every family in the country had the same income? Would the country be better- or worse-off? Would you be better- or worse-off?
5. Would you like to live in a society in which the government provided everyone with the basic necessities, such as housing and medical care, and then let people earn what they could beyond that? Is it the government's responsibility to do that? Is the government already doing that?
6. Are there some people who have a right to that kind of government help, but not others? Why is that?
7. Do you think the government would be able to set up the following programs successfully? (a) guaranteed jobs, (b) guaranteed income, and (c) equal family incomes.
8. Would you like to live in a society where the government does nothing except provide national defense and police protection, so that people would be left alone to earn whatever they could? How well do you think you would do in such a society?

L. General sense of equality and justice
1. The Declaration of Independence says that "All men are created equal." In what ways would you say that all people are created equal? In what ways are they unequal?
2. Are there people that you see as better than you? Who? How? Are there people that you feel better than somehow? Who? How?
3. What does the word *justice* mean to you? Are there groups or types of people who are treated unjustly in America today? (IF YES) Who?
4. Would you say that you are usually treated justly by the national government? Are you treated fairly at work? in society in general? by your coworkers and neighbors?

5. Can you think of any times, even when you were a child, that something happened to you that made you mad because you thought it was really unfair?
6. How about to someone else?

M. Justice and equality regarding race
   1. How would you explain the protests of black people in the past fifteen years or so? What is the best advice you could give to black people who want better jobs and more respect in our community?
   2. Do you think that all races should mix on an equal basis? Why?
   3. In your opinion, is the New Haven government fair to both blacks and whites, or does it favor one race over the other? (IF NOT FAIR TO BOTH) Why? Does that bother you?
   4. On the average, black people in New Haven have worse jobs, housing, and education than white people. How would you explain that? Should anything be done about it?
   5. Some people say that because of past discrimination we need to give special treatment to some people in minority groups; others say that special treatment is unfair. How do you feel? Why?

N. Justice and equality regarding the law and court system
   1. Do you feel that there are any kinds of people who get special treatment according to the law? Is that fair? Are there any who are discriminated against by the law?
   2. Are there any laws that you feel are unfair?
   3. Are there any kinds of people who get especially good treatment in courtroom practices or are likely to be especially successful in court cases?
   4. Are there people who are likely to be especially discriminated against, or hurt, in court cases?
   5. Do you feel that you would get the same treatment as everyone else if you were involved in a legal problem?

O. Progress and decline in own life
   1. If you could choose one thing that would make you really happy, what would that be? Do you think you are ever going to get (MENTIONED ABOVE)?
   2. When you think about what really matters in your life, what are your wishes and hopes for the future?
   3. What would you say is the biggest disappointment in your life? Why did (MENTIONED ABOVE) happen?
   4. If you imagine your future in the worst possible light, what would it look like? Do you think (MENTIONED ABOVE) is likely to happen? Can you do anything to prevent (MENTIONED ABOVE)?

P. General progress and decline in life

1. In general, would you say it is easy or hard for people to make their own lives better? Why?
2. Some people's lives don't ever seem to get any better, or sometimes even get worse. Why do you think that happens? Do you think that happens very much?
3. Would you say people now are happier or less happy than people were at the turn of the century? Why is that? Do you think our children will be happier in the future than we are now? Why?
4. Do you think people now are more or less moral compared with people at the turn of the century? Why? Will our children be more or less moral in the future? Why?

Q. Self-definition
   1. If you had to describe yourself to someone who didn't know you, what would you say? What are your best and worst qualities?
   2. What would you say are your most important values or beliefs? What do you think is the most important thing in life?

R. Utopia
   1. If you could design a utopia, a society where everything is just as you'd like it to be, what would it look like?
   2. What would be the best direction our country could go in?
   3. If you had to think of the worst society you could live in, what would it be like? What would be the worst direction our country could go in?
   4. Which way do you think we're moving? Why?
   5. Is there anything else you want to add? Are there any questions you want to ask me?

Notes

1. Why There Is No Socialism in the United States

1. Sir Arthur Conan Doyle, "Silver Blaze," in *The Annotated Sherlock Holmes,* ed. William Baring-Gould, 2 vols. (New York: Clarkson N. Potter, Crown Publishers, 1967), 2:277.

2. Werner Sombart, *Why Is There No Socialism in the United States?* trans. Patricia M. Hocking and C. T. Husbands (White Plains, N.Y.: M. E. Sharpe, 1976).

3. In 1977, the median money income of households in the United States was $13,572; the mean income was $16,100. The difference was $2,528. In 1970, there was a $1,978 gap (in 1977 dollars) between median and mean income. U.S. Bureau of the Census, "Money Income in 1977 of Households in the United States," *Current Population Reports,* P-60, no. 117 (Washington D.C.: U.S. Government Printing Office, 1978), p.2. This measure suggests what more sophisticated data confirm: income has become more unequally distributed since 1970.

4. Joseph J. Spengler, "Changes in Income Distribution and Social Stratification: A Note," *American Journal of Sociology,* 59 (November 1953): 253.

5. Robert J. Lampman, "Changing Patterns of Income, 1960–1974," in *Toward New Human Rights,* ed. David C. Warner (Austin: University of Texas Press, 1977), p. 122.

6. Alexis de Tocqueville, *Democracy in America,* ed. J. P. Mayer, trans. G. Lawrence (New York: Doubleday, Anchor Books, 1969), p. 9.

7. Louis Hartz, *The Liberal Tradition in America* (New York: Harcourt, Brace, and World, 1955), p. 206.

8. David Cameron, "Economic Inequality in the United States," paper presented

at the annual meeting of the Midwest Political Science Association, Chicago, April 1979, p. 9.

9. Morgan Reynolds and Eugene Smolensky, *Public Expenditures, Taxes, and the Distribution of Income* (New York: Academic Press, 1977), p. 77.

10. Ibid., pp. 82-88; Morgan Reynolds and Eugene Smolensky, "Post-FISC Distribution of Income: 1950, 1961, and 1970," Discussion Paper #270-75 (Madison: Institute for Research on Poverty, University of Wisconsin, May 1975), p. 21.

11. Eugene Smolensky, Leanna Stiefel, Maria Schmundt, and Robert Plotnick, "Adding In-Kind Transfers to the Personal Income and Outlay Account: Implications for the Size Distribution of Income," Discussion Paper #199-74 (Madison: Institute for Research on Poverty, University of Wisconsin, 1974), abstract.

12. Ibid., p. 20.

13. For discussions of policies that transfer goods, services, or wealth upward, see George J. Stigler, "Director's Law of Public Income Redistribution," *Journal of Law and Economics*, 13 (April 1970): 1-10; W. Lee Hansen and Burton Weisbrod, "The Distribution of Costs and Direct Benefits of Public Higher Education: The Case of California," *Journal of Human Resources*, 4 (Spring 1969): 176–191; Kenneth E. Boulding and Martin Pfaff, eds., *Redistribution to the Rich and the Poor* (Belmont, Calif.: Wadsworth Publishing Co., 1972); W. I. Gillespie, "Effect of Public Expenditures on Distribution of Income," in *Essays in Fiscal Federalism*, ed. R. Musgrave (Washington, D.C.: Brookings Institution, 1965), pp. 122–186; Howard M. Wachtel and Larry Sawers, "Government Spending and the Distribution of Income," in *The Poverty Establishment*, ed. Pamela Roby (Englewood Cliffs, N.J.: Prentice-Hall, 1974): 63–104; and Henry J. Aaron, *Shelter and Subsidies* (Washington, D.C.: Brookings Institution, 1972).

14. Timothy M. Smeeding, "The Anti-Poverty Effectiveness of In-Kind Transfers," *Journal of Human Resources*, 12 (Summer 1977): 370.

15. Ibid., p. 372. Other analysts, making somewhat different assumptions, find a greater diminution of poverty as a result of in-kind transfers. See Edgar K. Browning, *Redistribution and the Welfare System* (Washington, D.C.: American Enterprise Institute, 1975), and Morton Paglin and Gerald Wood, *Poverty and Transfers In-Kind* (Stanford, Calif.: Hoover Institution Press, 1980).

16. Smeeding, "Anti-Poverty," pp. 367–378.

17. Ibid., p. 375. See also Timothy M. Smeeding, "The Trend toward Equality in the Distribution of Net Income," Discussion Paper #470-77 (Madison: Institute for Research on Poverty, University of Wisconsin, December 1977).

18. R. A. Musgrave and P. Musgrave, *Public Finance in Theory and Practice*, 3rd. ed. (New York: McGraw-Hill, 1980), chaps. 12 and 15.

19. See Martin Anderson, *Welfare* (Stanford, Calif.: Hoover Institution Press, 1978): chap. 2.

20. Joseph A. Pechman and Benjamin A. Okner, *Who Bears the Tax Burden?* (Washington, D.C.: Brookings Institution, 1974), p. 61. Okner has updated this analysis to consider the distributive effects of aggregate taxation in 1970 and concludes that "no significant changes in the pattern of relative tax burdens occurred between 1966 and 1970." See Benjamin A. Okner, "Total U.S. Taxes and Their Effect on the Distribution of Family Income in 1966 and 1970," in *The Economics*

of Taxation, ed. Henry J. Aaron and Michael J. Boskin (Washington, D.C.: Brookings Institution, 1980), pp. 69-84.

21. Roger A. Herriot and Herman P. Miller, "The Taxes We Pay," *Conference Board Record,* 8 (May 1971): 40. On Director's Law, see Stigler, "Director's Law."

22. Stanley Lebergott, *The American Economy* (Princeton: Princeton University Press, 1976), pp. 239, 245.

23. Jeffrey Williamson and Peter Lindert, *American Inequality: A Macroeconomic History* (New York: Academic Press, 1980), p. 33.

24. James D. Smith and Stephen D. Franklin, "The Concentration of Personal Wealth, 1922-1969," *American Economic Review,* 64 (May 1974): 162.

25. Williamson and Lindert, *American Inequality,* p. 107.

26. Aristotle, *The Politics of Aristotle,* trans. and ed. Ernest Barker (London: Oxford University Press, 1972), p. 215.

27. John Adams, *The Works of John Adams,* ed. Charles F. Adams (Boston: Little, Brown, 1850-1856), vol. 6 (1851): 8-9.

28. Lord T. B. Macaulay, "Lord Macaulay on American Institutions," *Harper's New Monthly Magazine,* February 1877, p. 461.

29. Stephen Simpson, "Political Economy and the Workers," in *Social Theories of Jacksonian Democracy,* ed. Joseph Blau (Indianapolis: Bobbs-Merrill, 1954), p. 146.

30. Huey P. Long, *Every Man A King* (New Orleans: National Book Co., 1933), pp. 293-294. See also pp. 290-298.

31. See also Walter Bagehot, *The English Constitution* (New York: D. Appleton, 1920); Henry George, *Progress and Poverty* (New York: Robert Schalkenbach Foundation, 1960); Upton B. Sinclair, *I, Governor of California and How I Ended Poverty* (New York: Farrar and Rinehart, 1933); and Daniel Webster, quoted in Long, *Every Man,* p. 296n.

32. See for example Brian Barry, *Political Argument* (London: Routledge and Kegan Paul, 1965), especially pp. 38-83.

33. See Gunnar Myrdal, *An American Dilemma* (New York: Harper and Brothers, 1944); and Otto Kerner, Chairman, *Report of the National Advisory Commission on Civil Disorders,* intro. by Tom Wicker (New York: Bantam Books, 1968). Arguing from a neo-Marxist, rather than a liberal perspective, Frances Fox Piven and Richard A. Cloward nevertheless agree that a liberal polity needs some downward redistribution to remain stable. See *Regulating the Poor* (New York: Random House, Pantheon Books, 1971).

34. John A. Brittain, *The Inheritance of Economic Status* (Washington, D.C.: Brookings Institution, 1977); John A. Brittain, *Inheritance and the Inequality of Material Wealth* (Washington, D.C.: Brookings Institution, 1978); Leonard Goodwin, *Do the Poor Want to Work?* (Washington, D.C.: Brookings Institution, 1972); Christopher Jencks et al., *Inequality* (New York: Basic Books, 1972); Christopher Jencks et al., *Who Gets Ahead?* (New York: Basic Books, 1979); Lester Thurow, *Generating Inequality* (New York: Basic Books, 1975); and Kay Lehman Schlozman and Sidney Verba, *Injury to Insult* (Cambridge, Mass.: Harvard University Press, 1979).

35. Joseph T. Howell, *Hard Living on Clay Street* (Garden City, N.Y.: Anchor

Press, 1973); Louis (Studs) Terkel, *Working* (New York: Random House, Pantheon Books, 1974); Louis (Studs) Terkel, *American Dreams* (New York: Random House, Pantheon Books, 1980); Robert Coles, *Children of Crisis* (New York: Dell, Delta Books, 1967); Robert Coles, *Children of Crisis,* vol. 2, *Migrants, Sharecroppers, and Mountaineers* (Boston: Little, Brown, 1971); Robert Coles, *Children of Crisis,* vol. 3, *The South Goes North* (Boston: Little, Brown, 1971); Harry Maurer, *Not Working* (New York: Holt, Rinehart and Winston, 1979); and Carol B. Stack, *All Our Kin* (New York: Harper & Row, 1974).

36. C. B. Macpherson, *Democratic Theory* (Oxford: Oxford University Press, 1973); Edwin Dorn, *Rules and Racial Equality* (New Haven: Yale University Press, 1979); Herbert Gans, *More Equality* (New York: Random House, Pantheon Books, 1973); Michael Harrington, *Socialism* (New York: Saturday Review Press, 1972); and John Schaar, "Equality of Opportunity, and Beyond," in *Equality: Nomos 9,* ed. James R. Pennock and John Chapman (New York: Atherton Press, 1967).

37. See Leon Festinger, "A Theory of Social Comparison Processes," *Human Relations,* 7 (May 1954): 117-140; Robert K. Merton, *Social Theory and Social Structure* (Glencoe, Ill.: Free Press, 1957); and Thomas Pettigrew, "Social Evaluation Theory: Convergences and Applications," in *Nebraska Symposium on Motivation, 1967,* ed. David Levine (Lincoln: University of Nebraska Press, 1967), pp. 241-318.

38. W. G. Runciman, *Relative Deprivation and Social Justice* (Berkeley: University of California Press, 1966); and Helmut Schoeck, *Envy: A Theory of Social Behavior* (New York: Harcourt, Brace, and World, 1969).

39. E. E. Jones, David Kanouse, Harold Kelley, Richard Nisbett, Stuart Valins, and Bernard Weiner, *Attribution* (Morristown, N.J.: General Learning Press, 1971).

40. Lee Rainwater, *What Money Buys* (New York: Basic Books, 1974).

41. Ibid.

42. Jacqueline Macaulay and Leonard Berkowitz, eds., *Altruism and Helping Behavior* (New York: Academic Press, 1970).

43. Jones et al., *Attribution.*

44. Zick Rubin and Letitia Anne Peplau, "Who Believes in a Just World?" *Journal of Social Issues,* 31 (Summer 1975): 65-89.

45. Leonard Berkowitz, gen. ed., *Advances in Experimental Social Psychology,* vol. 9, *Equity Theory* (New York: Academic Press, 1976), ed. Leonard Berkowitz and Elaine Walster; and Elaine Walster, Ellen Bersheid, and G. William Walster, "New Directions in Equity Research," *Journal of Personality and Social Psychology,* 25 (February 1973): 151-176.

46. Harold L. Wilensky, *The Welfare State and Equality* (Berkeley: University of California Press, 1975), pp. 30-31.

47. Malcolm Sawyer, "Income Distribution in OECD Countries," *OECD Economic Outlook: Occasional Studies* (Paris: Organization for Economic Cooperation and Development, 1976): 15.

48. Lloyd A. Free and Hadley Cantril, *The Political Beliefs of Americans* (New York: Simon and Schuster, Touchstone Books, 1968), pp. 101, 107-108.

49. George Gallup, *Gallup Opinion Index*, 117 (March 1975): 10-12.

50. George Gallup, *Gallup Opinion Poll*, 157 (August 1978): 3.

51. Robert L. Lineberry, *American Public Policy* (New York: Harper & Row, 1977), p. 19. Data are from United States Advisory Commission on Intergovernmental Relations, *Significant Features of Fiscal Federalism* (Washington, D.C.: U.S. Government Printing Office, 1976).

52. Ted Robert Gurr, *Why Men Rebel* (Princeton: Princeton University Press, 1970); Samuel A. Stouffer, Edward A. Suchman, Leland C. DeVinney, Shirley A. Star, and Robin M. Williams, Jr., *The American Soldier*, vol. 1, *Adjustment during Army Life* (New York: John Wiley & Sons, 1949); Robert K. Merton and A. S. Kitt, "Reference Groups," in *Sociological Theory*, ed. Lewis A. Coser and Bernard Rosenberg (New York: Macmillan, 1957), pp. 264-272; James C. Davies, "Toward a Theory of Revolution," *American Sociological Review*, 27 (February 1962): 5-19; Jack H. Nagel, "Inequality and Discontent: A Nonlinear Hypothesis," *World Politics*, 26 (July 1974): 453-472; Runciman, *Relative Deprivation*; and David O. Sears and John B. McConahay, *The Politics of Violence* (Boston: Houghton Mifflin, 1973).

53. Lebergott, *The American Economy*, p. 162.

54. David L. Featherman and Robert M. Hauser, "Changes in the Socioeconomic Stratification of the Races," *American Journal of Sociology*, 82 (November 1976): 629.

55. U.S. Congress, House of Representatives, Committee on Education and Labor, *Problems of Youth Unemployment*, 96th Cong., 2d sess. (Washington, D.C.: U.S. Government Printing Office, 1980), p. 1.

56. Note that we are dealing here with three distinct issues: putative equality of opportunity, actual equality of opportunity, and equality of results. One necessary, but not sufficient, indication of equality of opportunity would be similar median incomes for identifiable blocs of people. If equality of opportunity is only putative, as tables 5 and 6 suggest, then one might seek the realization of that goal or a different goal — equality of results or downward redistribution. I am suggesting that women and blacks might be expected to abandon the equal opportunity goal as a chimera and pursue the equal outcomes goal instead.

This discussion ignores important complexities hidden in the terms *individuals, blocs, equal opportunity,* and *equal results.* For a full treatment of these issues, see Douglas Rae, Douglas Yates, Jennifer Hochschild, Joseph Morone, and Carol Fessler, *Equalities* (Cambridge, Mass.: Harvard University Press, 1981).

Note also that inequalities of holdings usually translate into inequalities of political resources, so that the pursuit of greater political equality might well become tied to the pursuit of greater economic equality. See Robert A. Dahl, "On Removing Certain Impediments to Democracy in the United States," *Political Science Quarterly*, 92 (Spring 1977): 1-20; Charles E. Lindblom, *Politics and Markets* (New York: Basic Books, 1977), pp. 161-233; and Gabriel Kolko, *Wealth and Power in America* (New York: Praeger, 1962).

57. Albert O. Hirschman with Michael Rothschild, "The Changing Tolerance for Income Inequality in the Course of Economic Development," *Quarterly Journal of Economics*, 87 (November 1973): 546-548.

58. Ibid., p. 552.

59. Ibid., p. 552.

60. R. F. Hoxie, *Trade Unionism in the United States* (New York: D. Appleton, 1920); and Selig Perlman, *A Theory of the Labor Movement* (New York: Augustus M. Kelley, 1970).

61. Leon Samson, *Toward a United Front* (New York: Farrar and Rinehart, 1935); David A. Shannon, *The Socialist Party of America* (New York: Macmillan, 1955); and Sombart, *Why No Socialism*.

62. The data about Debs and Thomas appear in Schlozman and Verba, *Injury to Insult*, p. 21.

63. The left wing of the Democratic Party is best represented by DSOC (the Democratic Socialist Organizing Committee). See its newsletter, *The Democratic Left*, ed. Michael Harrington.

64. David DeLeon, *The American as Anarchist* (Baltimore: Johns Hopkins University Press, 1978); James R. Green, *Grass Roots Socialism* (Baton Rouge: Louisiana State University Press, 1978); Corinne Jacker, *The Black Flag of Anarchy* (New York: Scribner, 1968); Richard E. Rubenstein, *Rebels in Eden* (Boston: Little, Brown, 1970); and Henry Silverman, ed., *American Radical Thought: The Libertarian Tradition* (Lexington, Mass.: D. C. Heath, 1970).

65. Robert S. Fogarty, ed., *American Utopianism* (Itasca, Ill.: F. E. Peacock, 1972); Charles Nordhoff, *The Communistic Societies of the United States* (New York: Schocken Books, 1965); John Humphrey Noyes, *History of American Socialisms* (Philadelphia: J. B. Lippincott, 1870); and William Alfred Hinds, *American Communities*, intro. by Henry Bamford Parkes (Secaucus, N.J.: Citadel Press, 1961).

66. Joseph Feagin, "Poverty: We Still Believe That God Helps Those Who Help Themselves," *Psychology Today*, November 1972, pp. 107, 108; George Gallup, *Gallup Political Index*, 5 (October 1965): 22; George Gallup, *Gallup Opinion Index*, 37 (July 1968): 23; ibid., 43 (January 1969): 21; ibid., 144 (July 1977): 21-24; Susan Hansen, "Public Opinion and the Politics of Redistribution," unpublished paper (Urbana: University of Illinois, 1977); and Natalie Jaffe, "Attitudes toward Public Welfare Programs and Recipients in the United States," Appendix B in Lester Salamon, *Welfare: The Elusive Consensus* (New York: Praeger, 1978), pp. 221-228.

67. Schlozman and Verba, *Injury to Insult*, p. 222.

68. Hansen, "Public Opinion."

69. Feagin, "Poverty."

70. Schlozman and Verba, *Injury to Insult*, pp. 203-219.

71. See Hartz, *The Liberal Tradition*; Dahl, "On Removing Certain Impediments"; Tocqueville, *Democracy in America*; Frederick Jackson Turner, *The Frontier in American History* (New York: H. Holt, 1921); Friedrich Engels, "Letter to Friedrich A. Sorge," in *Marx and Engels: Basic Writings on Politics and Philosophy*, ed. Lewis S. Feuer (New York: Doubleday, Anchor Books, 1959); Walter Galenson, "Why the American Labor Movement Is Not Socialist," *The American Review*, 1 (Winter 1961): 31-51; and Selig Perlman, "Upheaval and Reorganization (since 1876)," in John R. Common et al., *History of Labor in the United States*, 4 vols. (New York: Macmillan, 1918), 2:195-537.

72. Thomas E. Weisskopf, "Capitalism and Inequality," in *The Capitalist*

System, ed. Richard C. Edwards, Michael Reich, and Thomas E. Weisskopf (Englewood Cliffs, N.J.: Prentice-Hall, 1972), p. 126.

73. See Lebergott, *The American Economy*, p. 165.

74. Lindblom, *Politics and Markets*.

75. [Alexander Hamilton, John Jay, and James Madison], *The Federalist*, intro. by Edward Mead Earle (New York: Robert B. Luce, 1976), especially no. 10.

76. Perry Anderson, "The Antinomies of Antonio Gramsci," *New Left Review*, 110 (November 1976–January 1977), all quotations from p. 28. On pluralism, see, for example, David Truman, *The Governmental Process*, 2d ed. (New York: Alfred Knopf, 1951).

77. Ira Katznelson, *City Trenches* (New York: Random House, Pantheon Books, 1981), chaps. 1 and 3.

78. Morris Rosenberg, "Perceptual Obstacles to Class Consciousness," *Social Forces*, 32 (October 1953): 122-127; Melvin M. Tumin, "Some Unapplauded Consequences of Social Mobility in a Mass Society," *Social Forces*, 31 (October 1957): 32-37; Michael Mann, *Consciousness and Action among the Western Working Class* (London: Macmillan, 1973); Edward E. Lawler, "Reward Systems," in *Improving Life at Work*, ed. J. R. Hackman and J. L. Suttle (Santa Monica, Calif.: Goodyear Publishing Co., 1977); David O'Brien, *Neighborhood Organization and Interest Group Processes* (Princeton: Princeton University Press, 1975); and Mancur Olson, *The Logic of Collective Action* (Cambridge, Mass.: Harvard University Press, 1965).

79. James E. Rosenbaum, *Making Inequality* (New York: John Wiley & Sons/Interscience, 1976); Samuel Bowles and Herbert Gintis, *Schooling in Capitalist America* (New York: Basic Books, 1976); and Michael D. Katz, *Class, Bureaucracy, and Schools* (New York: Praeger, 1975).

80. Sidney Verba and Kay Lehman Schlozman, "Unemployment, Class Consciousness, and Radical Politics: What Didn't Happen in the Thirties," *Journal of Politics*, 39 (May 1977): 291-323; Schlozman and Verba, *Injury to Insult*; Ely Chinoy, *Automobile Workers and the American Dream*, intro. by David Riesman (Boston: Beacon Press, 1970); Richard Sennett and Jonathan Cobb, *The Hidden Injuries of Class* (New York: Alfred Knopf, 1972); and Robert E. Lane, *Political Ideology* (New York: Free Press of Glencoe, 1962).

81. The best summary discussions of why there is no socialism in the United States are John H. M. Laslett and Seymour M. Lipset, eds., *Failure of a Dream?* (Garden City, N.Y.: Doubleday, Anchor Books, 1974); and Seymour Martin Lipset, "Why No Socialism in the United States?" in *Radicalism in the Contemporary Age*, ed. Seweryn Bialer and Sophia Sluzar, 3 vols., Studies of the Research Institute on International Change, Columbia University (Boulder, Colo.: Westview Press, 1977), vol. 1, *Sources of Contemporary Radicalism*, preface by Zbigniew Brzezinski, pp. 31-149.

82. It may not be clear to some why we should examine attitudes to begin with. After all, if great ideas, or vast economic trends, or random selection determines the course of human history, then individual beliefs and actions are merely expressions of those forces. Less grandiosely, if belief systems are mainly the result of childhood socialization, then we should study the socializing agencies, not the resulting beliefs. But studies of political socialization, not to speak of studies of

huge historical forces, are poor at predicting a person's actions and viewpoints. Furthermore, it does not at all deny their importance to insist that how people actually feel and behave is also important. Surely if the Western ideals of democracy and human dignity mean anything, they mean that we must take seriously what citizens want and what they value. Part of understanding why there is no socialism in America is understanding why Americans are not socialists.

83. Robert Redfield, *The Little Community and Peasant Society and Culture* (Chicago: University of Chicago Press, Phoenix Books, 1967), p. 81. See also *Phenomenology and the Social Sciences*, ed. Maurice A. Natanson, 2 vols. (Evanston, Ill.: Northwestern University Press, 1973), 1: 3-44; and Lane, *Political Ideology*, pp. 8-10.

84. I deliberately limited the study to whites, in order to minimize communication barriers between the respondents and myself and to keep the focus on economic and social, not racial, differences.

85. All incomes are in 1976 dollars. The interviews were conducted between January 1976 and March 1977. Some of "the poor" are not really poor and some of "the rich" are not really rich strictly in terms of money income; however, all of "the poor" are manual or at most low-level white-collar workers with virtually no wealth or assets; all of "the rich" have great wealth and assets, even if they have fairly low incomes. Thus I use the terms *rich* and *poor* as a shorthand to describe respondents' overall socioeconomic status. Appendix A has a summary description of the respondents and their holdings and prospects.

86. See Appendix B for the interview questions. The respondents completed the full set. They also filled out two sets of paper-and-pencil measures examining their beliefs in "the just world syndrome," their level of Machiavellianism, their perception of the locus of control in their lives, and their interpersonal values and skills. Because these measures were not used directly in this book, I will not discuss them further.

87. Karl A. Lamb, *As Orange Goes* (New York: W. W. Norton, 1974), p. viii. Lamb also suggests that intensive interviewing comes closer to the phenomenological truth of social reality than a "scientific" survey, which "reduces the responses of human beings to a numerical value" (ibid.). This suggestion seems to be a loose variant of my third claim about the value of intensive interviewing. Note, however, that I take no position on whether phenomenology or positivism better describes "truth." As a teacher of mine once put it, "I have no dog in that fight"; my point is only that the two methods yield different, perhaps complementary, truths.

88. Harry Eckstein, "Case Study and Theory in Political Science," in *Handbook of Political Science*, ed. Fred I. Greenstein and Nelson W. Polsby, vol. 7, *Strategies of Inquiry* (Reading, Mass.: Addison-Wesley, 1975), p. 93.

89. Ibid., pp. 95, 105.

90. Ibid., pp. 107-108.

91. For example, despite their elaborate and sophisticated debate over how to study political ideologies and public opinion, Robert Lane and Philip Converse agree that most Americans hold "unconstrained" beliefs, or are "morselizers" rather than "contextualizers." From a substantive, rather than a methodological,

perspective, there is little difference between their findings. See Lane, *Political Ideology;* Philip Converse, "The Nature of Belief Systems in Mass Publics," in *Ideology and Discontent,* ed. David Apter (New York: Free Press, 1964), pp. 206-261; Lane, "Patterns of Political Belief," in *Handbook of Political Psychology,* ed. Jeanne Knutson (San Francisco: Jossey-Bass, 1973), pp. 83-116; Converse, "Public Opinion and Voting Behavior," in *Handbook of Political Science,* ed. Fred I. Greenstein and Nelson W. Polsby, vol. 4, *Nongovernmental Politics* (Reading, Mass.: Addison-Wesley, 1975), pp. 75-169.

92. If the X's fell along the other diagonal, the structure of the argument would be the same, although its substance would be reversed. A surveyor would then find a high negative correlation, and an intensive interviewer might find support for equality at home *and* at work as the alternative finding.

93. Eckstein makes a strong argument in favor of case studies, which are at least similar to intensive interviews, in his article on "Case Study and Theory." I do not disagree with his claims, but they are not directly relevant here. For other strong arguments in favor of small-sample methodology, see Park O. Davidson and Charles G. Costello, $N = 1$ (New York: Van Nostrand Reinhold, 1969) and Aaron Cicourel, *Method and Measurement in Sociology* (New York: Free Press, 1964), pp. 73-120.

2. Support for and Opposition to More Equality

1. Quotations from respondents are verbatim, with two exceptions. Extraneous words or phrases ("uh," "you know," "like") or repetitious words have been omitted, except when they indicate significant hesitation or uncertainty; and words that might identify a person or place have been omitted or changed.

All identifying details have been changed with as little distortion of the salient characteristics of the respondent as possible.

2. Robert Redfield, *The Little Community and Peasant Society and Culture* (Chicago: University of Chicago Press, Phoenix Books, 1967), p. 81.

3. Norms of Distributive Justice and Three Domains of Life

1. Ralph H. Turner, "Value Conflict in Social Disorganization," *Sociology and Social Research,* 38 (May–June 1954): 301-302.

2. Peter L. Berger and Thomas Luckmann, *The Social Construction of Reality* (Garden City, N.Y.: Doubleday, 1966), pp. 21-22.

3. David L. Sallach, "Class Domination and Ideological Hegemony," *Sociological Quarterly,* 15 (Winter 1974): 41.

4. The best discussion of the idea of equality in American political thought and action is J. R. Pole, *The Pursuit of Equality in American History* (Berkeley: University of California Press, 1978). Another valuable work, which examines the idea of equality in American thinking more analytically than historically, is Amy Gutman, *Liberal Equality* (Cambridge: Cambridge University Press, 1980).

5. *Social resources* is a general term encompassing material goods (for example, money, jobs, property), social goods (for example, opportunity, privilege, prestige), and political goods (for example, rights, authority, freedom). The term

is deliberately loose, since it is meant to accommodate anything that a society deems to be valuable, assignable, and at least potentially subject to considerations of justice.

6. L. T. Hobhouse, *The Elements of Social Justice* (London: George Allen and Unwin, 1922), p. 97.

7. For a detailed analysis of these and other elements of a complete definition of equality, see Douglas Rae, Douglas Yates, Jennifer Hochschild, Joseph Morone, and Carol Fessler, *Equalities* (Cambridge, Mass.: Harvard University Press, 1981).

8. Few philosophers have systematically tried to array distributive claims along a single continuum or to place such an array into a context of everyday use. Thus although the concepts in this chapter are obviously not original with me, the classification scheme is completely my own.

9. For analyses of the relationship between philosophy and psychology, see Martin Hollis, *Models of Man* (Cambridge: Cambridge University Press, 1977); Albert O. Hirschman, *The Passions and the Interests* (Princeton: Princeton University Press, 1977); and David Miller, "The Ideological Backgrounds to Conceptions of Social Justice," *Political Studies*, 22, no. 4 (1974): 387-399.

10. Gregory Vlastos, "Justice and Equality," in *Social Justice*, ed. Richard Brandt (Englewood Cliffs, N.J.: Prentice-Hall, 1962), p. 43.

11. Hugo Bedau, "Egalitarianism and the Idea of Equality," in *Equality: Nomos 9*, ed. J. Roland Pennock and John W. Chapman (New York: Atherton Press, 1967), p. 17.

12. Henry A. Myers, *Are Men Equal?* (Ithaca, N.Y.: Cornell University Press, Great Seal Books, 1945), p. 32.

13. Joel Barlow, *Advice to the Privileged Orders in the Several States of Europe . . .* (Ithaca, N.Y.: Cornell University Press, Great Seal Books, 1956), pp. 15-16. His italics.

14. See Richard W. Wollheim and Isaiah Berlin, "Equality," *Proceedings of the Aristotelian Society* (London: Harrison & Sons, 1956), 56: 281-326.

15. See Isaiah Berlin, *Four Essays on Liberty* (New York: Oxford University Press, 1969), pp. 118-172; and C. B. Macpherson, *Democratic Theory* (Oxford: Oxford University Press, 1973), pp. 95-119.

16. Gal. 3:28, New English Bible.

17. Steven Lukes, "Socialism and Equality," *Dissent*, 22 (Spring 1975): 159-160.

18. Bedau, "Egalitarianism," p. 13.

19. Gracchus Babeuf, *Manifeste des égaux*, trans. Steven Lukes, cited by Steven Lukes, "Socialism and Equality," *Dissent* 22 (Spring 1975): 155. For more on Babeuf, see Leszek Kolakowski, *Main Currents of Marxism*, trans. P. S. Falla, vol. 1, *The Founders* (Oxford: Oxford University Press, Clarendon Press, 1978), pp. 184-187; and Frank E. Manuel and Fritzie P. Manuel, *Utopian Thought in the Western World* (Cambridge, Mass.: Harvard University Press, 1979), pp. 568-577.

20. Robert S. Fogarty, ed., *American Utopianism* (Itasca, Ill.: F. E. Peacock, 1972), pp. 64-65.

21. Ibid., pp. 65-66.

22. Morton Deutsch, "Equity, Equality, and Need: What Determines Which

Value Will Be Used as the Basis of Distributive Justice?" *Journal of Social Issues*, 31 (Summer 1975): 146.

23. John Dewey, *The Public and Its Problems* (Chicago: Gateway Books, 1946), p. 62.

24. Richard H. Tawney, *Equality*, intro. by Richard M. Titmuss (London: Unwin Books, 1964), pp. 107-108. It is possible, of course, to believe in a norm of strict equality but not to seek fellowship. An example is the conventional wisdom about Yankees: they are willing that blacks be equal to them in all respects, as long as they do not get too close. (My thanks to James Fishkin for this point.) This comment demonstrates that the psychological claims about human motivation discussed here are neither logically nor empirically necessary adjuncts to their corresponding philosophical norms for behavior. But exceptions do not invalidate my argument that a particular norm and a particular type of social relation are generally associated with each other.

25. Bertrand R. Russell, *Authority and the Individual* (Boston: Beacon Press, 1949), p. 47.

26. Ibid., pp. 26, 47, 57.

27. Alexis de Tocqueville, *Democracy in America*, ed. J. P. Mayer, trans. G. Lawrence (New York: Doubleday, Anchor Books, 1969), pp. 691-692. Russell also concludes that "a society in which each is the slave of all is only a little better than one in which each is the slave of a despot. There is equality where all are slaves, as well as where all are free" (*Authority*, p. 49).

28. Russell, *Authority*, p. 49.

29. Vlastos, "Justice and Equality," p. 43.

30. William Frankena, "The Concept of Social Justice," in *Social Justice*, ed. Richard Brandt (Englewood Cliffs, N.J.: Prentice-Hall, 1962), p. 20. See also John Dewey's argument that "equality does not signify that kind of mathematical or physical equivalence in virtue of which any one element may be substituted for another. It denotes effective regard for whatever is distinctive and unique in each, irrespective of physical and psychological inequalities" (*The Public and Its Problems*, pp. 150-151).

31. Vlastos, "Justice and Equality," p. 40. See also Rae et al., *Equalities*, chap. 5; David Thomson, *Equality* (Cambridge: Cambridge University Press, 1949); Bernard Williams, "The Idea of Equality," in *Philosophy, Politics, and Society*, ed. Peter Laslett and W. G. Runciman (New York: Barnes and Noble, 1962), pp. 110-131; and John N. Findlay, *Values and Intentions* (London: George Allen and Unwin, 1961).

32. Vlastos, "Justice and Equality," p. 41.

33. Tawney, *Equality*, pp. 49-50.

34. Hobhouse, *Social Justice*, p. 118.

35. Ibid., p. 118.

36. Compare with Vlastos's different, also apparently empirical, claim that a norm of need is possible only in affluent societies. If resources are very scarce, helping people with extraordinary needs hurts others, and "failure to meet the extremity will not be felt as a social injustice but as a calamity of fate." Since humanity has been so poor until recently, it is easy to see "why it has been so slow to connect provision for special need with the notion of justice, and has so often

made it a matter of charity." Vlastos, "Justice and Equality," p. 42. See also Walter A. Weisskopf, "The Dialectics of Equality," in *The "Inequality" Controversy*, ed. Donald Levine and Mary Jo Bane (New York: Basic Books, 1975), pp. 214-227.

37. Hobhouse, *Social Justice*, p. 109.

38. Joseph Morone, "Equality of Results," unpublished paper (New Haven: Yale University, 1976). See also Wilfredo Pareto, *Manual of Political Economy*, ed. Ann S. Schwier and Alfred N. Page, trans. Ann S. Schwier (New York: Augustus M. Kelley, 1971), for example, p. 45; and Lionel Robbins, "Interpersonal Comparisons of Utility," *The Economic Journal*, 48 (December 1938): 635-641.

39. But see Edward Bellamy, *Looking Backward 2000-1887* (New York: Lancer Books, 1968), for an argument that these problems can be resolved in an egalitarian way through a market system. For other suggested solutions, see Rae et al., *Equalities*, chap. 5; Ilmar Waldner, "The Empirical Meaningfulness of Interpersonal Utility Comparisons," *Journal of Philosophy*, 69 (February 1972): 87-103; and John C. Harsanyi, "Can the Maximin Principle Serve as a Basis for Morality?" *American Political Science Review*, 69 (June 1975): 594-606.

40. Hobhouse, *Social Justice*, p. 110.

41. For a review of the debate on functional stratification, see Melvin M. Tumin, *Readings on Social Stratification* (Englewood Cliffs, N.J.: Prentice-Hall, 1970), pp. 367-454.

42. Deutsch, "Equity, Equality, and Need," p. 146.

43. Just as support for strict equality need not entail a desire for fellowship, so a response to need does not have to entail the desire that all people develop their potential fully. The counterpart to the conventional wisdom about Yankee racism (see note #24) is the conventional wisdom about Southern racism: Southerners are willing to nurture and be nurtured by blacks, as long as the blacks do not rise too high. But again, neither exceptions nor partial agreement invalidates the general premise. Again my thanks to James Fishkin for a very helpful discussion of the relationship between the philosophy and psychology of a norm.

44. Dewey, *The Public and Its Problems*, p. 150. Dewey insists that the idea of equality "isolated from communal life" is a "hopeless abstraction . . . , a creed of mechanical identity which is false to facts and impossible of realization. Effort to attain it is divisive of the vital bonds which hold men together; as far as it puts forth issue, the outcome is a mediocrity in which good is common only in the sense of being average and vulgar" (ibid., pp. 149-150).

45. Deutsch, "Equity, Equality, and Need," p. 147.

46. Ibid., p. 148.

47. Shalom Schwartz, "The Justice of Need and the Activation of Humanitarian Norms," *Journal of Social Issues*, 31 (Summer 1975): 112. See also Peter Singer, "Famine, Affluence, and Morality," in *Philosophy, Politics, and Society*, fifth series, ed. Peter Laslett and James Fishkin (New Haven: Yale University Press, 1979), pp. 21-35.

48. See Leonard Berkowitz and Kenneth Lutterman, "The Traditional Socially Responsible Personality," *Public Opinion Quarterly*, 32 (Summer 1968): 169-185; and Harrison Gough, Herbert McClosky, and Paul Meehl, "A Personality Scale

for Social Responsibility," *Journal of Abnormal and Social Psychology*, 47 (January 1952): 73-80.

49. The term *investments* has an economic connotation; one usually thinks of investing money before one thinks of investing time or energy. The term need not, however, be associated with money or material goods. Strictly speaking, it refers to anything that one puts into a process or structure in the hope of getting something valuable out of it. For those who insist upon the economic connotation, however, one can measure other types of investment by economic criteria. For example, Anthony Downs calculates the cost of political participation in *An Economic Theory of Democracy* (New York: Harper & Row, 1957); and Gary Becker calculates the monetary returns to education and training in *Human Capital*, 2d. ed. (New York: National Bureau of Economic Research, distributed by Columbia University Press, 1975).

50. Gal. 6: 9-10, New English Bible.

51. Sanford A. Lakoff, *Equality in Political Philosophy* (Boston: Beacon Press, 1964), pp. 35-37.

52. Bellamy, *Looking Backward*, p. 100.

53. Ibid., pp. 100-101.

54. Lakoff, *Equality in Political Philosophy*; and John Locke, *Two Treatises of Government*, ed. Peter Laslett (London: Cambridge University Press, 1967), *Second Treatise*, secs. 5.27 and 5.31-34.

55. Booker T. Washington, *Up From Slavery* (Garden City, N.Y.: Doubleday, 1953), p. 39.

56. "Commencement Exercises," *Oberlin Alumni Magazine*, Summer 1980, p. 15.

57. The Right Reverend William Lawrence, "The Relation of Wealth to Morals," in *Democracy and the Gospel of Wealth*, ed. Gail Kennedy (Boston: D. C. Heath, 1949), pp. 69-70.

58. See Zick Rubin and Letitia Anne Peplau, "Who Believes in a Just World?" *Journal of Social Issues*, 31 (Summer 1975): 65-89.

59. Hobhouse, *Social Justice*, pp. 99, 121.

60. Ibid., pp. 121-122.

61. Bernard Williams, "A Critique of Utilitarianism," in J. J. C. Smart and Bernard Williams, *Utilitarianism: For and Against* (Cambridge: Cambridge University Press, 1973), p. 79. See also Lars Bergstrom, *The Alternatives and Consequences of Actions* (Stockholm: Almqvist and Wiksell, 1966).

62. Robert Nisbet, "The Pursuit of Equality," *The Public Interest*, 35 (Spring 1974): 115-116.

63. Not all Americans blur the distinctions between investments and results. Consider this letter to the *Duke [University] Alumni Register*, September–October 1980, p. 29:

Editors:
   I am alarmed at your commencement speaker, U.S. Rep. L. Richardson Preyer's advice to make "a quality effort, which is more important than achieving goals."
   I disagree with that statement. To have a goal and to strive to achieve that

goal is the key to happiness and success. It is a matter of attitude. To merely put in a "quality effort" is synonymous with "giving it the old college try" . . .

You must never make allowances for failure. Never say you'll try. Say you will do it, whatever it takes. Perseverance is the key to a life with purposeful goals, to a life of fulfillment and happiness, to a life you wish for Duke graduates.

Winners never quit and quitters never win! Always strive to be a winner.

Rockwell F. Davis '64, D.D.S.

64. Nisbet, "The Pursuit of Equality," p. 117.

65. See Robert Nozick, *Anarchy, State, and Utopia* (New York: Basic Books, 1974), pp. 213-231. Note, however, that Nozick subscribes to the norm of procedures and rejects all norms that prescribe patterned outcomes.

66. Daniel Bell, "On Meritocracy and Equality," *The Public Interest*, 29 (Fall 1972): 40.

67. P. T. Bauer, "Equal Shares, Equal Earnings," *The Times Literary Supplement*, July 23, 1976, p. 938.

68. Nisbet, "The Pursuit of Equality," p. 117.

69. The protean John Dewey argues for this element of a norm of results, as earlier he argued for norms of equality and need. He says: "The function of government is to serve justice which signifies chiefly the protection of property and of the contracts which attend commercial exchange. Without the existence of the state men might appropriate one another's property. This appropriation is not only unfair to the laborious individual, but by making property insecure discourages the forthputting of energy at all and thus weakens or destroys the spring of social process." See *The Public and Its Problems*, p. 92. See also Milton Friedman, *Capitalism and Freedom* (Chicago: University of Chicago Press, 1962), on the intimate connection between economic freedom (that is, capitalism) and political freedom (that is, republicanism). Another claim that private property is essential for freedom and for social justice is made by John W. Chapman, "Justice, Freedom, and Property," unpublished paper (Pittsburgh: University of Pittsburgh, n.d.). For various arguments on the relation of property to justice, see Virginia Held, ed., *Property, Profits, and Economic Justice* (Belmont, Calif.: Wadsworth Publishing Co., 1980).

70. Thorstein Veblen, *Absentee Ownership and Business Enterprise in Recent Times* (New York: B. W. Huebach, 1923), p. 104.

71. Hobhouse, *Social Justice*, p. 144.

72. See also Torstein E. Eckhoff, *Justice: Its Determinants in Social Interaction* (Belgium: Rotterdam University Press, 1974), pp. 227-229; and Bernard Mandeville, *The Fable of the Bees*, ed. and intro. by Phillip Harth (Harmondsworth, England: Penguin Books, 1970).

73. Rawls rejects any "conception of justice" that accepts "the accident of natural endowment and the contingencies of social circumstances as counters in quest for political and economic advantage." Therefore he is at most an uneasy companion of the philosophers discussed above. But his theory of justice is so closely related to the claim that one should reward people according to the social benefits of their productivity that it seems a variant of this norm rather than a

separate one. See John Rawls, *A Theory of Justice* (Cambridge, Mass.: Harvard University Press, Belknap Press, 1971), p. 15. See also pp. 103-104.

74. Ibid., p. 60.

75. Ibid., p. 62.

76. See Bell, "On Meritocracy"; Allan Bloom, "Justice: John Rawls vs. the Tradition of Political Philosophy," *American Political Science Review*, 69 (June 1975): 648-662; and Nisbet, "The Pursuit of Equality."

77. Brian M. Barry, *The Liberal Theory of Justice* (London: Oxford University Press, 1973), p. 46. My italics.

78. Rawls, *Theory of Justice*, p. 82.

79. Barry, *Liberal Theory of Justice*, p. 110.

80. Joel Feinberg, *Social Philosophy* (Englewood Cliffs, N.J.: Prentice-Hall, 1973), p. 114.

81. Ibid., p. 116. See also James Dick, "How to Justify a Distribution of Earnings," *Philosophy and Public Affairs*, 4 (Spring 1975): 260-264.

82. Irving Kristol, "What Is Social Justice?" *The Wall Street Journal*, August 12, 1976, p. 10. Note the similarity between this view and the norm of procedures. The difference lies in the causal sequence. Here the market is invented to achieve a result; there the result is merely whatever happens in a market, which is invented for other reasons.

83. Hobhouse, *Social Justice*, p. 145.

84. Deutsch, "Equity, Equality, and Need," p. 143.

85. J. Stacy Adams, "Toward an Understanding of Inequity," *Journal of Abnormal Psychology*, 67 (November 1963): 422-436; Elaine Walster, Ellen Bersheid, and G. William Walster, "New Directions in Equity Research," *Journal of Personality and Social Psychology*, 25 (February 1973): 151-176; and Leonard Berkowitz, gen. ed., *Advances in Experimental Social Psychology*, vol. 9, *Equity Theory* (New York: Academic Press, 1976), ed. Leonard Berkowitz and Elaine Walster.

86. On methodological individualism, see Steven Lukes, *Individualism* (New York: Harper & Row, 1973), pp. 110-122, and notes therein.

87. Richard M. Titmuss, *The Gift Relationship* (New York: Random House, Pantheon Books, 1971).

88. Deutsch, "Equity, Equality, and Need," p. 145.

89. Paul Diesing, *Reason in Society* (Urbana: University of Illinois Press, 1962).

90. Alvin Gouldner, "The Norm of Reciprocity," *American Sociological Review*, 25 (April 1960): 173, 171.

91. Diesing, *Reason in Society*, p. 93. See also Michael D. Young, *The Rise of the Meritocracy, 1870–2033* (Baltimore: Penguin Books, 1975); Christian Bay, "Freedom as a Tool of Oppression," in *The Case for Participatory Democracy*, ed. C. George Benello and Dimitrios Roussopoulos (New York: Grossman, 1971): 251-269; and Herbert Marcuse, *One-Dimensional Man* (Boston: Beacon Press, 1964).

92. Eckhoff, *Justice*, pp. 234-235. See also Richard Hernnstein: "The greater the opportunities for social mobility and for equal education, the greater the social stratification according to biological factors, like inherited intelligence. This does not make me disfavor social mobility, nor do I welcome hereditary classes. But

whatever we like or think, the former will tend to create the latter" ("Backtalk: More About I.Q.," *Atlantic Monthly,* December 1971, p. 110).

93. Robert A. Dahl, "On Removing Certain Impediments to Democracy in the United States," *Political Science Quarterly,* 92 (Spring 1977): 7-8.

94. Ibid., p. 8.

95. Age appears to be an exception, since it obviously is not permanent or fixed at birth. But because it is completely involuntary, graded, socially obvious, and independent of any individual traits or behaviors, it fits within this category.

96. Ewart Lewis, *Medieval Political Ideas* (New York: Alfred Knopf, 1954); Arthur O. Lovejoy, *The Great Chain of Being* (Cambridge: Harvard University Press, 1936); and Paul Sigmund, "Hierarchy, Equality, and Consent in Medieval Christian Thought," in *Equality: Nomos 9,* ed. James R. Pennock and John W. Chapman (New York: Atherton Press, 1967), pp. 134-153.

97. Samuel H. Beer, *British Politics in the Collectivist Age* (New York: Alfred Knopf, 1965), pp. 9-21.

98. Edmund Burke, *The Works of the Right Honorable Edmund Burke,* rev. ed., 12 vols. (Boston: Little, Brown, 1865-1867), vol. 4, *Appeal from the New to the Old Whigs* (1866), p. 174.

99. Ibid., p. 175.

100. Edmund Burke, "The English Constitutional System," in *Representation,* ed. Hanna Pitkin (New York: Atherton Press, 1969), p. 172.

101. Edmund Burke, vol. 3, *Reflections on the Revolution in France* (1865), p. 279.

102. Richard H. Tawney, *Religion and the Rise of Capitalism* (Gloucester, Mass.: Peter Smith, 1962), p. 169.

103. Edmund Burke, vol. 1, *Thoughts on the Cause of the Present Discontents* (1865), p. 437.

104. Ibid., p. 522.

105. See Russell Kirk, *A Program for Conservatives* (Chicago: Henry Regnery, 1954); Peter R. Viereck, *Conservatism Revisited* (New York: C. Scribner's Sons, 1949); George F. Will, *The Pursuit of Happiness, and Other Sobering Thoughts* (New York: Harper & Row, 1978); David M. Potter, *People of Plenty* (Chicago: University of Chicago Press, 1954), pp. 91-110; and Tocqueville, *Democracy in America,* for example, pp. 87, 561-562, 566.

106. John W. Gardner, *Excellence: Can We Be Equal and Excellent Too?* (New York: Harper & Row, 1961), pp. 8-9.

107. Ibid., pp. 8-10.

108. Erik H. Erikson, "Inner and Outer Space: Reflections on Womanhood," in *The Woman in America,* ed. Robert Jay Lifton (Boston: Beacon Press, 1964), p. 2.

109. Ibid., p. 9.

110. Robert Jay Lifton, "Woman as Knower: Some Psychohistorical Perspectives," in *The Woman in America,* ed. Robert Jay Lifton (Boston: Beacon Press, 1964), p. 31. His italics.

111. For the original psychoanalytic distinctions between the sexes, see Sigmund Freud, " 'A Child is Being Beaten': A Contribution to the Study of the Origin of Sexual Perversions" (1919), in *Collected Papers,* vol. 2, *Clinical Papers,*

Papers on Technique, ed. Ernest Jones, trans. Joan Riviere (New York: Basic Books, 1959); Sigmund Freud, "Female Sexuality," (1931) in *Collected Papers,* vol. 5, *Miscellaneous Papers, 1888–1938,* ed. Ernest Jones and James Strachey (New York: Basic Books, 1959); Sigmund Freud, "Some Psychological Consequences of the Anatomical Distinction between the Sexes," (1925), in *Collected Papers,* vol. 5, *Miscellaneous Papers, 1888–1938,* ed. Ernest Jones and James Strachey (New York: Basic Books, 1959); and Sigmund Freud, "Femininity," in *New Introductory Lectures in Psychoanalysis,* ed. and trans. James Strachey (New York: W. W. Norton, 1965).

For popular literature on the fundamental differences between men and women and their correspondingly different roles, see Midge Dexter, *The New Chastity* (New York: Berkeley Publishing Corp., Berkeley Medallion Books, 1972); Phyllis Schlafly, *The Power of the Positive Woman* (New Rochelle, N.Y.: Arlington House, 1977); and Lionel Tiger, *Men in Groups* (New York: Random House, 1969).

Examples of academic literature reviews on the subject of sexual differences are Donald M. Broverman, Edward L. Klaiber, Yutaka Kobayashi, and William Vogel, "Roles of Activation and Inhibition in Sex Differences in Cognitive Abilities," *Psychological Review,* 75 (January 1968): 23-50; and Beth L. Wellman, "Sex Differences," in *The Handbook of Child Psychology,* 2d. ed. rev., ed. Carl A. Murchison (New York: Russell and Russell, 1967), 2: 626-649. The best study of the political philosophy of sexual ascription is Susan Moller Okin, *Women in Western Political Thought* (Princeton: Princeton University Press, 1979). The best argument for sexual and class ascription may still be Aristotle, *The Politics of Aristotle,* trans. and ed. Ernest Barker (London: Oxford University Press, 1972).

112. Simon Raven, "Perish by the Sword," in *The Establishment,* ed. Hugh Thomas (London: Anthony Blond, 1959), p. 75. Since American psychologists have not studied noblesse oblige and deference, this section is based on writing about Great Britain. Does the omission indicate a lack of ascriptive norms in the United States or the fact that even academic research is blinded by our dominant liberal values?

The psychological motivations discussed here in class terms are applicable, *mutatis mutandis,* to other ascriptive hierarchies. See, for example, Gunnar Myrdal's discussion of the psychological similarities between blacks, children, and women, all of whom have low status, in *An American Dilemma* (New York: Harper & Brothers, 1944), App. 5.

One important difference is that status and power do not necessarily co-vary for racial and sexual groups as they do in a class hierarchy. This may lead to inter- and intrapersonal tension and social problems of status inconsistency.

113. Tocqueville, *Democracy in America,* p. 13. Note how he uses the same analogy for a very different purpose in his description of the dangers of equality (see p. 56). That comparison may illustrate an ascriptive norm as nothing else can.

114. Ibid., p. 14.

115. Walter Bagehot, *The English Constitution* (New York: D. Appleton, 1920), p. 7.

116. Frank Parkin, *Class Inequality and Political Order* (New York: Praeger, 1971), p. 85.

117. Robert T. McKenzie and Allan Silver, *Angels in Marble* (Chicago: University of Chicago Press, 1968), p. 249. In one study, 34 percent of low-income deferential workers described themselves as middle-class, compared to only 11 percent of low-income nondeferential workers. Deference apparently does not entail self-deprecation; instead, it enhances, in their own eyes, the social status of poor British Conservatives (ibid., p. 196).

118. David Lockwood, "Sources of Variation in Working Class Images of Society," in *Working Class Images of Society*, ed. Martin Bulmer (London: Routledge and Kegan Paul, in association with the Social Sciences Research Council, 1975), pp. 16-34; and Kurt B. Mayer, *Class and Society* (New York: Random House, 1955).

119. Duff Cooper, *Old Men Forget* (London: Hart-Davis, 1954), p. 66.

120. Beer, *British Politics*, pp. 9-21; McKenzie and Silver, *Angels in Marble*, pp. 197-199; and Eric A. Nordlinger, *The Working-Class Tories* (London: MacGibbon and Kee, 1967), pp. 30-35.

121. Abraham Lincoln, "First Debate With Senator Stephen Douglas at Ottawa, Illinois (August 12, 1858)," in *Abraham Lincoln: Selected Speeches, Messages, and Letters*, ed. Thomas H. Williams (New York: Rinehart, 1957), p. 94.

122. Curiously, given his strong support for the purely procedural norm of social Darwinism (see next section), Herbert Spencer exemplifies the belief that all men are inherently and importantly superior to all women. See *The Principles of Ethics*, II (New York: D. Appleton, 1896), chap. 20. See also Reo M. Christenson, *Heresies Left and Right* (New York: Harper & Row, 1973), pp. 35-40, for a slightly more subtle version of the same argument, and George Gilder, *Wealth and Poverty* (New York: Basic Books, 1980), for the economic implications of such an argument.

123. Bell, "On Meritocracy," pp. 37-38; his italics. For other arguments that affirmative action policies unjustly discriminate against white males, see Nathan Glazer, *Affirmative Discrimination* (New York: Basic Books, 1975); Barry R. Gross, *Discrimination in Reverse: Is Turnabout Fair Play?* foreword by Sidney Hook (New York: New York University Press, 1978); and Allan P. Sindler, *Bakke, DeFunis, and Minority Admissions* (New York: Longman, 1978).

For a somewhat different argument that also questions the justice of affirmative action policies, see Rae et al., *Equalities*, chap. 4.

124. See Edwin Dorn, *Rules and Racial Equality* (New Haven: Yale University Press, 1979), pp. 120-140; John C. Livingston, *Fair Game?* (San Francisco: W. H. Freeman, 1979); and Robert K. Fullinwider, *The Reverse Discrimination Controversy* (Totowa, N.J.: Rowman and Littlefield, 1980).

125. Eckhoff, *Justice*, pp. 237-239; and Parkin, *Class Inequality*, pp. 82-88.

126. Fred Hapgood, "Chances of a Lifetime," *Working Papers for a New Society*, 3 (Spring 1975): 37-42.

127. Eckhoff, *Justice*, pp. 215-220.

128. Nozick, *Anarchy, State, and Utopia*.

129. See also Friedrich A. Hayek, *The Constitution of Liberty* (Chicago:

University of Chicago Press, 1960); and Friedrich A. Hayek, *Law, Legislation, and Liberty,* vol. 2, *The Mirage of Social Justice* (Chicago: University of Chicago Press, 1976).

130. This formulation has one caveat — the principle of rectification. If property is not infinitely available, some acquisitions will be unfair because they will inhibit someone else's chance of acquiring holdings. Other acquisitions will be unfair because they involve cheating, force, or some other violation of free consent. In those two cases, subsequent acquisitions, transfers, or benefits from the use of the initial holding are unjust and must be rectified. The person initially harmed must be compensated or the holding returned. Nozick discusses compensation in detail, but drops the general principle of rectification almost immediately, perhaps because he realizes how irrelevant it makes the rest of his theory to any actual history. See Nozick, *Anarchy, State, and Utopia,* pp. 54-87, 152-153.

131. Thomas Hobbes, *Leviathan,* intro. by Herbert W. Schneider (New York: Bobbs-Merrill, Library of Liberal Arts, 1958), p. 120.

132. Jeremy Bentham, "Principles of the Civil Code," in *The Works of Jeremy Bentham,* ed. John Bowring, 11 vols. (New York: Russell and Russell, 1962), 1: 343.

133. Michael A. Slote, "Desert, Consent, and Justice," *Philosophy and Public Affairs,* 2 (Summer 1973): 338-344.

134. Ibid., p. 323.

135. Barry, *Liberal Theory of Justice,* p. 118.

136. Dick, "How to Justify," p. 256. See also Garrett Hardin, "The Tragedy of the Commons," *Science,* 162 (December 1968): 1243-48; and Thomas C. Schelling, "On the Ecology of Micromotives," *The Public Interest,* 25 (Fall 1971): 61-98.

137. Charles R. Darwin, *Origin of Species* (Chicago: Great Books Foundation, 1957), p. 86.

138. Ibid., p. 270.

139. Herbert Spencer, *Principles of Sociology* (New York: D. Appleton, 1880); Lakoff, *Equality in Political Philosophy,* p. 143. See also Paul F. Boller, *American Thought in Transition* (Chicago: Rand McNally, 1969).

140. Herbert Spencer, *Social Statics together with Man versus the State* (New York: D. Appleton, 1892), p. 369.

141. William Graham Sumner, *The Challenge of Facts and Other Essays* (New Haven: Yale University Press, 1914), p. 25. See also Richard Hofstadter, *Social Darwinism in American Thought* (Boston: Beacon Press, 1944).

142. Melvin Lerner, Dale Miller, and John Holmes, "Deserving and the Emergence of Forms of Justice," in *Advances in Experimental Social Psychology,* gen. ed. Leonard Berkowitz, vol. 9, *Equity Theory* (New York: Academic Press, 1976), ed. Leonard Berkowitz and Elaine Walster, p. 158.

143. Melvin Lerner, "The Justice Motive in Social Behavior," *Journal of Social Issues,* 31 (Summer 1975): 17.

144. Ernest Van Den Haag, *Passion and Social Constraint* (New York: Stein and Day, 1963), p. 137.

145. Ibid., p. 131. See also chap. 1, note 52.

146. Lerner, "The Justice Motive," p. 18.

147. Van Den Haag, *Passion and Social Constraint,* p. 133.

148. Lerner et al., "Deserving and the Emergence," p. 153.

149. Ibid., p. 153.

150. Hobbes, *Leviathan*, p. 107.

151. Anthony Downs, *An Economic Theory of Democracy* (New York: Harper & Row, 1957).

4. The Socializing Domain and the Principle of Equality

1. Carol B. Stack, *All Our Kin* (New York: Harper & Row, 1974).

2. I chose respondents for description in chapter two according to their usefulness in demonstrating a particular point; I chose respondents for description in chapters four through seven according to their usefulness in demonstrating a general pattern. The two criteria do not always coincide; thus some of the people described in chapter two are not discussed in detail and vice versa.

3. William Frankena, "The Concept of Social Justice," in *Social Justice*, ed. Richard Brandt (Englewood Cliffs, N.J.: Prentice-Hall, 1962), p. 20.

4. See Isaiah Berlin, *Four Essays on Liberty* (New York: Oxford University Press, 1969), pp. 118-172.

5. The Economic Domain and the Principle of Differentiation

1. Contrast this view with Vincent's refusal to vote for President Ford because he pardoned Richard Nixon: "Why should that guy get a pardon? *He* committed a *crime.* Hey, if I gotta go to court for a crime, I have to pay my penalty. And he did worser crimes. Then some people say, 'The guy suffered enough . . .' *What* did he suffer? Because he felt embarrassed because the public found out what kind of president he really was? Hey, [motion of disgust] know what I mean?"

6. The Political Domain and the Principle of Equality

1. It is striking that Pamela and Phillip, the most devout Catholics of the sample, use an argument that other respondents do not. Most prefer loans to "handouts," but only these two suggest that handouts will dissolve the moral fiber of their recipients as a loan, even of a great amount, would not. "Getting something for nothing" is not just impractical or unjust; it is a temptation to sin. This viewpoint is distinct from support for or opposition to equality or differentiation. Both Pamela and Phillip seek many social welfare policies; both question aspects of economic differentiation; and both describe egalitarian utopias. But both insist that equality that is given to people is dangerous and sinful, whereas equality earned—even with a tremendous boost from the government—is desirable and good. This particular distinction between good and evil forms of equality may be an especially Catholic construction.

2. Two poor respondents disagreed. Mary Lou Trask's utopia would "be having all types of people with all being productive individuals, getting there on their own without expecting a lot out of other people. No crime. But to me a utopia would not be seeing everybody rich. I can't visualize people being happy just having everything they wanted and not having to at least work for it."

Peter Schmidt, the only native European in the sample, fears that "if you pay everybody the same, maybe there'd be a revolution or something." The revolution would come, not from the dispossessed rich, but from the newly rich workers. "They would have it too good. If you have it too good, then you have no worries, and you do crazy things. It's just no good." His utopia would provide ample and equal opportunities for, but no guarantees of, well-being.

7. Alternative Patterns of Belief

1. *Webster's New Collegiate Dictionary* (Springfield, Mass.: G. & C. Merriam Co., 1980), p. 577.

2. Lawrence Kohlberg may be the best advocate of the position that the clearest indication of moral development is an improving ability to apply a few general principles or values to a wide range of issues or subjects. See, for example, Deanna Kuhn, Jonas Langer, Lawrence Kohlberg, and Norma Haan, "The Development of Formal Operations in Logical and Moral Judgment," *Genetic Psychology Monographs* 95 (February 1977): 77-188.

3. For example, John McConahay argues that identical treatment of blacks and whites, and efforts to develop "amicable relations" among racial groups, may be an undesirable form of behavioral and attitudinal consistency if blacks face "grossly unjust inequalities of opportunities and outcomes." In this case, different treatment, both materially and symbolically, may be most appropriate. See "The Effects of School Desegregation upon Students' Racial Attitudes and Behavior," *Law and Contemporary Problems*, 42 (Summer 1978): pt. 1, p. 77.

4. All respondents agree with at least one segment of the dominant three-part pattern; no one displays the diametrically opposite pattern of differentiation in the socializing domain, equality in the marketplace, and differentiation in the polity. Four other possible combinations of two principles and three domains exist; none appeared clearly enough among my respondents to be identifiable.

5. Sanford A. Lakoff, *Equality in Political Philosophy* (Boston: Beacon Press, 1964), pp. 8, 14.

6. A worker should not, however, be too eager to learn. Bernard will be "forced" to fire a new employee because she wastes too much time asking questions: "You first have to qualify, justify your time. Once you can do *that*, you've got room to expand in your knowledge. But it's unreasonable to expect a company to finance your education when they're not even making a profit on your time."

7. The electoral process is little help here. When politicians are "running for something, they'll come out, shake your hand, give you a cigar. After they get in there, they don't know you no more." Nevertheless, one should register to vote because, "say I was gonna open up a nightclub, I apply for a liquor license. You have to be a voter before you can get a liquor license. Otherwise they turn you down. That's one thing about voting, you gotta be a voter to get anything." So much for claims that citizens are not rational!

8. At least one other respondent, a poor one, believes that there can be too much of a good thing, regardless of how it is distributed. Steven Vistacco, an intermittently employed plumber's helper, explains that children in large families are happier, more obedient, and more responsible than other children because

"they don't *have* maybe what the other children have. They don't get a TV, go on vacation. So when they do go, they probably appreciate it." If parents "don't or can't afford to give them most of the things, maybe they grow up with a little more sense of values or a little more respect for them."

9. Bruce perhaps exemplifies Isaiah Berlin's fears of the excesses of positive freedom as expressed in *Four Essays on Liberty* (New York: Oxford University Press, 1969), pp. 118-172.

10. A study that does find associations between demographic and attitudinal variables on the one hand and norms of distributive justice on the other is Robert V. Robinson and Wendell Bell, "Equality, Success, and Social Justice in England and the United States," *American Sociological Review*, 43 (April 1978): 125-143. A study that finds no such associations is Guillermina Jasso and Peter H. Rossi, "Distributive Justice and Earned Income," *American Sociological Review*, 42 (August 1977): 639-651.

11. Philip Converse, "The Nature of Belief Systems in Mass Publics," in *Ideology and Discontent*, ed. David Apter (New York: Free Press, 1964), p. 207.

12. Roger W. Brown, *Social Psychology* (New York: Free Press, 1965), p. 549.

13. Converse, "The Nature of Belief Systems," pp. 216, 229, 255.

14. Herbert McClosky, "Consensus and Ideology in American Politics," *American Political Science Review*, 58 (June 1964): 361-382; and James W. Prothro and Charles M. Grigg, "Fundamental Principles of Democracy: Bases of Agreement and Disagreement," *Journal of Politics*, 22 (May 1960): 276-294.

15. W. Lance Bennett, *The Political Mind and the Political Environment* (Lexington, Mass.: D. C. Heath, 1975); John C. Pierce and Douglas D. Rose, "Non-attitudes and American Political Opinions: The Examination of a Thesis," *American Political Science Review*, 68 (June 1974): 626-649; and John L. Sullivan, James E. Piereson, George E. Marcus, and Stanley Feldman, "The More Things Change, the More They Stay the Same," *American Journal of Political Science*, 23 (February 1979): 176-186.

16. C. Anthony Broh, *Toward a Theory of Issue Voting* (Beverly Hills, Calif.: Sage Publications, 1973); Norman R. Luttbeg, "The Structure of Beliefs among Leaders and the Public," *Public Opinion Quarterly*, 32 (Fall 1968): 398-409; and James A. Stimson, "Belief Systems: Constraint, Complexity and the 1972 Election," *American Journal of Political Science*, 19 (August 1975): 393-417.

17. Robert Lane, "Patterns of Political Belief," in *Handbook of Political Psychology*, ed. Jeanne Knutson (San Francisco: Jossey-Bass Publishers, 1973), pp. 83-116; and Bennett, *The Political Mind*.

18. Norman H. Nie, Sidney Verba, and John Petrocik, *The Changing American Voter* (Cambridge, Mass.: Harvard University Press, 1976). But see Sullivan et al., "The More Things Change."

19. Robert P. Abelson, "The Structure of Belief Systems," in *Computer Models of Thought and Language*, ed. Roger Schank and Kenneth Colby (San Francisco: W. H. Freeman, 1973), p. 287.

20. Lane, "Patterns of Political Belief," p. 102.

21. Hannah Arendt, *The Human Condition* (Chicago: University of Chicago Press, 1969), pp. 9-10.

22. Silvan Tomkins, "Left and Right: A Basic Dimension of Ideology and Per-

sonality," in *The Study of Lives*, ed. Robert W. White (New York: Atherton Press, 1963), p. 391.

23. Theodor Adorno, Else Frenkel-Brunswick, Daniel Levinson, and Nevitt Sanford, *The Authoritarian Personality* (New York: Harper and Brothers, 1950); Daniel J. Levinson, "Personality, Political: Conservatism and Radicalism," in *International Encyclopedia of the Social Sciences*, ed. David Sill (New York: Macmillan, 1968), 12: 21-30; Herbert McClosky, "Conservatism and Personality," *American Political Science Review*, 52 (March 1958): 27-45; Gardner Murphy, Lois Murphy, and Theodore Newcomb, *Experimental Social Psychology* (New York: Harper and Brothers, 1937); and Norman H. Nie with Kristi Anderson, "Mass Belief Systems Revisited: Political Change and Attitude Structure," *Journal of Politics*, 36 (August 1974): 540-591.

24. Converse, "The Nature of Belief Systems," p. 216.

25. Ibid., p. 219.

26. Milton Rokeach, *The Nature of Human Values* (New York: Free Press, 1973), pp. 166-168.

27. Lloyd A. Free and Hadley Cantril, *The Political Beliefs of Americans* (New York: Simon and Schuster, Touchstone Books, 1968), pp. 30, 33.

28. Richard M. Scammon and Ben J. Wattenberg, *The Real Majority* (New York: Coward-McCann, 1970), pp. 43, 44.

29. Stimson, "Belief Systems."

30. George E. Marcus, David Tabb, and John L. Sullivan, "The Application of Individual Differences Scaling to the Measurement of Political Ideologies," *American Journal of Political Science*, 18 (May 1974): 405-420.

31. Converse, "The Nature of Belief Systems," p. 229.

32. Lane, "Patterns of Political Beliefs," p. 103.

33. Walter Mischel, *Personality and Assessment* (New York: John Wiley & Sons, 1968), pp. 60-68.

34. Ibid., p. 282.

35. Philip Converse, "Public Opinion and Voting Behavior," in *Handbook of Political Science*, vol. 4, *Nongovernmental Politics*, ed. Fred Greenstein and Nelson Polsby (Reading, Mass.: Addison-Wesley, 1975), pp. 87-88.

36. Ibid., p. 88.

8. Ambivalence

1. Health here is used as Robert Lane defines it: "The healthy person has multiple values, and he finds them often in conflict; his health is revealed in his toleration of the conflict and the means he chooses to reconcile the conflicts." See Robert Lane, "Patterns of Political Belief," in *Handbook of Political Psychology*, ed. Jeanne Knutson (San Francisco: Jossey-Bass Publishers, 1973), p. 102. This is, of course, a quintessentially pluralist definition of political and personal health. One could also define it as commitment to a single positive, overarching goal; fulfillment comes through dedication to that goal. One would need to distinguish this radical, transcendent vision from the "obsession" or "fixation" discussed by Lane, but it is relevant to so few of my respondents that we need not consider it here in detail. Keep in mind, however, that for some people, exchang-

ing the three-part pattern for a single overarching value might be a step toward health. At that point, Converse's ideal of unidimensional constraint, purged of its liberal-conservative assumptions, becomes useful again.

2. Garry Wills, *Nixon Agonistes* (New York: New American Library, Mentor Books, 1979), p. 224.

3. Richard H. Tawney, *Equality*, intro. by Richard M. Titmuss (London: Unwin Books, 1964).

4. See chapter 9 for more on this point.

5. Morton Deutsch, "Equity, Equality, and Need: What Determines Which Value Will Be Used as the Basis of Distributive Justice?" *Journal of Social Issues*, 31 (Summer 1975): 144-145.

6. Antonio Gramsci, *The Modern Prince and Other Writings*, trans. and ed. Louis Marks (New York: International Publishers, 1957), p. 66.

7. Survey research provides broader evidence of this type of ambivalence. In a sample of 354, Joan Huber and William Form found that 85 percent of their white respondents, including 90 percent of the poor, agreed that "there's plenty of opportunity, and anyone who works hard can go as far as he wants." But a specific question about equal chances for the rich and poor to earn the same amount of money received agreement from only 42 percent. A majority also agree that equal opportunity exists in general, but not in particular cases, in response to questions about legal equality, political influence, and the chance to attend college. Both rich and poor follow this pattern, although the poor are consistently less sanguine. See *Income and Ideology* (New York: Free Press, 1973), pp. 88-94.

In an analysis of a variety of public opinion polls, Michael Mann also finds "a disjunction between general abstract values and concrete experience," such that dominant values are supported in general, but deviant ones receive more support in specific cases. In particular, "Respondents are more likely to be cynical about the opportunity structure that confronts them in their actual working lives" than about general opportunities. See "The Social Cohesion of Liberal Democracy," *American Sociological Review*, 35 (June 1970): 427, 429. David Garson finds that most auto workers describe themselves as somewhat or very satisfied with their work in general, but "when asked about details of life in the workplace, more workers than not are dissatisfied or very dissatisfied on a range of factors that impinge from all sides." See "Automobile Workers and the Radical Dream," *Politics and Society*, 3 (Winter 1973): 171. Finally, Free and Cantril present as their major finding the "schizoid" disjunction between general, ideological conservatism and specific, operational liberalism. See Lloyd A. Free and Hadley Cantril, *The Political Beliefs of Americans* (New York: Simon and Schuster, Touchstone Books, 1968). All of these findings show that there is tension between general support for differentiation and specific support for equality.

8. I make no claims about the number of respondents who feel ambivalent at all or who feel more than one form of ambivalence; I also make no claims about which forms are felt most often. Such analyses must await a larger sample.

9. Joseph Femia, "Hegemony and Consciousness in the Thought of Antonio Gramsci," *Political Studies*, 23 (March 1975): 33.

10. Garson found that 28 percent of his sample of automobile workers strongly favored the general idea of a "guild socialist shop model" when it was explained to

them. But at a specific level, only 12 percent or fewer agreed that workers should set the speed of production, determine job promotions, settle grievances, or elect managers and foremen ("Automobile Workers," pp. 174-177). In his more complex analysis, Mann first identifies "two types of deviant values . . . widely endorsed by working class people: firstly, values . . . expressed in concrete terms corresponding to everyday reality, and secondly, simplistic divisions of the social world into 'rich' and 'poor.' " Examples of the deviant, vague values include agreement that "the government should give everybody a good standard of living," that "the rich get the profits," that "big business has too much power," and that "the poor don't have a chance in law courts." Workers do not, however, connect these deviant values to form a coherent class-based political philosophy. "Instead, at the [intermediate] political level are rather confused values with surprisingly conservative biases." The combination of general conservative political values with deviant values about specific experiences corresponds to the fourth type of ambivalence; the combination of general conservative political values and even broader, as well as vaguer, class-oriented ideals corresponds to the type now under discussion ("Social Cohesion," pp. 430, 434, 436).

Alan Stern and Donald Searing found that 39 percent of their sample of American adolescents, as compared to only 20 percent of their British counterparts, agree that "the wealth of our country should be divided up equally." The most important finding in this context is that in both nations, 20 percent more middle-class than lower-class respondents endorse "abstract proposals such as economic equality. On the relatively concrete issue of taxation, [however], they slip behind working-class preferences for soaking the rich" ("The Stratification Beliefs of English and American Adolescents," *British Journal of Political Science*, 6 (April 1976): 195). No specific data are provided on this point. Stern and Searing's findings on how people explain wealth and poverty also support their conclusion that "blaming unjust systems is easier than censuring the individuals who benefit from them. Abstractions are always agreeable targets" (ibid., p. 197).

Finally, Frank Westie tested "the American dilemma" by comparing support for general principles and specific applications to situations involving blacks. In those relevant here, he found indications of this type of ambivalence; that is, more people agreed with a general egalitarian statement than with its specific application. For example, 99 percent agreed that "people should help each other in time of need," but only 64 percent would take a black family into their home for a night after a fire ("The American Dilemma: An Empirical Test," *American Sociological Review*, 30 [August 1965]: 527-538).

11. Gramsci, *The Modern Prince*, p. 67.

12. Joseph A. Schumpeter, *Capitalism, Socialism, and Democracy*, 3rd ed. (New York: Harper & Row, 1950), p. 262.

13. V. O. Key, Jr. with Milton Cummings, *The Responsible Electorate* (Cambridge, Mass.: Harvard University Press, Belknap Press, 1966), pp. 7-8.

9. Political Orientations: Why the Dog Doesn't Bark

1. This generalization, like so many others, has exceptions. Someone who is deeply ambivalent may seek to reduce his or her cognitive dissonance by search-

ing for a resolution and eventually taking a leap of faith in one direction or another. Bruce Abbott exemplifies this phenomenon; the discrepancies between his beliefs in individual rights and in the public interest push him to challenge his own views and those of others. But this active involvement in one's own ambivalence is rare, at least in my sample.

2. There is a certain lack of rigor in the distinctions being presented here. Just as domains of life and norms of justice blur into other domains or norms, so ambivalence and emotions seem hard to pull apart. This blurring is neither very surprising nor particularly worrisome. After all, people believe and feel all of these things at the same time and as a unified whole. The very attempt by a social scientist to pull strands apart and to make distinctions necessarily violates the true nature of a person's belief system. We must, of course, do it, but we should not expect to be completely successful. Perhaps the best way to think about all of these distinctions and especially about figure 5 is that each dimension is like one facet of a complex crystalline structure. Turning the quartz crystal around and describing each vantage point is necessary, but insufficient, for getting a full picture of the rock. Each new turn sharply illuminates some features of the rock, suggests others, and ignores the rest. As the crystal is turned, what was sharply illuminated becomes vague; what was ignored comes into the full glare of observation. Each description is different from the others, yet each describes the same object as the others. So it is with the distinctions I am using here. They are kept separate from one another in order to allow us to concentrate on a particular feature of a belief system; they blur into one another because they are all describing the same belief system.

3. Joseph Femia, "Hegemony and Consciousness in the Thought of Antonio Gramsci," *Political Studies*, 23 (March 1975): 32.

4. Ibid., p. 32.

5. Raymond Williams, "Base and Superstructure in Marxist Cultural Theory," *New Left Review*, 82 (November–December 1973): 8-9.

6. Roberta Sigel, "Assumptions About the Learning of Political Values," *Annals of the American Academy of Political and Social Science*, 361 (September 1965): 1.

7. Louis Hartz, *The Liberal Tradition in America* (New York: Harcourt, Brace, and World, 1955); Robert A. Dahl, "On Removing Certain Impediments to Democracy in the United States," *Political Science Quarterly*, 92 (Spring 1977): 1-20; and John Dewey, *The Public and Its Problems* (Chicago: Gateway Books, 1946), chaps. 3-4.

8. Charles E. Lindblom, *Politics and Markets* (New York: Basic Books, 1977), pp. 202-212.

9. See chapter 1, notes 71-81.

10. Robert A. Dahl, *Pluralist Democracy in the United States* (Chicago: Rand McNally, 1967), pp. 329-330. These views probably no longer reflect Dahl's political orientation.

11. Bernard R. Berelson, Paul F. Lazarsfeld, and William N. McPhee, *Voting* (Chicago: University of Chicago Press, 1954); Robert A. Dahl, *Who Governs?* (New Haven: Yale University Press, 1961), bk. VI; David Truman, *The Governmental Process* (New York: Alfred Knopf, 1951), pp. 501-535; and Jennifer

Hochschild, "Why the Dog Doesn't Bark: Income, Attitudes, and the Redistribution of Wealth," *Polity*, 11 (Summer 1979): 486-500.

12. Frank Parkin, *Class Inequality and Political Order* (New York: Praeger, 1971), pp. 81-86; see also Lindblom, *Politics and Markets*.

13. Perry Anderson, "The Antinomies of Antonio Gramsci," *New Left Review*, 100 (November 1976–January 1977): 22; see also chap. 1, sec. on "My Research" above. Still others assume this disjunction. For an extreme contrast between economics and politics, see John Rawls, *A Theory of Justice* (Cambridge, Mass.: Harvard University Press, Belknap Press, 1971), pp. 359-360. Here, if nowhere else, Rawls agrees with Milton Friedman, *Capitalism and Freedom* (Chicago: University of Chicago Press, 1962), pp. 1-36. Brian Barry discusses and critiques this sharp disjunction in *The Liberal Theory of Justice* (London: Oxford University Press, 1973), pp. 134-143, 154-165. So does Sheldon Wolin in *Politics and Vision* (Boston: Little, Brown, 1960).

14. Michael Mann, "The Social Cohesion of Liberal Democracy," *American Sociological Review*, 35 (June 1970): 425; see also Hochschild, "Why the Dog Doesn't Bark," pp. 500-505.

15. Peter L. Berger and Thomas Luckmann, *The Social Construction of Reality* (Garden City, N.Y.: Doubleday, 1966), pp. 23, 65, 66. See also Richard Hoggart, *The Uses of Literacy* (New York: Oxford University Press, 1970).

16. Femia, "Hegemony and Consciousness," p. 33.

17. Berger and Luckmann, *The Social Construction of Reality*, pp. 60, 65-66.

18. Ibid., pp. 89-91.

19. Tim Patterson, "Notes on the Historical Application of Marxist Cultural Theory," *Science and Society*, 39 (Fall 1975): 264.

20. Hannah Arendt, *The Human Condition* (Chicago: University of Chicago Press, 1969), pp. 9-10.

21. Louis (Studs) Terkel, *Working* (New York: Random House, Pantheon Books, 1972), pp. xxxii, xxxiv.

22. Abram Chayes, "The Role of the Judge in Public Law Litigation," *Harvard Law Review*, 89 (May 1976): 1281-1316; Geoffrey Aronow, "The Special Master in School Desegregation Cases," unpublished paper (New Haven, Yale University Law School, March 1979); and Owen Fiss, "The Supreme Court 1978 Term—Foreword: The Forms of Justice," *Harvard Law Review*, 93 (November 1979): 1-58.

23. Patterson, "Notes on the Historical Application," p. 265.

24. Ibid., p. 265.

25. David L. Sallach, "Class Consciousness and the Everyday World in the Work of Marx and Schutz," *The Insurgent Sociologist*, 3, 4 (Summer 1973): 33.

26. Patterson, "Notes on the Historical Application," p. 278.

27. Berger and Luckmann, *The Social Construction of Reality*, p. 91.

28. George Lukacs, *History and Class Consciousness* (Cambridge, Mass.: MIT Press, 1971), p. 100.

29. Femia, "Hegemony and Consciousness," p. 33. Others have discussed the role of schools as socializing agents. See Samuel Bowles and Herbert Gintis, *Schooling in Capitalist America* (New York: Basic Books, 1976); Robert D. Hess and Judith V. Torney, *The Development of Political Attitudes in Children*

(Garden City, N.Y.: Doubleday, Anchor Books, 1967); Michael B. Katz, *Class, Bureaucracy and Schools* (New York: Praeger, 1975); Kenneth P. Langton, *Political Socialization* (New York: Oxford University Press, 1969); and James E. Rosenbaum, *Making Inequality* (New York: John Wiley & Sons/Interscience, 1976).

On churches, see Hess and Torney, *The Development of Political Attitudes;* Parkin, *Class Inequality and Political Order;* for examples see the Right Reverend William Lawrence, "The Relation of Wealth to Morals," in *Democracy and the Gospel of Wealth,* ed. Gail Kennedy (Boston: D. C. Heath, 1949), pp. 68-75; and Richard Hofstadter, *Social Darwinism in American Thought* (Boston: Beacon Press, 1944), p. 18.

On television and other mass media, see Herbert Gans, *Deciding What's News* (New York: Random House, Pantheon Books, 1979); Hoggart, *The Uses of Literacy;* and Michael J. Robinson, "Television and American Politics: 1956-1976," *The Public Interest,* 48 (Summer 1977): 3-39.

On political repression of alternative visions, consider the Civil War, the Chicago Seven conspiracy trial, the killing of Communist Workers Party members and subsequent acquittal of their killers in Greensboro, North Carolina, the deaths of Black Panther Party leader Fred Hampton and other Panthers, the disavowal of congressional candidates who belong to the Ku Klux Klan and Nazi Party by both Republicans and Democrats, and so on.

30. Lester Thurow, *Generating Inequality* (New York: Basic Books, 1975); consider also the Homestead strike, Pullman strike, and other examples of "labor unrest."

31. Frances Fox Piven and Richard Cloward, *Regulating the Poor* (New York: Random House, Pantheon Books, 1971); Barbara Boland, *Studies in Public Welfare: Participation in the Aid to Families with Dependent Children Program (AFDC)* Paper no. 12, Pt. 1, Joint Economic Committee, U.S. Congress, November 1973; and Larry R. Jackson and William A. Johnson, *Protest by the Poor* (Lexington, Mass.: Lexington Books, 1974).

32. Patterson, "Notes on the Historical Application."

33. G. David Garson, "Automobile Workers and the Radical Dream," *Politics and Society,* 3 (Winter 1973): 164, 177.

34. Mann, "The Social Cohesion of Liberal Democracy."

35. Ralph H. Turner, "Value Conflict in Social Disorganization," *Sociology and Social Research,* 38 (May–June 1954): 307.

36. William James, *The Writings of William James,* ed. John McDermott (New York: Modern Library, 1968), p. 16.

37. See also Femia, "Hegemony and Consciousness," p. 48; and Carl Friedrich, *The New Belief in the Common Man* (Boston: Little, Brown, 1942), pp. 62-63, 152-156.

38. Dewey, *The Public and Its Problems,* p. 159.

39. Ibid., p. 160.

40. Lloyd Etheredge, personal communication (n.d.), p. 3.

41. Mann, "The Social Cohesion of Liberal Democracy," p. 435.

42. Amitai Etzioni, *A Comparative Analysis of Complex Organizations* (New York: Free Press, 1961), shows that workers' normative orientations in industries and other "utilitarian" organizations are irrelevant to their role performance.

43. For example, Gramsci "predicted a turn to reaction as early as the summer of 1920, and Leon Trotsky wrote in 1932 that none of the Italian Communists 'except Gramsci' had seen the possibility of a Fascist dictatorship." See John M. Cammett, *Antonio Gramsci and the Origins of Italian Communism* (Stanford, Calif.: Stanford University Press, 1967), p. 159.

44. Berger and Luckmann, *The Social Construction of Reality*, pp. 95-108.

45. Ibid., pp. 103, 106.

46. Parkin, *Class Inequality*, pp. 96-98.

47. Femia, "Hegemony and Consciousness," p. 35.

48. Parkin, *Class Inequality*, p. 98; see also Philip Selznick, *TVA and the Grass Roots* (Berkeley: University of California Press, 1949); and David M. Potter, *People of Plenty* (Chicago: University of Chicago Press, 1954).

49. Patterson, "Notes on the Historical Application," p. 278.

50. Williams, "Base and Superstructure," p. 10.

51. Ibid., p. 12.

52. Parkin, *Class Inequality*, pp. 88-94; and W. Carey McWilliams, *The Idea of Fraternity in America* (Berkeley: University of California Press, 1973).

53. Williams, "Base and Superstructure," pp. 11, 12.

54. See "Radical Chic" in Tom Wolfe, *Radical Chic & Mau-mauing the Flak Catchers* (New York: Farrar, Straus and Giroux, 1970), pp. 3-94, for a hilarious description of how alternative cultures are absorbed and diffused by even the most well-meaning dominant culture.

55. Williams, "Base and Superstructure," p. 10.

56. Parkin, *Class Inequality*, pp. 88-94.

57. I am not castigating pollsters for not having asked as many questions as I would like them to. Such criticism would be petty and boring. Also unjust. Students of public opinion are beginning to ask why people hold the distributive beliefs they hold and what kinds of people hold these beliefs. See, for example, Robert V. Robinson and Wendell Bell, "Equality, Success, and Social Justice in England and the United States," *American Sociological Review*, 43 (April 1978): 125-143; James R. Kluegel and Eliot R. Smith, "The Organization of Stratification Beliefs," unpublished paper (Riverside, University of California, 1978); and Eliot R. Smith and James R. Kluegel, "Sources of Beliefs about Social Inequality," unpublished paper (Riverside: University of California, ca. 1979). My point is that only after we have a solid conceptual framework, which this analysis seeks to provide, can we know what questions to ask in the much more tightly organized format of a public opinion poll.

58. For a discussion of the aggregate consequences of this fact, see Anthony Downs, "Why the Government Budget Is Too Small in a Democracy," *World Politics*, 12 (July 1960): 541-563.

59. Robert E. Lane, *Political Ideology* (New York: Free Press of Glencoe, 1962).

60. Lindblom, *Politics and Markets*, pp. 210-211.

61. See L. Richard Della Fave, "On the Structure of Egalitarianism," *Social Problems*, 22 (December 1974): 199-213, for a discussion of the elements necessary to generate a political demand for equality.

62. Raymond Williams, *Marxism and Literature* (Oxford: Oxford University Press, 1977), p. 112.

63. Todd Gitlin, "Prime Time Ideology: The Hegemonic Process in Television Entertainment," *Social Problems*, 26 (February 1979): 264.

64. Berger and Luckmann, *The Social Construction of Reality*, p. 106.

65. Daniel Bell, *The Cultural Contradictions of Capitalism* (New York: Basic Books, 1976).

66. Dahl, "On Removing Certain Impediments."

67. Femia, "Hegemony and Consciousness," p. 34.

68. David Sallach, "Class Consciousness and the Everyday World in the Work of Marx and Shutz," p. 35.

69. Berger and Luckmann, *The Social Construction of Reality*, p. 103.

70. James E. Carter, Energy Speech to the Nation, Washington, D.C., July 1979. See also Alvin Toffler, *Future Shock* (New York: Random House, 1970), and the many best-sellers advising people how to survive the coming world crisis.

Index

Abbott, Bruce: use of norms in economic and political domains, 41-42, 223-227; use of norms in socializing domain, 221-223; and ambivalence, 226-227, 333n1

Acquiescence in given distributions, 261, 265-272, 278

Adams, John, 8-9

Affirmative action policies, 74; respondents' attitudes toward, 117, 157-158, 174, 257

Ambivalence: in respondents, 34, 137, 238; and relation to dominant three-part pattern of beliefs, 239, 258-259, 262, 266-272, 278-279; manifestations of, 239-242; definition, 239; as normative versus pragmatic judgments, 242-246, 266-268, 282, 332n7; as normative versus normative judgments, 246-249, 269, 282; political effects of, 246, 247, 249, 258; as encroachment of economic values on other domains, 250-254, 268; as egalitarian experiences versus differentiating beliefs, 254-256, 266-267, 282-283; as differentiating experiences versus egalitarian beliefs, 256-258, 266-267, 282, 283, 332n10; and relation to emotional responses to distributive beliefs, 261-263,

334n2. *See also* specific respondents

Aristotle, 8

Ascription, norm of: explanation of, 52, 70-75; specific use by respondents, 91, 98-99, 119-120, 123, 128, 134-135, 139-140, 146, 153, 157, 164, 169, 194-195, 198-203, 217; respondents' emotional response to, 99-100, 103, 133-136, 139-140, 146, 217-218

Australia, income distribution in, 11

Azlinsky, Barbara: use of norms in economic domain, 32-34, 126-129; use of norms in political domain, 32-34, 165-169; and ambivalence, 32-34, 127-129, 166-169, 241-242, 252; use of norms in socializing domain, 95-98

Babeuf, Gracchus, 54

Barry, Brian, 311n32, 323nn77,79, 327n135, 335n13

Baum, Judith: use of norms in socializing domain, 107; use of norms in political domain, 183, 187-188; and ambivalence, 244-245, 251

Bellamy, Edward, 61, 320n39

Bentham, Jeremy, 76

Berger, Peter L., and Thomas Luckmann,